CW00924365

Fabulous Flying Boats

Fabulous Flying Boats

A History of the World's Passenger Flying Boats

Leslie Dawson

Pen & Sword
AVIATION

First published in Great Britain in 2013 by
Pen & Sword Aviation
an imprint of
Pen & Sword Books Ltd
47 Church S treet
Barnsley
South Yorkshire
S70 2AS

ISBN 978 1 78159 109 3

A CIP catalogue record for this book is available from the British Library

Typeset in Palatino

Printed and bound in England by
CPI Group (UK) Ltd, Croydon, CR0 4YY

Pen & Sword Books Ltd incorporates the Imprints of Pen & Sword Aviation, Pen & Sword Family History, Pen & Sword Maritime, Pen & Sword Military, Pen & Sword Discovery, Wharncliffe Local History, Wharncliffe True Crime, Wharncliffe Transport, Pen & Sword Select, Pen & Sword Military Classics, Leo Cooper, The Praetorian Press, Remember When, Seaforth Publishing and Frontline Publishing

For a complete list of Pen & Sword titles please contact
PEN & SWORD BOOKS LIMITED
47 Church Street, Barnsley, South Yorkshire, S70 2AS, England
E-mail: enquiries@pen-and-sword.co.uk
Website: www.pen-and-sword.co.uk

Contents

To those whose lives and memories created this book.

What is a flying boat?	–	An aeroplane supported by a hull on the water.
And a float plane?	–	An aeroplane fitted with floats
And a seaplane?	–	It can be either.
Isn't that confusing?	–	Possibly

Acknowledgements

As someone drawn to clear sparkling water and to the lure of a windsock beckoning from a summer green airstrip, I wanted to learn more about the pioneers, passengers and piloting experiences of a largely forgotten and unique form of flying that utilised the natural waters that separate the land masses and islands of our world. Many kindly gave of their time to portray events enacted a good fifty years before our meeting, a part of their youth, pride and a way of life, tempered by the times, while invention and controlling factors have inevitably combined to ensure the like will never come again.

I have attempted to keep a chronological list of the individuals and organisations that kindly aided my research and enquiries, frequently with personal anecdotes and treasured photographs, and though my appreciation would have been given at the time, I can only apologise for the oversight if your contribution does not appear amongst the following – but here goes.

Michael Cobham sanctioned pictures of his parents, Sir Alan and Lady Cobham, and the refuelling trials, the Poole Plate and Aeromaritime poster were supplied by Katy Armstrong of Millers Antiques and Collectibles, the Museum of Transport and Technology (Auckland) sent photos of their model of Richard Pearse and his aeroplane and the restored *Aranui*, and Roy Tassell a nice shot of the Supermarine Sea Eagle.

I first learnt what it was like to fly a twenty ton flying boat at the harbour side home of Captain Tommy and Connie Rose, followed by a meeting with Captain Bob and Audrey Harwood. Their different entries into BOAC formed the basis of my first authorship on flying boats (*Wings Over Dorset*, published by Dorset Publishing Company) and I thank Bernard Dyer (another former instructor with 622 Gliding School) for putting me in touch with Peter Rose who passed me on to brother Christopher in Australia, who very, very kindly perused his father's log book in detail (particularly the 'remarks' column) and then went through the photograph collection. I also have to thank Audrey for allowing me to collate Bobs log books and for her search for the missing one!

A drive to Orcheston in Wiltshire to meet Mrs Harman, former Woman Seaman Mollie Ann Skinner, revealed a box full of publicity pictures and a small, clandestine photo (cameras were not encouraged during the war) of *Hailsham's* last landing at Poole. And she still had her 'woolly pully'. Colleague Eileen Wigg wrote with details of her own service with the riggers launches and to let me know she was 'the tall one' at the end of the line of girls pictured on the quayside. Perusal of former catering assistant Ivor Coleman's ring-bound BOAC Brats Newsletters unearthed an unusual photo of the cycling flying boat captain and traffic assistant, while former water controller Peter Davidson explained in detail the alighting area activities and the night sortie of the 'Ploughman'. He also sent me a letter from Stan Gibbs which recalled the radio room equipment installed at the Marine Terminal.

Lilliput resident Jeremy Waters contributed photos of the pre-war club at Salterns from his collection, while Beverley Helliwell Smith unearthed a fascinating framed aerial photo which showed the lower wing tip of the circling biplane. Specialist navigator Vic Pitcher kindly provided his log book and photos of his time aboard the giant Boeing Atlantic flights, supplemented with memories of the Lilliput Marine Terminal by Patricia, the former station assistant who had instantly claimed his heart.

Bob Doe's descent to Poole was related to me in person during our meetings at his West Surrey home during the course of my research for his biography, while the catching of the spy at Lulworth Cove formed part of a fascinating letter from Air Vice Marshal 'Birdie' Bird-Wilson, another survivor of the Battle of Britain, who, having shot down six of the enemy before being himself shot down in flames, had recovered sufficiently to enjoy swimming with equally young WAAFs in a nearby stream after arriving at Warmwell in 1941!

Harry Pusey provided a rare insight to the largely forgotten pre-war presence of Imperial Airways at Poole, among his 'other' experiences, while Bob and Margaret Rayner showed me the original photographs and letters concerning the activities of two generations of the family about the harbour. Mrs Margaret Lee also wrote to me from Bideford in Devon. Agnes and William Fyson sent me a superb snapshot of their trip in a Supermarine Channel flying boat at Bournemouth, while Doctor Nigel Pearce provided another unique pre-war snapshot taken by his father, a ships pilot, of *Maia* and *Mercury* moored off the Vickers factory.

Shorts Publicity Dept kindly sent data and photos, and the Public Record Office of Northern Ireland the *Golden Hind* photo (Bombardier collection). Adrian Meredith sent a reflective shot of *Centaurus*, Philip Glover the cockpit detail of *Hythe* with his father and Joe Parker at the controls, and Dave Fagan a classic image of the Southampton terminal.

Richard Tazwell offered his own research on wartime Poole and arranged a meeting with John Newall to view the photo shoot at Hamworthy, and Keith Hayward and Jim Davis (B.A.Heritage Centre) kindly confirmed events at Poole and Malta – after descending two floors to peruse the relocated archives!

Martin Hayle, who foresaw the need to collate the history of the lesser known Royal Naval Air Stations at Sandbanks and Lawrenny Ferry, kindly sent a copy of his booklet on Daedalus 11, while a morning coffee spent in company of Peter Devlin revealed the initiative of a young naval cadet in wartime Britain. A visit to the home of Ivor and Norma Faulconer, combined memories of naval pilot training and catapult operations with those of the post-war Seaplane Club of Great Britain, together with framed photographs of pre-war pilots and aeroplanes and an unexpected collection of vintage model biplanes. June Topham (née Bamford) topped off her experiences as a young wartime Wren posted out to Africa, with publicity shots of the bevy of 'lovelies' positioned about the Walrus, during a sunny afternoon at her home opposite the former Royal Navy Air Station at Sandbanks.

John Witcombe recounted the activities of 461 (RAAF) Squadron and led me to Sunderland author John Evans who immediately sent the photo of *Mister Blue* at La Baule. Further information came from Christine Campbell of the Imperial War Museum at Duxford, and Nina Burls of the RAF Museum at Hendon, where I had my very first flight as an A.T.C. cadet.

The essential 'Bible' of Sunderland data, Aeromilitaria No 3 1979, was combined with copies of the allocation amendments made at the Belfast factory, kindly forwarded by G-Info, and with the assistance of Richard Gibbons (via Bryan Ribbans' Seawings Flying Boat Forum) and aviation historian Carlos Mey in Argentina (which included the nice shot of *Uruguay*) used to confirm the Sunderland conversions to Sandringhams and their final operators in South America. The RAF Halton Apprentices Association 10th Roll of Honour provided a concise summary of the ditching of 'Sunderland' *Golden Fleece* in remembering 32 year-old RAF Pilot Sergeant Henry Richard Mason of 119 Squadron, while the National Australian Archives include the post-war recollections of former air gunner Leonard Corcoran in remembering Pilot Officer James Barry of 10 Squadron RAAF.

210 Squadron Assocation secretary Martin Balderson kindly assisted my enquiries into the crew of Barry Aikman. He also suggested I contact former Aquila traffic assistant Norman Hull, who answered all my questions and put me in touch with José Carvalho, who forwarded his collection of photos taken at Madeira. The Madeira Museum Story Centre guided me to José, the son of Captain Durval Mergulhão, who responded with photos of *Porto Santo* while waiting in Florida for the

snows to clear for a return home to Ottawa. Stan Piet of the Maryland Aviation Museum sent the shot of the Mariner (Glenn L. Martin Collection) and Rick Leisenring (Glenn H. Curtiss Museum) typically sent an image of the pilot and his flying boat glider.

Former launch coxswain 'David' Rose provided memories of Poole and Lake Nyasa, while an invite from Kevin Patience to attend a Bournemouth Air Crew Association dinner led to former BOAC stewardess Joan Mills, whose daughter Amanda brought in the Springbok panel during our meeting. Captain Jim Peers effortless related his 'Horseshoe' experiences and the Solent float problem in the absence of surviving log books, while Jean, a former Pan Am stewardess, provided a youthful picture of him taken at Durban.

An illustrated talk for Parkstone Yacht Club members in their delightful 'private residence' just yards from Poole harbour shore, resulted in Boeing 747 Captain Richard Gurney contacting his mother Kathleen, who kindly forwarded a fascinating collection of memorabilia from her Solent flight to Tanganyika. While admiring the view across the Blue Lagoon from the club balcony, I was joined by Bob Kent, whose clear recollection of the German bomber emerging from the night sky was a delight for any writer to chance upon, as were his equally unique memories of the unexpected landing of *Southern Cross* and his meeting with the glamorous Maureen O'Hara.

Margaret O'Shaughnessy took time from her busy schedule to portray the founding of the Foynes Flying Boat Museum and creation of the world's sole Clipper replica, and I have to thank Jennifer Stepp (Stars and Stripes) for permission to use the photo of Charles and Maureen (O'Hara) Blair taken during the 1969 retirement flight for Pan Am, when the actress postponed filming to accompany her husband. Mary Kane of Boeing Images kindly provided the shot of the prototype Clipper by the factory slipway.

Lene Myrdal of the Norwegian National Archives (Riksarkivet) at Oslo unearthed the engineers report of the sinking of *Jutulen* in Africa and Birger Larson of the National Aviation Museum (Norsk Luftfartsmuseum) at Bodø sent details of the last flights of the Vingtor Catalina and the two Norwegian Sandringhams, with photos of *Bamse Brakar* bring craned from the water. Karl Sandberg of the Scandinavian Airline Museum at Gardemoen sanctioned the rare 1939 DNL timetable cover showing a Junkers floatplane in the Lofoten islands, while Marcelo Bordim allowed me to include his photo of Savoia *Jahú* at the Museu TAM (Wings of a Dream Museum) São Carlos, believed the largest museum in the world maintained by a private airline.

I am grateful for all the help given by Virginie Claverie-Lumalé and by Fabrice Bregier of the Musée de l'Hydraviation at Biscarrosse. Virginie also put me in touch with Marc Fabre who kindly sanctioned the image of his father Henri and *Le Canard*. The museum is also home to des Amis du Musée de l'Hydravion, whose president Jacques Lauray described his colleagues as a benevolent bunch of hydro fanatics!

A chance perusal of the PPRuNe Forum (Professional Pilots Rumour Network) led to an unexpected reply from Bristol, where Melbourne based Captain Henry de Courcier just happened to be visiting his mother-in- law before rejoining the Airbus fleet of Cathay Pacific, and I was pleased to be allowed to use the rare photograph of *Rigel Star* fortunately saved by his mother from her wartime work at Rose Bay.

An email to Booh Crisp resulted in a mass of information from Pierre Jaunet concerning the Catalina Safari operations in Africa, and I have to thank Antoinette for digging out the phone number for Tim Spearman, who allowed use of his atmospheric image of Z-CAT on lake Malawi. Mike Shirley-Beavan also sent details of the Bushbuck Safaris.

Jenn Whiteman contacted me from the New York office of the Christian and Missionary alliance with details of *Gospel Messenger* and its heroic pilot Albert J. Lewis, while former TV reporter Peta Carey recalled the Catalina's crash landing at night while en route to New Zealand. Phillip Treweek sent his airborne view of the Catalina Club of New Zealands XX-T and David Barrie (Rédacteur en chef d'AeroWeb-fr) kindly supplied images of both the Canard replica and the Plane Sailing Catalina at Biscarosse in 2010.

Oakland Aviation Museum's Lori Fogerty and husband and wife team Scott and Pamela Buckingham provided details of the museum and *City of Cardiff*, complemented by Joseph May, who writes for the aviation blog Travel for Aircraft. A phone call to California and Tom Moore (China National Aviation Corporation website), then led to Michael, the grandson of Captain Edward "Eddie" Smith, who kindly sanctioned images of the Douglas Dolphin amphibians.

Executive director Larry Wood and curator Stewart Bailey provided an awesome view of the '*Goose*' in its impressive glass fronted lair at the Evergreen Aviation & Space Museum at McMinnville, Oregon. By contrast, Doctor Andreas Zeitler (flying-wings.com) sent a superb shot of the Dornier 24 piloted by Iren Dornier during a September 2004 photo session over the Bavarian Alps, taken at 11,000 feet from the draughty open doorway of a single-engined Dornier 27.

I have to thank curator Squadron Leader Alan Jones MBE and the staff of Solent Sky for my welcome over the years and to former Sunderland and Boeing 707 captain Vic Hodgkinson who invited me home to view his bound photograph collection after my very first visit, when I was exceptionally allowed into the cockpit of *Southern Cross* (displayed as *Beachcomber*). My repeated thanks also go to Ron and Noreen Gillies for a recorded interview during a very informative evening following the return of the flying boat to Calshot.

Gina Maria Alimberti (New England Air Museum) sent a photo of the restored *Excambian*, latterly operated by Antilles Air Boats, with further information forwarded by director Mike Speciale. Mick Bajcar provided the action shot of an Antilles Goose taxiing across Charlotte Amalies harbour, while Bob Winkworth and Colin Lee (South Hampshire Historic Aviation Society) respectively provided a rare shot of *Corsair* at Hythe and the last airworthy civilian Sunderland leaving Calshot for the Kermit Weeks Fantasy of Flight Museum in Florida. Once owned by Charles Blair, the former *Excalibur V111* is festooned with lights at the end of the runway at Christmas!

Dave Homewood of Wings Over New Zealand Aviation Forum put me in touch with Peter Lewis, whose photo of *Aotearoa* on the waterfront at Mission Bay (credited to Peter and Marcus Bridle) shows what could easily have been done elsewhere. The Mars fire-fighting flying boats are still actively pursuing their craft however and I am grateful to Wayne Coulson (Coulson Aircrane Ltd) for checking my research and to son Britton for forwarding the excellent action shot taken over California in September 2009.

My meetings with Jack and Gemma Harris were always filled with laughter and I had to be prised away from the fabulous collection of aviation memorabillia within the spacious library of their waterside home at Lilliput. The floatplane Spitfire incident over Poole was recounted in detail in a nine page letter to Jack from former test pilot Lieutenant Commander Don Robertson from his Bembridge, Isle of Wight home in 1990. A particularly happy re-union with *Southern Cross* was arranged courtesy of Alan Jones in 2010 when Jack again sat at the controls which he had operated under the guidance of Charles Blair thirty-four years earlier. This time the right hand seat was occupied by Gemma, who even on their honeymoon had had to endure a diversion to see what was going on at the local airfield!

Paul Warren Wilson patiently answered all my emails on keeping a vintage flying boat in the air, while Rachel Morris and the Plane Sailing team kindly allowed me to sit at the controls of '915' as Flying Fortress Sally B watched from the rear of the hangar, perhaps remembering my awe at being allowed inside her own cockpit during an air display at Bournemouth many years ago. Both aircraft are the sole examples flying in this country and rely heavily on contributions from all of us, however modest.

A close friend of Bryan Monkton, Trevor Dean (Australian Aviation Museum) kindly sent the wartime photo of the pilot as a 'Black Cat' RAAF Squadron Leader, and Phil Vabre (The Airways Museum and Civil Aviation Historical Society) sanctioned use of the pre-war view of Rose Bay taken by Milton Kent. Iwona Hetherington (The Powerhouse Museum) provided the image of Captain Taylor, and Ron Cuskelly

(Queensland Air Museum) sent several images of 'Le Bermuda'. Frank Stamford telephoned from a hot and humid Victoria early in 2012 (we were experiencing minus ten degrees) in time to include his photo of *Beachcomber and Islander* at Lord Howe Island in 1974 , while the arrival of Sikorsky replica *Osas Ark* at Duxford, prompted a call to Jacquelyn Borgeson (The Martin and Osa Johnson Safari Museum, Chanute) when director Conrad Froehlich forwarded the image of the pioneer husband and wife wildlife photographers, who had acquired two Sikorsky amphibians and pilot licences for their 1933 Africa safari.

Pippa Leech, and Roger Hopkins (Movie Media), patiently transformed faded seventy year old photos into pristine copies, and I have to thank Olivia Spencer of Loch Lomond Seaplanes for the shot of the Cessna Caravan moored off a Brownsea Island look-alike stretch of Scottish coastline. Now that really would be something to look forward to.

Happy Flying.

Leslie Dawson
Bournemouth
England

© Loch Lomond Seaplanes.

Chapter One

First to Fly

While not forgetting the monks, said to have thrown themselves off church steeples with outspread hands clutching their voluminous robes, as others of their calling simply levitated themselves without any visible means of support, a method yet to achieve its true commercial potential. Nor the pioneering balloon ascents made in France by Joseph-Michel and Jacques-Étienne Montgolfier. Nor the first practical glides made by Otto Lilienthal in Germany using bird-like wings – the true dawn of flight is generally accepted to have cast its light on a cold and virtually deserted beach at Kitty Hawk, North Carolina, in December 1903.

Orville and Wilbur Wright were inventive young men, designing a press to run their own print business and setting up a bicycle repair shop to market their own design. Believed enthralled by the antics of a toy helicopter however and then inspired by Otto and saddened by his death, which had come while seeking a means of controlling flight other than weight-shift, they had built their own experimental bi-plane gliders, using a wind tunnel and inventing the world's first three-axis control system – naturally!

The younger by four years, 35 year old Orville had won the toss of a coin on that windy seventeenth day of December. Lying head-first on the fabric covered lower framework of their *Flyer*, the fuel injected, 12 horsepower engine, built in their own workshop, had propelled him for twelve seconds and 120 feet above the sands of Kill Devil Hills, the safe landing confirming the honesty of the first, man-carrying, sustained flight of a heavier than air machine. Both flew twice that day, Wilbur exciting the few, curious, spectators by remaining airborne for fifty-nine seconds before crunching onto the sand over 850 feet away. The *Flyer* was irrevocably damaged by the wind as it was walked back however and the brothers had returned home to quietly seek protection for their inventions.

On the other side of the world, a shy, reclusive 26 year old young farmer may have beaten them to it by some nine months. Born into a farming and musical family, the son of a Cornishman who had emigrated to South Island, New Zealand, Richard William Pearse had, like the Wrights,

Richard Pearse. New Zealand (and world?) first 'heavier than air flight.
IMAGE COURTESY OF MOTAT LIBRARY.

patented his own (geared) bicycle design in 1902. Like Otto, he had also built a small (15 horsepower) twin cylinder petrol engine and in March 1903, had made his first real flight, as distinct from preceding hops, from a country road near the farmland donated by his parents at Waitohi, South Canterbury, remaining airborne for some 300 yards.

All the more remarkable when considering that the engine, made from tin pots and pans using hand-made tools, was mounted in front and not behind the airframe and had driven a variable pitch, hand-carved metal propeller. The single wing, another innovation, was made of bamboo, scrap metal and canvas, and was fitted with a wire- braced fin on top and a large elevator at the rear. There was also a steerable, tri-cycle undercarriage! The flight may have ended in a gorse bush, but in many ways, was years and not months ahead of the game. Sadly, no firm record survived and it took years for the event to surface. Richard went on to build a helicopter based on a tilting propeller, but quietly died in 1953 without any form of acknowledgement.

His effects included some of his designs however and gradually his prescience began to be recognised, if posthumously. In March 1979 a memorial was unveiled at Waitohi and three years later the local airfield at Timaru was re-named Richard Pearse Airport. Today, visitors to Auckland's Museum of Transport and Technology will find a replica of that inspired early aeroplane and its creator high above their heads – if they care to look up!

From designing and building balloons for wealthy clients such as the

Honourable Charles Rolls, which had required a move from rented premises in London's Tottenham Court Road to two railway arches at Battersea Park, Eustace and Oswald Short had decided to build aeroplanes after Eustace had been taken up for a flight by Wilbur Wright. Elder brother Horace was persuaded to join them and the brothers began testing their machines at Britain's first 'aerodrome' at Shellbeach, near the village of Leysdown on the Isle of Sheppey, where the brothers began building the first of six Short-Wright *Flyers* under license. In 1909 Orville and Wilbur visited the works in London and in Kent where the machines were being built to a higher standard than in France.

Henri Fabre. First successful flight from water. Marseilles March 1910.
© MARC FABRE

Though a lot safer to collapse into, flying from water had not progressed beyond towed gliders and the pioneers had mainly flown from dry land – until the spring of 1910. Born into a ship owning family in Marseilles, Henri Fabre had become fascinated with flight. Having studied advanced sciences at the Marseille Jesuit College and engineering in Paris, he had devoted his time to examining the effects of air-flow on model airframes and wings, but unlike others, had also studied the effects of water on a body. Helped by mechanic Marius Burdin and naval architect Léon Sebille, his first conventional monoplane design failed to leave the surface of the Étang de Berre, a large freshwater 'pool' of water to the north-west of the town, despite three engines driving the propeller! Things improved dramatically when he placed the main wing and engine at the rear, with a pair of small, controlling, biplane wings in front, though the first 'hop' from the lake at the close of 1909 was all too brief due to the limitations of the little Anzani engine.

The concept was successful however and three months later an improved design featured a spreading 46 foot, bird-like, dihedral main wing supported by outrigger floats. Positioned behind the rudder, the replacement 50 horsepower Gnome Omega rotary engine was fitted with an 8 foot wooden Chauviere propeller. Twenty-eight feet in front, the top and smaller of two biplane style winglets comprised the elevator,

A Canard at Monaco 1911. Pilot Jean Becu.
© COLLECTION CITY OF BISCARROSSE MUSEUM- ORIGIN HYDRAVIATION FABRE.

controlled by a large wooden lever angled above the skeletal airframe. The 'cockpit' was an exposed open weave 'basket' fitted mid-way along the top of two parallel wooden beams, braced by a vertical strut.

On 28 March 1910, the moustached 27 year old engineer climbed aboard his fragile looking creation and was rowed out to the centre of the lake. A large crowd had gathered on the shore and on seeing the rear mounted propeller, probably expected him to fly in that direction, or more likely crash, for he had never taken a flying lesson in his life. After a few, short, test runs, the sound of the engine echoed across the water and the 'clothes-horse' left the surface at the very first attempt, maintaining some 6 feet of daylight before safely set down, intact. Three more flights were made, the longest covering some 600 meters (1,600 feet), all of which was formally recorded by a court official from nearby Martigues.

Henri named his craft, the first to leave water under its own power, *Le Canard* (the duck) after the bird it resembled in flight, and was subsequently seen making much longer flights across the lake. A few examples were built and sold, while several of the patented hollow, aerodynamic floats, were snapped up by the pioneering Gabriel and Charles Voisin, whose conventional biplane design became the first to fly over the Seine that October. Fitted with floats and wheels, the modified Canard-Voisin became the first successful amphibious 'hydro-avion' and an example was delivered to the world's first 'seaplane' carrier *La Foudre*. Along with Richard Pearse, the achievement of Henri Fabre, the first to prove it was

Le Canard replica Lake Biscarrosse May 2010. © DAVID BARRIE.

possible to fly from water, has almost faded into obscurity, but on the one hundredth anniversary of his historic flight, a full-size replica faithfully constructed from wood and fabric by Airbus engineers Guillaume Bulin and Marc Anscieau was displayed at the May 2010 Biscarosse Seaplane Air Show.His meeting with a prominent American pioneer undoubtedly helped solve problems on the other side of the Atlantic.

Born at Hammondsport New York, Glenn Hammond Curtiss had also set up a bicycle repair business but had gone on to race 'motor cycles' at world record speeds powered by his own engines, before attracted to flight. Invited to join the Aerial Experiment Association led by Alexander Graham Bell, the inventor of the telephone, on 4 July 1908 his *June Bug* design remained airborne before an appreciative crowd for a measured kilometre, earning him the Aero Club of America pilots licence Number One. Displays and long distance flights followed, while finding time to teach one of the earliest women pilots Blanche Stuart Scott. A Curtiss biplane made the first take off and landing aboard a moored American battleship and his 1911 wheel and float equipped *Triad* (land, air and water) amphibian, was sold to the naval arms of America, Japan, Germany and Russia. Though meeting Fabre, the first to use lift-producing floats, he had not consulted the Wright brothers, who bitterly contested his copying of their patented airframes!

Glenn's particular contribution was in designing boat-like hulls to support the weight, with floats used purely to balance the wings. The provision of a 'step' was found to aerate the area in contact with the water and reduced the drag even further as the hull rose from the surface, as was demonstrated in 1912. The following year the Smithsonian Institute awarded the 35 year old the Langley Medal for his development of the 'flying boat' and Lord Northcliffe, owner of the *Daily Mail* newspaper, offered ten thousand pounds for the first heavier than air crossing of the Atlantic. Four years earlier, Frenchman Louis Blériot had won an identical sum from the newspaper for crossing the English Channel, but an Irishman would fly the Curtiss entry.

Tall, and with striking, aquiline, features, John Cyril Porte had commanded the earliest of Royal Navy submarines and was an excellent navigator, though the long hours spent on the exposed metal casings undoubtedly caused the onset of pulmonary tuberculosis. Flying interested him and with other officers he had launched an experimental glider from the slopes of Portsdown Hill near Portsmouth before flying a home-built aeroplane similar to the attractive little *Demoiselle* monoplane of Alberto Santos-Dumont, though his illness had caused the Admiralty to retire him in 1911.

Undaunted, he had gained his pilot's licence at Rheims in France and invested his money and services in the newly formed British Deperdussin Company. As technical director and test pilot, he won a host of trophies promoting the company's monoplane while privately flying a little float-plane called '*The Seagull*'. Unable to attract sufficient support however, the company had folded and he was fortunate to be taken on as a test pilot by White and Thompson, another new concern. A meeting with Glenn Curtiss at the Volks seaplane base at Brighton had resulted in a flight in the Curtiss flying boat shipped over for Ernest Bass of the famous brewing company. His new employers would maintain it, giving Porte an invaluable insight into the Curtiss hull design, though it would fall to another to make the worlds first scheduled passenger flight.

Like Curtiss, Tom Benoist had progressed from flying aeroplanes to building them and on 1 January 1914, his graceful (Type 14) single engined biplane flying boat, flew Abram Pheil, a former mayor of Saint Petersburg, who had bid four hundred dollars for the privilege, alongside pilot Tony Jannus for the 23 mile open-cockpit, over-water, inaugural flight of the Air Boat Line to Tampa, Florida. Financed by millionaire Rodman Wanamaker, Curtiss had designed a much larger flying boat to cross the Atlantic to Plymouth. The start of the First World War postponed the competition, but by the end of five years of war in Europe, the aeroplane had been developed as an important weapon, with floatplanes and flying boats serving the naval arms of the principal combatants and their allies.

Moving to a more suitable flying ground at Eastchurch and having

Frank McClean and Short S80 folding wing 'pusher' Hydro-Aeroplane on Nile Jan-March 1914. © SHORTS PUBLICITY DEPT BELFAST.

studied the rapid advance of French designer aviators such as Henri and Maurice Farman, the Short brothers had completed their first biplane for the Naval Wing of the Royal Flying Corps. In January 1912, Lieutenant Charles Samson had become the first British pilot to fly from a ship after taking the Short S38 from a wooden ramp fitted across the deck of HMS Africa, though it seems the event had been quietly pre-empted at Sheerness harbour in December. The ramp was re-fitted over the gun turret of the battleship HMS Hibernia in time for the May Naval Review off Portland, when Samson became the first to fly from a moving vessel. For each of the (three) flights the machine had been fitted with long streamlined 'flotation bags' adjacent to both wheels and the tail-skid, effectively making it an amphibian. A year later the company's Folding

Wing device revolutionised the storage of aircraft, especially on naval vessels, the subsequent rise in orders bringing yet another move to premises alongside the river Medway at Rochester. In 1914 Frank McClean even flew a Short 'Hydro-Aeroplane' in stages from Alexandria to Khartoum.

The war had increased floatplane production for the Seaplane Works, while over a hundred non-rigid SS (Submarine Scout) airships were built for the Airship Service and two rigid airships (R31 and 32) for the Admiralty. With so many new aircraft to be flight tested, John Lankester Parker was taken on as an assistant to John Kemp, though his youthful appearance caused Horace to famously suggest he refrain from flying the larger ones! John Parker would become company chief test pilot and would retire as a director, awarded the OBE for his services to aviation. The Rochester built biplanes were the first to deliver torpedo attacks on shipping, but in 1917 forty-five year old Horace died after an illness. By then, the problems of using water absorbing wood, unreliable glues and flammable materials were all too apparent.

Re-called by the Royal Navy, Lieutenant Commander Porte had joined the newly formed Royal Naval Air Service as squadron commander of a pilot training school at Hendon, North London, where he had given many displays. He had persuaded their Lords of the Admiralty to buy the *America* flying boat and the reserve for the Atlantic attempt and was largely responsible for the 1915 order of Curtiss H4 flying boats, following trials with the first British flying boat at Calshot and by the German Navy! Built by the Cowes, Isle of Wight, boat building company of Samuel Saunders, the hull of the Sopwith Bat Boat featured Samuels patented method of sewing strips of laminated mahogany and water-proofing calico with copper wire, named Consuta after the steam launch which had tested the idea on the Thames in 1898. The little flying boat had won the 1913 five hundred pound Mortimer Singer prize for the first 'All-British' amphibian, despite the wheels having to be kicked into place by the observer in the second seat, and though seen with bomb racks at the 1914 Naval Review, the trials had ended early the following year, when the navy dismantled their example.

Having led mixed formations of floatplanes and flying boats against German submarines and airship bases, John Porte was given command of the RNAS Seaplane Experimental Establishment at Felixstowe, where the Curtiss flying boats had been evaluated. From simply improving the American flying boat he proceeded to develop a completely new British-built flying boat, the Felixstowe, using his own hull design powered by Rolls Royce Eagle engines. The German 'ace' Manfred von Richthofen would forever be associated with the bright coloured machines of his Jasta, high over the misery of the mud-filled trenches. But few would remember the coloured stripes and zigzag painted hulls of some of the

Licence-built Short Felixstowe, former military F3.

RNAS Felixstowes towards the end of the war: the 'Dazzle' effect created by the marine artist Norman Wilkinson to distort the outline and direction of merchant ships to German submarines.

The guns ceased firing in November 1918. The following May just one of a trio of three-engined 'Navy-Curtiss' flying boats alighted at Plymouth having become the first fixed-wing craft to cross the Atlantic, though the route owed much to Porte's ideas by stopping at Newfoundland, the Azores and Lisbon. But at twenty minutes to ten on the Sunday morning of 15 June, a modified twin-engined Vickers Vimy bomber landed in Ireland after flying non-stop from Newfoundland in less than sixteen hours. Former Royal Flying Corps pilot Captain John William (Jack) Alcock and former observer Lieutenant Arthur Brown duly received the ten thousand pound *Daily Mail* prize and were knighted by King George V, while the contents of the sealed white bag that had also survived the traumatic flight was acknowledged as the first air mail to be carried over the Atlantic.

A Porte flying boat may well have conquered the ocean, but in August, just one day away from departing for South Africa, the huge five-engined *Felixstowe Fury* triplane stalled and crashed after being lifted too soon from the water. The Felixstowe 5 would replace all other flying boats operated by the newly formed Royal Air Force however, with fifteen bought by the Imperial Japanese Naval Air Service and two operated between Key West and Havana by Aeromarine West Indies Airways.

Years would pass before a flying boat conquered the ocean. But in September the resumption of the Schneider Trophy Race at Bournemouth saw the floatplanes joined by the Sea Lion flying boat, designed by 24 year old Reginald Joseph Mitchell of the Southampton based Supermarine Company, and the 'winning' Savoia S13 flying boat entered by Italy, later disqualified for completing the wrong course in the mist!

Retired as a wing commander and made a companion of the distinguished order of Saint Michael and Saint George (CMG), John Porte became chief designer for the Gosport Aviation Company, having sensibly patented his ideas for improving floats and hulls. His illness had never left him however and he died suddenly in October, leaving his wife Betty and the world of aviation to mourn the loss of Britain's greatest flying boat pioneer. Just 35 years old, he was posthumously awarded the American Distinguished Conduct Medal by President Woodrow Wilson.

SHORT BROTHERS

The post-war shortage of timber and the need to diversify in order to survive, caused the brothers Short to manufacture metal bus and tram bodies for London Transport, though the use of duralumin in airship construction and the research into metal hull and float designs by Oscar Gnosspelius and Arthur Gouge would later prove invaluable. Having built Felixstowe flying boats for the RAF and Japanese Navy, in 1921 Shorts first large flying boat design, the Cromarty, built in response to the Admiralty's requirement for a long range military flying boat, was fitted with a pair of Rolls Royce 650 horsepower Condor engines believed capable of keeping the five and a half tons in the air for up to eleven hours. Prophetically, the name began with a C, but the hull was still of water absorbing wood (spruce) and a fatal taxi across a reef in the Scilly Isles in August 1922, by the RAF Seaplane Development Flight, saw the fifty-nine foot long biplane scrapped on the spot.

The previous year the company had produced the first British all-metal (duralumin) aeroplane, and though government cut-backs precluded the Silver Streak fighter from achieving the prominence it deserved, in 1923 the company completed a single seat flying boat for a private buyer. Just under 25 feet long with a 36 foot wingspan, it was thought to be the world's smallest flying boat, but more importantly was the first to be built at Rochester with an all metal hull. Grossly underpowered by the pair of 16 horsepower motor cycle engines however, the S1 Cockle failed to leave the water until the wing setting was adjusted, by which time the buyer had lost interest. Passed to Felixstowe for evaluation, the engines were later replaced by a pair supplying three times the supposed 'power de cheval'. But nothing came of it and the Cockle was eventually scrapped, though subsequent flying boats would continue the distinctive smooth profiling. Flown at the beginning of 1925, the experimental Felixstowe S2 was the first Short-built 'large' flying boat to feature an all-metal hull. By then, the government had disbanded all four of the heavily subsidised independent airlines in favour of a single state-controlled concern.

Aside from Daimler Airway and the British Marine Air Navigation Company, Handley Page Transport had been the first to provide lunch boxes filled with sandwiches, chocolate and fruit for passengers boarding their converted bombers, while Instone Airway had been first to introduce formal attire for its staff. Funded equally by the government and the British, Foreign and Colonial Corporation, Imperial Airways was formed on 1 April 1924. Granted a capital sum of one million pounds with a further million pound subsidy to be spread over the next ten years, the 'all-British' personnel and thirteen aircraft were expected to provide regular flying services to the British Empire and its Dominions. Not all the collection were landplanes however.

Supermarine

The son of a Birmingham iron founder, Noel Pemberton-Billing had run away to South Africa and had subsequently been wounded in the Boer War. Returning to England he had opened one of the first motor-car garages at Kingston-on-Thames and had qualified as a barrister before opening his own steam-yacht brokerage, when he took on a young Hubert Scott-Paine as his assistant. Believed to have won a bet by qualifying as a pilot within a single day, in 1913 Noel is thought to have used the money to open the riverside factory of Pemberton-Billing Ltd at Woolston, near Southampton, to build his own aeroplanes and flying boats. Interested in flying and fast boats, Hubert was made works manager and when Noel was called up for the Royal Naval Air Service (when he constantly campaigned for an air arm independent of the army and navy), Hubert bought and renamed the business as the Supermarine Aviation Works Ltd.

Designed by Lieutenant Linton Chorley Hope RNVR, who had created strong, lightweight, yacht hulls before being called up, AD flying boats were built for the Admiralty towards the end of the war, the end of hostilities enabling several to be bought back and modified to seat up to three passengers in front of the pilot. Known as Channel flying boats, they were used to deliver newspapers and to give pleasure flights from Southampton, Bournemouth and the Isle of Wight. In April 1920, three were delivered to Southampton railway station to be shipped out to Bermuda for pleasure flying with the Bermuda and West Atlantic Aviation Company. Three more went to Det Norske Luftfartsrederi A/S,

Channel flying boat off Bournemouth 1919.
© WILLIAM AND AGNES FYSON.

which opened Norway's first airline service, and four were bought by the Royal Norwegian Navy, which opened the country's first airmail service. Others went to Japan, New Zealand, Venezuela and Chile.

Hubert had then joined with Southern Railways, the owners of Southampton Docks, in forming the British Marine Air Navigation Company. The following June the first of three new commercial flying boats was launched from the east shore of the river Itchen. Designed by Mitchell, now chief company engineer and designer, the Supermarine Sea Eagle continued the 'pusher' engine format, the 360 horsepower Rolls Royce Eagle engine supporting up to six passengers, sat within an enclosed cabin, at just over 90 miles an hour. The boat-like hull was fitted with fixed wheels to enable it to power ashore unaided, but if needed to be moored the pilot had to leave his open cockpit and carefully make his way across the cambered surface to the bow, using the handrail fitted beneath the windows of the passenger cabin. If no buoy was available, he had to unship the coiled rope and sea-anchor lashed to the hull above the starboard wheel strut. A flight to Guernsey on 25 September 1923 was recognized as the first scheduled passenger service of a British flying boat (technically an amphibian) and though services continued to the Channel Islands, Cherbourg and Le Havre, Hubert sold his interest in Supermarine Aviation to pursue his passion for power boats, but accepted a directorship when Imperial Airways took over in April 1924.

Launched that March in response to the Air Ministry's intention to replace the Felixstowe 5s, the Mitchell designed Swan featured a wheel retraction system driven by a fan exposed to the slipstream. Emerging a year later, the production Southampton, became the second longest-serving flying boat in RAF history. Fitted with ten seats in 1926, the Swan was used by Imperial on cross-channel services for just a year before retiring. Of the three Sea Eagles, G-EBFK had crashed in May 1924, GR

British Marine Air Navigation Company Supermarine Sea Eagle.
COURTESY ROY TASSELL COLLECTION.

was hit by a ship while moored at night in Saint Peter Port in January 1927, leaving GS to continue the Guernsey service until late 1928, the year the company was absorbed and re-named as the Supermarine Aviation Works (Vickers) Limited.

Vickers had produced its own amphibious flying boat at the close of 1918, though Sir John Alcock had encountered fog en route to the 1919 Paris Exhibition and both he and Viking 1 had perished during the forced landing at Côte d'Evrard in Normandy. A year later, Viking 3 had secured first prize in the Air Ministry trials for amphibians and a pair of Viking 4s were briefly operated on passenger services between Buenos Aires and Montevideo by the Rio Platense Aviation Company until the cash ran out. Within a few years Supermarine and R.J Mitchell would find lasting fame for producing a legendary fighter for the RAF, while Short Brothers would forever be associated with the British flying boat story.

SURVEYS

Having risen from a veterinary assistant to a commissioned RAF flying instructor in the final year of the Great War, thanks to the bridge party contacts of his mother at their Camberwell home, Alan (John) Cobham had joined with two other former service pilots in giving seasonal 'joy-rides' using a converted Avro 504 trainer and had met his future wife,

Pastoral picnic. Alan and Gladys Cobham(later Sir and Lady Cobham). COURTESY MICHAEL COBHAM, FLIGHT REFUELLING LTD.

actress Gladys Lloyd, while operating from Yorkshire. The demise of the Aircraft Manufacturing Company, which he had joined to pilot an aerial photographer, then caused him to join his friend Captain Geoffrey de Havilland as a test and charter pilot.

In 1923 he was awarded the Royal Aero Club's Britannia Trophy for crossing the English Channel in a light aeroplane, though the 26 horse-power engine of the tiny, single seat *Humming Bird* was left with just half a gallon of fuel in the tank. Having prudently acquired large refuelling funnels and pumps, he had then won the 1924 Kings Cup Air Race with the new DH 50 biplane. Aware that Sir Sefton Branckner, the newly appointed director of civil aviation, intended sailing to India to assess possible landing sites for an Australian service, he took the opportunity to fly him there in the enclosed cabin of the biplane, though the cockpit still lay open to the elements. The first to fly over the Himalayas, they were welcomed as heroes on their return in February 1925.

South Africa was a particular goal of the airlines however and having again fought hard to attract sponsors for a survey, in particular Sir Charles Wakefield of Castrol Oil, a year later the pilot flew out to Capetown via India and Rangoon, accompanied by his faithful engineer Arthur Elliott and by Gaumont British Films cameraman Basil Emmott. Intent on filming, they were lucky to clear a momentarily forgotten ridge, while the pilot's instinctive reactions saved them from disaster when moisture flooded the carburetor while circling 1,000 feet above Victoria Falls. Having sat alone at the controls for a total of over ninety hours and some 16,000 miles, he brought them home in March, beating by a full two days the simultaneous return to Southampton from Capetown by the Union Castle liner Windsor Castle. Other flyers provided an airborne escort to Croydon Airport and Gladys was taken aloft in a two seater

Moth to watch her husband's arrival, when his aeroplane was engulfed by an adoring British public. Film and book credits followed.

Three months later he was off again on an equally eventful 28,000 mile survey to Australia, receiving a knighthood and a second Britannia Trophy in October, when the float-equipped DH 50 was skillfully landed, as requested, on the Thames between the crowd-packed bridges at Vauxhall and Westminster, though without Arthur Elliott. The weight of the metal floats had allowed just one other aboard and faced by fierce dust storms after leaving Baghdad, they had been forced to skim the Tigris, unwittingly disturbing the aim of a gazelle- hunting Arab who had fired a single shot at them instead. An emergency landing was made at Basra. But the bullet had entered Arthur's lung and the pilot had needed a lot of persuasion to continue after the death of his friend, though greeted by one hundred thousand admirers at Melbourne.

In 1927 four Southampton flying boats of the RAF Far East Flight left to survey the route to Australia via Italy, North Africa, India and Malaya, the all metal hulls reducing the all up weight by five hundred pounds with a corresponding increase in range. After circumnavigating Australia, the crews crossed the South China Sea to Hong Kong before returning to Singapore where they were reformed as No 205 Squadron. Sir Alan had also left Britain that November.

Having co-founded Cobham-Blackburn Airlines as a prelude to operating regular flying boat services between Alexandria and Capetown, he convinced the Air Ministry to loan him the experimental (1926 built) all-metal Short Singapore flying boat for the 'Sir Charles Wakefield Flight of Survey Round Africa'. Lady Gladys had joined the crew as an airborne secretary to allow her husband to attend the many conferences with government officials, for their co-operation and financial support was vital to the success of future services. The route was planned to cross the Mediterranean and make a clockwise circuit of Africa, from the Nile to the Indian Ocean and to Capetown, returning along the Atlantic seaboard to Gibraltar. A truly remarkable survey followed, for many areas were uncharted and had never heard the sound of aircraft engines, let alone seen a flying boat.

After flying an exhausting 20,000 miles across Egypt, the Sudan, South Africa and Southern Rhodesia, and a 2,000 mile survey between Lake Victoria and Khartoum for the Colonial Office, which was considering an air mail service, Sir Alan brought them home on the last day of May 1928, but immediately embarked on a publicity tour of the major ports of Great Britain. The government would always favour the state airline however and in December, Imperial Airways bought out the Cobham-Blackburn company to secure the rights to operate services in South Africa.

In the summer, *City of Alexandria,* the first of five metal-hulled Calcutta flying boats evolved from the Singapore design, began flying between

Calcutta *City of Alexandria.*

Southampton and Guernsey. The rest would be named after the city of Athens, Rome, Khartoum and Salonika. Accompanied by Oswald Short, on 1 August John Parker brought the sound of the three, 550 horsepower Bristol Jupiter engines to the Thames, landing between the Vauxhall and Lambeth bridges before mooring off the Albert Embankment to allow Chancellor of the Exchequer Winston Churchill and other dignitaries of the Houses of Parliament to tour the aircraft. The following year Calcuttas began linking Genoa with Alexandria for the London to India airmail and passenger service.

Flown from Croydon to Basle by a three-engined Armstrong Whitworth Argosy airliner, passengers boarded a train for Genoa where the fifteen seat flying boat awaited them. Unlike the two pilots, they (and the radio operator) were sat within an enclosed cabin where drinks and light meals were served by a steward while crossing the sunny Mediterranean to Naples, Corfu, Phaleron Bay (west of Athens) and Spinalonga Bay (off north east Crete); the final landing made in Ras-el-Tin harbour at Alexandria. A second train journey ended at Cairo from where eight-seat de Havilland Hercules airliners completed the seven-day service at Karachi. An early casualty to the fleet came in October 1929 when *City of Rome* was forced to descend to the sea when some 10 miles off Spezia, north-west Italy. Discovered by chance by a merchant vessel late that night, the transfer of passengers proved impossible in the high seas and gale force winds. Though taken in tow, the line soon parted and all seven occupants were never seen again.

Keen to start a Cairo to Capetown service, Imperial Airways needed to see how a floatplane would tackle the natural lakes and rivers of Africa. Approached by the Air Ministry while building an all-metal and soundproofed, seventeen seat, single-engined passenger aircraft, complete with washing and toilet facilities, Shorts added two more engines and a pair of 40 foot floats to give a fair comparison with a Calcutta. Alan Cobham was the natural choice of pilot. Manned by three crew and two (movie and still) photographers, between July and August 1931, the Valetta was flown across Africa to Lake Kivu (west of Lake Victoria) and into the

Congo, returning to Rochester after a survey of over 12,000 miles. Floatplanes would never seriously compete with commercial flying boat services, but in September, Reginald Mitchell watched Flight Lieutenant John Boothman of the RAF High Speed Flight, fly the S6B at over 340 miles an hour above Cowes to win Britain's third Schneider Trophy Race. Two weeks later, the Rolls Royce R engine powered Flight Lieutenant George Stainforth to over 407 miles an hour, a world record.

Mitchell's Sea Lion flying boat had prevented Italy winning the trophy outright in 1922 and the following year his S4 had raised the world speed record for floatplanes to 226 miles an hour. With America needing just one more win to secure the trophy after the 1925 race, the far-sighted Air Chief Marshal Trenchard had provided Air Ministry funds to form an RAF team, the High Speed Flight, at Felixstowe. Supermarine S5s had come first and second in 1927 and despite opposition from treasury officials, Air Ministry funds had again been used to purchase two Supermarine S6s, enabling the 1929 race to be won at almost 330 miles an hour. The state of the economy had deterred the government from sponsoring the all important third race however and the victory owed everything to the patriotic gift of one hundred thousand pounds from Lady Lucy Houston. Without her, the lovely sculpture would not be permanently installed within the Royal Aero Club in London and Mitchell's legendary Spitfire design, born from these triumphs of speed, may never have materialized. A year later the world's largest flying boat began a protracted tour of Europe.

Dornier

Born to a French wine importer and his German wife at Kempten (Bavaria), Claudius Dornier had graduated from the Technical University at Munich. When in his late twenties, his working knowledge of strengthening light metals had seen him appointed personal adviser to Count Ferdinand von Zeppelin, whose airship works were at Friedrichshafen on the Bodensee, the German name for the 39 mile long freshwater Lake Constance, bordered by Germany, Austria and Switzerland. Given his own department to develop all-metal aircraft, by the end of the First World War his use of thin, load bearing panels in the construction of the wings and hulls had transformed the designs. Moving to Manzel, the department became his own, independent Dornier-Metallbautten, which in 1922 moved to larger premises at Altenrhein on the Swiss shore of the lake, to avoid the ban on building military aircraft imposed on Germany and her allies. He also opened a factory at the Marina di Pisa, on the west coast of Italy, where his delightfully streamlined Wal (whale) flying boat flew at the end of the year.

Powered by two Rolls Royce Eagle engines fitted in tandem to reduce the frontal area and maintain equilibrium should one fail, the hull accommodated fourteen passengers and featured aerodynamic stub-wings (sponsons) rather than wing floats. The tail had a single fin and rudder. Built under license in Spain, the Netherlands, Switzerland, Japan, America and Russia, the reliable flying boats were snapped up by airlines and the military. The 1925 expedition of the renowned explorer Roald Amundsen landed a pair on the most northern Arctic ice and in January 1926 one of sixteen operated by the Spanish Air Force made an east-west crossing of the South Atlantic to Buenos Aires, though with several intermediate stops. Pilot Ramón Franco became a national hero. Two years later, the hydrogen-filled airship Graf Zeppelin began a seasonal trans-Atlantic service to New York, but in July 1929 a much larger flying boat, specifically designed to cross the Atlantic non-stop, emerged from the factory at Altenrhein.

Known simply as the Do-X, with the appropriate registration D1929 boldly stenciled across the wing and fuselage, the twelve (tandem) Bristol Jupiter air-cooled engines built by Siemens, lifted some 40 tons from the lake to become the world's largest heavier than air flying machine. In October, almost a hundred and sixty passengers were flown for an hour over the lake. The following year the four year-old state airline Deutsche Luft Hansa began operating three Wals on a South Atlantic airmail service, with ships positioned off West Africa and South America to winch them up for refuelling and maintenance before catapulting them on their way. Having made three hundred test flights, and refitted with Curtiss water-cooled engines, in November 1930 the Do-X began a lengthy tour of Europe and West Africa and the following August completed a thirteen hour crossing of the South Atlantic to New York. Calshot was visited during the outward flight and during the return in May 1932, after which the colossus was landed on Lake Müggelsea in the eastern suburbs of Berlin. Underpowered and uneconomical, the giant never conquered the Atlantic and lasted less than a year with the re-named Lufthansa.

From October 1931 Calcuttas had begun flying from Cairo to Mwanza on Lake Victoria and in January, Imperial had begun a ten and a half-day, weekly through-service to South Africa, though the Capetown sector was retained by South African Airways. The design evolved into the military Rangoon flying boat which re-equipped 203 Squadron at Basra in the Persian Gulf during the year, the last of them fitted with stainless steel Alclad planing bottoms to lessen the corrosion. The year also saw the introduction of the Short Kent flying boats *Scipio*, *Sylvanus* and *Satyrus*. Born of the political decision by Italy to stop British flying boats refuelling in the ports of its colonies, the 450 mile range enabled them to fly non-stop from Mirabella (Crete) to Alexandria.

* * *

The Kent class introduced a luxurious form of travel soon to be associated with flying boats. The enclosed cockpit had a separate compartment at the rear for the radio operator/navigator, while an increase of over nine thousand pounds all-up weight enabled a higher mail payload to be carried. The fitting of four engines proved more reliable, the long exhaust pipes and collector rings reduced the noise for everyone aboard, while the wide cabin allowed much more space for the fifteen passengers. Unlike the Calcutta's forward-facing seats, arranged in a double and single row either side of a narrow walkway, the Kent had four rows of facing pairs on both sides of an aisle which led aft to the stewards 'pantry', toilet and washroom. As a measure of the times, the twin-burner oil stove could be used by a ladies 'travelling companion' to serve her mistress her usual fare. The same applied to a gentleman travelling with his own servant or valet.

In May 1932 Eustace Short died of a heart attack while landing the single engined, all-metal Mussel floatplane on which he had first learnt to fly. Oswald was left to carry the family name forward and in June the prototype all-metal Sarafand flying boat, emerged as the second largest aeroplane in the world. Though still a biplane, the 31 tons were lifted by six Rolls Royce Buzzard engines in tandem (as was the cockpit seating), the lower of the 120 foot wings strengthened against the drag of bracing hull/wing struts. Designed for ten crew, with a range of over 1,250 nautical miles, the flying boat proved more efficient than the Do-X , with half the engines and typically none of the publicity.

The RAF could only use it for experimental work, but the concept of a large and reliable, multi-engine flying boat, had been proven. Just over a year later, the company's first large monoplane flying boat, the twin-engined Knuckleduster, was launched in response to an Air Ministry requirement for a general reconnaissance flying boat, the distinctive thirty degree gull-wing necessary to clear the propellers of the steam-cooled Rolls Royce Goshawk engines from the water. Alliot Verdon Roe, founder of the A.V. Roe (Avro) aircraft company, and his brother Humphrey, had joined Samuel Saunders on the Isle of Wight and both Saunders-Roe and Supermarine received contracts for their military (London and Stranraer) biplane flying boats. The revolutionary Knuckleduster never progressed beyond the prototype, but Shorts continued development of the monoplane would soon bear fruit.

Long- distance

Aside from contesting the Schneider Trophy, Italy had investigated the practicalities of long-distance flying. In 1925, the year the race was held at

Baltimore, Major Francesco De Pinedo had taken a standard Savoia-Marchetti S16 flying boat away from Rome on what would prove to be a significant test of reliability and endurance. Accompanied by mechanic Ernesto Campanelli, his outward flight took in India, Burma, Singapore, the Dutch East Indies and Broome on the west coast of Australia. Flying on to Perth, Adelaide, Melbourne, Sydney and Brisbane, he reached the Cape York Peninsula before crossing to Thursday Island, continuing via the islands of the Dutch East Indies to the Philippines and Shanghai. Korea was next and then Japan (Tokyo) when the flying boat headed back to Italy via India. Powered by a single 450 horsepower engine, the S16 had crossed vast tracts of land and water during the 30,000 mile journey and had convincingly proved that flying boats were capable of flying long distance. Pinedo was understandably fêted and ranked amongst the finest pilots of the time – though his next flight almost ended in disaster.

In February 1927 he and his crew boarded a Savoia-Marchetti S55 flying boat powered by a tandem pair of 500 horsepower engines, positioned high above a cockpit set within the leading edge of the mainplane separating the two wooden hulls. Leaving Sesto Calendi, they followed the African coast to Dakar before crossing the South Atlantic to Pernmbuco, Brazil. Reaching Buenos Aires, they turned north to the West Indies and from New Orleans headed west to land on the lake formed by the Roosevelt Dam in Arizona. The refuelling over, a young man sat in a boat alongside, lit up a cigarette and without thinking threw the match into the water. Within seconds, the contaminated surface ignited and the *Santa Maria* exploded and sank. Pinedo was ashore, but co-pilot Captain

Savoia S55 *Jahú*. COURTESY MARCELO BORDIM.

Carlos del Prete and engineer/mechanic Curlo Zacchetti Vitale had to dive for their lives. Another machine was flown out for them to complete the return journey.

By contrast, in April, 27 year old Joâo Ribeiro de Barros and his crew (co-pilot, navigator and mechanic) made a heroic 'private' crossing of the South Atlantic between Cape Verde and Fernando de Noronha, having used all his savings to buy a second hand S55 and suffered malaria, arrest and sabotage en route from Genoa to Gibraltar. Today, his beautifully restored *Jahú* is displayed within the Museu Transportes Aéreos del Mercosur at São Carlos, São Paulo, Brazil, as the sole surviving example in the world.

The largest display of long-distance flying came in 1933, when twenty-four triple finned Savoia S55X flying boats, led by the Italian Air Minister General Italo Balbo, crossed 6,000 miles of the Atlantic in tight formation during appalling weather conditions. Powered by a tandem pair of 700 horsepower Fiat engines, the front driving a double bladed propeller and the rear a 'pusher' four-blader, the Savoias had refuelled in Ireland, Iceland, Labrador and Canada, landing at New York in time for the Chicago Century of Progress World Fair. Though the type was subsequently used by the appropriately named Societè Aerea Mediterranea, a three engined commercial version, the S66, would be operated by the airline and by Aero Expresso Haliano and Ala Littoria, with up to eighteen passengers seated inside the smoothly contoured twin hulls.

In November 1920, 20 year old Wilmot Hudson Fysh had joined with his friend and fellow former Australian Flying Corps officer Paul McGuiness and three Queensland graziers in forming the Queensland and Northern Territory Aerial Services Company (Qantas), which received a government subsidy to carry the mail in western Queensland. In January 1934 the company was joined by Imperial Airways in forming Qantas Empire Airways Ltd (QEA) to operate services between Brisbane and Singapore, with Fysh as managing director. A year would pass before the first 'through' service of mail and passengers left Croydon for Australia, but the surveys of Africa, India, Malaya and Australia would be of huge value to the forthcoming flying boat services.

Forced to restrict the choice of landing fields during his surveys to those long enough to be exited with a full fuel load, to the detriment of crew numbers and equipment, Sir Alan Cobham had evolved a system of in-flight refuelling to achieve a lighter take-off without affecting the range and payload. Trials using the new Airspeed Courier monoplane, which featured a retractable undercarriage, involved trailing a weighted line from a tanker aircraft. Caught by a shepherds crook from the cockpit of the Courier, the hose and trigger nozzle were drawn down before gravity assisted the flow of fuel from the higher flying converted airliner. Not at all easy to perform stood in a buffeting slipstream threatening to send you and the long swaying hose into the Courier's propeller. But in September 1934 Sir Alan and Squadron Leader Bill Helmore left Portsmouth airfield to demonstrate the system during a non-stop flight to India.

Though successfully topped up over England, the second refuelling over Malta was followed by the engine and propeller coming to a stop (a throttle linkage problem) and they were lucky to clear the stone walls of the island to complete a wheels-up 'dead-stick' landing on Hal Far airfield. Even worse was to follow, with one of the two tankers crashing on returning to England with the loss of all aboard, while the parked Courier was destroyed by a badly handled Italian Air Force machine at Rome Airport. Determined to continue, Sir Alan went on to form Flight Refuelling Ltd at Ford Aerodrome near Littlehampton, his former Flying Circus base. A second, momentous decision, following the formation of Imperial Airways, would greatly affect British commercial flying boat operations,

Empire Air Mail

Announced in Parliament that December, the government's new Empire Air Mail Postal Scheme, would enable a half ounce letter to be sent by air across the whole of the British Empire, for no more than the one and a half penny stamp seen on everyday letters, and from the same red pillar boxes. Postcards required a one penny stamp. Aware of the booming air travel market and the possibility of carrying some 200,000 tons of mail a year, Imperials technical adviser Major Robert Mayo envisaged a fleet of large aircraft, each able to carry one and a half tons of mail and freight and twenty four passengers in comfort for some 700 miles before having to refuel.

Public opinion would not have agreed to the costly purchase of land for runways, but the RAF and Alan Cobham had proved it was possible to operate across Africa and to the Far East, while the size and weight, take-off and landing distances, meant the aircraft just had to be flying boats. The decision was made to use them on the two main Empire air routes and Short Brothers received an unprecedented, one and a quarter million pound order to build twenty-eight radically new flying boats. With no design on the drawing board and no such specification flying, the company expressed a wish to test a prototype. Imperial said there simply was no time, the money was there, and each machine would be worth £45,000. Pressed hard, Chairman Oswald Short signed the contract! Today we would refer to it as a 'Catch 22' situation, for without the expected increase in demand for the mail there would be no profit, and without Imperial's nudge to the government there would have been no subsidy towards the airlift and development costs. The combination, which included an extra subsidy from the Post Office for the Christmas mail, virtually paid for the whole of the order. The idea to carry all the British mail to all of the Empire (the 'all-up' scheme) for no more than the shipping companies were charging at the time, had come from the airline's secretary while accompanying managing director George Woods-Humphrey and chairman Sir Eric Geddes on a promotional flying visit to Capetown. The details had been worked out, the government had been informed and the rest as they say is history, though few remember Mr S.A. Dismore whose foresight had ensured the scheme would work.

C-CLASS

Using the basic layout of the attractive Scion Senior floatplane as a half-scale model, Shorts chief designer and general manager Arthur Gouge doubled the linear dimensions, installed more powerful engines, created a 17 foot deep all-metal hull with two decks and a new planing bottom and added his own, patented, drag-less flap design to improve the take-off and landing runs. Both distances proved shorter than those of the significantly smaller biplane flying boats! A total advance in all-metal design and performance, the British aircraft industry had seen nothing of such size and complexity. Short Brothers simply got on with it, producing their own machining presses and recruiting a largely unskilled labour force to be trained at the riverside factory. For their contribution to aviation in the locality, Oswald Short and Arthur Gouge would both be awarded the Freedom of the City of Rochester.

The new monoplane flying boat was 88 feet long and over 31 feet high, the 114-foot wingspan supporting an all up weight of 18 tons, including twenty-four passengers, seven crew and one and a half tons of mail. Smoothly contoured into wings set high above the water without the need for a gull-wing, and fed by two (325 gallon) cylindrical fuel tanks, the four Bristol Pegasus engines produced a comfortable cruising speed of 165 miles an hour. Each wing float was joined to the main spar by a pair of tandem struts, the intervening bracing wires fitted with a shock absorber to allow 4 inches of backward movement during rough-water landings, rather than overload the wing. Designed to maintain services to South Africa and Australia, the 'Empire' flying boats had a still air range of well over 700 miles but required regular refuelling and oiling stops.

Things had come a long way since those early plywood hulls, part covered in weight saving fabric, had been replaced by copper-riveted mahogany planks laid in diagonal skins separated by oiled fabric. An alloy of aluminium and one third the weight of steel, duralumin could be used in much greater thicknesses while the new monocoque construction (French for 'single shell') allowed much more space within the hitherto cramped interiors. Wing construction had progressed from fabric covered wood to fabric covered metal, but at Rochester they were enclosed by flush riveted metal with doped linen cloth on just the moving control surfaces.

It was just not that simple to leave the water. At full take-off power, a partly immersed hull will create a bow-wave until sufficient speed takes it over the 'hump' to begin skimming or aquaplaning across the surface, and much thought had gone into designing a 'step' or upward cut in the planing bottom to draw in a cushion of air. The balance (centre of water pressure) was equally important. Too far forward and the hull will pitch up with insufficient flying speed. Too far back and it will dig in, with potential fatal consequences for both. In addition, as Richard Pearse had found all those years ago, there was a need to alter the angle or pitch of a propeller to develop sufficient power to take off and then cruise at a higher speed without over-revving and wrecking the engine.

Built under licence by de Havillands, the American Hamilton-Standard constant speed propeller was separated from a hub in which a piston turned each of the three blades, to either fine pitch (for take off) or coarse (for cruising). Fitted to super-charged engines (supplied with high pressure air) such as the Pegasus, they provided a pilot with the best power available at altitude. Primarily responsible for developing the nine cylinder air cooled radial engine in Britain, the Bristol Aeroplane Company had seen an increase in power of one hundred and thirty per cent when using the new high octane fuels, while fuel consumption had dropped by as much as one quarter, due largely to a forty per cent reduction in weight from the development of light alloys and metals.

Ideally pilots would come from current flying boat operations with Imperial in the Mediterranean and would simply require type conversion. Landplane pilots would be converted by Air Service Training Limited at the former Armstrong Whitworth Flying Club premises on the river Hamble. Military pilots would also be allowed to transfer from the RAF and would be awarded acting First Officer (co-pilot) status after gaining civilian engineering and wireless operating licences at Croydon. As Air Superintendent of the airline, Major H.G.Brackley was responsible for the selection and training of all of them and with the very experienced Captain F.J.Bailey, would personally check out the first to be given command of the new 'Empire' boats. Most held Master Pilot certificates. Others would fly as supernumerary crew under their supervision.

It was not just a matter of introducing larger aircraft on the routes however. The far-flung marine bases required mail and passenger handling facilities, overnight accommodation, radio and weather stations, fuel, supplies, water and land transport. The terminals would require concrete slipways, maintenance hangars and workshops and it was not surprising that many would have their origins with the military. In 1936 the Air Ministry opened a new factory on Queens Island at Belfast, Northern Ireland, to build aircraft and seaplanes, the shares jointly owned by Shorts and the ship builders Harland and Wolff – Short and Harland Ltd.

Chief test pilot John Parker lifted *Canopus*, the first of the new flying boats, away from the Medway and the assembled media on 4 July 1936, though having to pull off an unexpected and fortunately un-noticed, flap-less landing on his return! Fitted with eight fuel tanks for longer range, *Caledonia* followed on 15 September from when up to two flying boats a month appeared on the slipway, delivered to Imperial the day of the launch or soon afterwards. The factory knew them as the S23 or C-Class, as each of the names began with the third letter of the alphabet. The initial order comprised *Canopus, Caledonia, Centaurus, Cavalier, Cambria, Castor, Cassiopeia, Capella, Cygnus, Capricornus, Corsair, Courtier, Challenger, Centurion, Coriolanus, Calpurnia, Ceres, Clio, Circe, Calypso, Camilla, Carinna, Cordelia, Cameronian, Corinthian, Coogee, Corio* and *Coorong*. Flown out to Genoa in October, *Canopus* made the first scheduled flight at the hands of Captain Bailey, who flew between Alexandria and Brindisi in seven hours and twenty minutes, having refuelled at Mirabella Harbour (Crete) and at Athens.

The results of the RAFs refuelling trials had been forwarded to Ford by the Air Ministry and with the director of civil aviation agreeing to sponsor trial flights across the Atlantic. Flight Refuelling had modified the hull of *Cambria* to take a winch and hose. Obsolete Armstrong Whitworth transports were converted into tanker aircraft. The initial trials were not without humour. The increased weight in flight could not be absorbed by the tanker undercarriages on landing and the sacks of clay and sand used as ballast were jettisoned on the seaward leg of the circuit – causing embarrassment to one public spirited observer after he had alerted rescue services and the local lifeboat to search for the bodies portrayed as tumbling from an aircraft over the beach! In December, *Caledonia* entered the Christmas spirit by flying some five and a half tons of Christmas mail each way between Britain and India.

Situated opposite Supermarine's factory and slipway at Woolston, Hythe had first become involved with flying boats towards the end of the First World War, when the boat builders, May, Harden and May had begun constructing hulls for AD and Felixstowe flying boats within sheds built by the Admiralty.

Hulls had continued to be built for Supermarine Aviation and by 1924 a large hangar had been erected. Four years later the site was absorbed by Vickers-Supermarine. Having utilized Supermarine's slipway and the former premises of British Marine Air Navigation at Woolston for its biplane flying boats, Imperial had begun using Hythe and by 1937 had installed a new maintenance, hangar. A second was built and passengers arriving by train at Berth 50 in the Southampton Western Docks, were ferried by launch to Hythe and a waiting flying boat.

On 8 February 1937, Captain H.W.C. (Jim) Algar finally took *Castor* away with eight passengers and over a ton of freight and mail (and gold bullion) on the first regular passenger service to Alexandria. Two days earlier he had been forced to return and circle Southampton for an hour with oiled up plugs, and had then been delayed by rough water. Fitted with special fuel tanks for the Atlantic, which increased the range to almost 2,900 nautical miles, ten days later *Caledonia* was flown non-stop to Alexandria in just over thirteen and a half hours by Captain Cumming, having left Southampton at four fifteen in the morning. Captain Powell and *Cambria* ended the month by circumnavigating Britain in just under eight and three quarter hours.

Early in May, Imperial withdrew its landplanes from as far as Kisumu (Kenya), in preparation for the new 'Empire' flying boat services, expected to take over in June using the stops on the Nile pioneered by the Calcutta crews. On 22 May *Cambria* arrived at Durban looking rather sightless without the customary row of portholes, thought unnecessary for proving flights, after Captain Egglesfield had off-loaded radio equipment for the East African stations en route. Seven days later, *Courtier* was flown in by Captain Edward Alcock, whose brother had famously conquered the Atlantic. Departing two days later, on reaching Lindi he was asked to return to inaugurate the first passenger service to Southampton, begun with five passengers and less than half a ton of mail on 6 June . Two days later, Captain E. Attwood brought *Canopus* in to complete the first, six-day through-service from Southampton. Operating from waters of equal attraction to the sailing community could be tricky however, for the day that *Cambria* arrived at Durban, *Castor* had collided with a yacht on Southampton Water prior to leaving for Karachi. The passengers and mail were transferred to *Cygnus*.

On 22 June , the Secretary of State for Air and the Postmaster-General, arrived to mark the formal start of the un-surcharged Empire Air Mail service, when *Centurion* powered off with three and a half thousand pounds of mail for the Sudan, East and South Africa. The increased range meant crews no longer had to be positioned along the routes and the No 5 Operating Division at Southampton replaced Croydon as the hub of the Empire services, becoming known as the Number 5 Line. In July *Calypso* extended the airmail service to Australia and the following month *Camilla* and the Qantas 'boat *Carpentaria* left Sydney with the first of the Australian airmail. But at the close of the first year of operations three flying boats had been lost, though through no fault of the design nor the construction. Though given the best equipment available, crews had nothing like today's global positioning and communication systems beamed down from satellites orbiting in space and had to make the best of changing weather patterns.

Delivered to Imperial on 16 March, eight days later *Capricornus* had left

Southampton on the first through-service to Australia, with a single passenger and ten thousand pounds worth of gold bullion stowed in the 'secret' compartment beneath the floor of the aft cabin. The radio operator was in (morse) touch with French ground stations, but reception had become difficult due to the deteriorating weather conditions and the aircraft had entered cloud while heading for Lake Marignane, near Marseilles. Unable to maintain height and forced to descend in a blinding snowstorm, one wing had collided with trees on a 2,000 foot high ridge in the Beaujolais Mountains, near Macon in the French Alps, sending the big flying boat back into the air before impacting, more or less level, on the edge of a pine forest. Fortunate to survive with just a broken arm, the radio operator had struggled painfully through the snow to a nearby farmhouse, though both pilots, the flight clerk, steward and lady passenger died from their injuries.

By contrast, *Courtier* had descended in perfect October weather to the calm but deceptively clear water of Phaleron Bay near Athens, though the failure to round out in time ended the lives of three of the nine passengers. Two months later *Cygnus* fatally ended a nine month career at Brindisi Harbour. The large, electrically operated flaps were very effective if used correctly, and in time. But if abused, the swiftly displaced lift and centre of gravity caused the 24 tons of metal to 'porpoise' with increasingly long bounces and none of the grace of the friendly marine mammals. With full (drag) flap run out and a choppy surface, *Cygnus* failed to take-off, porpoised, overturned and sank with the loss of the steward and one passenger. Others were injured. A fine line balanced

British Long Range Atlantic Trials. Harrow tanker refuelling *Cabot*.
COURTESY MICHAEL COBHAM, FLIGHT REFUELLING LTD

triumph from tragedy, for *Calypso* had made the first scheduled service between Alexandria and Karachi in October and John Burgess brought *Centaurus* safely home in December after safely surveying the route to Australia and New Zealand.

Imperial ordered another eleven flying boats, bringing the total to thirty-nine, the largest single order for a British civil aircraft at the time. The first of the new order, *Carpentaria, Coolangatta* and *Cooee* (delivered in March 1938) were the last of thirty-one S23s and completed the six ordered by Qantas for the Singapore to Sydney service. The remaining eight, *Champion, Cabot, Connemara, Clyde, Captain Cook, Canterbury, Cumberland* and *Cathay* would be S30s. With the exception of *Cabot,* they were powered by four, 890 horsepower Bristol Perseus sleeve-valve engines. Though rated at 30 horsepower less than the Pegasus, the output was matched by cleverly fitting nacelles of exactly 3 inches less diameter to reduce the (profile) drag. Built from a heavier gauge of metal sheet, the strengthened hulls and wings enabled nearly two and a half extra tons to be lifted from the water, while the still-air range of some 1,870 miles and an eight hour endurance, more than doubled the performance.

Chapter Two

Bigger and Further

France

With coastlines ending on the shores of the English Channel, the Atlantic and the Mediterranean, and wide coastal estuaries and fresh water lakes, it would have been unnatural if France had not become involved with flying boats. Born at Bagnères-de-Bigorre in August 1883, within the Pyrénées region of south-west France, more famous for its thermal spa than anything to do with aviation, Pierre-Georges Latécoère had distinguished himself at the local college and gone on to study engineering at the École Centrale in Paris, as had Louis Blériot, the first pilot to cross the English Channel. Following the death of his father, at 22 Georges had joined his mother in running the family sawmill which supplied rolling stock for the railway. Poor eyesight brought a swift return to civilian life after the start of the First World War, but in 1917 he was commissioned to supply shells and aeroplanes for the war effort, which had seen the two-seat, single engined biplane FBA (Franco-British Aviation) flying boat produced for the Royal Naval Air Service and other allied air arms.

Two new factories were built on the outskirts of Toulouse, the aeroplane factory at Montaudran soon having its own little airfield to test the licence-built Salmson reconnaissance biplanes. A year later Pierre formed his own airline to fly mail and a limited number of passengers on pioneering services to Spain and Africa, and from South America to Brazil, later using his own float equipped 'hydroplane' design on African services. Launched in 1926, his first flying boat featured a monoplane wing, a pair of tandem engines, and sponsons rather than wing floats, but in 1927 the company was taken over by his chief financier and renamed. From then on he devoted himself to building bigger and better flying boats. With no suitable fresh water (non corrosive) waterway nearby to test his designs, in 1929 he erected a large wooden shed on the shore of the six mile long Lake Biscarosse in Aquitaine, sheltered by dunes and by the pines of the surrounding Landes forest.

In October 1933 a merger between his old company (Aéropostale) and four others created the national carrier Air France. Having acquired fourteen luxuriously equipped Lioré et Olivier ten seat, four engined, metal hulled, H242 flying boats from Air Union, the new airline was able to fly non-stop over the Mediterranean, linking Paris with Algiers and Tunis via Marseilles. In December, twenty-three years after Henri Fabre's historic flight, his four (tandem) engined (L300) *Croix du Sud* also lifted from the Étang de Berre, to the west of Marseille, though landing over two thousand miles away at Saint Louis on the West African Atlantic coast, an international record. The longer range was used by Air France to carry mail between France and South America, using the shortest Dakar – Port Natal route.

Three years later the six-engined (L521) *Lieutenant de Vaisseau Paris*, heralded as the largest aircraft in the world and able to carry seventy-six passengers on two decks, flew from Natal to Florida – but was sunk after dramatically becoming airborne at the end of the mooring cable when a hurricane crossed Pensacola Bay. Dismantled and shipped back to France, it was fitted with more powerful, 960 horsepower engines and in October 1937 flew between Kenitra (Morocco) and Maceio (Brazil) in thirty-six hours, a new long distance record. Operated by Air France-Transatlantique, two years later it flew non-stop between Port Washington and Lake Biscarosse. Though seen with its successor, the (L522) *Ville de Saint Pierre*, at Bermuda, world events would see both impressed into the Aéronavale and both would be destroyed in 1944 when retreating German forces dynamited the hangar alongside the Étang de Berre.

AMERICA

Juan (Terry) Trippe had learned to fly at the Curtiss Flying School in Miami, and with the help of his equally wealthy friends, had founded an air taxi and an air charter company. In 1927 he absorbed two embryonic concerns, which included Pan American Incorporated co-founded by Air Corps Majors Arnold and Spaatz, and at 28 became president of the resulting Pan American Airways. Six years before a similar scheme was launched in Britain, the 1928 Kelly Foreign Air Mail Act, enabled private companies to be subsidised to effectively compete with the state-backed Aéropostale of France, German Luft Hansa and Britains Imperial Airways in carrying United States mail across the world. Among the first to use the twin engined, eight-seat S38 amphibious flying boat designed by the Russian-born Igor Sikorsky, Trippe ordered three four-engined models in October 1931. Designed to carry up to thirty-eight passengers for almost 1,000 miles, the S40 was the largest commercial airliner of the time. Named by First Lady Lou Henry Hoover in November, *American Clipper* was the first to be named by Trippe after the fast China-tea 'Clipper' sailing ships of the 1860s that had dominated world trade routes, including the Atlantic, though the array of struts 'suspending' the engines between the wing and hull, and the twin booms connecting the tailplane soon caused them to be known as 'Flying Forests'! The reliability of *American Clipper, Caribbean Clipper* and *Southern Clipper* firmly established 'Pan Am' with the public, but even as they began flying mail and passengers to the Caribbean and Latin America, Trippe was planning a larger version capable of flying over 2,000 miles of the Pacific without refuelling.

Built expressly for Pan Am by the Vought-Sikorsky division of the United Aircraft Corporation at Connecticut, the S42 was fitted with eight elliptical fuel tanks (over 1,200 gallons of petrol) to feed four, 700 horse-power, Pratt and Whitney Hornet engines, each driving three-bladed variable pitch Hamilton-Standard propellers. Put on the South American route in May 1934 *Brazilian Clipper* was followed by *West Indies Clipper* in December and a third (un-named) the following May. Graceful and supremely state of the art, they were approached from a gangway laid from the quayside to the ribbed walkway atop the fuselage, where an outward opened hatch revealed a staircase immediately in front of the twin tail fins. Inside, four ventilated and sound proofed cabins were provided with fully adjustable seats and individual baggage space beneath. The all-up weight had risen to 17 tons, 4,000 pounds more than the S40, and there was a 30-mile an hour speed advantage, but an even larger flying boat was about to join the airline.

Glenn L. Martin had progressed from kites to flying his own aeroplane in 1909 and had gone on to found two aircraft factories. Though initially pipped by Sikorsky in supplying Pan Am, his giant M-130 flying boat was certainly more advanced. Constructed of riveted aluminium alloy with a corrugated duralumin roof 25 feet above the hull, the four, 830 horse-power, Pratt and Whitney engines, could support up to 23 tons at a comfortable cruising speed of 163 miles an hour, just sixty per cent of the available power. Strutted sponsons provided lateral stability and concealed extra fuel tanks. The 'control cabin' accommodated two pilots and a radio officer with the flight engineer sat within the wing super-structure. The lower deck held the galley, lounge and three cabins, each with eight seats capable of being converted into six sleeping bunks. In addition, the starboard side of the twelve-seat lounge provided a pair of dressing rooms, with four fold-back wash basins, supplied with hot and cold running water. *China Clipper* first flew in December 1934 and was followed by *Hawaii Clipper* and *Philippine Clipper*.

Known as Martin Ocean Transports by the factory in Pan Am service, the trio came to be known as 'China Clippers' by the public. Trippe had expensively equipped the remote Pacific islands of Midway, Wake and Guam with refuelling facilities, radio and navigation aids, and luxurious hotel accommodation for passengers and crews. In November 1935 *China Clipper* brought the first American airmail to a magnificent new seaplane terminal at Manila, having taken six and a half days and less than sixty

CNAC Douglas Dolphin amphibian.

flying hours to arrive from San Francisco, over 8,000 miles away, a third of the time required by ocean liners. The naval-style uniforms of the crews became as popular on the 'island-hopping' routes as they had throughout South America. Released by First National Pictures in August 1936, the movie *China Clipper* featured the Martin flying boat and a rising star by the name of Humphrey Bogart. Each Clipper could seat forty-eight passengers, but the fuel required for the long-distance flights brought a drastic reduction in the pay load, and despite the publicity following the inaugural October service to Hong Kong by *Philippine Clipper,* and a six day service to Manila by *Hawaii Clipper*, the trio were the first and last of the line. Unlike the Douglas Dolphin. Developed from the 'air yacht' design which had included Bill Boeing among its clients, a pair of the twin engined, six seat amphibians was operated between Hong Kong and the Chinese mainland from 1934, latterly by the Chinese National Aviation Company part owned by Pan Am. Modified versions served the US Coastguard, Army and Navy.

Four more Sikorsky flying boats joined Pan Am between July 1935 and April 1936, the S42As *Jamaica Clipper*, *Antilles Clipper*, *Brazilian Clipper* and *Dominican Clipper* given 750 horsepower Hornet engines and longer, more efficient wings to increase capacity and range. Hoping to capitalise on this wave of enthusiasm, in February 1936 a factory and slipway were built west of the Hamble peninsular to build the 'A's under license in Britain. Nothing was concluded and in December the British Marine Aircraft Company was bought and re-named Folland Aircraft by the former chief designer of the Gloster Aircraft Company.

Trippe had already considered the two ultimate airmail destinations however and in September Pan Am had taken delivery of the S42Bs *Pan American Clipper 11* and *Bermuda Clipper. Pan American Clipper 111* would follow in the New Year. Given the new 'constant-speed' propellers developed by Frank Caldwell for the Hamilton-Standard division of United Aircraft, the Hornet engines could support up to 23 tons for some 3,500 thousand miles. But having agreed to jointly fly the Atlantic with Imperial Airways, Pan Am could not now start on its own and instead proceeded to survey the Pacific. Britain was not prepared to allow landing rights in Australia however and in March 1937 New Zealand welcomed the airline's chief pilot Ed Musick and *Samoan Clipper* (the renamed *Clipper 11*) at the end of a 6,900 mile proving flight from San Francisco.

After painstaking research and planning, the crew had flown 2,400 miles to Pearl Harbour, Honolulu, before heading for the incredibly small island of Kingman Reef, 1,100 miles further south, virtually at the centre of the Pacific Ocean, guided in by direction finding equipment aboard the Pan Am supply vessel North Wind, anchored in the coral lagoon. Sixteen hundred miles of ocean had then been crossed to Pago Pago and the island of Tutuilla, in the middle of the American Samoan Islands, before setting off for Auckland, 1,800 miles away. *Samoan Clipper* returned to New Zealand on Boxing Day and subsequently brought the first New Zealand airmail into Hawaii on 3 January . A Martin Clipper completed the service at San Francisco three days later.

By now Pan Am had become America's premier airline, receiving huge subsidies due to the influence of Trippe and the expertise of technical director Charles Lindbergh, famous for his 1927 solo flight to Paris. In a little over a year, an even bigger, Boeing flying boat would join the airline, while another long-range success was already patrolling high in the heavens.

PBY

Similar to 'Bill' Boeing, Reuben Hollis Fleet had made a successful career in the lumber business and had also been inspired by a flight in a Curtiss seaplane from Seattle in 1914. The First World War had gained him his pilot wings and the rank of major, responsible for setting up military flight training schools for the air division of the army before joining the engineering test centre at McCook Field. On returning to civilian life he had become general manager of the Gallaudet Aircraft Corporation before forming the Consolidated Aircraft Company. Firm orders from the Army Air Service enabled a move to much larger premises in 1924 (used by Curtiss during the war), when landplane trainers for the navy were simply given floats and a bigger engine to convert them into seaplanes. With the army and fledgling airlines taking interest in all-metal monoplanes however, he had appointed Isaac Machlin Laddon as chief designer, a position he had held at McCook Field. Akin to Supermarine and Mitchell, Consolidated and 'Mac' Laddon became synonymous with new and innovative designs which continued up to and beyond the Second World War.

Amid growing concern for Japan's ambitions in the Pacific, American aircraft companies were invited to bid for a contract to produce an all-metal, 2,000 mile range monoplane flying boat to provide early warning to the far-flung American bases. Though new techniques would be required to form and rivet large sheets of aluminium alloy for the envisaged 60 foot hull and 100 foot wingspan, Laddon's design won. Just under a year later, in January 1929, the XPY-1 (Experimental Patrol bomber, built by Consolidated) Admiral was lifted from the Anacostia River by a naval pilot with Laddon as observer. Glen Martin won the subsequent bid for production. In retaliation, Fleet used the materials bought in anticipation of the military order, to swiftly produce a civilian version, the Commodore. He also bought a majority stockholding in the New York, Rio and Buenos Aires Airline (NYRBA), to ensure only his flying boats would fly a new 7,000 mile service between Miami and Argentina, though founder, World War One 'ace', Colonel Ralph O'Neill, was first to buy the new Sikorsky S38.

Reuben had the wings of the Commodores painted coral, the black painted hulls merged into an attractive cream above the waterline, where the name of the airline was painted across the dramatically tapering fuselage, preceded by a long forward- pointing arrow. Thirty-two passengers were accommodated in four fabric panelled cabins, individually decorated in pastel shades, with fully upholstered seats and thick carpeting, though with little protection from the noise of the two uncowled, 575 horsepower Pratt and Whitney Hornet engines. Crewed by two pilots and a radio operator doubling as a steward, with names such as *Cuba*, *Havana* and *Rio de Janeiro*, the Commodores proved reliable and popular, but with an all-up weight of less than 9 tons (including fuel), fewer than fourteen passengers could be flown on the longer sectors. Operating costs were off-set by airmail contracts with the governments of Argentina, Uruguay and Brazil, but Juan Trippe took steps to prevent the hardworking company from receiving a vital subsidy from the American Government, and in 1930 made a typical 'hostile' bid for control on behalf of Pan Am.

Determined to win a military order, Fleet improved his design and early in 1933 began supplying the Navy with Ranger flying boats, fitted with a shortened lower wing to support the floats. Within twelve months, a formation flew non-stop to Coco Solo Island to the north-west of Panama. Another flew to Pearl Harbour, a new base on the Hawaiian island of O'Ahu in the Pacific, over 24 hours and over 2,000 miles from San Francisco. A specification had already been issued for a 3,000 mile range flying boat however and in 1935 the (model 28) XP3Y-1 was successfully test flown at Anacostia Naval Air Station. Gone were the array of struts between the wing and the hull, brilliantly replaced by Laddon with a single pylon with space inside for the engineer. Integral fuel tanks were housed within the wing centre section, while electrically operated floats, incorporated under licence from Saunders-Roe, formed the wingtips in flight. The moulding of the engine nacelles into the leading edges of the wing, first seen on the later Rangers, further lessened the drag and there was a single rudder – all of which presented a remarkably slim profile, the key to performance and endurance. Worth six million dollars to the company, the first order for sixty PBY-1s came that August, the month a move was made to even larger premises at Lindbergh Field, adjacent to San Diego Bay, California.

The Navy had requested certain improvements and when delivered in May 1936, the prototype was powered by 850 horsepower Pratt and Whitney Twin Wasp engines, driven by three bladed Hamilton propellers. The internally braced metal wing was covered by unbleached, doped cotton fabric, and the hull extended beneath the rudder, ending the lack of lateral control when loaded to operational requirements. The first entered service with VP-11 (Heavier than air, Patrol) Squadron in October. A naval training school was established on North Island in San Diego Bay, from where Charles Lindbergh had lifted away from the Rockwell Field premises of the Ryan Airline factory to head for New York at the start of his epic solo flight to Paris.

Climbing aboard, pilots moved forward and up into the enclosed cockpit beneath the two propeller arcs, leaving the bombardier to squeeze between the two seats and down into his own compartment in the nose, where he also manned the turret. A separate compartment behind and a step down from the cockpit, housed the radio operator's equipment on the starboard side with the navigators desk opposite. Both men faced outwards, given a square window to light the interior. A metal hatch led beneath the pylon, where the flight engineer sat 'suspended' on his metal seat, reached by a short and fixed vertical ladder. A throat mike kept him in touch with the rest of the crew and a pair of clear vision panels gave him an intimate view of both engines and floats. Below him, on the starboard side, the sink, cupboards and galley equipment projected from the metal ribbed concave interior.

Both wing centre sections had two internal bomb racks, with exterior racks for torpedoes, depth charges or bombs. Emergency jettison handles were fitted below the cockpit instrument panel, on both sides of the bombardier hatch. The crew compartment had space for three 'stretcher' style metal bunks, the upper of two on the starboard side partly supported by strops secured to the roof. Next was the waist gunner compartment. Initially fitted with a pair of sliding hatches, in the summer of 1939 the last batch of PBY 4s would have upward sliding transparent cupolas, attracting use of .5 calibre machine guns ('twin fifties') rather than the standard issue .303 rifle calibre. The life raft was usually stowed here, with a chemical Elsan toilet at the rear.

The last compartment had a sliding hatch in the 'tunnel' on the bottom of the hull (beyond the step) for a kneeling gunner to protect the belly and rear from attack, a precaution denied British flying boats and the four engined 'heavies' of RAF Bomber Command, many of which would be shot down by upward firing cannon specifically installed in German night fighters. There was also the flare tube and camera hatch. The tapering stern was used for stowage. In all, the hull had seven watertight compartments before the smoothly cambered flanks rose up to the tail.

Sat before his own instrument panel inside the pylon, his feet dangling beneath the seat or resting on a shelf above the hatch from the cockpit, the engineer would begin to prime the starboard engine first to power the pump for the hydraulic system. With the throttle advanced about one fifth by the pilot, cowl flaps opened, propeller set for maximum revolutions, carburetor mixture control set at 'Idle Cut Off' and both ignition switches on, the starter button was pressed until the engine fired, when the mixture lever was quickly moved to 'Auto Rich'. With both engines running and the pumps maintaining the fuel pressure, the senior pilot ran through the checks, not least of which was the windscreen wiper, before taxiing away to line up into the wind, taking care not to overheat an engine while turning. The closeness to the centerline created a natural resistance, even in the air.

Advancing the throttles, the three spoke, oval, control wheel was held firmly back to bring the nose above the water, resisting the down force created by the lift of the wings, timed to coincide with the rising of a wave during heavy swells to avoid plunging in. Laddon had mounted the elevator high up on the vertical 'stabiliser' to avoid much of the spray. Once on the step, back pressure was reduced to allow the speed to build to some 65 knots and re-applied to help the hull break free of the surface. Another levelling brought the speed up to 80 knots, below which control would be lost if an engine should falter, and the climb-out begun, having applied the appropriate throttle and propeller pitch setting. The PBY was forgiving if stalled and would descend with wings level until the nose was lowered and power applied. In calm conditions, a landing approach was usually made at just under 90 knots, reduced to around sixty after the final turn, when the altitude was maintained to steadily fly onto the water. Long hours in the air demanded simplicity and 'cats' were more often climbed,

Canopus refueling on the Nile.
COURTESY MICHAEL COBHAM, FLIGHT REFUELLING LTD.

cruised and landed at 90 knots indicated. For an open sea landing, a power-off, held-off stall was recommended at no more than 50 feet above the surface to allow the hull to settle without a damaging bounce, or worse. Before taking off and landing, a sliding shutter was drawn down in the extreme nose to protect the bomb aiming panel of the (Norden) gyroscopic bomb sight, coupled to the automatic pilot for the bombardier to take over when approaching a target. The highly secret Stabilised Bombing Approach equipment would be perfected by British-based Liberator and Flying Fortress crews during daylight bombing missions over Germany.

Fleet had not lost sight of the civil market and in February 1937 a model 28-1 was bought by Richard Archbold and the American Museum of Natural History for a third expedition to New Guinea in November. The first sanctioned for non military use, it was named *Guba* after the Papuan word for 'sudden storm'. A wealthy zoologist and private pilot, Archbold flew it non-stop across America before the expedition, but in August sold it to the Soviets to help the search for Sigizmund Levanevsky and his crew, missing over Alaska during a flight to New York. The Soviets had ordered three 28-2s to carry cargo and mail and would subsequently build over a hundred PBYs under licence (Gydro Samoliot Transportnyj or GSTs) until 1941, when the Taganrog factory, by the Sea of Asov, was overrun by the Germans.

A replacement (model 28-3) *Guba 11* was bought for the expedition and was landed in Dutch New Guinea by expedition chief pilot Russell Rogers, the six thousand mile journey broken by refuelling stops at Pearl Harbour and Midway Island.

FOYNES

Much had been achieved since twenty-seven year old Jack Alcock and his thirty-three year old friend and navigator Arthur Brown had ended their non-stop Atlantic crossing on the deceptively green, boggy surface of Derrygimla Moor in Connemara, just yards from the telegraph station where Guiglielmo Marconi had transmitted the first message to Canada. In 1933 Charles and Anne Lindbergh had landed their Lockheed Sirius single engined floatplane in Galway Bay while surveying potential airline routes, and two years later America, Britain and Canada had agreed to jointly develop a transatlantic air service with an Irish airport as the North Atlantic terminal. After extensive surveys, drainage work had begun at Rineanna to support four grass runways. Situated on the south bank of the sheltered Shannon estuary, with rail links already in place to Limerick, Foynes was chosen to be the flying boat terminal.

Home to less than five hundred people, the pace of the quiet little west coast settlement would change dramatically with the arrival of the flying boats. Wireless and telegraphy stations were installed at Rineanna and within the Monteagle Arms, the sole hotel in Foynes, which also housed the equipment of Air Ministry meteorological personnel sent from Croydon. Imperial and Pan Am had agreed to make two return Atlantic services a week, but with Britain as yet without flying boats able to carry fuel and passengers across the virtually unknown expanse, the long-range *Caledonia* and *Cambria* were chosen to fly a government sponsored, experimental Atlantic air mail service, though facing ice-bearing clouds and sixty mile an hour headwinds.

The previous year Bill Forbes and his team of specialists from Cable and Wireless had been shipped out to Bermuda to install the first radio direction finding equipment to guide ships and aircraft safely to the islands. Fitted with long-range tanks, *Cavalier* had been dismantled and shipped out, and in May 1937 Captain Neville Cumming lifted away from the Great Sound at Daniells Island bound for New York as Captain Robert Sullivan brought *Bermuda Clipper* in from America. On June 12th both flying boats flew in from New York for the official opening of the new, multi-million, Marine Air Terminal on the island and six days later passengers began flying the six hundred and seventy air miles to LaGuardia. Between 5/6th July Captain Arthur Wilcockson took just over fifteen hours to fly a stripped out *Caledonia* from Foynes to Botwood as Captain Harold Gray brought *Pan American Clipper 111* in from the other direction. *Caledonia* then flew on to Montreal and New York as the

Clipper headed for Southampton. *Cambria* and *Caledonia* went on to make five crossings by September when *Caledonia* ended the trials.

MAIA & MERCURY

First long-range S30 *Caledonia*. Rod el Farag on the Nile.
© JACK HARRIS COLLECTION.

From the start, the ability to economically fly long distance was the ultimate goal. But in 1916 height was the overriding concern of Flight Lieutenant Day as he climbed aboard a diminutive Bristol Bullet fighter secured to a Porte Baby flying boat with John Porte at the controls, to find a response to the high-flying Zeppelin airship raids. Though the two safely separated 1,000 feet over Harwich, nothing more had been done and the concept of releasing a fully fuelled aeroplane at an operational height lay dormant for twenty years. Until July 1936, when the government announcement of it's intention for Imperial Airways to undertake trial crossings of the North Atlantic, prompted Major Mayo to form his own company to take the concept across the ocean. Having convinced the Air Ministry to sponsor the trials, a float-plane and supporting flying boat were completed by Shorts in 1937. Named after the Greek goddess and mother of the messenger Hermes, *Maia* resembled the C-Class, but with a wider fuselage, extra wing and control surfaces, the outer engines fitted further out to take the floats of *Mercury*, the Roman name for Hermes.

Enacted high above the Thames Estuary in February 1938, the first separation of the 'Short-Mayo Composite' was a success: John Parker in *Maia* and Harold Piper in *Mercury* using the combined power of eight engines to climb to 5,000 feet before pulling their respective handles to allow *Maia* to drop cleanly away. The Atlantic was next. But Lufthansa was already operating a South Atlantic mail service between Bathurst and Natal using 16 ton Blohm und Voss Ha 139 'float seaplanes', catapulted on their way from the Shwabenland, stationed west of Horta, and on March 27 the sole Dornier 18F piloted by Lufthansa Captain von Engle was catapulted from the Westfalen positioned off Start Point in Devon. Just over forty-three hours later, the graceful twin engined flying boat landed at Caravellas, Brazil, after a record, non-stop flight of over five thousand miles. Intended to give the German national airline a genuine passenger service across the North and South Atlantic, the giant Blohm und Voss Bv222 Wiking (Viking) flying boat would not fly before 1940 however. Powered by six diesel engines, it would be the largest and heaviest flying boat in the Second World War, though unarmed transports required fighter escort and armed maritime versions would fall easy prey to Allied fighters.

Trials continued however and just before eight pm in the evening of July 21st, twenty-eight year old Australian Donald Bennett took *Mercury* away from Captain Wilcockson and *Maia* high over Foynes, with radio operator and Air Ministry observer A.J. Coster sat beside him. Despite a headwind, they remained airborne for twenty hours and as many minutes until landing at Boucherville (Montreal), the cargo of newspapers and newsreels having made the east-west Atlantic crossing in a record thirteen hours and twenty-nine minutes. Separations continued until October when Captain Bennett and radio operator First Officer Ian Harvey landed on South Africa's Orange River just over forty-two hours after leaving the Tay in Dundee, almost six thousand miles away. A long distance, straight-line record for seaplanes, it has never been beaten. As with the 1916 trials, the composite idea was never fully developed. A second 'launch' aircraft would have been necessary on the other side of the Atlantic, while the size and weight of the passenger aircraft would have been prohibitive.

The final blow came on August 10th 1938, when the prototype four engined Focke-Wulf Condor airliner was flown direct from Berlin to New York in just under twenty-five hours. Donald Bennett would go on to play a leading role in the 1940 Atlantic Ferry Organisation however and within

Maia & Mercury. © DR. NIGEL PEARCE.

a few years would command the RAFs Pathfinder Force as the youngest Air Vice-Marshal in the service.

SOUTHAMPTON

Following the success of the un-surcharged Empire Air Mail Scheme to South Africa in June 1937, the second stage to India and Malaya opened the following February when *Centurion* and *Coolangatta* departed for Karachi. Qantas crews flew on to Singapore. *Coorong*, the last of the original order, was launched at the end of the month and with *Cooee* and *Corio* joined *Carpentaria*, *Coolangatta* and *Coogee*. To keep pace with the envisaged passenger movements, the Southampton terminal had moved from Berth 101 to a pair of offices between Berths 107 and 108, and then Berth 108 itself, where two pontoons were positioned in front of the new two-storey building. From March, the flying boats were towed across from Hythe and with a pair of cables attached to the tail mooring hook, winched backwards into the floating docks, designed to enable a simultaneous entry and discharge of mail and passengers from both sides of the aircraft.

The third and final stage of the Empire Air Mail Scheme, the Australia and New Zealand service opened between June and August 1938. On June 26th *Camilla* and *Cordelia* left Southampton on the first through-service to Australia, with *Challenger* flying on from Singapore to Sydney. On July 5th *Cooee* left Sydney on the return service. Twenty-three days later *Calypso* left Southampton with the first of the 'all up' mail to Australia and New

Corio & Calypso at Southampton.
© DAVID FAGAN COLLECTION.

Zealand. Hong Kong would be included from September.

The Australian service took nine days instead of the thirty required by ocean liners, with overnight stops at Athens, Basra, Karachi, Calcutta, Bangkok, Singapore, Surabaya, Darwin and Townsville. The surface route delivered just one post a week. Letters to Alexandria now arrived after three or four days instead of from four to six, the Calcutta post took a week instead of sixteen days and Singapore took ten days rather than twenty-two. Seven flights a week began leaving Southampton for Egypt, with four to India, three to East Africa, two to South Africa and three to Malaya and Australia. As at Southampton, pontoons and gangways led passengers ashore as barges pumped over a ton and a half of petrol into the tanks.

On August 4th 1938, Lord Huntingfield, the acting Governor-General of Australia, formally opened the new flying boat terminal at Rose Bay (named after an 18th century secretary to the British Treasury) to the east of Sydney Harbour, New South Wales. A ribbon connecting *Camilla* to the shore was cut, and having brought *Centaurus* in on Christmas Eve during a proving flight, Qantas Senior Captain Lester Brain began the journey to Southampton loaded with mail, freight and eight passengers.

Five days later, *Coriolanus* inaugurated the thrice-weekly Empire Air

Camilla & *Coriolanus* Rose Bay terminal 1938.
COURTESY MILTON KENT & CAHS VICTORIA.

Mail service to Southampton. Apart from the two-storey terminal building and the jetty, to one side of a public swimming enclosure, the Rose Bay facilities were far from complete, and another year would pass before the slipway, apron and maintenance hangar were entirely ready for use.

HYTHE

Though no longer a passenger terminal, Hythes rôle as a maintenance base was of vital importance in maintaining the increasing volumes of air mail. Returned from a 'service' flight, a C-Class 'Empire' flying boat was moored off the slipway to allow the floor coverings, tables, chairs, curtains, lifebelts, galley equipment etc to be removed for cleaning and renovation, reducing the weight to around 24,000 pounds, clearly painted on the hull for reference. After checking the depth of water complied with the maximum (loaded) displacement of 4 foot 6 inches for safety, the aircraft was then towed to a mooring at the end of the slipway and out of the tidal run, when a wheeled beaching leg was fitted beneath each wing root and adjacent to the hull, as a steerable wheeled cradle was secured under the tail. A final check to ensure there were no large craft or liners about to add their own mini tidal wave to the proceedings, and the aircraft was hauled rearwards from the water by a tractor moving at right angles to the slipway, the hauling cable passing through fixed pulleys aligned with the slope as the cable to the buoy was paid off from the mooring compartment. Once clear of the water, a power hose cleared the accumulated salt and slime from the fully exposed hull. Having checked the beaching gear was properly aligned, an inspector then climbed aboard as a winch began hauling the machine to the top of the incline for the tractor to complete the tow to the hangar.

The Hythe work force was divided into two eight-hour shifts which began work on the flying boats at six-fifteen in the morning and at two-thirty in the afternoon. To retain the Certificate of Airworthiness, virtually everything was examined, from wing floats, petrol pipes and batteries, to flying controls, instruments, accessories and the radio. A 'rolling' program of inspection ensured an aircraft flew for as long as possible, with major engine overhauls performed in the main workshops at Croydon. At Hythe, engine maintenance was assisted by a wheeled framework fitted with a platform, two funnels and two pipes to allow the drained off engine oil and oily rags to be passed to separate receptacles, rather than stain the apron below or splash those meticulously inspecting the hull's protective coating. Propellers were overhauled every two hundred and seventy hours, when each of the three blades was dismantled, inspected for cracks, and re-balanced. Engines were tested outside on the concrete apron, where the cardinal points of the compass were clearly marked to align the on-board compass. With everything signed up and ready to go, bags of ballast were loaded aboard to simulate a full load of passengers and mail for the test flight. A normal 'turn around' was accomplished in two days. More extensive overhauls were carried out by Folland, within the former British Marine hangar erected on the eastern shore at Netley.

C-Class to Africa

Almost half the passengers on the Empire routes were employed on government business, taking advantage of the speedy services during their leave periods, a smaller percentage making private journeys to perhaps visit relatives far from home. Children under three were charged a tenth of the full fare, with those aged between three and seven charged half-fare and given a separate seat. Irrespective of their own weight, passengers could take up to 44 pounds of luggage on board. The fare included meals in the air and on the ground and included first class hotel accommodation during the stop-overs. Imperial claimed to be the only airline serving full restaurant meals in flight and with so many countries involved on the Eastern service in particular, passengers sampled French, Italian, African, Indian and Malayan dishes and the more exotic platters of the East Indies.

Typical of the return fares to the Middle East and Australia at this time, Alexandra was costed at £72, Calcutta £171, Singapore £234 and Brisbane £274. Among the pre-war élite, the famous and titled found they could return from visiting the large game reserves of central Africa in no more time than it took to spend a more mundane holiday at home. Imperial charged £109 pounds to reach Nairobi (£196 and four shillings return), £110 to reach Mombasa and Accra (£112 pounds return) and £112 to reach Dar Es Salaam (£201 pounds and twelve shillings return). Work had begun on a new Empire Terminal building in Buckingham Palace Road, between the Victoria coach and train terminals of South London, where the impressive art-deco, concave design of Albert Lakeman featured the creative stonework of Eric Broadbent in the form of a globe surmounted by a god like figure with arms outstretched to a large bird, surmounted by the words Speed Wings Across the World. The Africa service was a success from the start.

The fare from London to Durban would have set you back £125, with just £13 added for the return, and in keeping with the First-Class thême, you would have received a gold edged card confirming the booking. Having completed the formalities on arriving in London, which included having your weight taken and recorded, and that of your luggage, you were passed through to the adjoining rail platform reserved exclusively for Imperial Airways. A notice board boldly proclaimed the Empire Air Service, the name of the RMA. (Royal Mail Aircraft) reserved for the flight, departure time and platform number. As it is a Friday evening, the hands of the little 'clock' are set at seven thirty and the chalked numeral beneath indicates platform nine, where you find the two Pullman carriages at the rear of the train displaying the name of the flying boat. Within a short time the doors are closed and whistles announce the start of the adventure. Had Hythe sent word of a delay, a tea-dance might have been arranged rather than have passengers waiting around in the lounges. Travelling in comfort to the Southampton Flying Boat Terminal Station, a uniformed airline traffic officer conducts you aboard a coach which stops in front of the imposing architecture of the South Western Hotel. On entering, you receive a little card which amongst other information says you will be called at four o'clock the following morning!

Though having dozed during the longish train journey, the call finds you only half awake at that hour. Having again checked your inoculation certificate, airline ticket and stiff backed British passport, you join the others boarding the coach for the short trip to the dockside terminal, where the formalities are completed and you are invited to wait in the lounge until the aircraft is ready to receive passengers.

Winched within a pontoon, the bow of the 'Empire' flying boat had been secured to a buoy anchored further out in the Solent, and mooring lines run from bollards to recessed cleats on both sides of the forward and aft entry doors. The doors and loading hatches had been opened, and with the 'ship to shore' electrical cable plugged in above the pantry port and fuel hatch on the starboard side of the aircraft, the wingtip and tail navigation lights, 'at anchor' light (on the mast above the cockpit) and interior lighting had all been switched on – presenting a welcoming sight on an otherwise gray and drab British dockside at that time in the morning.

Conducted outside by the traffic officer, and down a gangway onto the pontoon, you are aware of the cables emerging from the water to the tail hook of the aircraft, and passing the unblinking tail light, find Royal Air Mail printed in a half circle on the side of the long fuselage. The nearest passenger door, which leads into the promenade cabin, was more often used, but today you are allowed to enter from the forward door in order to have a good look at the interior. Moving towards the nose of the aircraft, a glance above reveals the two flags run up on the removable flag staff behind the aerial mast as the Air-Force blue Civil Air Ensign, featuring a dark blue cross edged in white, and the triangular Air-Mail blue pennant of the Royal Mail – the crown, title and hunting horn (from the horse-drawn carriage days) proudly picked out in gold.

With your foot guided from the gently swaying pontoon, you step down into the aircraft, where a curtain has been drawn back to one side. A look inside the door of the forward or 'smokers' cabin on the left (cigarettes only), reveals the familiar winged head-rests of the Pullman-style seats fitted throughout the aircraft, though these have metal ash trays set within the padded arm rests. To the right is a lateral pair of seats and a folding table, with another three on the left and two more facing. A pair of floor to ceiling metal pillars supported two pairs of longitudinal bunks at night. Some ten feet away, behind the central folding table, two inset metal handles mark the door to the mooring compartment. On the other side, a short metal ladder led down to the interior, which in flight is taken up by a large sea anchor, two metal bins (one each side) for a pair of canvas 'sea anchors', their warp and trip lines, the slip release line, and a variety of long, shackled ropes and cables, together with a long-handled boat hook and the fenders which protect the doors when alongside a jetty or pontoon. A retractable Harley (landing) lamp was mounted on a hinged panel to the left, while a short ladder at the far end led up to the mooring hatch. A pair of circular metal louvres either side of the mooring compartment door allow controlled amounts of fresh air into the smokers cabin, while each of the six viewing ports (one can be opened in an emergency) is fitted with a roller blind. Sectioned by slim metal strips, the curve of the roof descends to light green tinted walls. Above each seat, a wall light fitting incorporates a control switch and a button to summon the steward and in keeping with the Pullman thême, the familiar chord-strung, lightweight luggage rack supported by leather strops is fitted on both sides of the cabin. Recessed metal compartments stow overnight bags.

Leaving the entrance 'lobby' with its curtain and vertical ladder to the flight deck, and passing along the corridor, with adjoining ladies and gentleman's toilets on the right and pantry opposite, you arrive at the opened door of the centre or 'mid-ship' cabin. Some 4 feet shorter than the forward cabin, there are three viewing ports on either side with two of the three seats on the right. Four bunks could be made up here, provided with an extra pair of high level window panels as standard throughout the aircraft.

Compensating for the rise in the hull, a step takes you up into the aptly named promenade cabin, though not without noticing the little sign strategically placed above the arch of this and every doorway, to remind passengers there was to be no smoking! The cabin has three pairs of seats and tables on the left, the remainder taken up entirely by the promenade aisle, the jewel in the crown for the C-Class, provided with a slender, twenty foot long handrail, four shoulder-high viewing ports with taut, sliding curtains, and a long luggage rack.

Arriving at the far end, partly taken up by the open concave entrance door (both doors have a viewing port to prevent an unexpected watery exit!) two steps take you up and into the aft cabin, a folding ladder positioned by the bulkhead to reach the escape hatch in the roof. A pair of inward facing seats on the left and two facing pairs on the right of the aisle are each separated by a fold-back table fitted with the customary pair of wheels, and another long hat rack extends above the three right hand viewing ports. Four bunks could be made up here, the overall supply of mattresses, bed linen, covers, curtains and equipment stowed at the rear of the upper deck and accessed from a roof panel. Most flights were completed in daylight or by late evening, which was just as well, for the movement of the aircraft had been found to cause considerable difficulty in assembling and entering the bunks, particularly when mounting the short ladder to the top. As a consequence, they were very rarely used.

The central aisle ends before a final bulkhead, above the end of the planing bottom. To the left, another pair of metal handles mark the door to an eleven foot long freight and baggage compartment. Accessed from a hatch on the starboard side of the aircraft, the hold continued into the unlined and tapering tail, used to stow excess baggage, bilge pumps, engineering equipment, a propeller or two and even an engine if requested by one of the line stations. Aware of the regular positioning of brass Pyrene fire extinguishers, you had appreciated the steadying hand rail positioned by the entrance to each of the cabins, and the fitted carpet beneath your feet, which also protected the metal-framed plywood floor panels. By contrast, the exposed floor of the flight deck was scarred and a touch oily.

Well before your arrival, the passenger details had been phoned through to the flight clerk. A combination of load-master and post office clerk, he was responsible for determining the weight and balance of the aircraft, servicing the technical logs and maintaining all the paraphernalia required by the passengers; from manifests, passports, tickets and landing proforma, to cash and currency, magazines, daily papers, stationary and postcards. He also typed up the menu cards for each cabin and ran up the appropriate flags for each port of call. Not for nothing was he provided with a little portable typewriter. He held the key to the bullion store beneath the floor of the mid-ship cabin, helped secure the launches as they came alongside, supervised the loading of the baggage and mail and joined the steward in ensuring the interior was always in tip top condition. The steward and the radio officer (who occupied the mooring compartment at the beginning and end of each flight), are issued with a pair of working overalls, known as a boiler suit, while first officers received two pairs to perform their own external checks and non-flying duties.

With your name checked off his list by the clerk, who had relieved you of your passport and accompanying paperwork, you are shown to a seat by the steward, who deftly shows how five simultaneous little movements of the arm levers take the seat to the reclining position (not to be used during take-offs or landings) and how to secure the straps. Lifebelts were carried for every passenger and could be supplemented by the inflatable seat cushions. A well illustrated little pamphlet covers all the relevant emergency procedures.

After asking whether you would like a rug or a foot muff at that time in the morning, the steward disappears into another cabin. Placing your hat and overcoat in the overhead rack and a small overnight bag in one of the recessed compartments, you settle into the comfortable green upholstery, perhaps feeling a little hollow in the stomach after leaving the darkened hotel in the dawn, the mind and body beginning to attune, like any sailor, to the restless pitching of the hull. Others, who will be sharing all or some of your own journey, settle in alongside and you try not to doze before the arrival of the flight clerk as he makes his way to the front of the aircraft, checking all hatches are closed and the toilets vacated. His own seat is at the rear of the upper deck, opposite the starboard mail loading hatch and lighting control panel. Though separated by a longitudinal partition from some 3,000 pounds of mail and freight, his prodigious paperwork suffers whenever a window or hatch is opened up front and he will soon occupy his own little office within the forward cabin, which will be stripped out to increase the mail payload to 2 tons. As a consequence, the passengers will be reduced to seventeen and the smokers relegated to the aft cabin, when their wafted presence will become rather more noticeable than before.

Following the clerks arrival by the forward door, the attendant traffic officer is told everything is ready for departure and after exchanging pleasantries, retires to the pontoon as the clerk retrieves the last fender: the closing of the door against the rubber sealing gaskets and the sound of whistles ordering the release of the mooring ropes, heightening the expectation of everyone aboard.

Rather than disturb the pilots pre-flight routine, the radio officer has used the ladder near the flight clerks position to descend to the pantry, and moving forward to the bow, eased his upper body from the mooring hatch to await the command to slip the mooring. Not the easiest of tasks in pouring rain or in windy conditions, though prompted by a whistle blown by the captain. Having closed the curtain and stowed both fenders, he had then mounted the ladder to confirm the closing of hatches and seating of passengers to the first officer. Moving to the rear of the flight deck, he had donned his lifejacket, unclipped the fire extinguisher from the underside of the roof and climbed a short ladder to stand in the opened escape hatch, ready to deal with any engine problems. Sat high above the water with a sliding 'direct vision' window on both sides, the captain and first officer had only to incline the head to have a clear view of everything outside. Yesterday, both had come to the airlines dockyard operations office to check the weather forecast to enable the route to be chosen by the captain, who this morning had mounted the stairs to the cockpit some fifteen minutes before the planned departure, about the same amount of time after the rest of the crew had arrived.

Moved into action after hearing his whistle, the radio operator releases the bow mooring, and raising a hand towards the cockpit, retracts the mooring bollard and secures the hatch behind him before stowing the slip line and removing his overalls. The first officer pulls a lever on the cabin roof to release the tail mooring hook and the flying boat moves away from the pontoon to allow the captain and first officer to begin priming and starting the engines. Though forewarned by the steward, the sudden burst of sound and vibration, accompanied by brief bursts of flame, momentarily ends any conversation in the cabins as each of the three bladed metal propellers is forced into action. In winter or on cold mornings, the heating system, nominally set at twenty degrees centigrade, would be felt only after the starboard inner engine had been running for at least half an hour.

With all four engines operating smoothly, the clerk confirms the closure of the upper hatch to the captain and moves to his seat as the machine begins moving under power, the sound of the water sharply slapping against the hull beneath your feet, just another sensation to get used to. There is no running up of engines on the brakes to check the 'mag' drop as with a landplane however. There are no brakes. Just a practiced advance of throttles in pairs, preferably down-wind to avoid unnecessary spray being thrown up by the propellers. Perhaps turning in a wide circle if the cylinder head temperatures were slow in coming up, before moving towards Calshot, where a large area was reserved off the Netley shore to avoid conflicting with the liners. Again warned by the steward, the turning into wind is followed by a high-pitched whine and rumble as the flap motor extends the under wing flaps. If all has gone to plan, at half-past five, the first officer triggers the Aldis lamp to flash the series of dots and dashes requesting take-off from the control launch, the steady white light in reply bringing a booming roar as the propellers disappear and rising spray covers the windows.

Unlike the uncomplicated thrust of modern day jets, all four propellers rotate in the same direction causing an opposite movement of the nose known as torque. To oppose the yaw, the opposite throttles are advanced first to avoid the anticipated swing in that direction, with a foot pressed against the corresponding rudder pedal. If a swing continued, the outer engine was throttled back until the rudder took effect. Using aileron to balance the floats, the captain holds the control 'wheel' hard back to enable the elevator to capitalise on all that lift, as the big boat comes up on to the planing bottom, the Rochester-machined metal having to withstand all that weight though just over one millimeter thick. A flat calm would have required a much longer distance to rise on to the 'step', whereas today the light chop on the water has helped break the surface tension. The engine note deepens as the dripping hull breaks free of the foaming water and is held down to establish some 95 precious knots to avoid an ignominious and destructive collapse back to the surface.

Climbing and banking away over Calshot, the gain in height enables the radio operator to trail his transmitter aerial prior to tapping out code letters to inform the next ground station the time of take-off, intended landing place, estimated time of arrival and cruising altitude. The reduction in power is evident as the wings are levelled and the whining motor returns the grumbling metal back under the wings. As with some of the fine houses of the era, there is a marked contrast in the sensations experienced between those 'upstairs' and those 'downstairs'. The concentration of the pilots totally and necessarily absorbed within the sound and vibration of the engines during the take-off, while those below, strapped in close proximity to one another, could only listen to the rapid increase in frequency and volume of the staccato slaps as the hull was thrown against the water. It would be the same on landing, when a crews 'smooth', perhaps 'classic' view of their pilots return to the water, would more often be transmitted to the lower deck passengers sat so much closer to the surface, by a definite thud as the hull took the initial shock, accepted and virtually forgotten amongst the host of fond memories.

Accustomed to the sight and sound of the strutted, twin-finned flying boats emerging for RAF service from the Saunders- Roe factory at Cowes, the inhabitants of the Isle of Wight had soon identified the cleaner outlines of the Empire boats, routed close to the island before crossing the channel to France. Based on the previous day's information which, unlike other forms of aerial transport, included the tide and water state at the next destination, the captain had chosen one of four main outward routes.

The two most northerly both turned over the Nab Tower Lighthouse off the east coast of the island, and either crossed the French coast at Fécamp before heading for Mâcon, a subsidiary refuelling stop on the Saône river, before turning south to follow the Rhône river towards Lake Marignane – or crossed the coast to the west of Le Havre to head for the Velay region of central southern France before heading for the lake near Marseilles. The lack of deviation made this the most direct route to the Mediterranean, weather and other unforeseen problems considered.

The two remaining tracks turned over Calshot and headed for the Needles off the western extremity of the island before turning out over the channel. They then either made landfall to the right of the lighthouse at the Pointe de Barfleur, crossed the Cotentin Peninsular to Avranches to avoid the busy Cherbourg airspace, and followed the low lying coast of the Bay of Biscay (fuel was available at Lake Hourtin-Carcans) to pass between the Isle de Ré and La Rochelle and across the Isle d'Oléron before heading for Lake Marignane – or approached the French mainland via the Channel Islands and Jersey, crossing in over Dinard to cut across Brittany to Saint Nazaire (a naval port and refuelling station) on the wide estuary of the Loire, before heading directly across France for Marseilles.

With no sound proofing aboard, the drone of the engines has defeated the resolve of your eyelids after the early morning start and you had succumbed until offered a refreshing cup of tea, followed in turn by an English breakfast and coffee, served by the ever attendant steward following your selection from the typed breakfast menu. Most of the flight is carried out below 10,000 feet and in sight of land or water (today's 'visual flight conditions'), the wide river valleys, high peaks, large forests and coastal estuaries visibly confirming the aircrafts position to the crew. The C-Class were fitted with radio (voice) transmitters, but coded morse transmissions occupied a narrower band width and free of most atmospheric disturbances, were used to communicate with the ground stations positioned across mainland France. A sixty second transmission, comprising the aircrafts call sign and a ten second holding down of the key, overcame any language barrier and received in exchange the bearing of the aircraft to the station. A more accurate bearing, based on a triangulation with two other stations, was officially known as a D/F (direction finding) bearing, laconically referred to by aircrew as a 'fix'.

Free to make whatever stops were deemed necessary, the captain has descended to Lake Biscarosse, the home of the Latécoère flying boats and among the popular étangs or 'pools' of fresh water that attracted summer visitors to the Aquitaine region. Winston Churchill and Charlie Chaplin enjoyed holidays at the Duke of Westminster's villa on the shore of the Étang d'Aureilhan. After watching the wake of the take-off disappear behind, you decide to stretch the legs by visiting the promenade cabin. With a smile and a nod to those seated at the nearest table, you lean on the rail to watch the changing landscape below as the wide Garonne is succeeded by the winding Tarn, the sun shining brightly from the bluest of skies. In the distance, the Alps retain their customary wisps of cloud, balanced on the unseen air.

Descending towards Marignane, the sunlight lends a sparkle to the radiantly clear waters of the lake and the landing run ends with a turn toward the jetty. Stepping ashore, you can either relax outside, in the warmth of the day, watching the landplanes circuiting the aerodrome nearby, or take a seat in the lounge shared with the passengers of Ala Littoria.

Rejoining the aircraft, you notice the circular cooling gills on the engine cowlings have been opened, proof indeed that you have entered warmer climes. Airborne again, the coast of the French Riviera steadily recedes as you are flown deeper into the Mediterranean, making landfall above the northern peninsular of the island of Corsica before crossing the Tyrrhenian Sea to the Italian mainland and Lake Bracciano. Just over 20 miles to the north-west of Rome, this loveliest of Italian lakes is in reality a sunken volcano, the modern two-storey terminal bearing the words Idroscalo Civile and positioned, rather picturesquely, on the south-western shore against a backdrop of wooded olive groves rising to a medieval hilltop fortress. The comfortable lounge is again available courtesy of the Italian airline.

Brought back to the aircraft, you notice the flight clerk had added the Italian flag to the display during the taxi in, the ensuing and now familiar spray of foam across the window contrasting with the intense blue clarity of the lake as you ascend to head for Brindisi, on the eastern side of the 'heel' of the Gulf of Taranto. Today, the captain heads across Italy via Benevento rather than waste precious fuel by climbing an extra 6,000 feet to the 10,000 required to directly approach the strongly fortified Italian naval base. Round about mid-day, the steward enters the cabin wearing an immaculate white jacket and proceeds to transform the baize covered tables for lunch, the white linen, silver-service cutlery, ceramic plates and drinking glasses deftly topped off by a small posy of fresh flowers. As in ocean liners, the table has a raised metal rim to avoid accidents.

Prepared and cooked by top quality catering companies, the hot and cold food, fruit juices, cereals, marmalade, honey, eggs, bacon, ham, bread and butter, rolls, tea, coffee and wine ordered by him beforehand, had all been brought alongside by launch at Southampton and passed through the window port of the pantry, above the stainless steel sink. Secured within hot boxes, baskets, the ice chest, or on the many fitted racks within this airborne Aladdins Cave, the contents of the vacuum flasks, bottles, trays and containers are replenished en route and presented to the highest standard by the knowledgeable airborne 'Maitre d'. Before leaving Southampton, he had ensured the 5 gallon fresh water tank was topped up and that the emergency rations and first aid box were in place. Positioned in a recess, a fixed ladder gave him direct access to the flight deck where the crew have their meals served on a tray at their stations. The least mobile, the radio operator maintains a constant listening watch and rarely leaves his seat, directly behind the captain and in close contact with both pilots. Should circumstances allow either pilot to leave the cockpit (known as a coupé) to enjoy a full meal, the steward would clear and set the centre cabin where a passenger or celebrity might be invited to join the 'Captains table'. Exceptionally, a clock and altimeter are fitted inside this cabin, above the forward entrance door.

Constantly on the move, for the pressing of any of the buttons in the aircraft lights a coloured bulb on a wall panel in the pantry, distributing reading material and his own brand of reassurance to younger passengers and those making their first trip, the steward is greeted as a friend by those regularly using the services, for whom his demeanour encapsulates the spirit of the era. Understandably, the fold-down seat in the pantry sees little use.

Losing height over the attractive low lying coastal plain bordering the Adriatic, dotted with olive groves and citrus trees, the aircraft approaches the breakwater of Brindisi Harbour, where the Kent 'boat *Sylvanus* had tragically burnt out in November 1935. Cameras have been collected by the clerk and placed in a sealed bag until customs have been cleared. A launch of Ala Littoria arrives alongside to take passengers ashore to again use the facilities and lounge of the airline. Airborne once more, you head across the Straits of Otranto during the late afternoon and make landfall above the island of Corfu before crossing the mountainous Greek mainland to the Gulf of Corinth and Phaleron Bay.

The landing is made almost at dusk, but Imperial are proud of the accommodation included within the price of the ticket and you are taken by car to the Hotel Grande Bretagne for the first night stop-over. As at Southampton, you receive a little card which answers most of the questions that might come to mind, such as the current rate of exchange of the currency coupons purchased from the flight clerk and the name of the local airline rep on hand to ensure our brief stay passes as smoothly as possible, the stated four-fifteen Saturday morning call seemingly not nearly as bad to contemplate as it would have been in Britain. Luggage will be collected from outside the door half an hour later and cars will arrive at five fifteen, allowing a comfortable drive to the refuelled and mailed-up aircraft for the six am take-off. Breakfast and lunch will be served in the air.

Having enjoyed an excursion to Athens and a night's sleep without the noise of engines, the bright early morning sun warms the senses as the aircraft climbs out over an island studded sea before crossing some 370 miles of the Mediterranean to North Africa, to descend in full view of Royal Navy battleships moored in Alexandria Harbour, the end of the line for the Calcutta and Kent class. On the way, you had glimpsed the distant outline of Crete, where Imperial had moored the 100 ton motor yacht Imperia off Mirabella harbour to accommodate pilots and passengers while acting as a radio and refuelling station, and where *Scipio* had lain clearly visible for years after a disastrous rough water landing in August 1936.

The day now ends at Rod-el-Farag on the river Nile, with an overnight stay in the Egyptian capital of Cairo (El Qahira). Transported by coach, you enter the famous Shepheard's Hotel, a favourite haunt of the rich and famous, though the driver might equally have drawn up at the splendid Continental Savoy. Refreshed, breakfasted and airborne again, with perhaps half the passengers having left to continue eastwards on the Australian service, you watch the changing landscape of East Africa as you follow the Blue Nile to Luxor, where there is time to view the landscape of the Valley of the Kings before retiring for the night. The following day you reach Wadi Halfa on the Egyptian border, emerging into a wall of heat which continues unabated to Khartoum in Sudan, the confluence of the Blue and White Niles, alighting to a moored houseboat before spending the night at the Grand Hotel, grateful for the large, airy room and a chance to really stretch the legs.

Surrounded by panels of cellulose acetate, the flight decks rapidly heated in such temperatures and extra blinds had been fitted in addition to those above the sliding windows. The standard navy blue uniform of the crew, worn with white shirt, separate collar, dark tie and peaked cap, had been supplemented by another of khaki drill. Uniform was not to be worn off duty, but when ashore, a shorts-clad and sunburnt right or left leg, revealed not only a pilot's seat in the cockpit but also his capacity as captain or first officer. Some had sensibly taken to wearing pith helmets.

Passengers might include members of the Royal Family, an experience that had come quickly to 31 year old First Officer Lawrence Glover when joining Captain John Burgess, a fellow New Zealander, to be shown the Africa service.

Granted a Short Service Commission with the RAF he had risen to Flight Lieutenant with No 24 Communication Squadron, among only four serving officers approved to fly members of the Royal Family and cabinet ministers. An assessment flight for Imperial Airways had been followed by a conversion course at Hamble with Air Service Training, equipped with two Cutty Sark amphibians, two Calcuttas and a former 203 Squadron Rangoon. The Duke and Duchess of Gloucester had boarded the Empire flying boat at Alexandria and had departed at Kisumu, but not before Prince Henry and Princess Alice had personally signed his logbook and he had been pleasantly surprised to receive a solid silver cigarette case engraved in appreciation of his services. They had met again in November when the duke and duchess were flown from Port Bell to Cairo.

Driven to the quayside by an Imperial Airways bus after an early morning breakfast, the next landing is made on a comfortingly straight stretch of the Nile at Malakal, where the aircraft is approached by dugout canoes paddled across from their riverside village by surprisingly tall

Captains Parker and Glover in *Hythe* cockpit.

members of the Shilluk tribe. By now you have come to feel an association and affection for this machine which, amid an unforgettable mixture of hot metal and aviation spirits, has provided a host of experiences and memories: your body unconsciously riding the 'bumps' caused by large areas of ascending hot air, and the downward lurch on encountering the inevitable descent of the expanded and cooled air mass. At every refuelling and oiling stop, your smartly attired companions have been offered light refreshments, coffee or iced tea and cakes, as the mail is unloaded and fresh taken aboard. Care had always to be taken by the coxswains of the passenger launches and by the long refuelling barges, manned by black, smooth-skinned natives overseen by pith helmeted engineers, charged with making a safe connection with the fuel cock set within the fire-proof hatch above the pantry port.

With the engines constantly in use, a long sector followed by a longish taxi to a landing stage could result in overheating and continued firing, even when switched off, for which Shorts had fitted two large cut-out levers either side of the throttle quadrant, to stop fuel reaching the carburetor jets. The drag of a 3 foot diameter canvas drogue streamed from the mooring hatch could slow things in an emergency and was deployed on the inside of a turn when strong surface winds opposed the south-north flow of the Nile. The Kent crews were first to attach a large drogue to the tail hook to maintain direction when moored. Though anodised and coated with lanolin in the factory, the metal surfaces were susceptible to corrosion, especially from salt water, and the Hythe engineers would tighten and coat the internal rivets of the hull with beeswax. Fresh-water rivers and lakes were much less destructive.

Though fascinating to contrast the lush green surrounding the irrigation ditches bordering the Nile with the seemingly endless desert stretching into the distance, flying at such low levels could bring unexpected detours to avoid dust-storms and even swarms of locusts, which would litter the flying surfaces. Encountering monsoon rain and strong headwinds after leaving Karachi, on 12 June 1938 *Ceres* had landed on a small lake (Dugari) between Raj Samand and Lake Gwalior, though drought had lowered the water level by 8 feet and the hull had sunk into the soft mud. After an overnight supper and rest, the passengers and mail bags had been respectively taken by car and bullock cart some 30 miles to the nearest rail head and had continued from Gwalior aboard *Capella*. To the disappointment of the inquisitive crocodiles, *Ceres* was flown out eight days later.

The waters of the Nile are well up, enabling a refuelling stop to be made at Juba (Southern Sedan), rather than having to divert to the more southerly Rijaf, the facilities of both an improvement on those initially set up at Butiaba on the eastern shore of Lake Albert, in the Southern Rift Valley. The next landing is made at Laropi and then Port Bell (Uganda) on the ocean-like expanse of Lake Victoria, where a coach takes everyone to a hotel at Kampala, where the altitude keeps the sticky heat at bay. In the morning, a large brass bell is struck to announce the aircrafts departure from the lake for Kisumu (Kenya), the dry desert sands below gradually replaced by swamplands, small tributaries and glistening lakes, before descending for a refreshing night's rest within the Kisumu Hotel.

Each of the C-Class flying boats had its own, crested, stationery, containing a literary extract associated with the name of the aircraft, and captains would personally add their signature to the certificates issued after crossing the Equator. If requested, a landing could be made at Lake Naivasha (Nairobi), where a watchful eye had to be kept open for basking 'hippos'. Passengers in-flight folders included well illustrated maps giving potted histories of the various regions and it was not at all unusual for captains to lose height over places of interest, the flying boats regularly seen circling low over prominent Indian palaces, the pyramids of Egypt, the cascading Nile at the Murchison Falls and even large herds of game animals.

Leaving Kisumu behind, you are flown across Kenya toward the East Coast of Southern Africa and Mombasa, landing at Dar Es Salaam and Lindi (Tanganyika) before passing the sedimental delta of the Rovuma river (Cape Delgardo) on the edge of the Indian Ocean. With no need to divert to Quelimane, situated on an unmistakable bend of the Bons Sinais River, your day ends within the harbour of Mozambique Island with an overnight stop at Lumbo. The crew lodge within the houseboat Richard King. Then on to Beira and Lourenço Marques (Portuguese East Africa), losing height to follow the coastline, where you can see large shoals of fish and even sharks in the clear waters surrounding the off-shore reefs and islands. The arrival of the steward to ensure everyone is strapped in their seats, heralds the approach to Durban harbour. The previous September, Captain Alcock had brought *Calypso* in from Kisumu (having taken over from *Cassiopeia,* which in turn had replaced *Centaurus,* which had lost an

Houseboat Richard King. © ROSE COLLECTION.

engine over the Mediterranean) to record the very first arrival on time, as scheduled, for the Africa service.

After saying your goodbyes on the quayside, you take a final, rather wistful look back at the flying boat, where the national flag had joined the royal mail pennant and civil air ensign above the cockpit, and each of the three-bladed propellers had been turned over by the first officer blipping the engines until one blade remained vertical – as you had found on your arrival at Southampton, five days and over 7,000 miles away.

Chapter Three

Peace to War

Losses

Having changed crews at Alexandria for the onward flight to Australia, *Calpurnia* had refuelled at Lake Tiberius, the biblical Sea of Galilee. A second stop was scheduled for Lake Habbaniya some 60 miles west of Baghdad. But a raging sandstorm caused a rapid loss of height in the darkness, ending in a fatal crash in the shallow waters of Lake Ramadi on Sunday, 27 November 1938. First Officer Alex Spottiswoode had previously made a name for himself as a speed trials racing driver, but was among the three crew who lost their lives due to the seasonal lowering of the water exposing marsh and mudflats.

Launched on 8 December, *Cabot* was the first of the long range S30s, though without fittings and retaining Pegasus engines to be used as a test aircraft ahead of *Champion, Caribou, Connemara* and *Clyde.* John Parker took just twenty-one seconds to lift her off the Medway at the higher all up weight of 46,000 pounds. By then QEA had moved to Sydney, where the six Empire 'boats had commenced services to Singapore, with Imperial Airways crews flying on to Southampton. Four days after *Cabot* had flown off the Medway, a high tide generated by a violent storm, succeeded in forcing *Coorong* away from the mooring at Darwin and across the harbour, ending up hard against a wooden jetty with the watchman and four engineers still aboard. Lashed with ropes and timber, she was later dismantled and shipped back to Shorts for repair.

Cavalier had inaugurated the Bermuda service. But on Saturday, 21 January 1939, two hours after leaving Port Washington, Captain Marmaduke Alderson was faced with severe icing of the carburetors of all four engines. With only the outer engines functioning to any extent, the descent from 12,000 feet ended with a forced landing on a stormy ocean at just after one o'clock on Sunday morning. The punctured hull sank within fifteen minutes. Unlike Pan Am's ocean-flying Sikorsky *Bermuda Clipper*, the exhaust heaters were not up to the job and equally there were no life rafts aboard. All thirteen aboard had to cling to hastily inflated seat cushions during the night. By the morning, two passengers and a steward had died from their ordeal. The remainder were rescued by the crew of the tanker Esso Baytown, who had accurately pin-pointed their position in the darkness after receiving the S.O.S transmission. The rescue featured in newspapers across the world and a plaque was later installed within the Bermuda Cathedral. Remarkable as it seems today, the post accident recommendations suggested that passengers should be strapped in before take-offs and landings, adequate safety equipment should be carried and passengers instructed in their use. They should also be told where the emergency exits were!

Formed in 1935 by the amalgamation of Hillman Airways with Spartan Air Lines and United Airways, Allied British Airways had absorbed British Continental Airways the following year, when the name was changed to British Airways and a patriotic winged lion adopted as the company motif. In 1937 the company was the first independent airline to attract a government subsidy, the Stockholm airmail service the first to leave Britain without surcharge. Backed by a forward-looking management and a modern fleet of all-metal German and American monoplanes, BA may have become Britain's premier airline, for the heavily subsidised Imperial Airways continued to operate mostly outdated British-built biplanes on the Empire routes. But early in 1939 a bill proposing a merger of the two into a new national airline (British Overseas Airways Corporation) was supported by the government and by both managements, though Imperial would lose five more flying boats before the year was out, four of them permanently.

Taxied close to the shore at Batavia on Sunday, 12 March , an unseen object punctured the hull of *Capella* and with Captain Hussey and the crew ordered ashore, the flying boat was left to settle in the water. As with *Coorong,* the components were shipped back to Shorts, but were beyond repair. Two days later, *Corsair* failed to arrive at Juba on the Nile. In-bound to Southampton from Durban with thirteen passengers, the crew had reached the night stop-over at Kisumu on Lake Victoria, where replacement direction-finding equipment had been fitted following the radio operator's report that his set had packed up. Leaving early in the morning, a routine landing had been made at Port Bell further down the lake, departing shortly after six-fifteen the following Tuesday morning. The new equipment had not been tested however and Juba was nowhere in sight at the expected time. After an extra two, fuel consuming and fruitless, hours trying to identify ground features in increasingly misty conditions, Captain Edward Alcock (brother of the famous Atlantic flier Sir John) pulled off a skilful forced landing between the trees bordering a narrow and winding river scarcely wider than the wingtips, though having to rapidly open up the engines and head for the steep bank of the muddy shore when the hull was torn

Corsair on the Hythe slipway, possibly after the return from Faradje. © BOB WINKWORTH COLLECTION.

open by a submerged rock at the very end of the landing run. Held in position by the engines until the passengers were disembarked, *Corsair* slid back and sank, though the engines remained above the water level.

The crew and sleepy passengers, some of whom had been unaware of anything amiss, were greeted by a rather surprised Belgian commissioner who had arrived to tell them they had landed on the river Dungu, near the village of Faradje in the Belgian Congo, some 200 miles south-west of Juba. Kindly taken to his home, they were driven 50 miles to the town of Aba from where they and the mail, salvaged by cutting open the hull, were taken to Juba to await the scheduled arrival of *Centurion.* Though *Connemara* and *Clyde* were delivered toward the end of March, Shorts could not afford to abandon so much equipment and sent a salvage team out to the Congo. In their absence, three more aircraft were lost: *Challenger* crashing at full speed on 1 May while attempting to go round again in the narrowest part of Mozambique Harbour, while in June, *Centurion* overturned and broke up on landing on the Hooghly river (Calcutta) and *Connemara* burnt out at Hythe after a refuelling barge exploded alongside. *Corsair* was found to be repairable, but on 14 July the first attempt to leave was hampered by engine failure and ended up in the mud of the riverbank with fresh damage caused by a rock on the starboard side!

In the meantime, *Caribou* and *Cabot* were about to be delivered and two of Cobham's Harrow tankers had been shipped out to Montreal and flown on to Newfoundland for the Atlantic trials. By now, Shell Petroleum had taken over the controlling financial interest held by Imperial Airways in Flight Refuelling. Several contact methods had been tested at Ford, the approach, using a nose-mounted set of metal jaws, to be adapted and used for many years to snatch downed airmen from inaccessible locations. A practical transfer of fuel was finally established by flying a tanker alongside the modified *Cambria,* when a cable fitted with special attachments was fired by rocket across the cable trailed by the flying boat. The tanker was then re-positioned behind, above and to one side, to allow the joined cables to be drawn in and the fuel hose to be attached. Signaled by Aldis lamp or by flag, waved from behind a perspex side panel in the Harrow, the cable and hosepipe were drawn down to *Cambria* to allow gravity to assist the transfer of 800 gallons of petrol, preceded by a precautionary supply of nitrogen to prevent a discharge of electricity.

Motorised winches soon replaced the pair of large winding wheels turned by white overalled crewmen inside the tanker, while the thought of engine failure with an extra 1,000 pounds of aviation fuel on board caused Sir Alan and Arthur Gouge (to be knighted in 1948) to fit a jettison trunk aft of the hull of the flying boat. To Shell's undoubted relief, the company received the contract to refuel a scheduled airmail service between Southampton and New York and when nearing completion, the first four S30s were modified to enable another 7,000 pounds of fuel to be transferred in the air. The Air Registration Board required the empty and all-up weights to be displayed near the tail. The S30s now added a third – the all up weight after refuelling.

BOEING

In July 1936 the Boeing Airplane Company was awarded the contract to supply Pan Am with six flying boats of sufficient range and capacity to reliably fly economic and speedy passenger services across the Atlantic – exactly twenty-two years after Michigan lumber executive William Edward Boeing had taken a joy ride in a Curtiss-style floatplane from the freshwater Lake Union in North Seattle. Impressed, but believing he could improve on the open framework design, the 33 year old had financed the building of a floatplane by his friend and fellow passenger, 32 year old U.S Navy Lieutenant, George Conrad Westervelt, though neither had any such experience. Taught to fly by the Glenn Martin School in Los Angeles, in September 1915 'Bill' Boeing had bought a 60 horsepower Martin 'float biplane' and had divided his time between flying and studying the construction in his own lakeside hangar. The following June he had taken their own floatplane design, the 'B&W1' *Bluebill,* safely away from the lake. In July they had formed the Pacific Aero Products Company. Re-named in April 1917, a month after America had declared war on Germany, the Boeing Airplane Company produced floatplane trainers for the Navy during the remaining months of the war, at the end of which *Bluebill* and its successor *Mallard* were shipped out to the New Zealand Flying School at Kohimarama, Auckland.

Launched in 1919, the B1 flying boat resembled the Curtiss biplanes.

Though able to carry two passengers in the second open cockpit, it was bought to carry mail between Seattle and Vancouver Island. As with Short Brothers, the company had to diversify with the post-war military run down, building bedroom furniture, Curtiss flying boats, de Havilland fighters, and even speedboats, but went on to produce float-plane trainers for the navy and pursuit (fighter) planes for the navy and army. The Model 204 flying boat first flew in 1928, the year Boeing began operating its own airmail and passenger service. Similar to the B1 in appearance, the biplane could carry a pilot and four passengers at 95 miles an hour for over 300 miles. By 1934 however, the company had progressed to metal monoplanes with multiple engines and retractable landing gear.

First flown in 1937, the revolutionary giant XB-15 long-range bomber was underpowered and slow, and obviously needed the new automatic pilot system. The wing was capable of supporting a large flying boat however, but with limited space within the factory alongside the Duwamish River at Seattle, the first Boeing 314 was largely assembled on the concrete ramp outside. One hundred and fifty two feet long, the wing was fitted with four, 1,500 horsepower Wright Twin Cyclone engines to lift an all up weight approaching 37 tons, the 15 ton cradle fitted with flotation tanks to ensure it would return to the surface! Barged down the river, NX18601 began water trials in Elliot Bay at the end of May 1938 and in June was lifted from the water by test pilot Edmond 'Eddie' Allen.

So clean was the design, the single rudder was found to have no air to 'bite' on and the only means of turning was by throttling back the engines on one wing! The tailplane was finally given three 'stabilisers' with rudders on both outboard units. Aerodynamic Dornier-style sponsons were chosen rather than wing floats, but without the struts of the Martin Clippers, able to provide a boarding platform and concealed extra fuel tanks.

Named *Honolulu Clipper* in Hawaii, when Captain McGlohn and his crew were traditionally garlanded in leis, in January 1939 the giant flying boat left San Francisco on Pan Am's first six day service to Hong Kong. Named by First Lady Eleanour Roosevelt, in April *Yankee Clipper* was flown to Foynes by Captain Harold Grey and in May was loaded with almost a ton of mail before Captain La Porte departed to Horta (on Faial island in the Azores), Lisbon and Marseilles on the first scheduled Atlantic airmail service. By contrast, on Tuesday 6 June Captain Henri Guillaumet brought the 22 ton Latécoère 522 *Ville de Saint Pierre* into Foynes after a six-hour crossing from Lake Biscarosse, for the facilities (and those at Rineanna) to be inspected by three senior Air France officials. On 24 June Captain La Porte and *Yankee Clipper* inaugurated the airmail service to Southampton, using the northern route via Sheldiac

(New Brunswick), Botwood (Newfoundland) and Foynes, where the select few passengers greeted by members of the Irish government included Julian Trippe, who had been given a spontaneous party above the ocean when it was discovered it was his birthday!

Situated on Long Island, the New York marine and land airport was named after Fiorello LaGuardia, a three term mayor of the city, who had instigated the project. On 28 June 1939, Captain O'Sullivan and *Dixie Clipper* inaugurated the passenger service to Marseilles (via Horton and Lisbon) with Elisabeth Trippe among the twenty-two passengers, the landing on the Étang de Berre made twenty-nine years after Henri Fabre had first left the surface. On 8 July , Arthur La Porte took *Yankee Clipper* and seventeen passengers on the northern route from LaGuardia to Southampton. All six Clippers (*Honolulu, California, Yankee, Atlantic, Dixie and American*) would be delivered by the end of the year. The largest civil aircraft in service, they were the first to use one hundred octane fuel and with a range of 3,500 miles, were easily the Jumbo-jets of their day.

On 5 August Captain John Kelly-Rogers took *Caribou* away from the mouth of the Shannon. Topped up by the first Harrow, flown from the grass at Rineanna by Geoffrey Tyson, he was refuelled over Newfoundland by H.C Johnson, the former chief pilot of Sir Alan's Flying Circus. A star aerobatic pilot with the 'circus', former RAF fighter pilot and Avro test pilot Geoff Tyson had had an amazing escape during one of his customary low-level and inverted finales, when the pin of his Sutton harness had slipped out. Hanging on for dear life to the spade-grip of the control column as he fell from the seat, the weight of his body had pulled the aeroplane into a half-loop and he was thrown back inside the cockpit as the machine righted itself a few feet from the floor of a deep valley alongside the display ground! He would join John Parker's test team at Shorts and later became chief test pilot with Saunders-Roe on the Isle of Wight, awarded the OBE for his services to aviation.

Though the British weekly airmail service to New York brought the concept of in-flight refuelling to the eyes of the world, and would ultimately send Squadron Leader Martin Withers and Vulcan XM607 to the Falklands on the longest bombing raid in history in 2007, Boeing and Pan Am had conquered the North Atlantic without it.

The Boeing Clippers were simply magnificent. Passengers were immediately aware of the length (106 feet) and of the jutting nacelle of the port inner engine as they crossed the cambered metallic surface towards the entrance to be greeted by large letters announcing *Pan American Airways System*. Up to seventy-four could be carried by day, with ten in each of the main lounges. Only six per cabin could be accommodated overnight however and the over-night ocean flights were duly limited to forty passengers, the seats converted to two tier bunks with high quality bedding and floor to ceiling curtains. Luxurious and well soundproofed, each lounge had two facing rows of three-seat settees on the left of the aisle with two doubles on the right. Soft lighting graced an alternating décor of either a thick turquoise carpet and pale green walls or a rust coloured carpet with beige walls. Large rectangular windows gave superb views of the outside.

The first lounge was in the nose, directly beneath the cockpit, followed by the galley and facing (crew) toilet and twin washroom, with semi-spiral stairs to the flight deck. Three more lounges followed, the second noticeably larger and converted to a dining room at meal times, when white coated stewards deftly served gourmet-style meals for up to twelve passengers at a single sitting. The central aisle continued up through two more lounges to the dressing rooms; a pair of two seat couches on the right facing a door to the luxurious ladies twin dressing room/toilet on the left and a door to the men's facility on the right. The very last compartment contained the much publicised 'bridal' or VIP suite. The luxury and range had unsurprisingly attracted the wealthy and famous, film stars and politicians.

The normal flight crew comprised a double roster of pilots, radio operators, flight engineers and two stewards. While the luxury rivalled that of ocean liners, the flight deck was comparable to the operations room of a battleship; the semi spiral staircase emerging into an area 21 feet long and 9 feet wide, high enough for the tallest crew member to stand in comfort. Immediately in front of the stairs was the seven foot long plotting table of the navigating officer, with inset master compass and periscope-style drift sight. To the right of the stairs, behind a pair of full height heavy maroon curtains, were the raised seats of the pilots, each with a floor to ceiling handrail. In addition to the curtains, which were drawn at night, the cockpit interior was lined in black to preserve the pilot's night flying vision.

Both pilots had a standard instrument panel (airspeed, turn and slip, rate of climb, artificial horizon, gyro compass and altimeter) and a magnetic compass. In addition, the captain had a suction gauge, clock, flap indicator and pressure gauge for the automatic pilot, the co-pilot with his own pressure gauges and an outside air temperature indicator. The central 'Sperry' panel had controls for the gyro compass/automatic pilot system, with a row of manifold pressure and engine revolution gauges above. Above the windscreen, the captain had a wing flap (up/down) switch, engine starter buttons (1,4,2,3) and landing lights (on/off) switch. A central panel held the master (on/off) ignition switch and individual (off-left-right-both) engine starter switches. The co-pilot had switches for navigation and taxi lights, pitot head heater and his own flap control. An angled panel above both sets of rudder pedals had a 'tilt' adjustment dial and a pair of instrument lighting switches. There was no central console, the throttle, trim controls and indicators noticeably set to one side of both pilots, as the engineer fine-tuned everything once the captain had set things rolling. A central hatch led down into the nose, which had space for two rest bunks aside from the marine equipment, with a special door providing an outside mooring platform. The lower nose held a cargo bay.

At the top of the flight deck stairs, on the starboard side of the aircraft, a full height handrail was positioned by the side of the radio operators position, his padded swivel chair set before an array of forward facing knobs and dials, with a typewriter and angle-poise lamp. The roof held a manually operated direction-finding loop aerial. Immediately behind him, the levers, knobs and wall mounted multi instruments of the flight engineer are set at right angles to the rest of the crew, lit by an angled roof lamp. On both sides, a pair of oblong panels (fitted with venetian blinds) brought the maximum amount of natural daylight into the cabin.

To the right of the engineer, a hatch opened to a catwalk within the leading edge of the wing, to allow inspection and repair of an engine in flight, once the propeller had been feathered. Rescued from the abandoned bomber project, the tunnels had proved particularly helpful when turning on water against strong cross-winds, when the rising upwind sponson would force its opposite number beneath the surface, sending water streaming from the outboard propeller. Moved inside the lit and noisy interior, crew members were shielded from the elements as their weight helped balance the wings. The rear of the cabin had a briefing table and chair reserved for the 'commander'. Immediately behind, a door led to the ladder of the observation dome, the main cargo hold and crew rest room.

On the far side of the world the governments of New Zealand and Australia had reached agreement with Great Britain for a new airline to cross the Tasman Sea separating New Zealand from Australia. *Centaurus* had made a proving flight to Auckland in December 1937 and in 1938 three of the original Qantas order for the improved S30 had been transferred to Tasman Empire Airways Ltd (TEAL). Captain Cook, Canterbury and Cumberland had been re-named at Rochester as *Awarua* (Maori for 'twin rivers'), *Aotearoa* ('land of the long white cloud') – and *Australia,* which departed for New Zealand in August 1939. But while taxiing along the flare path at Shatt al Arab (the confluence of the Tigris and Euphrates) for a pre-dawn take-off on 9 August , a collision with the ironwork of a floating flare ripped open the planing bottom. The rapid attempt to 'beach' the aircraft on the mid-river Coal Island punched in the nose, displaced the flight deck structure, crumpled the hull and ripped away the port wing float. None of the twelve passengers and crew was injured, but the semi submerged flying boat required

Aotearoa Southampton 1939. Capt. Burgess, First Off. Craig, Radio Mr Cussans, Steward Mr Phillips, Ground Eng. Mr McNamara.

three months of repairs before cleared to fly back to Britain, when it was rebuilt, fitted with long-range tanks – and retained as *Clare*.

Nine days later, 30 year old John Burgess lifted *Aotearoa* away from Southampton just before a quarter to five in the morning. The flight out to Singapore required night stops at Athens, Basra, Karachi, Calcutta and Bangkok before continuing to Sourabaya, Darwin, Townsville and Rose Bay, though the gyroscopic automatic pilot system, first tested by 20 year old pilot and inventor Lawrence Sperry on a Curtiss floatplane in 1913, helped ease the load for Captain Burgess and First Officers Craig and Chapman. A following wind enabled the 1,200 mile crossing to Mechanics Bay, Auckland, to be completed in seven and three quarter hours, exactly one hour ahead of schedule. Six days later Europe was at war. German troops had entered Czechoslovakia in March, Poland was invaded on 1 September and with no response to their ultimatum, Great Britain and France had been forced to act, ending the Atlantic hopes of Imperial Airways and Air France. Pan Am announced that from now on the Atlantic services would end at Foynes, in neutral Ireland.

A few months earlier, concerned for the 'Empire' route between Australia and Britain should Japanese forces, which had already invaded China, reach Singapore, the two governments had funded a 5,600 mile survey of an alternative route across the Pacific and Indian oceans. Chartered by the Australian Government, *Guba 11* had been flown across Australia to Sydney to pick up the long-distance pilot and expert navigator Captain P.G. Taylor, famously awarded the Empire Gallantry Medal for having (six times) climbed onto the wings of Sir Charles Kingsford-Smiths Fokker tri-motor *Southern Cross* to transfer oil (in a thermos flask) from a failed engine, during an aborted airmail flight to New Zealand to celebrate the 1935 Silver Jubilee of King George V.

Centaurus - with open starboard loading hatch.
© ADRIAN MEREDITH PHOTOGRAPHY.

Flown on to Port Hedland on the west coast, on 4 June 1939 *Guba* had headed out across the South Pacific to Batavia, Christmas Island and Cocos Island, and to Diego Garcia and Mahe Island in the Indian Ocean, the final landing made at Mombasa (Kenya) thirteen days later. Each of the island groups were found capable of hosting a marine base, and the crew had arrived in America in time for the opening of the New York World's Fair, having become the first to fly a flying boat non-stop across Australia, the first to fly any aeroplane across the wide Indian Ocean, and the first to fly a flying boat across equatorial Africa – effectively circumnavigating the world at its maximum diameter.

Formed at Port Moresby in March with the Supermarine Seagull, No 11 Squadron RAAF was allowed to impress two of the bigger flying boats from the national airline rather than deplete Imperial Airways. Piloted by Qantas Captains Bob Gurney and Eric Sims and First Officers Bill Purton and Godfrey Hemsworth, called up from their reserve Air Force status, A18-10 *Centaurus* and A18-11 *Calypso* began to shadow Japanese shipping. Positioned at Southampton, *Corio* and *Coorong* were released to balance the loss for Imperial, about to receive the largest flying boat to emerge from the Rochester factory.

G- CLASS

Intended to cross the North Atlantic Ocean non-stop in association with the Pan Am Clippers, the S26 was the final development of the C-Class design. Three were built, the government subsidy to Imperial ensuring the long range would be available for military use. Over thirty-seven and a half feet high, the hull ended in a Sunderland style knife-edged vertical blade before curving up to the tail, expected to support up to thirty-three and a half tons, some 16 tons more than an Empire and nearing that of a Boeing Clipper. Visibly larger than anything before, the wing stretched to over one 134 feet, the four, 1,380 horsepower Bristol Hercules sleeve valve engines comfortably cruising at over 175 miles an hour, even against a 40 mile an hour headwind. Developed by engineer Roy (later Sir) Fedden and draughtsman Len Butler, the revolutionary sleeve valve, fitted inside a cylinder, dispensed with the traditional camshaft, pushrod and rockers, saving weight, energy, and absorbing high engine revolutions. Eleven and a half tons of fuel would be carried.

The first of the giants was launched in June 1939 and cinema goers were treated to a typically brisk British Pathé News commentary, which stated that the one hundred and three feet was just twice that of Drakes own *Golden Hinde,* yet able to encircle the world in one hundredth of the time! Designed for maximum comfort, the four luxurious cabins seated twenty-four passengers by day and twenty by night, provided with a cocktail bar and a lounge.

As with the Clippers, the flight deck had an additional 'Commanders' seat and table to the rear, with a 'settee' for off-duty crew, the remaining space available for stowage and the mail.

Golden Hind off pre-war Shorts slipway Rochester.

The G-Class trio would have names beginning with the corresponding letter of the alphabet, though world events would preclude Short Brothers from achieving perhaps their ultimate goal of providing a British airline with a flying boat capable of flying non-stop scheduled passenger services across the Atlantic. *Golden Hind* was delivered to Imperial Airways for crew training on 24 September, the day *Cabot* took just thirteen hours to fly between Foynes and Botwood. Six days later her crew completed the sixteenth and last Atlantic airmail service, though landing at Poole and not Southampton, for Imperial Airways had transferred its operations to Dorset.

Imperial Airways Poole

The increasing possibility of war with Germany had aroused concern for Southampton, considered a prime target for the Luftwaffe, particularly as the new Supermarine Spitfire fighter was in production for the RAF at Woolston and Itchen. In August 1939, Station Superintendent Clive Adams was asked to survey Poole Harbour as a possible wartime base for Imperial Airways and had taken along John Lee to write up the report. Arrangements had subsequently been made for a speedy evacuation and launches had begun taking marine equipment down the coast to Dorset. Moved to Poole on 1 September, the flying boat traffic section were housed in two boats moored alongside the quay and were 'allowed' to use the single telephone in the harbour master's office. Flying was controlled by vessels moored off Brownsea, the largest of the islands, within the second largest natural harbour in the world. After a few weeks, with no immediate bombing of Southampton as feared, the staff were returned to Southampton – until May 1940 when German forces invaded the Low Countries.

Returned to Poole, the administrative staff now occupied No 4 the High Street, just across the road from the Post Office, the former Mission to Seaman building given a bright new coat of paint and named Airways House. Today the site is occupied by Poole Museum, and the Post Office has become a gift shop. At the time, Will and Gladys Rayner lived above Cullens, a corner grocer shop that William managed at No 39 the High Street. Their son Bob attended the Henry Harbin School in Poole and when nearly 14, was told of an office vacancy in the town. Having had a successful interview, he was only aware his employer was Imperial Airways on arriving for his first morning's work as a messenger boy in January 1940. The ground floor lounge (and toilet) of No 4, was now coping with passenger arrivals and departures and from previously using the billiard room of the Antelope Hotel, a few yards away, the immigration officer would be seen here, together with Captain Carter. A member of the local pottery family, Cyril Carter was the resident

Imperial Airways office boy.

security officer, tasked to vet all those using the flying boats as part of the British Army Intelligence Service.

Billeted at the Antelope, Station Superintendent Gerald Hawtin occupied an office on the first floor of Airways House, the remainder providing an open-plan work area for the administrative staff. Here worked his secretary Victoria Stone, with George Ashton and Johnny Lee running the export section, Harry Terry in charge of imports and Malcolm Brown and others involved with passenger handling. Miss Jones manned the switchboard/telex, assisted by temporary operator Sheila Smith and occasionally by Bob Rayner, fitted out with a brass-buttoned, double breasted uniform jacket and a peaked cap bearing the Imperial Airways badge.

Among his other duties, Bob would take Air Ministry Aircraft Movement Orders to the water guard and customs offices within the former pottery premises on the quay. Begun in the 1870s by Jesse Carter and developed by his two sons, from 1921 the pottery had been managed by the partnership of Carter, Stabler and Adams. By the 1930s 'Poole Pottery' had gained international fame for the elegant hand-painted ware individually marked by the painters and 'paintresses'. On receipt of Air Raid Warnings Yellow and Red, Bob was entrusted to open the side door of a house near the church of Saint James, where stairs led down to a basement shelter for use by the airline staff.

A special non-stop train now brought VIP passengers from London to Bournemouth West Station rather than to Southampton, the three coaches fully blacked out to preserve the identity of those within and frequently coupled to a Pullman carriage. In the early days a Rolls Royce conveyed them to Poole, with Ray Hodges or Reg Windows at the wheel, or perhaps taxi driver Arthur Mathews. Later, an unmarked coach would take them to their hotel prior to an early morning departure. In similar fashion, wartime security measures required the blinds of the flying boat cabins to be pulled down when leaving and approaching major ports and harbours, the desperate state of the nation brought home to Bob during late May and early June as he watched troops evacuated from the beaches of Dunkirk being landed on the quayside and given bread by the employees of Baverstocks bakery in New Street. Unknown to him then, his future father in law was also employed about the harbour.

Born in Guernsey, George Ellis Wetherall had entered the Royal Navy as a boy seaman and had seen action at the Battle of Jutland. Retired as a Petty Officer on the reserve (later Chief Petty Officer), he had become the 'Sole Hand Skipper' of the 19 ton, 45 foot *Emoh*, owned by a Mr K. Lankester. The job had entailed several relocations but faced with another move, this time from the Parkstone Yacht Club, his wife had said enough was enough. A praiseworthy letter written by his employer at his Shore Cottage, Sandbanks, address, had secured employment with the Poole Harbour Board however and George was given his own office at New Quay on the Ferry Port side of the harbour. As coxswain for Harbour Master Commander Charles Euman, he was responsible for the motor launch Grey Shadow and in his spare time manned the helm of the commander's J class racing yacht. No two days were the same. Aside from ferrying the commander on his duties about the harbour, he would don a bronze helmet and diving gear to retrieve the occasional car that had fallen off the concrete ramp of the chain-ferry linking Sandbanks with Studland Bay. He had also positioned the first mooring buoys prior to the arrival of the flying boats.

BOAC Poole

Having pioneered services across Europe to the Far East for an incredibly short two years, the flying boat division of Imperial Airways was officially absorbed by BOAC on 1 April 1940, from when the Poole terminal embarked on eight full years that would prove unmatched in the annals of British flying boat operations. At the time of the Munich crisis, car tyres had marked the water 'runways'. But with the move from Southampton, the RAF had properly marked and maintained five alighting areas, though two were only useable at high water. The prevailing westerly winds ensured the longest, from Sandbanks to the Wareham Channel, would be the main area – to the dismay of the residents at Arne, over which the flying boats would turn at low level before setting course for France. The village would be depopulated and used as a battle range by the army.

As former Signalman and Water Controller (the latter term used from about 1947) Peter Davidson explained to me, a signalman had three vessels with which to operate local control of the alighting area. Comparable to the control tower of an airfield, his own vessel, an ex-naval air-sea rescue pinace, was positioned to port of the area in use.

Ministry of Civil Aviation Alighting Area pinnace Poole. © PETER DAVIDSON.

Crewed by a coxswain, engineer and two deckhands it was equipped with a windsock, derrick, searchlight, Aldis lamp and a very high frequency radio transmitter. A 20 knot Upwind Launch, crewed similarly but without an engineer, would join the coxswain and two deckhands/firemen of a Fire Launch in sweeping the area for debris. Launch 39, known as the 'Crash Launch' and fitted with a towing post in the centre of the open deck, would parallel the landing until the flying boat emerged from the spray, when it led the way to a mooring in much the same way as the 'Follow-Me' vehicle on airfields.

The cabins of the alighting area launches were painted yellow to distinguish them from others bustling about the harbour, the crews maintaining contact by Aldis lamp and Morse code until after the war. If all else failed, they were trained to signal with flags (semaphore). Wind direction permitting, the existing channel-marker buoys were used to indicate the area in use, with pyrotechnic flares used in difficult conditions. For night operations, battery lamps were installed in pram dinghies roped in a line, not an easy task for the towing launch in a changing wind and tide, but once clear, the aircraft would radio back to enable them to be towed away.

One of the worst in history, the winter of 1939/40 had seen snow and ice completely cover military airfields across Britain, rendering them useless for operations. At Poole, the flying boats were frozen at their moorings for days, unavoidably delaying services to Africa and Australia. A wartime Restricted Area, Sandbanks was occupied by troops, with acres of barbed wire about the shoreline, though Peter remembered the relatively deserted harbour could still offer peace-time attractions such as swimming and rod-fishing in the summer, if you were careful. Of the pilots, he particularly remembered Captain Stone who was in charge of testing and ferrying the flying boats. Initially employed as an engineer, his accurate diagnosis of faults in the air saved time and money, a typical air test begun by a speedy take-off in the wake of the departing passenger launch to prevent the engines from cooling. If a trip to Hythe was unavoidable, his three man skeleton crew were treated to a steep-banked turn on leaving the water, followed by an ebullient, low-level (fuel-saving) cross country to the engineers. He was the only pilot Peter had seen side-slip a Sunderland!

The outbreak of war had caused the London offices of Imperial Airways to be evacuated to the Grand Spa Hotel in Bristol. Employed as a signals clerk at Hythe, conveniently at no great distance from the family cottage, 17 year-old Harry Pusey had been posted to Bristol as a night duty telephone and signals clerk before swiftly returned to Hythe to be trained as an operations clerk. He had then been sent to Poole to be trained in marine operations, signalling, meteorology and air navigation. The airline, Air Ministry and meteorological office staffs all shared a building situated on the left hand corner of the Lower High Street where it meets with the quayside, the narrow pavements and close-packed buildings indicative of times long past, when the little fishing port was isolated from the rest of the country and the mariners had divided their time between fighting the French and Spanish and bringing home the brandy!

Aside from the telex room, the ground floor was occupied by two forecasters and clerks of the meteorological section, a narrow corridor ending in a wooden staircase leading up to the first floor domain of senior Air Ministry air traffic control officer Stanley Baker and his staff and an Air Ministry signals office. The remaining triangular-shaped area was entirely taken up by the desks of Imperial Airways Operations Superintendent Alan Dewdney, marine section foreman Tom Perry, and the operations assistant (Harry), which unfortunately had to be passed by everyone on their way to the only toilet in the building. With space at a premium, bicycles were parked in the downstairs corridor, permanently cluttered by the charged hydrogen cylinders used to fill the met office weather balloons. Having decided whether a red, white or blue balloon would best show against the prevailing sky, inflation was performed inside the building and only judged to be ok if the balloon remained motionless when two penny pieces were balanced on the top! Release was carried out from the quayside, using a theodolite to check the rate of climb, drift, and the cloud base. At night, it was great fun to watch the silent ascent marked by the glimmer of a little cake candle.

The roof of the building was painted with the black and yellow stripes usually seen on the control caravans of land 'aerodromes'. Aircraft returning from occupied France had to maintain strict radio silence and would fly over the easily recognisable building to be identified. Standard departures were flown via Wimborne Minster, Cerne Abbas and Lundy, setting course when 10 miles west of the Scilly Isles – or if making for Foynes, at Fastnet.

Bob Rayner was not the only 'boy-entrant' at Poole. Believed the youngest taken on by the marine section at the time, 16 year-old Douglas Rose had joined Imperial Airways in 1940 as a trainee seaman, and was thereafter known as 'David' due possibly to an earlier entrant having the same name. With others, he was shown how to splice wire and rope hawsers by a rather fearsome Chief Petty Officer known as Ossy Osbourne, within the 'riggers loft', in reality a cellar under the King Charles pub. In the High Street behind, the cargo section operated from the yard of the Antelope Hotel, where the airline staff ran their own canteen and social club in an upstairs room. The catering department had taken over a shop on the other side of the narrow street. Morse was taught and examined by former Royal Navy Chief Petty Officer Fielder within a hut at the end of a jetty at Hamworthy.

A quayside building had been requisitioned for the station engineer and his staff and also provided an office and rest room for the launch crews of the marine section. The Davis boatyard had supplied two motor launches, Silver Spray taken over by the riggers and Felix by the engineers. Maintenance was carried out at a launch house and slipway on the left bank of the inner harbour, just after the lifting bridge, where a fuel barge was usually moored on the opposite bank. Passenger and baggage launches departed from the stone steps on the quay known as the Shambles, believed named after a large shed where fresh fish was once sold by the local fishermen. A few yards away was the Swan public house, otherwise known as the 'Dirty Duck', later to become The Flying Boat, complete with appropriate sign board.

With an average of two flying boats arriving in the afternoon and departing early the following morning, the quayside was a hive of activity: the four cabin launches of the marine section taking passengers to and from the moorings as stevedores of the cargo section loaded and off-loaded baggage and mail using long-tillered open launches. The main BOAC moorings, the half-diver buoys, were positioned off the deep water channel near Brownsea and were generally referred to as 'trots', the name given by crab and lobster fishermen to the lines of bobbing bait-pots.

When ready to leave, a pilot would request 'permission to slip' from the attendant MCA launch, and on receiving the customary 'green' from an Aldis lamp, the radio officer would remove the bow mooring, the first officer would release the tail line and the aircraft would taxi to the runway in use. Having waited to ensure it was not about to return, the riggers boat would then close up to the buoy, where as a trainee, David was obliged to retrieve the dripping wet 4-inch rope, hand over hand. During the next two years he would progress to Coxswain 2nd Class, with control of the small launches that held up to five marine section personnel, until called up for war service aboard H.M. minesweepers.

Following the transfer of Imperial Airways to Poole, the British Power Boat Company had taken over factory premises in West Quay Road and built the twelve high-speed launches used by BOAC and the fourteen operated by the Ministry of Aviation. Having finished with flying boats, Hubert Scott-Paine had formed the company in 1927 to develop his passion for speed. Six years later he had become the first to pilot a single engined powerboat at over 100 miles an hour, though *Miss Britain 111* was badly damaged by a fire after the run across Poole harbour. He and Gordon Thomas formally broke the 100 mile an hour barrier on Southampton Water, while the trials of his design for a high speed seaplane tender for the Air Ministry, had brought a close association with a hero of the First World War.

Lieutenant-Colonel Thomas Edward Lawrence, the famous 'Lawrence of Arabia', had served Winston Churchill as an adviser in Middle Eastern affairs after the First World War and had joined the RAF as a lowly aircraftsman, using the pseudonym John Hume Ross to escape attention by the press. Based at the Cattewater seaplane base at Plymouth (the future Mount Batten) he had helped his commanding officer arrange the 1929 Southampton Schneider Trophy Race, and two years later had witnessed a tragic flying boat crash at Cattewater. Frustrated by the lack of rescue launches, he had vigorously campaigned for better equipment. Posted to the Hythe factory to test and oversee production of seaplane tenders for the RAF, he had used his considerable influence to promote Scott-Paine's designs, which employed a hard planing surface to aquaplane across the water, rather than through it. He also assisted the dangerous testing of an armoured target launch for the RAF. Just weeks after leaving his last RAF posting in Yorkshire, in May 1935 the 46 year old had died after swerving his Brough Superior motorcycle to avoid two little boys on bicycles that had appeared in a dip in the road, a short distance from his Dorset cottage. He was buried in the village of Moreton. Now owned by the National Trust, the Clouds Hill cottage is opened for public viewing, while a stone effigy of the former hero of Arabia can be seen within the little Saxon church at Wareham.

Corsair had finally escaped the Congo during the early morning of 6 January 1940, when Captain Jack Kelly Rogers flew her away from the river Dungu. The rescue saga had involved rebuilding the damaged hull, an incredible feat of engineering in the middle of nowhere, and the equally innovative building of a dam from trees, mud and rock to raise the water level. As elsewhere, the native workers soon found use for the discarded metal, nuts and bolts and upholstery, while the collection of mud huts erected by the riverside to house them all, inevitably came to be known as Corsairville! Refuelled at Juba, some nine months after her intended arrival, the flying boat was comprehensively overhauled and re-fitted at Alexandria and returned to service.

Short Brothers had received an order for a ninth S30 in 1939 and *Cathay* was delivered in March, the month a second flying boat was ferried out to Qantas. Commanded by Captain Oscar Garden, who had first learnt to fly with the Norwich Aero Club, *Awarua* was flown across France at tree-top height to avoid being shot down by enemy fighters, and landed at Waitemata harbour, Auckland, on 3 April, twelve days after leaving Southampton. Of three more flying boats ordered by Imperial in 1939, only two S33s were completed. Though similar to the Empires, the S30 type hulls were strengthened to lift a maximum 53,000 pounds, as with *Cabot* and *Caribou*, though having a much shorter-range. Effectively the last of forty-two C-Class Empire flying boats, *Clifton* and *Cleopatra* were respectively delivered to BOAC in April and May 1940.

NORWAY

Aside from enthusiastic ascents in balloons, the first heavier than air flight from Norwegian soil was made by a Blériot monoplane in October 1910, followed in September 1913 by that of the first 'seaplane', when a float equipped Maurice Farman Longhorn biplane left the river Niteelven. With few airfields, Curtiss flying boats were shipped over for demonstration flights and in 1920 the three Supermarine Channel flying boats began flying for Det Norske Luftfartsrederi A/S, together with a pair of Friedrichshafen FF.49 floatplanes, though the company was short lived. In 1927 Deutsche Luft Hansa AG was granted a concession to operate international services from Gressholmen Island in the Osløfjord to Gothenburg (Sweden), Copenhagen (Denmark) and the Baltic. In the following eight years the fleet progressed from Dornier Wal flying boats, to the more capacious seventeen seat Junkers tri-motor floatplanes.

Granted national airline status in 1935, together with an all important subsidy for carrying the mail, Det Norske Luftfartselskap A/S Fred. Olsen & Bergenske (DNL) leased and later bought the Ju52 *Fritz Simon* from the German airline. In June, the re-named *Havørn* (sea-eagle) opened a summer service from Gressholmen to the Bergen peninsula, with intermediate landings at five coastal towns. Conducted along a jetty to the seaward facing floatplane, where the trailing edge of the port wing clearly showed the long 'detached' flap/aileron that gave the land-plane version a particularly short take-off and landing, passengers mounted a short fixed metal ladder atop the port float to access the opened cabin door, hinged on the corrugated metal fuselage. Inside, they found two single rows of comfortable adjustable leather 'recliner' seats on either side of the aisle. Each had an oblong window giving a good view of the outside, while the sedate cruising speed of around 130 knots, ensured a pleasant and unhurried passage to their destination, usually ended with a smooth touch down on clear, unruffled water.

In July, the company's single engined, six seat Junkers, named *Ternen* after the seagull seen on the Fred Olsen (shipping) Line logo, began flying from Bergen to Tromsø, the capital of the Arctic region. Nine coastal towns were visited on the way north and the service, which stretched for over 1,250 kilometers, became known as the Midnattssolruten or Midnight Sun Route. The larger capacity *Havørn* took over in the new year, with the smaller floatplane flying more localised routes, surveys, and a night airmail service from Gressholmen to Göteborg (via Moss), on the west coast of Sweden. In March 1936 DNL secured a contract with Julian Trippe for Pan Am to fly from New York to Reykjavik in Iceland with DNL continuing on to Bergen and to Europe.

The company bought a brand-new twin engined Sikorsky S43 flying boat, which was named *Valkyrien* after the legendary Norse maidens, but with Pan Am pulling out of the agreement in favour of a Newfoundland-Foynes route, the amphibian was stored at Malmö in Sweden. A second Ju52 arrived in June and was named *Najaden* after the flagship sunk by British warships during the Napoleonic war.

Since the days of the Vikings ('vikingr'), sea mists have cloaked the coasts of Scandinavia, especially during autumn and winter, though the northern coastal waters experience the phenomena in spring and summer due to the contrasting warmth of the surface with the exposed land mass. Leaving Bergen for Trondhjem on the sixteenth of the month, *Havørn* encountered fog and flew into the Lihesten mountain, miles off track, on the north side of the Sognefjord. All seven aboard died in the worst aviation accident experienced in Norway. In 2008 a memorial was erected part way up the mountain.

The arrival of *Falken* in July brought the fleet back up to three floatplanes, and *Ternen* inaugurated a service to Balestrand on the north bank of the Sognefjord, the longest and deepest of the Norwegian waterways. In June 1937 *Valkyrien* inaugurated a service to Stockholm, but the relatively high-cost fares ended the flights in July. Sold to Aéromaritime, formed by the French shipping company Compagnie Maritime des Chargeurs Réunis, the Sikorsky joined four others in flying coastal services through French West Africa, south of Dakar. Soon afterwards, *Hauken* increased DNLs fleet to four Junkers floatplanes. The government had already considered opening new airports to assist the burgeoning air services, though the cost limited construction to a site at Fornebu, some 8 kilometers from Oslø, to replace the airport at Kjeller and the marine base at Gressholmen, with a second at Kjevik near

Aeromaritime poster. COURTESY ONSLOWS AUCTIONEERS VIA MILLERS ANTIQUES & COLLECTABLES.

Kristiansand, on the southern tip of Norway. Both were officially opened on 1 June 1939.

A consortium made up of the Swedish Aerotransport (ABA), the Danish Det Danske Luftfartselskab A/S (DDL) and the influential DNL of Norway, had begun negotiations with Julian Trippe for a shared trans-Atlantic service, using a Boeing 314 Clipper chartered from Pan Am to fly from Bergen to New York, via Reykjavik and Botwood. But in the early morning of 9 April 1940, Denmark and Norway were invaded by German forces, partly to gain access to the Atlantic for German battleships and submarines, and partly to use Narvik to deliver iron ore from Sweden, rather than the seasonally frozen port of Lulea. The first airborne assault in history, the skies over the key airfields at

DNL 1939 timetable. Junkers 52 floatplane. © THE S.A.S MUSEUM GARDEMOEN.

Boeing 314 prototype by factory slipway. © BOEING.

Sola/Stavanger (only the second in Europe to have a concrete runway) and at Fornebu/Oslø, were filled with parachutes supporting the elite paratroopers of the 7th Flieger Division.

The declaration of war with Britain had prevented *Cabot* and *Caribou* from flying a regular trans-Atlantic service intended for 1940. Instead, the aircraft and crews of Captains Long and Store had been impressed for service with 119 Squadron, RAF Coastal Command, flying a series of radar trials from Invergordon and Islay. The need to deliver radar equipment direct to the main allied naval base at Harstad in the Lofoten Islands, to the north-west of Narvik, was not a problem for the longer range S30s, tasked with surveying possible landing areas for the RAF before flown home. Stripped of military equipment, V3137 (*Cabot*) left Invergordon just after midnight on 3 May and after off loading equipment and military passengers at Harstad, flew off to Bodø, over 130 miles away to the south. V3138 (*Caribou*) followed a day later.

By then, the Luftwaffe occupied the Norwegian airfields. Confusingly, both sides operated the sleek and efficient looking twin-engined Heinkel 115 floatplane, the first two Küstenfligerstaffeln (coastal flying squadrons) of Kü.Fl. Gruppe 506 based at Trondjhem. Flown by a crew of three, the floatplane carried torpedos or bombs and was armed with a machine gun in the belly and at the rear, for use by the observer and radio operator.

About an hour after *Caribou* had arrived, the sound of church bells alerted both crews to an incoming air raid. Though quick to respond, the two large flying boats were attacked by a Heinkel while taxiing towards the harbour mouth. Despite defensive fire, the last pass injured five of the crew aboard *Caribou*. Wounded in the leg, with the starboard outer engine out of action, smoke streaming from both wings, a shattered nose, and fuel sloshing about the lower deck from pierced fuel tanks in the badly holed hull, Captain Store used the remaining power to run *Caribou* onto the muddy shore. Captain Long followed suit with *Cabot.* Norwegians ferried the wounded to hospital and as the tide receded, the sensitive equipment was removed and sunk and the machine guns gifted to the commander of the Norwegian troops in the town. As attention centred on *Caribou,* another attack was delivered, this time by a Dornier, the second of two bombs exploding close enough to set the flying boat ablaze before settling into Bodø Fjord. Denied the cover of darkness in that latitude, *Cabot* was floated on the late tide and towed further north. Though covered with bushes and blankets across the roundels, it was strafed by a Junkers 88 the very next day and burnt out. Both crews were retrieved by British destroyers. Retreating to the north, the Norwegian Royal Family and government were evacuated to Britain by HMS Devonshire.

Equipped with six Heinkel 115 floatplanes before the invasion, the Marinens Flyvevåben (Norwegian Naval Air Arm) was also able to use two captured 115s against the enemy until the country capitulated on 10 June . Of these, six serviceable aircraft were used in a brave escape from their moorings. Four, including a Luftwaffe aircraft, landed safely in the Orkneys. Three would subsequently be used in clandestine operations in support of the resistance in Norway. A fifth was landed in Finland. A sixth crew was sadly lost somewhere over the North Sea.

In September, DNL was allowed to operate a thrice weekly service from Trondjem to Tromsø and a twice weekly service on to Kirkenes, though the crews were supplemented with Germans as a security measure. But the escape to neutral Sweden by Captain Finn Lambrechts in particular, the regular pilot of *Havørn,* whose invaluable knowledge led to the clandestine Heinkel flights, saw the company banned from resuming operations in the spring and closed down. Seen with swastikas since 1936, Lufthansa floatplanes took over the seasonal services.

Italy had joined with the Axis forces on 11 June . Twelve days later France had signed an armistice with Germany, bringing a hurried evacuation of the former Imperial Airways staffs and a loss of vital communication equipment, for the Mediterranean could no longer be flown in safety by civilian aircraft. Crews were reluctant to let their flying boats be captured however. Amongst the upheavals, *Caledonia* continued on from Corfu to reinforce the Africa service and *Clyde* flew back to Poole – having barely cleared the Maltese shore at Kalafrana Bay when a mis-firing engine and heavy swell deterred Kelly-Rogers from taking off towards the sea. *Cathay* was flown back from Ajaccio.

Pioneer wildlife photographers Martin and Osa Johnson aboard Sikorsky S38 amphibian *Osas Ark*. They were first to photo Mt. Kilimanjaro and Mt. Kenya from the air.

© THE MARTIN AND OSA JOHNSON SAFARI MUSEUM, CHANUTE, KANSAS.

At the end of June, a ban on flying over French colonial territory effectively cut Britain off from Europe – save for the vital Poole to Lisbon flying boat service (surveyed by *Cambria* three years earlier) which linked up with the Pan American Clippers flying the Atlantic.

Several 'Empire' crews had been stranded in Africa but within a few weeks BOAC had equipped and staffed fresh stations on a new route to Australia from Durban, an enormous undertaking in those uncertain days. Imperial Airways had had a slipway and hangar built adjacent to the Prince Edward Graving Dock, with an office in the town's Club Arcade. To meet the new demands, extensive engine overhaul and maintenance facilities were set up in premises in Sydney Road. At home, Imperials engine and propeller workshops at Croydon were dispersed to Treforest in South Wales to avoid attention from the Luftwaffe. From July, crews flew northwards from Durban to Cairo to link up with the pre-war Empire route to Australia, the seating increased to twenty-nine to keep the twice weekly service open. When viewed on a map, the Africa to Australia route resembled a slightly distorted and inverted item of equine appendage and inevitably became known as the 'Horseshoe Route'.

Five days out from Durban, the route turned eastwards and away from the Nile to cross the Suez Canal and the Sinai Desert before reaching Lake Tiberius. Kalia, on the 'Dead Sea' would later be added to the schedule. A seemingly unending expanse of Syrian Desert was crossed to Lake Habbaniya near Baghdad, with another long stretch of desert ending at the Persian Gulf and the confluence of the Tigris and Euphrates rivers at Basra, where the night was spent in a large and airy hotel. A pre-dawn take-off was followed by breakfast on the island of Bahrein, before reaching Dabai (near Sharja) and Jiwani (on the Arabian Sea), with the day ended at Karachi; the bustling port and meticulous customs and immigration procedures in great contrast to the remote desert stations.

The following day, landings were made on the sacred Lakes of Raj Samand and Mahdo Sugar (Delhi) and on the wide river Ganges (Allahabad), before descending over the Willingdon Bridge for a final, evening, landing on the Hooghly river; the night stop-over at Calcutta again bringing noise and bustling humanity to senses more attuned to the confines of the flying boat. Up early in the morning to chase the bright sun to Rangoon (Burma), Bangkok (Siam) and Singapore (Malaya), where a Qantas crew took over to fly on to the lush, tropical islands of Klabal (Sumatra), Batavia, Soerabaja, Soembawa (Java) and Koepang (Timor) before crossing to Darwin, on the north-western tip of Australia. On again to Groot Eylandt and Karumba, passing down the east coast to Townsville, Gladstone and Brisbane before finally approaching the Rose Bay terminal at Sydney.

The outbreak of war had delayed starting for Tasman Empire Airways, though the crew of *Aotearoa* had been kept busy since arriving in New Zealand; First Officer William Craig completing his 'commander' training after night take-offs and landings in Auckland Harbour. Born in England, his family had brought him to Wanganui when he was about six months old and he was among the first pupils at the Western Federated Flying Club. When 21 he had been commissioned into the Dominian Territorial Air Force and was one of four New Zealanders recommended for a commission in the Royal Air Force. He had paid his own passage to Britain and had subsequently joined No 20 Army Co-operation Squadron on India's North-West Frontier. Promoted to Flight Lieutenant, he had joined Imperial Airways in May 1937 and on completing the required engineering and navigation courses, was posted to Hythe, flying several times around Britain with *Connemara* and Captain Griffiths, who was due to arrive in New Zealand on the next flying boat – as was Mrs Craig.

With two of the three flying boats delivered in April, TEAL opened offices at Wellington prior to extending the Empire Air Mail service to New Zealand. BOAC and Qantas held the largest shares, the remainder divided between the New Zealand Government and Union Airways.

Given charge of operations, at the end of the month, company chief pilot Captain Burgess took *Aotearoa*, nine passengers and over forty thousand air mail letters, from Waitemata to Rose Bay in nine hours to record the first commercial crossing of the Tasman Sea. On 6 June the newly promoted Captain Craig flew to Sydney in just over seven and a half hours due to the strong tail-winds. The sole connection by air with Australia, the weekly return service was maintained by *Aotearoa* and *Arawua* throughout the war, when the airmails kept those fighting in the Middle East in touch with their families, though diplomatic mail had always to be given priority. The service was trebled from 1944.

Re-named in the factory at Rochester, the two remaining G-Class boats Grenville and Grenadier were launched as *Golden Horn* and *Golden Fleece* in May and August 1940. With *Golden Hind* they were impressed for military service by the Air Ministry and converted at Rochester, where a power operated four-gun turret was installed behind the tail fin and a pair of two-gun turrets fitted on the long spine. Under-wing racks were fitted for eight, 500 pound bombs, the cavernous interiors given stowage for twenty reconnaissance flares, twenty-eight flame floats and eight smoke floats. Air to surface radar was also fitted. Intended to fly the mail before commencing Atlantic passenger services, all three retained faired-over windows which, with the newly applied wartime camouflage, presented an altogether sharper profile. Airborne surveillance radar was fitted by the Blackburn Aircraft factory at Dumbarton, on the north shore of the Firth of Forth. Flown to 119 Squadron, at the newly opened RAF Coastal Command Station of Bowmore on Loch Indaal, on the Isle of Islay off the west coast of Scotland, the trio were appropriately known as 'G Flight'.

Chapter Four

Battle for Britain

Atlantic Terminal

The European War had caused Pan Am to abandon the service from Lisbon to Marseilles, while the American Neutrality Act prevented the Clippers from bringing VIP passengers directly to Britain. The Atlantic service now ended at Foynes in neutral Southern Ireland rather than Southampton. Aside from maintaining the West Africa service, the long range S30s *Champion*, *Cathay* and the retained, re-fitted, *Clare* operated a shuttle between Poole and Foynes. Mooring buoys were already in place, thanks to the proving flights, while Esso and Shell had provided fuel storage tanks and fuel launches. Passenger reception and departure formalities were carried out from a transit lounge within a building near the west quayside, with fast passenger launches to the moorings. Along with the radio and meteorological staffs, the airport building housed staffs of the airport management, customs and the airlines.

Difficult to predict, the Atlantic winds would largely determine the arrival times of the Clippers, while it was no mean feat to coincide the arrivals from Poole with the landplane passengers brought from Rineanna by BOAC coach, the British airline having taken overall responsibility for passenger handling and consequently more in evidence. Accommodation remained scarce in Foynes, where the locals had rented rooms to the airlines, which had their own management, office and engineering staffs. Aside from immigration, customs and police personnel, a British and American security (consular) official was on hand. Both were accommodated courtesy of BOAC at Bolands Meadow, outside Foynes, where a hotel would later lodge the airline staffs. With many wartime movements conducted at night or at dusk, a dedicated control launch laid flares across a mile of the estuary, complemented by parachute flares fired from a mortar fixed at the stern. Aircrew received instructions from a hut on Foynes Island. By 1945, a fixed flare path and channel marker lights would be in place, together with two timber piers connected by gangways to a floating pontoon. There would also be a two-storey, glass-enclosed control tower on top of the airport office building.

Having received confirmation of an in-bound Boeing, control launches swept the landing area for debris as a BOAC launch headed out to prepare the mooring. Led to the mooring by a BOAC (towing) launch, the Clipper was boarded by a customs officer, who after checking the documentation with the purser, and the health aspects of the aircraft and occupants, would authorise the unloading of passengers, mail and freight. An operations officer collected the secret (Morse) codes and ciphers from the captain and the navigation equipment, while the station engineering officer checked the serviceability of the aircraft with the flight engineer to arrange the day's activity for the ground staff. A launch then took the flight crew ashore to be escorted through the customs, immigration and health sections. The captain and navigator would then proceed to the meteorological office to report the weather encountered during the flight with the duty senior forecaster, and in return would receive a weather report for the evening departure to Lisbon. Passengers and crews were offered coffee, tea and biscuits and on clearing formalities, were free to breakfast in the restaurant. High tea or a late lunch was available for passengers awaiting the Poole shuttle, while those bound for Rineanna would have left by coach. For night stop-overs, passengers were taken by BOAC bus to the Dunraven Arms Hotel, some 10 miles away in the picturesque village of Adare, as was the captain. Crews usually lodged at the Royal George.

With no direct passenger service to America from Britain and with the G-Class impressed into the RAF, it was decided to establish a Trans-Atlantic service by fitting extra fuel tanks within the longer range flying boats. Intended to replace *Cavalier* in the Atlantic, *Clyde* was flown into Poole. As was *Clare,* and in the early morning of 3 August 1940, Captains Kelly-Rogers and Wilcockson took a party of VIPs away to Foynes, and maintaining complete secrecy reached Botwood after a flight of just over fifteen and a half hours. Flying on to Montreal, they arrived at New York during the evening of 4 August , when Lord Balfour, the Under Secretary of State for Air, two government officials and a representative of the Secretary of State for the United States Navy, became the first passengers to complete a British Trans-Atlantic crossing. Tasked to secure facilities for trainee pilots in America and American training aircraft for the RAF, Lord Balfour also learned that the war in Europe had caused Juan Trippe to consider reducing his order for an improved Boeing 314. Strong tail winds helped the darkly camouflaged *Clare* re-cross the ocean a minute short of thirteen hours, the subsequent landing at Poole enabling a handful of American pilots to proceed on their way to assisting the men and women of the newly formed Air Transport Auxiliary to deliver aircraft direct from the factories to the front line squadrons.

Unable to fly the Mediterranean and with North Africa invaded by Italian forces, Britain had no direct communication with Cairo or with British Forces in Africa and the Middle East. Air power was vital.

Dismantled and shipped to the Gold Coast of West Africa, British and American war planes destined for the Desert Air Force were re-assembled at Takoradi, where buildings had been commandeered and a large landing strip laid down for an RAF Station. Following much the same route as the pre-war internal service operated by Imperial Airways (Khartoum to Lagos) and Elders Colonial Airways (to Takoradi via Accra), but with extra landing grounds constructed and defended by Free French forces, the mainly fighter aircraft flew over 4,000 miles to Abu Sueir near Cairo, where the previously factory fresh machines were completely overhauled to remove dust and sand from the engine filters, wings and fuselage. The Fleet Air Arm used the route to equip aircraft carriers in the Mediterranean. Should Lisbon fall to German forces, passengers and cargo vital to the war effort would have to be flown non-stop from Poole to Takoradi. But thanks to Lord Balfour's deal with Pan Am on behalf of the British Government and BOAC's Subsidiary Airways (Atlantic) Ltd, the airline would receive the first of three long-range Boeing flying boats within a year.

CLYDE & THE CONGO

Expected to follow *Clare*, on 5 August *Clyde* was being prepared at Poole for the Atlantic crossing. But at four o'clock in the afternoon, Captain 'Tony' Loraine was told he would instead be flying a party of senior officers of the newly formed Free French Army on a diplomatic mission to Lagos first thing in the morning. Led by 45 year old Général Edgard de Larminat, who had survived the First World War and had now escaped imprisonment by the Germans for refusing to accept his country's surrender to the same enemy in a second world conflict, the eight officers duly arrived in civilian clothes. The first refuelling was made at Lisbon, where a flare path was laid across the water for the departure to be made at night. With the landing lights switched on to assist forward vision, *Clyde* was barely airborne when co-pilot Captain May spotted the vague outline of a vessel in their path. Both pilots flung the controls to the left, narrowly avoiding digging in the port wingtip. Levelling out, they climbed safely through the darkness and on through the night until the welcoming sunrise revealed the deserted coastline of West Africa to port.

It also revealed a jagged tear on the underside of the starboard wing, beyond the outer engine, and a chunk of missing aileron. They had not missed the ship after all. Alighting on the long, wide expanse of the river Gambia at Bathurst, after a leg of nearly 2,000 miles (equal to an Atlantic crossing) that had required accurate astral navigation, the damage was patched up using a discarded length of aluminium found at the pre-war Lufthansa base a few miles away. An assortment of heavy brass nuts and bolts were supplied by the Royal Navy! The following evening they landed at Freetown, over 400 miles away. Faced with refuelling from a large and unwieldy steel barge, with nothing like the proper equipment, they waited until the early morning before taxiing *Clyde* to a sheltered bay where an old buoy had been marked with a flag. Despite the heat and the onset of heavy rain, large drums of aviation fuel were laboriously hoisted topside from native canoes until around five o'clock in the evening, when 1,000 gallons had been poured into the wing tanks using a hand held funnel sheltered by Loraine's uniform raincoat. By then he was soaked through.

The following morning they departed for Lagos, some 1,300 miles away, where the damage to the wing was more properly repaired. But with no boat available to take the officers on to Leopoldville in the Belgian Congo, Captain Loraine received instructions from London to land on the unknown river Congo, 1,200 miles further on. Flown over largely uncharted areas, without radio contact or weather information since leaving Lisbon, and despite no safety launches in the river, *Clyde* was landed safely and without incident. The temperature had risen to over one hundred degrees however, over thirty degrees higher than the normal operating oil temperatures of the Pegasus engines, and had brought real fears of simultaneous engine failure over a very inhospitable area.

Leopoldville (now Kinshasa) lay on a bend of the southern bank of the widening river. Brazzaville, the French capital of the region, was on the far side. If the governor was allowed to continue to support the Vichy French Government, Equatorial Africa would be denied all allied air communication with the Middle East. A coup d'état, formulated by Général Larminat and Colonel Carretier, the leader of the Free French Army, within a cabin of the flying boat, saw Brazzaville taken a few days later, enabling the region to declare for Free France and De Gaulle. With the officers safely back on board, the flying boat soon left the river, but the lack of servicing in such a climate soon made itself felt with a leak in the fuel system and oil cooler. The automatic pilot also failed on leaving Freetown, and for the rest of the return journey (some three and a half thousand miles) both pilots had to remain at the controls by day and by night, the landing at Poole ending twenty-three days and some 12,000 air miles of military service. There was no immediate respite for Tony Loraine however, who had contracted malaria and was confined to his bed for six weeks. In late September, *Corinthian*, *Cassiopeia* and *Cooee* arrived independently at Durban to reinforce the 'Horseshoe' – having safely continued on from Leopoldsville.

Poole had become unrecognisable to those who know it today. Wartime had brought refugees from Southampton and elsewhere into the town, entered only by a pass, while the parks and recreation grounds not taken over by the military were in use as 'dig for victory' allotments to supplement the meagre and rationed wartime diet. Decades before becoming a millionaire's playground of luxury 'second' homes and apartments,

Sandbanks was barricaded at Banks Road, where residents were required to show a pass signed by the town clerk.

Controlled by the Admiralty, the harbour was defended by a boom with Royal Artillery gun batteries positioned on the coast and on Brownsea Island, owned at the time by Mrs Mary Bonham-Christie. The war had brought 6-inch guns to her island together with a reception centre for Belgian and Dutch refugees. Two naval 'examination' ships, HMS Rosa and HMS Roger Robert, were positioned in turn outside the harbour to escort the boats to Brownsea, where the occupants were screened before allowed onto the mainland. An older vessel, the Empire Sentinel, had been filled with explosives and positioned as a 'blockship' in the main channel, swept regularly by harbour defence launches for mines dropped by the Luftwaffe and by mine sweepers from Portland Naval Base after a particularly heavy raid.

Post-war, huge cross-channel ferries would bring welcome visitors from France (though lights would continue to mark the submerged hulk of a tank landing craft), and a yacht marina and luxury high-rise apartment block would occupy the quayside just yards from the former Carter pottery premises. For now, metal 'tramways' cut in the quayside serviced the merchant vessels loaded with coal, oil and petrol, the ships engineers obliged to keep a head of steam in the boilers in case of an air raid. Local yards such as Bolsons and Dorset Yacht had turned from building and repairing leisure craft, to building and testing military gun boats, high speed launches and landing craft. Poole had also become an important repair base for the armed motor launches of the Royal Navy, the weapons and ammunition stored on the Baiter Peninsula until the craft were ready, when they were tested at HMS Bee at Weymouth. The lifting bridge was almost always up and the quayside packed with moored naval and cargo vessels. A German bomb sank a vessel moored by the bridge, but was probably logged as a near miss by the brown overalled bomb aimer, crouched thousands of feet above.

It would be wrong to forget just how exposed to the war the civilian flying boats were. Historians regard 10 July 1940 as the start of the Battle of Britain, when the first 'seventy plus' raids of the Luftwaffe began winging their way over the channel from newly acquired bases and fields in Northern France, bringing intense fighting for RAF fighter pilots defending the south west. The naval base at Portland attracted swarms of dive-bombers with fighter escort, and by August raids of '200 plus' were coming in from Cherbourg; the more numerous Hurricanes of RAF Fighter Command reinforced by Spitfires flown in at first light from Middle Wallop in Hampshire to the grass airfield at Warmwell near Chesil Beach. Tuesday, 13 August was trumpeted by the Luftwaffe as the start of Adlertag or Eagle day, when the Royal Air Force was going to be driven from the sky. But around four o'clock in the afternoon, a Messerschmitt Bf

109E of the Second 'Pik-As' (Ace of Spades) Wing of Jagdgeschwader 53 (11/JG53) based at Rennes, ended up in Poole harbour after being shot by a 609 (West Riding) Squadron Spitfire flown by Pilot Officer David Crook. The pilot, Unteroffizier Hohenseldt, was captured.

The very next day *Clare* left Poole for a second crossing to America, when the Under Secretary of State for Air purchased three of the six new Boeing 314A flying boats ordered by Trippe, to replace the losses incurred by BOAC. The Pan Am trio would be named *Pacific Clipper*, *Anzac Clipper* and *Capetown Clipper*. BOAC had no claim to the 'Clipper' title held dear by Trippe however and the 'Speedbird' pre-fix would accompany their Boeings, named *Berwick* for Canada, *Bangor* for America and *Bristol* for Great Britain.

The German Seenotdienst (Air-Sea Rescue Service) was a well-organised affair, with fast launches, and large twin engined bi-plane Heinkel 59 floatplanes, fitted with a hatch and telescopic ladder, hoist, respirator machines and heated sleeping bags. At this time, Britain had nothing by comparison and aircrew had to hope that lifeboats, fishing boats and naval vessels, would spot them and fish them out of 'the drink'. Ordered to set up a rescue service, the Naval Officer at Poole had acquired two Speedlarks from Bolsons shipyard, though their 25 knot potential was

Rescue Role Walrus. © AUTHOR COLLECTION.

undermined by an inability to handle heavy seas and rough weather. Further to the east, aircrew had been relieved to see the quaint little Walrus amphibian from RAF Tangmere arrive overhead, splashing down in a whirl of prop-wash and spray before staggering off to dry land, where a hot meal and a change of clothing awaited them. The aerial battle for supremacy, the greatest ever known, rose to a peak in late August and September – when a Walrus may have come from Poole.

The Royal Flying Corps and Royal Naval Air Service had begun training seaplane pilots at Lee on (the) Solent in 1917, the personnel given temporary tented accommodation while the floatplanes had to be craned over the cliff and into the water. Absorbed within the newly formed Royal Air Force the following year, when over thirty surviving FBAs were assembled at Lee, 209 Training Depot was equipped with a hangar and slipway for the Short 184 (folding wing) biplanes, which had famously sunk the first surface craft by torpedo three years earlier. In the 1920s, the greatly improved facilities of the Seaplane Training School also trained observers. Begun five years earlier by 28 year old Charles Richard Fairey, who had spent two years as chief engineer to Short Brothers, the Fairey Aviation Company had become a major supplier to the Royal Air Force and Royal Naval Air Service. Built at the Hayes, Middlesex, factory and assembled and test flown at Hamble, the wood and fabric Fairey 111 D biplanes seen at Lee, had floats fitted alongside the wheels. Later versions of the final F variant would be of all metal construction.

In 1934 Lee was also provided with an airfield. Five years later the Admiralty took control and opened HMS Daedalus, named after the mythical Greek whose son Icarus supposedly singed his bird-feathered wings flying too close to the sun. On completing their training and wearing their wings on the left sleeve of the uniform, rather than on the chest as with RAF flyers, trainee seaplane pilots began a basic course with No 765 Naval Air Squadron. Formed in May 1939 from the Seaplane Training Flight, 765 was equipped with Fairey Seafox and Fairey Swordfish floatplanes and the Supermarine Walrus flying boat. The navies of the world still catapulted spotter aircraft from battleships and from April 1940, graduates were passed to 764 Naval Air Squadron for an advanced seaplane course. But with increasing wartime activities competing for space on the water, in August, 764 was deployed to the naval base at Pembroke Dock in South Wales. 765 was sent to Dorset.

SANDBANKS NAVAL AIR STATION

Officialdom knew R.N.A.S. Sandbanks as H.M.S Daedalus 11. But the locals soon referred to the requisitioned Royal Motor Yacht Club premises as 'HMS Tadpole' and the assortment of little seaplanes as 'Tiddlers'. With lovely first floor views across the water, the Mountbatten Room was fitted out as a war room for the officers (naturally) and the remainder used as cabins, offices and kitchens. A sentry box was positioned outside the entrance, and the car park put to use as a parade ground. Sleepy cottages in Panorama Road (yet to achieve millionaire luxury home status) were requisitioned as a Petty Officer's Mess, billets for the ratings, station sick quarters, and billets for members of the Womens Royal Naval Service.

Most 'Wrens' were recruited locally and able to live out, but a mess was provided for them at Sandbanks. The premises of the adjacent Sandbanks Yacht Company (the later Davis Boatyard) was requisitioned and cleared of yachts and the immediate shoreline cleared of barbed wire to enable the timber boat shed (longer in those days) to maintain the marine aircraft. Fourteen could be accommodated if the wings were folded, and a sign soon appeared on a wall to remind everyone that 'A hot engine is always on contact'. It still survives today. The yard was given a concrete slipway, a winch, workshop and fuel tanks. The station even had its own Fire Service.

The training floatplanes were all biplanes. Delivered to the Fleet Air Arm in 1937, the Seafox was a twin float version of the Fox light bomber that had ended RAF service six years earlier. Designed for catapult operations from light cruisers, with the observer sat facing rearwards within a bulky cockpit, the 390 horsepower Napier Rapier engine had proved inadequate. It also tended to overheat and landings were made at relatively high speeds. At Sandbanks, nothing could be worse than an attempted take-off in light and changeable wind conditions, when your predicament was announced to all and sundry by the screaming engine, and then finding a lack of corrective power on arriving back at the mooring. Equipped with the more reliable 690 horsepower Bristol Pegasus engine, the three seat Swordfish (pilot, observer and telegraphist/ air gunner) had entered squadron service a year earlier, and would achieve fame as a torpedo bomber aboard fleet carriers, when it was known affectionally as the 'Stringbag'. The higher power available was undoubtedly responsible for its omission from most of the collisions incurred within the restricted confines of Poole harbour.

Designed by Reginald Mitchell, the Walrus flying boat had also begun service with the Fleet Air Arm in 1936, with production shared by the Saunders-Roe factory at Cowes due to the pressing need for Spitfires. Positioned as a 'pusher' at the rear of the 46 foot strutted wings, the Pegasus engine produced over 700 horsepower and drove a four bladed wooden propeller to support a four-man crew, the nose and dorsal machine-gun positions exposed to the elements. The first amphibious aircraft in the world to be launched by catapult with a full military load, up to 760 pounds of bombs or depth charges could be carried beneath the lower wing. Known by crews as the 'Shagbat', the biplane had been used for ground attack and reconnaissance during the ill-fated Norwegian campaign and at Sandbanks fulfilled an invaluable air-sea rescue role in addition to the training flights. The amphibian avoided the more familiar training accidents, but had inevitably been powered up the concrete ramp with the wheels unlocked, though some of the 'aces' bravely fighting high in the skies above had landed wheels-up when converting to Hurricanes and Spitfires from fixed undercarriage biplanes. Air-raid shelters were swiftly built at the base as the air battle reached a climax during those hot, endless summer days of 1940, when aircraft of both sides became scattered about the Dorset countryside, causing many to ponder why such lovely weather should only arrive when the country was at war.

On 13 September Captains Kirton and Shakespeare took *Clare* from Poole for the fourth of the Atlantic crossings, though the forecast of bad weather over the ocean caused the whole of the next day to be spent at Foynes. The war had brought security restrictions on all movements and activities surrounding the terminal. Intelligence personnel had arrived and as part of the Secrets Act passengers were briefed to refrain from discussing their movements with anyone, especially the departure times.

The arrival of a flying boat from Poole enabled a bundle of newspapers to be transferred to *Clare* which left in the evening, arriving safely at the Bay of Exploits (Newfoundland) before flying on to Boucherville (Montreal) and LaGuardia, where the camouflaged wings and hull were in stark contrast to the twinkling lights of New York City. Swiftly photocopied by the New York Post and other leading newspapers to save time, the defiant and inspiring headlines of the London newspapers were distributed to a readership that had been subject to German propaganda for far too long and was eager to read how the young RAF pilots were rising time and time again to counter the raids of the Luftwaffe. There was also the matter of an unarmed British flying boat crossing the Atlantic at the height of the conflict.

The Luftwaffe had expected their Adlerangriff (Attack of the Eagles) to win aerial supremacy in a month, but on 15 September 1940 the defending fighter pilots defeated enormous daylight raids on London, saving this island from invasion and preserving the future for Europe and America. From then on it would be celebrated as Battle of Britain Day. Though the invasion was postponed, London and the major cities were now bombed by night, with hit and run attacks on coastal areas by day. Shorts factory at Rochester had been bombed throughout the battle, while the Supermarine Spitfire factory at Woolston was virtually destroyed on the 26th. The following day, Germany, Italy and Japan formed a tripartite (Axis) military alliance.

NAVAL PILOT TRAINING

The country may have been at bay, but pilot training had continued and 20 year old Ivor Faulconer was among those learning to fly Miles Magisters at No 24 EFTS at Luton airfield. His mother had been taught to fly by Herbert Travers, the chief instructor of the popular London Aeroplane Club at Stag Lane, who had also taught the famous long-distance flyer Amy Johnson. With flying subconsciously in his blood, Ivor had taken advantage of the wartime one year (geography) degree course offered at Oxford University, but with no University Air Squadron there, had volunteered for the Fleet Air Arm. Indoctrinated into service life at HMS St. Vincent at Gosport, he had begun flying training wearing the bell-bottom trousers of a leading airman beneath his overalls.

Passed to the Hawker Harts and Hinds of No 1 Service Flying Training School at Netheravon in Wiltshire, one of the oldest military airfields in the world, he was awarded the coveted Above Average rating and promoted to acting Sub-Lieutenant within the Air Branch of the Royal Naval Volunteer Reserve, known as the 'Wavy Navy' due to the serpentine stripes on the uniform sleeves. Posted to Sandbanks, he joined four others of his course in learning to fly from water, principally with the Walrus, their future operational aircraft. Introduced to the biplane by Petty Officer Snaith with further instruction by Sub Lieutenant Stephens and Lieutenant Bateman, Ivor completed forty-six flights, each of some forty-five minutes, and invariably begun on the slipway where the engine was coaxed into life by an airman using a hand crank. The last five flights of his course were made on the Seafox and the float Swordfish. He was then posted to HMS Argus for deck training, his first flight made in a Swordfish before resuming with the Walrus, adding two and a quarter hours to his dual totals and forty to his solo time. He was then transferred to 764 Squadron, now at Lawrenny Ferry, some 12 miles inland from Milford Haven in Pembrokeshire.

Once at sea, naval vessels could not be put in danger by slowing down to retrieve a catapulted aircraft. Nor could they wait for a suitable sea state. They could however 'calm' the surface by swiftly steering sixty degrees out of wind to port and then forty to starboard. A pilot was allowed two minutes to land on the 'slick', when the air gunner hooked onto a boom projecting from the starboard side of the ship. With the engine throttled back, the Walrus was allowed to slip to the rear while being towed at 12 knots, the gunner climbing onto the top of the mainplane to attach a winch line. Hoisted back onto the launch rail, an aircraft hand removed a pin from each side for the wings to be folded, when the aircraft was returned inside the hangar. There was normally no second chance, for the 'big-ship' captains were only too aware of the target they presented to a submarine at that speed. At Lawrenny Ferry the slicks were simulated by a fast launch. The docks and oil tanks in the area had been targeted by the Luftwaffe and two yachts, the Comilla and Zaza, respectively accommodated officers and ratings. At lunch time, the handling crews would occasionally crowd onto the wings of a Walrus to be taxied down to Milford Haven to avail themselves of the excellent facilities at the Sunderland flying boat base.

Though winter was approaching, the shorter evenings drew no respite for the defenders of these islands. Taking off from Sandbanks during the evening of Monday 7 October 1940 to search for a downed aircraft in the channel, a 765 Squadron Walrus was shot down some 8 miles off Anvil Point, with the loss of observer Mike Hoskins and pilot Tommy Rose-Richards, a well known Brooklands racing driver before the war. The bandleader and pilot Billy Cotton had also raced at Brooklands and with a family home in Panorama Road, had joined the Royal Motor Yacht Club, where his yacht 'Wakey Wakey' would be seen after the war. Just three days after the loss of the two naval lieutenants, the famous Dorset landmark of Corfe Castle took a near miss in the afternoon – from one of our own fighters.

ONE OF *THE FEW*

Scrambled away from Chilbolton airfield at one o'clock, the four 238 Squadron Hawker Hurricanes led by Pilot Officer Doe were soon enveloped in solid cloud extending upwards from 3,000 feet. A veteran of the Battle of Britain, Bob Doe had been posted to the squadron in September and had seen both his flight commander and commanding officer shot down in a matter of days. With fourteen enemy aircraft destroyed, making him joint third, highest scorer in the battle, and awarded the Distinguished Flying Cross, the twenty year old was virtually flight and squadron commander as he led the small formation upwards, feeling on top of the world and a little over-confident, though for him this was entirely out of character.

Robert Francis Thomas Doe had left school when fourteen and had worked as an office boy with the News of the World in Fleet Street. War was obviously coming and he had joined the RAF Volunteer Reserve, taught to fly during the evenings and at weekends. With over seventy hours in his log book, he had gone to the RAF Recruiting Centre in Kingsway and simply said he wanted to be a pilot. The RAF would soon need every pilot it could fly and Bob passed all the preliminaries (having been advised to memorise a loading equation by a friendly senior officer) and was awarded a Short Service Commission early in 1939. He had proved to be an excellent shot and would owe his survival to an awareness that you were always shot down by the one you never saw, causing him to spend nine-tenths of his time in the cockpit looking behind.

Privately, he had nursed a conviction that his flying was poor and had suffered a slight inferiority complex due to having taken a few hours longer to solo than his fellow course members at Hanworth. Determined to prove himself, after every sortie he had analysed everything in the quiet of his room and had survived unscathed until that afternoon.

Climbing to 17,000 feet, the Hurricane's shadowy outline would have been visible to those above cloud just before the Merlin engine pulled him clear. In the life and death, heart-stopping moments that followed, the cockpit was hit from in front and from behind. Steel plate had been fitted to the rear of the seat after the lessons learned by No 1 Squadron in France, though the Hurricane's wood and fabric offered little resistance to enemy fire, other than the quick wits and training of its young pilots. Above the sound of the engine, Bob's mind registered an audible thump as an armour-piercing bullet slammed against the seat armour, the core of the bullet passing through the steel and on through his shoulder, colliding with the watch on his left wrist before passing between the first and second fingers. Almost immediately there was an explosion beneath the seat as a cannon shell, probably fired from beneath the tail, ended it's days in the silken folds of the parachute pack, a burning fragment painfully cutting the tendon of his right leg as a tracer bullet simultaneously exploded with a blinding white flash on hitting the petrol tank, inches in front of his face.

The searing flash of flame, dreaded by all fighter pilots, never came and there was no fire, at least providence granted him that. Though badly wounded, his shocked senses recalled the emergency actions impressed in his mind each night in his lonely room, and the stick was automatically pushed forward, sending the Hurricane into a noisy vertical dive within the safety of the swirling cloud. Fighting the gravitational forces, he jerked back the handles on the cockpit roof and pulled the release pin from the Sutton harness that bound him to the seat. Clad in bulky flying suit, with 'Mae-West' rubber life jacket, parachute harness, gloves and flying boots, he filled the space completely, trapped by the mounting 'g' as the engine pulled him down. Struggling hard, he suddenly found he was free and remembered to pull the metal D-ring on the shoulder harness: the slender connecting wire releasing the parachute from its canvas pack and jerking him upright. Only half aware of his surroundings, his brain registered the single thought that he would not now be able to get married as planned!

Descending quicker than he would have liked, he looked up and was surprised to see shell holes in four of the silk panels of the canopy. He also found he only had one good leg to land on. Unseen by him, Hurricane P3984 had crashed at the edge of a small quarry near the railway viaduct at Corfe Castle (now a car park and office for the National Trust), the wings projected across the road to the foot of the steep and grassy castle mound, barring the way as the ammunition exploded. The cloud ended around 2,000 feet and he saw he was descending towards the largest of the islands in Poole harbour. The owner of Brownsea, Mrs Bonham-Christie was an ardent nature lover and had applied a firm dictum forbidding the loss of life to any living creature on the island, applied equally to bait-diggers in their quest for worms. Having no intention to spoil her wishes, Bob landed heavily on his bottom and promptly passed out. On coming round, he found his face was resting on a rose briar and was aware of a man standing over him, asking in an Irish accent, what are you? The swift oath given in reply left no doubt to his identity before he passed out again.

Taken by boat to the Naval Air Station at Sandbanks, an ambulance drove him to Cornelia Hospital in Poole for an operation. Appalled by what was found in the wounds, nurses quickly syringed the hand clear of infection, for the heavy landing that would bring lower back problems in later life had been made in a drainage pit, virtually an open sewer! The pilot could only lie helpless in his bed as bombs subsequently approached the hospital. One exploded close to the double ward he shared with an army sergeant and they both knew the next was meant for them, though the sergeant managed to douse the flames from the incendiary with his dressing gown. Later, a visiting army padre took time to enquire after the pilot's welfare and the following day returned with two army officers who each had a bottle concealed in a newspaper. Made all the more special for knowing that soldiers evacuated from Dunkirk had been less than polite to the 'Brylcreem Boys', who had of necessity fought their air battles away from the beaches rather than above them. Bob Doe was able to return to operations, hobbling to his fighter and helped up to the cockpit by his ground crew. One of Churchills legendary 'Few', he went on to fly Spitfires, formed a Hurricane squadron in Burma and commanded a Vampire jet fighter squadron in the Middle East before retiring as a Wing Commander, awarded the British and Indian Distinguished Service Order medals and two Distinguished Flying Crosses.

The Poole Plate

On 9 January 1941 the American president's personal representative arrived at Poole after crossing the Atlantic to Lisbon aboard *Yankee Clipper*. Met by MP Brendan Bracken on behalf of Winston Churchill, Harry Hopkins was escorted to London aboard the special train reserved for VIPs. A close friend of Roosevelt, whom he had served since his days as Governor of the State of New York, Hopkins had been influential in his re-election for a third term in 1940. Able to 'get things done', his tireless work and heavy smoking belied the fact that he too had survived a serious illness (an attack of polio had left Roosevelt unable to walk), having almost died of cancer in 1939, though the remains of his stomach required a daily diet of calcium and vitamins. A lean and ill looking man, his ability to express himself frankly and openly and his love of life had endeared him to the Churchill family. Returned to Poole in February for the flight to Lisbon, he took with him a reminder of his visit to England.

Potted in 1940 and hand painted by Margaret Holder, the commemorative earthenware plate featured a stylised impression of *Canopus* by artist Arthur Bradbury, together with a passenger launch and wave-skimming seagull in the foreground and the words 'Port of Poole Empire Airways' (technically incorrect, though the meaning was obvious). The reverse stated that Harry Hopkins had landed at the ancient port of Poole on 9 January 1941 and had departed on 10 February after making 'what may prove to be the most important mission in the history of democracy'. The American 'Lend Lease' Bill had already been passed by the House of Representatives however and Hopkins was simply following up on Churchill's requirements, though the sentiments, expressed by makers Carter, Stabler and Adams, were no doubt greatly appreciated. The bill had had an overwhelming majority on 11 March , but for the British people, the long term ramifications would only be realised during the immediate aftermath of the war, when the payment for the much needed war planes, tanks and naval vessels would bring a huge balance of payments deficit, continuing wartime austerity and food rationing. The final instalment would be made in 2006. For the moment, the much needed equipment enabled Britain to continue the fight for freedom – alone.

Bob Rayner had seen a variety of people using the flying boat services at Poole, from politicians and VIPs such as Anthony Eden and Harry Hopkins to movie stars such as Gracie Fields (who owned a house at Sandbanks), Jean Simmons, Bette Davis – and Stewart Granger who had much closer ties with early aviation and the area than most people remember. Born James Stewart, he had had to change his name as it was the same as the famous American actor. The family home was at Boscombe and his sister Iris had married Captain Francis Colebourne Fisher, founder of the airfield at Christchurch. In 1936, after only twenty-five hours of solo flying, Iris had been presented with the Northesk Cup by the Duchess of Bedford at Woodley aerodrome near Reading, for being the 'Best Woman Pilot in Britain' and her brother had joined other famous personalities in visiting the flying club at Somerford. His namesake James Maitland 'Jimmy' Stewart had held a commercial licence before the war and rose to the rank of Colonel in the wartime American Air Force (later reserve Brigadier General) after flying Liberator heavy bombers deep into Germany from Tibenham, Norfolk.

Clyde had completed the fifth and final series of Atlantic crossings in October, when the winter headwinds had become too strong, and with *Claire* had employed the extra range on the Poole-Lisbon-Lagos West Africa service until February 1941, when Lisbon was battered by a hurricane. Having endured 100 mile an hour winds and huge waves for eight hours moored on the Tagus, *Clyde* was wrecked beyond repair when flying wreckage holed the port wing float, freeing the starboard wing and rolling the flying boat onto its back. In March, an American flying boat flew in from Poole to replace the loss. Named simply *Guba* by BOAC, the aircraft was in fact the famous *Guba 11* that had surveyed the Indian Ocean. Purchased by the British Air Commission in 1940, *Guba* had re-crossed the Atlantic to Prestwick loaded with a valuable cargo of aluminium. Four

The Poole Plate. COURTESY WOOLLEY & WALLIS (SALISBURY) VIA MILLERS ANTIQUES AND COLLECTIBLES.

more flights were made after arriving at Lisbon, including one to Lagos, though the flying boat would be fortunate to survive the dramatic events soon to be enacted at Poole.

Alan Dewdney was posted to Foynes and 19 year-old Harry Pusey had taken over at Poole, given specific responsibility for advising flying boat pilots at Lisbon whether it was safe to proceed northwards to Dorset, or not. On receiving a forecast from the met office at Gloucester, he would take into account the more localised (orographic) forming of cloud over the Purbeck hills, the tree-clad expanse of the New Forest – and the opinion of Mr Matthews, the knowledgeable skipper of the Poole sprat fleet! The weather report was vital to the war effort and as such was classified. Unable to send a radio message in clear, Morse was used with CQ (All Stations) followed by QGN (clear to continue northwards) or QGO – the exact opposite of what it seemed. No explanation could be given as to whether the decision was due to enemy activity or to allied operations in the area, the captains having to rely on the judgement of the young officer at Poole. His advice was only over-ridden on three occasions, one pilot in particular opting to return to Dorset in thick cloud, when his radio operator was forced to trail his aerial to check exactly where the water was (his finger poised on the electric motor switch) until creeping in over Poole harbour at an extremely low level.

The diplomatic mail occasionally arrived at Poole without a courier and the staff had taken it in turn to be locked within a 1st Class compartment of the train to deliver it safely to London, where the night stop-over would include a visit to Piccadilly Circus to view the naked but contractually motionless girls of the Windmill Theatre. When Harry's turn came he was refused the trip as he was under 21 and could not be trusted with the mail, so they said. Never mind the fact, he thought, that it was his decision and his alone to bring a flying boat home with all it contained, which included the diplomatic bag!

With the transfer of the flying boat operational headquarters from Hythe, the ops and engineering staffs had moved from Poole to more spacious accommodation available at the Trinidad Ashpalt factory on Hamworthy Quay. The passenger handling facilities were transferred to the Carter Pottery building at Poole quay and the Airways House staff relocated by flying boat to Neyland, to the east of Milford Haven. Having earlier joined the others in taking a short flight in one of the giant Boeings, which had required a speedily signed chit from his parents due to his age, Bob Rayner had to be 'vouchsafed' for the flight to Wales as he was still under 18. Within a short time he would be called up for service with the Household Cavalry, though by now the Royal Horse Guards had exchanged their steeds for armoured cars.

Leased to BOAC, the ground floor Pottery retail showrooms and tea room had been converted to provide reception and departure facilities, with a lounge and restaurant on the floor above. Incoming flights arrived during the afternoon, but with premises at a premium, crews and passengers were inspected by medical staff at the moorings before allowed ashore, an inefficient and inconvenient process for everyone involved. As more and more men were called up for war service, the government took the radical decision to replace them with women. BOAC had followed suit and among the sixty staff involved with passenger movements, were eighteen 'Women Seamen' of the marine department. Mostly local girls in their twenties, they added considerable glamour to the wartime harbour. Clad in blue trousers, white sweaters and sea boots they were trained to assist passengers out to the moorings and in the handling of the larger, cabin-equipped passenger launches. Most would qualify as Coxswain 2nd Class. Among them was former pottery paintress Mollie Ann Skinner, who was photographed with a number of personalities, including George Formby and his wife Beryl Ingham, both members of the wartime ENSA troop entertainment service, her uniform lapel badges confirming she was trained to communicate by Aldis lamp and by flags.

Other girls, such as Eileen Wigg, who had come to Bournemouth as a teenager and had attended Talbot Heath School, chose to man the Riggers Boat. Taught to drive a launch and to sling a line, she helped tow and secure the flying boats, changed buoys and took fitters out to the moorings to work on the engines. You soon became strong, tying knots and hauling

Women Seamen at Poole. Isobel Rickard, Mary Hill, Bosun Frank Hewitt, Bunny Reece, Molly Skinner, Nora Bevis, Eileen Wigg. COURTESY MRS MOLLIE HARMAN (NÉE SKINNER).

in 6-inch hawsers while standing on the stern of a launch, clad in thick navy-style issue sweater and trousers. If you fell in you could easily sink wearing all that gear. She had once, but fortunately was a good swimmer! Twelve hour shifts were the norm. Depending on when a flying boat was expected she either arrived at six in the morning or six at night after cycling the 12 miles from her parent's home on the old Wallisdown Road. If there was a delay, the marine crews would have a sing-song in a pub on the quay, telling 'silly stories' and playing darts. There wasn't a lot of time for anything else and anyway she was too tired: the usual routine to get home, have a bath, go to sleep, wake up, get dressed and cycle back to work again. For more formal occasions the girls had been issued with a heavy officer-style overcoat and peaked cap. Eileen had been known as 'Bugs' from her boarding school days and when with fellow Woman Seaman 'Bunny' Reece had inevitably formed a pair known as Bugs Bunny! She loved the open air and it was all good fun. Strong and active, when the flying boats left, Eileen would volunteer for the Womens Land Army and work on farms in the Christchurch and New Forest area.

Woman Seaman Mollie Skinner. Lapel badges show proficiency in semaphore & morse. MRS. M. HARMAN.

On the other side of the Atlantic *Pacific Clipper*, the first of the six Boeing 314A's originally ordered by Pan Am, was launched in March

Mollie with George Formby and his wife (manager) Beryl.
MRS M. HARMAN

and was duly joined by *Anzac Clipper* and *Capetown Clipper*. The remaining three, bought by the British Government at over a quarter of a million pounds each, went to BOAC. Fitted with 1,600 horsepower Twin Cyclone engines driving larger diameter propellers, *Bristol*, *Bangor* and *Berwick* supported a gross take-off weight of thirty-seven and a half tons. To enable them to fulfill their purpose with BOAC, they had enlarged fuel tanks (over 5,400 gallons, an extra 1,200 gallons) to give a maximum cruising range of over 5,000 miles, some 1,200 more than the 314. A special galley had been designed to maximise the accommodation for the ten-man crew. *Bristol* was the first to arrive and from May 1941 began operating the Foynes-Lisbon-Lagos West Africa service, though the early refuelling in Africa had to rely on canoes to bring the fuel drums alongside.

Woman Seaman Eileen Wigg.
MRS E. ARMSTRONG.

ATTACK ON POOLE

Air raid wardens regularly patrolled the streets of Britain at dusk to ensure that curtains were drawn to deny any reference to enemy bomb aimers (Turn that light out!). But the early morning of 12 May 1941 was lit by strong moonlight which clearly revealed the Poole terminus and moorings to the crew of a Heinkel bomber, heading home after failing to locate RAF Bicester. The first run in from the east went unchallenged, but was far from being unobserved by those on the ground.

Leaving his mother to routinely take twelve year old twins Rita and Ronald to the underground brewers vaults in West Street for the night, which had been hastily converted to public shelters near the church of Saint James, sixteen year old Bolsons shipyard apprentice Bob Kent had accompanied his father to the shore near Wilkins Way to check on his fishing boats. An armed sentry guarded the way, but his father was well known, and receiving a nod from the man, they had continued on without having to show the pass issued to those whose occupation required them to be in the area. Hearing engines, Bob had looked up and excitedly called out to his father 'Look an aeroplane. An aeroplane!' as the bomber emerged from the darkness surrounding Holes Bay and began to skim the surface of the moonlit water.

A mainstay of the Luftwaffe's Blitzkrieg across Europe, the Heinkel 111 had found RAF fighters to be a different proposition. Shot down in October 1939 near the village of Humbie, East Lothian, the equipment aboard 1H+JA of the Stabskette (Staff flight) of Kampfgeschwader 26 had confirmed that the Lorenz 'beam' system was in use over Britain, while on 6 November 1940, equipment salvaged from 6N+AH of KG 100, force landed on a beach near West Bay, Dorset, had revealed that British jamming equipment, which included a set installed in the rural police station at Wimborne, was on the wrong frequency!

Within seconds, Bob and his father clearly heard the burst of power as the pilot opened up the 1,150 horsepower Daimler-Benz engines to clear the iron-studded supports of the lifting bridge connecting Old Poole with Hamworthy. He and his observer, recently made squadron-commander of the Eighth Staffel of 111 Gruppen of the famous Kampfgeschwader 55 Bomber Wing, would have had an excellent view of the surroundings. Withdrawn from the day battle, the twin-engine bomber featured a smoothly contoured, fully glazed nose, the instrument panel attached to the roof and the universal joint for the nose gun, manned by the observer/bomb-aimer, off-set to the right to give the pilot maximum visibility.

Coming round for a second run, the Heinkel continued on down the main channel, this time drawing a response from the harbour and shore gun batteries controlled by the Naval Headquarters Ship Sona, the requisitioned luxury 500 ton motor yacht of Lord Camrose (the British newspaper magnate William Berry) moored alongside Poole Quay. Machine gunning from the nose, the bomber sent two bombs tumbling down onto the Parkstone Shoal Moorings, where one exploded close to the starboard side of *Maia*, moored to No 34 Buoy. Almost immediately, the tail of the Heinkel was struck by shells and tore away, sending G1+ES plunging down between the Wytch and Middle channels.

The ninth and last of the 'composite' separations had taken place in November, when *Mercury* had flown a nine-hour night mail service from Southampton to Alexandria. *Maia* had then been used to train navigators, in between testing new instruments and equipment, until converted to C-Class standard to operate the Foynes shuttle. Though not a direct hit, the explosion tore two large holes in the planing bottom and the hull slowly rolled over, leaving the left wing jutting accusingly from the water. Led by Superintendent Hawtin, engineers cut a hole in an attempt to save night watchman Francis (Frank) Smith believed trapped inside, but the escape of air allowed more water to flood in and *Maia* settled deeper in the water.

The Heinkel appears to have been the only one that failed to return to the occupied French airfield at Villacoublay, near Paris. Of the five Luftwaffe aircrew, only the flight engineer Unteroffizier Karl Sheuringer and gunner Gefreiter Karl Röhl survived the impact of the crash. When fished from the water by the naval duty boat Ptarmigan, it seems the engineer objected to the way he was being treated and spat in the face of a seaman, who promptly knocked him overboard. The gunner was found aimlessly wandering about the darkened mudflats. Word had spread and Bob was among the crowd of people from Old Poole that gathered on the quayside as the two airmen were brought ashore, noticing the armed guard and hearing the inevitable shouts of abuse as they were taken away. The bodies of observer Oberleutnant/Staffelkapitän Horst Gündel and wireless operator Feldwebel Heinrich Neuber were retrieved from the harbour, while the body of their pilot, Feldwebel Willy Wimmer, was eventually washed ashore on the Isle of Wight, having been dragged the length of the harbour and through the conflicting currents at the Havens before making the long journey across Bournemouth Bay.

The wreckage of *Maia* was dumped on a mudflat near Hamworthy Quay, though the starboard wing, which had taken the full force of the blast that had killed the watchman inside, had fallen off when raised from the water. With the engines and instruments removed, the hull and port wing were offered for sale by tender at fifteen and eighteen pounds! Peppered by shrapnel and unable to make the early morning departure from Buoy 35, *Guba* flew out to Lagos three days later. Withdrawn for overhaul in August, a lack of spares would keep her unserviceable until July 1942.

Disbanded in 1918, 119 Squadron had reformed at Bowmore in March 1941 and had operated the G Flight trio on long range reconnaissance and convoy protection. In April they had been joined by two former 'Empire' flying boats. Extensively modified to Sunderland standard at Belfast, *Clio* (AX659) and *Cordelia* (AX660) now had radar aerials and after the Norway experience, a power operated gun turret on top and at the rear. They also carried six depth charges. In May the long-range Atlantic 'boats were moved to Mountbatten for special flights to Gibraltar and the Middle East.

X8274 (*Golden Fleece*) was temporarily attached to 10 Squadron RAAF for the missions, but on 19/20 June 1941 engine failure caused Pilot Officer James Barry to force-land in the Bay of Biscay, 100 miles out from Cape Finisterre and the Spanish coast. On 24 June, the Australian Associated Press simply announced five names known to be aboard the 'missing Coastal Command flying boat', whilst revealing that Berlin Radio had stated nine had drowned and Brigadier Taverner, Sergeant Major Long, Sergeant Anderson, Sergeant Hill and Corporal Corcoran had been 'picked up' by a German aircraft from the 'Sunderland'. Liberated after four years as a prisoner of war, in 1945 former air gunner Len Corcoran recalled a starboard engine had failed at 2,000 feet due to oil trouble, and the survivors had manned the dinghy and drifted for five days until rescued by a U-boat directed to their position by a German aircraft.

SURCOUF FLIGHT

The largest submarine in the world, the Surcouf was commissioned in 1934 and named after Robert Surcouf, a privateer revered by the French for his capture of British ships. Three hundred and sixty-one foot long, the giant displaced over 4,000 tons when submerged. More akin to a surface battleship, its armament comprised a power operated turret for a pair of 8 inch guns, anti aircraft cannon and machine guns, torpedo launchers – and a crane and cylindrical hangar for a spotter floatplane. In true pirate tradition, there was also a hold for forty captives. The crew had abandoned a

Golden Fleece. ©SHORT BROS & HARLAND.

refit at Brest after the fall of France and had crossed the channel to Devonport Naval Base on one serviceable engine. Repairs had been completed, though with other French warships, the submarine was subsequently commandeered lest it should fall into German hands. Trials with the Royal Navy had highlighted the lack of radar, instability on the surface in a heavy sea, and the slow rate of dive, while the crewing complement (one hundred and eighteen) was considered comparable to an eighteenth century privateer! Presented to the Free French Navy, it had escorted convoys sailing from the Canadian port of Halifax, but on returning to Plymouth, had been damaged during an air raid in April 1941. Three months later, the submarine had departed for Bermuda, though without its spotter 'plane which had been flown to Sandbanks.

Designed by Marcel Besson and constructed by Atelier du Nord de la France in the Les Mureaux region of central France, the (ANF-LM) MB411 Pétrel was powered by a 175 horsepower Salmson radial engine in front of two open cockpits, the underside of the thirty-nine foot wing cluttered with an array of struts connecting a closely configured set of triple floats. As 'Surcouf Flight', it afforded a chance for the instructors to fly something different, but without having to attach the wooden wings and floats beforehand as on the submarine. The appearance in the skies over Sandbanks presented a rather stubby outline to those sufficiently interested to look up, while the complete lack of a tailplane above the rear fuselage may have suggested that the local gunners had already had a crack at it! A lack of spares inevitably brought problems and after considerable ingenuity to keep it flying, the little floatplane was stored at Mount Batten and later broken up. A second production model had gone to Escadrille 7-S-4 of the Aéronavale, based at Saint-Mandrier, to the south of Toulon.

Following the successful flights of *Clyde*, *Corinthian*, *Cassiopeia* and *Cooee*, from July 1941 the West Africa route was extended eastwards to link with the Horseshoe services, the new sector coming to be known as the trans-African or 'Congo' route. Leaving Foynes at dusk, crews steered west of ten degrees to head for Lisbon in order to avoid meeting the Luftwaffe over the Bay of Biscay, followed by a night departure for the long leg to Bathurst where passengers alighted at the marine airport buildings, built for the RAF on the quayside at Half Die, before driven to a rest house a few miles along the coast at Faradje. The next landing was on the river Bunce near Freetown, where a rest house had been built at Jui on Hastings Creek. Next was Lagos, the West Africa terminal, followed by Libreville, Pointe Noire and Leopoldville: turning inland for Coquilhatville, Stanleyville, Laropi and the Horseshoe route to Cairo, or continuing on to Port Bell on Lake Victoria for the southern route to Durban. By the end of July, the West Africa route was being flown by *Clare, Cathay, Champion, Bristol, Bangor, Berwick, Guba* – and a second PBY named *Catalina*, transferred from RAF service during the month.

Though the Boeings maintained the luxury of the pre-war Pan Am flying boats, the Cyclone engines required regular, one hundred and twenty hour servicing to de-scale the valves; the concern for spares and size of the aircraft causing BOAC to set up a specialist maintenance base at Baltimore Municipal Airport, on the shore of the Patapsco River and Colgate Creek. Pan Am had begun flying from the man-made peninsula in 1932 and in 1937 the Sikorsky S42s had joined *Cavalier* of Imperial Airways in flying to Bermuda. LaGuardia (New York) was comparatively ice-free however and the American airline had relocated most flying boat services there in 1939, though continuing to use Baltimore for shorter journeys and for maintenance, the huge terminal building providing hangar space, offices, passenger concourse, lounge and a scenic viewing platform. The flight to Baltimore initially provided an ad hoc Atlantic service for the Boeings which, with the onset of winter at Newfoundland, crossed the South Atlantic between Bathurst and Belém (Brazil) and continued via Trinidad and Bermuda. The return to Foynes was made via Bermuda and Lisbon.

Having escaped to Britain with some of their sturdy twin-engined Fokker floatplanes, in June 1940 pilots of the Royal Netherlands Naval Air Service had been mustered as No 320 Squadron of the RAF. A year later, Captain Bennett flew *Mercury* from Hythe to RAF Felixstowe to provide crew training for the squadron, but in August, the sleek, record-breaking floatplane was returned to Rochester and broken up for scrap. The month saw AX659 (*Clio*) crash inland when a starboard engine failed on leaving Loch Indaal, though without loss of life, and with AX660 (*Cordelia)* loaned to the newly formed 413 RCAF Squadron at Stranraer, 119 Squadron was moved to Pembroke Dock. *Cordelia* was returned to BOAC in September.

The war had ended the unsurcharged air mail service. But the loss of routes and shortage of space with the change in priorities had caused the Post Office to introduce a lightweight letter sheet for service personnel in 1941, swiftly supplemented by a more innovative system known as the Airgraph Service. Written on a dedicated form, letters were photographed and reduced in size before flown overseas when they were reproduced, enlarged, sealed and forwarded by ordinary post to their destination. And all for three pence.

Though German forces occupied both sides of the Mediterranean, it was decided to reopen the faster Mediterranean route to Egypt. In October, the month X8273 (*Golden Horn*) and X8275 (*Golden Hind*) were withdrawn from military service, Captain May used the cover of night to fly the long range *Clare* from Foynes to Lisbon, Gibraltar, Malta and Cairo without attracting the attention of enemy fighters. *Clare*, *Champion*, *Cathay*, *Guba* and *Catalina* would maintain the service until mid 1942, when the German advance across the desert would cause them to be withdrawn to reinforce the Africa service.

In December, the demilitarised *Golden Hind* and *Golden Horn* flew in to Poole, the month the new Boeings began flying across the Atlantic to New York. Made Flight Captain in charge of the Trans-Atlantic Service, John Kelly-Rogers was about to make one of the most important ocean crossings of his career.

Chapter Five

Survival

Churchill and Berwick

Having absorbed its subsidiary at the end of 1941, BOAC now owned the Boeing trio outright and while at Baltimore for a routine servicing of *Berwick* in January 1942, 'Jack' Kelly-Rogers was summoned to Washington and received orders to captain an important flight from Norfolk (Virginia) to Bermuda, intended to confuse German intelligence as to the departure of Winston Churchill after his meeting with President Roosevelt. Two Pan Am Clippers would follow close behind with the remainder of the ninety-strong British contingent. Invited to take over the controls during the flight, the Prime Minister was very impressed and after questioning Kelly-Rogers at Bermuda, decided to fly all the way home, rather than board the battleship Duke of York, a saving of nine days on his agenda.

Berwick was flown throughout the night of 16 January, mostly in radio silence to avoid detection by the Luftwaffe, with Captains Shakespeare and Loraine sharing the load. Reports received from Pembroke Dock (their destination), Plymouth and Poole all indicated lowering cloud and poor visibility however, causing Kelly-Rogers to divert to Mount Batten, where he made a skilful approach amidst rolling fogbanks surrounding Plymouth Sound. The extended non-stop flight had taken just under eighteen hours, during which time Churchill had had his slippers warmed in the galley oven and had again handled the controls. Keenly interested in aviation, he had taken flying lessons before the First World War and again in 1919, but had given up after surviving a crash whilst leaving Croydon that August. Though without the VIP facilities at Pembroke Dock, and given short notice, a mooring had been prepared, launch crews had been alerted and a guard of honour assembled on the breakwater as a special train was speedily coupled together to return Churchill to London. The first British Prime Minister to complete a trans-Atlantic crossing, he subsequently invited Kelly-Rogers to join him and his family for lunch, enabling the pilot to 'dine-out' on his experience for months!

SALVAGE OPERATIONS

George Wetherall had helped retrieve a variety of aircraft and vessels from Poole harbour and on 8 January 1942, Lieutenant Commander Vandy RNR, OBE, had written to the Navy Officer in charge of Poole, requesting recognition for Petty Officers Luff, Wetherall and Fisher following their devotion to duty and outstanding qualities of leadership, while under his command during the salvage operations. In December 1940, a Walrus had been deposited, undamaged, on Poole Quay after a crash in the harbour, followed in February by a Seafox forced down by heavy weather and rain. The wreckage of the Heinkel bomber that had ended up off Half-Way Diver, had been landed in May after a week of hard work and in September, a Fleet Air Arm launch had been lifted onto the slipway at Sandbanks, despite being written off after sinking in deep water. The letter stressed that the four salvage operations had required hard work and long hours, generally without food or rest, using the exposed launches Skylark and Gondolier. In addition, December had seen the War Department vessel Gondolier King towed to Christchurch after thirty-seven hours without rest, following forty-seven hours spent to the east of Christchurch Bay in November, lightening the vessel and saving valuable equipment in the teeth of a south-westerly gale.

DURBAN

January had seen six pilots transferred from No 70 (Far East) Squadron of the RAF to Imperial Airways at Durban. Among them was Jim Peers. Brought up in Barry on the south-east coast of Wales, James Melvyn Peers had come to love the water and sailing. Though close to taking his final exams as an architectural surveyor and working towards his yacht master certificate, he had applied to join the RAF Volunteer Reserve the day after war was declared, but was told he had a reserved occupation. He was also told that his background would have taken him into the Royal Engineers. The next day, the 21 year old re-applied, saying he was a book-keeper! Sent to RAF Padgate in

Jim Peers. © MRS JEAN PEERS.

Lancashire for basic training, he found he was in at the start of the 'phoney war' period. Posted to RAF Feltwell, he had endured a variety of 'stooge' jobs which included constructing a papier mâché relief map of the Ruhr Valley and the Möhne Dam, using reconnaissance photos taken by the station's Wellington bombers, whose designer Barnes Wallis, was already working on a 'bouncing bomb'. Eventually passed to an Initial Training Wing at Cambridge, Jim's sailing experience undoubtedly helped him achieve top marks in navigation. He also learnt to handle machine guns before shipped out to Rhodesia within the first of the Empire Air Training Schemes.

Taught to fly Tiger Moths at Salisbury before converting to twin-engined Airspeed Oxfords, he had received his Rhodesian Pilot Wings but had frustratingly been shipped to Durban, Mombasa and Nairobi, narrowly missing the Sunderland equipped 230 Squadron, and had joined 70 Squadron at Kabrit, which in 1940 had replaced its lumbering Vickers Valentia biplanes with the Wellington. Made operational almost immedi-

The Vaal Dam South Africa, completed 1938. COURTESY CAPT JIM PEERS.

ately, he was among the crew when skipper 'Stan' Baldwin decided to dive-bomb the docks at Benghazi, the near vertical dive almost ending in disaster when the elevators locked-in as the airspeed indicator reached a new high. A memorandum swiftly followed, restricting the speed to 250 knots, with the elevator trimmed beforehand! On completing a tour of operations with the squadron, Jim had heard that Imperial Airways at Durban were running out of flying boat pilots and was interested in taking on RAF bomber pilots. A conversion unit had been set up at Vaaldam, the service pilots expected to replace some of the more experienced first officers to enable them to be upgraded to captains.

On graduating, Jim was rostered among the C-Class crews 'trapped' in East Africa by the war, flying from Durban to Cairo and from Karachi to Calcutta, where Qantas crews took over to fly to Australia and New Zealand. Lodged in a hotel at Durban, his entitlement to wear civilian clothes when off duty considerably annoyed one of the other guests, a lady, who loudly berated him for not being involved in the fighting 'up north' until the situation was explained to her, when her attitude changed dramatically!

A natural harbour formerly within Zulu territory, in 1835 Durban was named after the Cape Governor Sir Benjamin D'Urban. Seventy-one years later dredging allowed far larger vessels to enter, thanks to the foresight of George Maydon, a twice elected Natal Member of Parliament who subsequently became Colonial Secretary and Natal's Minister of Harbours and Railways.

Following the decision by the Union Government to create a flying boat base within the Congella basin, the Maydon Channel had been dredged to a depth of 35 feet, though the flying boats of Imperial Airways had to moor off Salisbury Island until provided with a slipway and hangar, sheltered from the south-eastern gales by a green headland nearly 200 feet high (the Bluff) and an easterly spit of land (the Point). The Zulus had entered their sheltered lagoon from a narrow channel between the two headlands. Not unlike Poole, where the deep, inland 'pool' of water and narrow waterways had also been paddled by the ancients, and where a log boat retrieved from the mud is preserved within the town museum a short distance from the quayside.

For the flying boat crews, Durban afforded an average seasonal temperature between sixty to eighty degrees, while the midday heat was equable rather than oppressive. Before each service flight, crew members undertook a medical check-up by the company doctor within the twenty-storey Trust Building in Congella, which apart from the ground floor shops and restaurants, had largely been taken over by BOAC. A dentist was also available. On the morning of departure, the first officer would arrive at Maydon Wharf and donning a freshly laundered pair of white overalls (at company expense) would pause to check the tail line was secure and the locking nut had been removed from the release hook, before entering the rear of two entry doors, left open by the station engineers as were the starboard pantry, mail and baggage loading hatches.

A walk-through check of the cabins on the lower deck ended with mounting the pantry ladder to the flight deck, where a notice board held pertinent comments made by the previous crew, a mandatory read before proceeding further. Though the station engineers would have thoroughly prepared the aircraft, he was obliged to make his own independent pre-flight checks. With company engineers found only at the overnight servicing stops, he was qualified to certify the serviceability of the aircraft, engines and instruments before each sector departure. Some had seen the sense in qualifying as a wireless operator. He would also supervise refuelling, a task not be taken for granted, for fire was an ever present risk, even at Durban. In December 1942 an explosion would sink *Ceres* at her mooring. Crews were expected to cope with everything that might befall them en route, including an emergency engine change, and Jim had prudently spent some of his time in the engine workshops at Congella.

Moving to the flight deck ladder and emerging from the roof hatch onto the top of the wing, over thirty feet above the water, you had a unique impression of the sights and sounds of the harbour, where masts and rigging from a former age mingled with the camouflaged flying machines of the 20th century. From here, you could see whether the pitot head covers had been removed from the mast and check the housing for the anchor and steaming lights, before ensuring the leading edge engine maintenance platforms were closed and locked, rain plugs were removed from the exhausts, the engine cowling gills were closed and the nacelle oil filler caps and main fuel filler caps were closed and flush.

A final look to ensure nothing had been left on the wing surfaces and it was time to re-enter the aircraft, leaving the hatch open for the purser to take up his position prior to the engine starts. BOAC had altered the title of flight clerk to purser at the beginning of the war, but the reduction in wartime catering requirements had dispensed with a steward, leaving the purser to cope should the need arise.

The next checks were carried out at the rear bulkhead near the former clerk's position, the interior lit by the opened hatch and by the light from the two starboard window ports: the nearest inset within the upward opening half of the mail loading hatch, and the second above the navigator's folding chart table. Positioned below the roof of the bulkhead, each of the four (Telelevel) fuel gauges was operated by using a thumb and finger to slowly turn a 'butterfly' handle to the left, when a pointer would stop at the fuel level inside that particular tank. The gauge was zeroed by reversing the turn. Beneath the fuel gauges, two air intake shutter control wheels were checked for free movement (hot to cold) as was each of the cooling gill handles on either side of the fuselage (opened and closed), before looking up to check the fuel cocks were all off. A glance at the wall panel to ensure the voltage switch was down, the emergency starting switch (Desiderio) was unscrewed and the two-way starter button switch positioned for the ground plug, and it was time to move forward to the cockpit to remove and stow the boiler suit.

The days of a crew operating a particular flying boat were long gone and it was vital to check the previous occupant had not left the right hand seat in such a position that you were unable to see out of the windscreen and had difficulty reaching the rudder pedals. A glance at the side pocket to ensure the navigation and instrument logs, daily log and emergency procedure manual were in place, while a turn of the head to the right confirmed the Very pistol and cartridges were stowed securely. The Aldis signal lamp was plugged in and tested, making sure that both red and green filters were available, before turning on the instrument heating and lighting. The best available at the time, they comprised a Hughes rate of climb indicator, turn indicator, compass, Sperry artificial horizon and directional gyro, a liquid pitch indicator, Marconi homing indicator and a Smith's chronometer. Seemingly out of place within such a marine environment, the C-Class airspeed indicators were calibrated in miles per hour rather than knots, to be remedied in the post-war fleets.

At some point in the proceedings, the station engineer would have made his way up the stairs and presented the equivalent of the RAF Form 700 for signing that the aircraft was considered serviceable, when the fuel record was matched with the refuellers chit. The next to arrive, the radio officer had also slipped on his boiler suit before mounting the stairs. Depositing his satchel, containing the requisite codes, ciphers and his pencils, he would look under his desk to ensure the control lock had been removed and stowed on the bulkhead and with a final glance to ensure the trailing aerial was raised, moved down to the mooring compartment. Having checked everything was properly stowed away, he mounted the short metal ladder at the end and partly emerging from the roof hatch, ensured the slip line was in place beneath the mooring hawser.

Moving over to the captains seat, the two levers fitted below the window for operating the retractable bow searchlight were tested (out, and up and down) by the first officer, before turning the selector switch to operate the second landing light within the leading edge of the starboard wing. The outward course was then set by turning the calibrated face of the compass in the left hand corner of the cockpit, and the mean sea-level pressure set on the dial of the Kollsman altimeter by turning a milled knob at the base of the instrument. Having set the oil valves for the Sperry automatic pilot and carefully ensured the trip clock was fully wound, with a quick look behind to ensure the trailing aerial was up, he moved across to his own seat to set his own compass and altimeter.

With the arrival of the captain, the passengers reported as all aboard (mostly VIPs and mostly male) and both doors clamped shut, the mooring rope was slipped from the bow and a lever on the right of the cockpit roof pulled to release the tail line and allow engine starting to begin. All four throttles were moved forward about an inch, with mixture controls set to normal and propellers set to fine pitch. Moving back from his seat, the first officer opened the engine cooling gills, ensured the carburettor air intakes were set at hot and opened the fuel cocks. A colour code, signifying red for port and green for starboard was displayed on the central console levers and on the various fuel cocks and levers. The outer engines were normally started first to control the swing on the water. Positioned near the cooling gill handles on either side of the cabin, the primer controls consisted of a cock, which was turned to the engine in question, and a primer: the plunger of which normally required just four pumping actions at those latitudes to suck in sufficient fuel to fill the carburettor. A hinged box to the rear of the hatch between the seats had a ring-pull to access the carburettor test cock control levers.

Hearing his first officer call that the fuel cocks were open and the first engine was primed, and with a good look outside to ensure there had been no last-minute arrival of a launch beneath the wings, the captain pushed the ignition switch up and flipping up the cover on the top of the instrument panel, pushed the first starter button until the engine fired, when the throttle was advanced to register some 500 revolutions per minute on the rev counter. When all four engines were running smoothly, the purser would re-appear to report the bow hatch was closed and with the engine oil temperatures registering above fifteen degrees centigrade and the oil pressures constant, all four engines were steadily opened up to 1,200 rpm. Time for the first officer to again leave his seat to screw the emergency starter switch back in, move the changeover switch to the aircrafts battery and return the carburettor air intakes to cold.

Returned to his seat, he would use his left hand to briefly move each of the propeller pitch levers, fitted at floor level at the rear of the console, beneath the autopilot engaging lever, to coarse (cruising) pitch (confirmed by a drop in engine revolutions) as the captain carefully taxied the aircraft downwind towards the appointed take-off area in the Maydon channel. Back at the bulkhead, he would then test the fuel pumps, using the port and starboard test cock control wheels and wing root cock, when the uninterrupted sound of the engines confirmed that all four pumps were feeding fuel to their respective engines.

Commercial aircraft had two sets of magnetos fitted to each engine. While the captain held the throttle levers in the forward position, the first officer, back in his seat, would briefly switch off each magneto in turn. If an unacceptable rev drop persisted and could not be cleared (by briefly advancing the throttle and running 'rich' to clear an oiled up plug), a return would be made for the station engineer to sort things out. Maintaining a steady rpm, the smaller fuel/air carburettor mixture levers on the console were brought fully back to rich and then fully forward to the full boost position before returned to normal.

Looking up to the centerline of the cabin roof, the flap operating switch was checked to be in the off position before the electric motor was switched on (confirmed by a blue light) and the controller switch turned to flaps out, when the sliding pointer began confirming the flap position. It took just twenty seconds for the 26 foot span wing flaps to be moved to the one third out indication (eight degrees) for take-off. A warning red light would appear alongside the blue should the setting be exceeded. To the right of the flap controls, above and behind the second pilot seat, an inward opening hatch and wind screen had been fitted for 'observation' purposes. The distances flown rarely warranted use of a sextant however and the hatch was mostly used by the purser to mount the 6 foot ensign staff, stowed behind the second pilot seat. A more suitable and bulged 'astro dome' was fitted as standard on the longer-range S 30s.

Arriving at the take-off position, with the oil pressures indicating 70 pounds per square inch and the cylinder head pressures and temperatures respectively registering over fifteen and one hundred degrees 'C ', having set the roof mounted elevator trimmer and given the rudder handle a couple of turns to the left to offset the expected swing to the right, the captain asked his first officer to flash the abbreviated 'ready to take off' signal (OKTO) to the upwind control launch. In response to a steady white light, he would then call for full boost, when all four mixture controls were moved through the gate and they were away – as distanced in procedure from the forthcoming nonchalant jet fighter pilot's 'Kick the Tyres an' Light the Fires!' as you could get.

At most stops, the first officer stayed aboard while the rest of the crew went ashore and that was that. Dudley Travers was different. On his return he always sent Jim Peers off to enjoy his own time away from the aircraft and needless to say, was considered a 'real gentleman'. Once, when Jim was not particularly hungry, his revered captain polished off both their flight rations and would regularly consume numerous chocolate bars. Cruising altitude was anything between 3,000 to 5,000 feet, though some did descend lower, causing the trailing aerial to play havoc with fishermen!

Jim's landings were considered satisfactory enough for him not to be sent to Vaaldam for first officer training. But seeing others (considered less competent) wearing the coveted extra stripe, he had decided to attend the course, when it was suggested he might as well do the 'nav' test (a modified wartime 1st Class certificate) as well. Aware the course in question had been running for two months, Jim considered it an impossible task to catch up in the few weeks left to him – but was passed out with top marks!

When moored and finished with all engines, the captain switched off the ignitions and pulled the inboard and outboard fuel cut-out levers. His first officer would then briefly blip the starter buttons to turn each airscrew until all four blades were vertical. The captain would then centralise the rudder bar, level the control wheel and push the control column fully forward, when the first officer inserted the control lock before moving aft to close the fuel cocks, set the engine starting to shore battery, and check the remaining fuel levels indicated by the gauges. If the captain had not done so already he then pushed the throttle levers to Full Open, moved the mixture controls fully back, turned off the carburettor test cocks and brought the flaps back to the closed position. He then followed his captain outside. At the end of a service flight, the captain was required to submit a full report, written in long hand, of each of the sectors involved.

BOAC LILLIPUT

By now the substantial brick premises of the Harbour Club at Salterns Way, Lilliput had been taken over on behalf of the director general of the Ministry of Civil Aviation. Built in 1935, the club and hotel premises benefitted from a long wooden jetty at the rear which extended as far as the deep water channel – a throw back to the days when the site was cluttered with factory buildings and railway sidings associated with the pottery

Harbour Club Lilliput pre-war. COURTESY BEVERLEY HELLIWELL SMITH.

Pre-war Harbour Club. Without todays marina and luxury apartments
© JEREMY WATERS COLLECTION.

industry. Relocated from Poole and Hamworthy, BOAC staffs had moved into offices on the right hand side of the building, which became known as the Marine Terminal. Passenger reception, medical, customs and immigration personnel now worked in more suitable surroundings and were joined by accounting, catering and postal staffs. Ministry of Aviation personnel joined with surface transport, flying control, signals, operations and traffic sections in performing the more immediate tasks. There was also an RAF meteorological office. Launches were berthed at the basin to the front left of the building, as they are today, where the car park occupies the site of the pre-war tennis court.

In a detailed letter to Peter Davidson, Stan Gibbs remembered the Approach Control office using high frequency radio and direction finding equipment to guide descents through cloud (QGH) to some 20 feet from the water, years before the introduction of sophisticated instrument landing systems (ILS). Two triangular loop aerials set at right angles to each other on the roof formed part of a Bellini-Tosi direction finder system linked to a Marconi receiver in the radio room. When rotated, the large left-hand dial gave the bearing-seeking Morse transmissions from the airborne radio officer a no-wind magnetic homing (QDM) to Poole; his own receivers and transmitters mounted within shock-proof supports, with a retractable loop aerial fitted in the roof of the cabin. Another medium frequency beacon radiated a continuous note from the terminal, interrupted every thirty seconds by the station call-sign GJX. High frequency radio transmissions were normally only used to talk to crews prior to the landing approach, though contact was maintained with those flying the Atlantic from Foynes, Baltimore and the Azores, considered quite magnificent for those early wartime days. At the end of the war, Peter would go on to work in air traffic control at Hurn, Northolt and Heathrow and would marry Marian, a former Poole Grammar School friend, whom he had met again at Lilliput where she was employed as a telephonist.

The Harbour Heights Hotel had been requisitioned to provide overnight accommodation for the aircrew and passengers, though captains were usually billeted elsewhere. The Sandacres, Sandbanks and Haven Hotels were within easy reach. Picked up by coach early in the morning, passengers were driven by way of Evening Hill to Lilliput, where a notice-board positioned almost opposite the rather concealed little road leading to the terminal, proclaimed the presence of the airline. A blue carpeted and freshly decorated lounge enabled them to relax while awaiting their turn to be weighed and documented. They might breakfast in the newly decorated restaurant, frequented by airline staff and flight crew, where bright coloured Poole Pottery ware, rather than the usual drab white glaze of wartime, helped dispel the anxieties associated with the war and with flying. An armed guard was in position at the entrance to the terminal and VIPs received a guard of honour at the end of the jetty, provided by soldiers from Bovington Army Camp. The secluded waterside setting inspired a happy working and social environment, the Airways Club equipped for billiards, table tennis and badminton, while over a hundred people attended dances featuring the Melody Makers band of marine fitter Percy Douglas.

BOAC board opposite the Salterns Way terminal.
©JEREMY WATERS COLLECTION

America's entry into the war following the attacks made on Hawaii during the morning of Sunday, 7 December 1941, had freed the Boeings from the restrictions of the Neutrality Act, enabling crews to fly direct from Poole to West Africa. The existing channel marking and mooring buoys were much too small and too difficult to see from the high cockpits however. Using old tyres from Halifax and Stirling heavy bombers supplied by the Ministry of Aircraft Production, Tom Perry had created the Perry Dan Buoy and after a lot of work by everyone concerned, the first was anchored twelve hours before the deadline set for the arrival of the first Boeing 314A.

MALTA

Situated between the coasts of Italy and North Africa, Malta had been constantly bombed since Italy's entry into the war, the supply convoys from Gibraltar mercilessly attacked by Italian bombers based just 70 miles away. Few merchantmen reached the island and though severely starved, Malta never surrendered, defended initially by obsolete Royal Navy Gloster Gladiator biplanes found stored in crates at the RAF flying boat base at Kalafrana, on the south side of the island.

Recalled to the RAF for war service, on 3 April 1941 Flight Lieutenant Lawrence Glover positioned his 228 Squadron Sunderland off Galatea Island to guide a badly needed force of fighters flown off HMS Ark Royal and saw the six Hurricanes and lead Skua safely end their perilous 400 mile journey on the bomb-scarred runways. Another six Hurricanes arrived later. On 27 April, the day German troops entered Athens, twenty-three Hurricanes and three Skuas were flown off *Ark Royal*. But having helped guide them in, Sunderland L5807 was attacked and burnt out on returning to Kalafrana by Me 109 fighters of 7 Staffel of Jagdgeschwader 26, which had moved to Gela (Sicily) in February. Used to flying ten-hour patrols off the coasts of Sicily, Italy and the Ionian Sea, the surviving squadron Sunderlands were flown to West Africa in June.

The Hurricanes were relieved by Spitfires in 1942, when pilots such as the Canadian ace George Buerling, reached a peak in their lives that would never be satisfied again. Until then, submarines and aircraft were the only safe means of arrival. Turning to BOAC for help, the RAF used long-range flying boats detached from the West Africa Service to fly out (six) priority passengers and a ton of freight, made up of engines, ammunition and armaments. A shuttle was flown to Gibraltar during the return to Poole.

Arriving from Gibraltar at a quarter to six in the morning of 3 February 1942, *Clare* was targeted at Kalafrana by a single aircraft and one of a number of incendiary bombs pierced the roof, setting a seat on fire. The blaze was extinguished by a launch crew led by Traffic Officer P.C. Armour, enabling *Clare* to leave at five thirty that evening, with a safe arrival in Cairo at forty minutes past midnight. Kalafrana was virtually wrecked on 7 April . Eight days later, King George V1 awarded the George Cross Medal to the island for the heroism and sacrifice that had denied invasion of a vital allied base in the Mediterranean. In November 1943 BOAC would present Mr Armour with a Certificate of Commendation for his gallantry and devotion to duty in saving *Clare* and for outstanding service whilst station superintendent at Guba and Malta during 1941 and 1942.

WALRUS PASSENGER

A uniform could give access to areas normally quite unapproachable in peacetime and several cadets were treated to 'rides' in American bombers after making their way out to airfields in the New Forest. Initiative was not just a preserve of the Air Cadets however. Though the beaches and cliff-top were surrounded by barbed wire and a gun battery of 25 pounders had been positioned a short distance from the family home in Southbourne, the seriousness of the situation in 1940 had only really been made apparent to schoolboy Peter Devlin when taking the dog out for a walk one evening. Accosted by someone he knew as the local plumber, but now an acting coastguard, he had been asked just what he was up to and hustled along to a requisitioned house with soldiers visibly entrenched a few yards from the front door. Let off with a warning, he had no illusions about the imminent threat of invasion, though the arrival of attractive ATS recruits for training enabled him and his chums to present themselves as bag-carriers to the girls, who were billeted at the Grange Hall Hotel. Tempted to join the Royal Navy, the Merchant Service appeared to offer a much better prospect should Britain survive the war and his parents had sacrificed a great deal to send him to the School of Navigation for Merchant Navy Officers at Warsash, for which he would always be grateful to them.

© PETER DEVLIN.

The news was far from encouraging however, and in April 1942 the 17 year old had taken a days leave from training to visit his family. Deciding to catch a bus to Sandbanks, his naval uniform allowed him to pass into the hangar without any difficulty and he had simply asked whether it would be possible to be taken up for a flight. A smart Lieutenant pilot had said 'Yes' and pointing to an equally smart looking Wren had told him to 'get equipped'.

Little more than a teenager like himself and very efficient, the girl handed him a Mae West and parachute from a pile on a table, saying with a laugh, 'don't worry it won't work!' Moving out to the concrete slipway, trying hard not to waddle with the seat-type 'chute between his legs, he was helped aboard a launch by a friendly naval airman for the short trip to a moored Walrus.

The first military aircraft to have an enclosed cockpit and retractable undercarriage, the little amphibian would simply disappear from view when making rescues in choppy seas. Stressed to take catapult launches, the biplane was remarkably sturdy and with the elevator almost immediately behind the propeller, very responsive in the pitching plane, though the first clandestine loop usually brought an unexpected soaking in bilge water from the inverted cockpit floor, all too apparent to a grinning mooring party on the return. Take-offs and landings were made with the roof hatch closed, though fine conditions might see the hinged flat surface left open.

Helped down into the cockpit, Peter strapped himself in as the pilot became occupied with his checks. A fixed metal ring was fitted to the starboard wing float for mooring and once the engine was running satisfactorily, the rope was released, and taxiing clear of the buoy and launch, they quickly left the water with just the two of them aboard. Likely to have been an excuse for a test flight, they made a wide circuit of Poole, the sliding window at his shoulder presenting Peter with a clear view below and a lasting memory of a surprising number of vessels moored about the harbour. All too soon they were lining up to land, the undercarriage warning horn automatically sounding off as the throttle lever was closed. Designed to ensure the rather large wheels were correctly positioned for a land or water landing, the system is thought to have caused the unusually high number of wheels-up incidents on runways due to an over-familiarity with the sound! Emerging from a customary cascade of spray across the lower wing and rear fuselage, a short taxi returned them to the mooring buoy and waiting launch. Going back into the busy hangar to return the parachute and inflatable lifebelt, Peter was greeted in mock surprise by the Wren who said 'So you didn't need them then?' A trip to savour on the bus home, especially as he had omitted to mention he had never flown before!

Fitted with a single wing and two enclosed cockpits, the American Vought-Sikorsky Kingfisher began replacing the older floatplanes at Sandbanks during 1942. The prototype Supermarine Sea Otter visited the station the following year but with fewer requirements for catapult launches, 765 was disbanded in October. The Admiralty relinquished Sandbanks in July 1945 and members were allowed back in September, thankful for the care and preservation of the premises. All associated with the Naval Air Station remember it as a happy place, uniquely removed from the prevailing atmosphere at some of the pre-war bases at the time. Even at the height of the Battle of Britain, Squadron-Leader George Darley of 609 Squadron, had been forced to break into the kitchen at RAF Warmwell to personally cook bacon and eggs for his young Spitfire pilots returned from defending this country, due to the station commander ordering the door to be locked outside of the statutory mess opening hours – war or no war!

STARFISH

By 1942 a naval decoy site had become established on Brownsea Island, intended to draw Luftwaffe bombers away from the Poole area by simulating a burning target at night. Created by an expert from Sound City Film Studios at Elstree in Hertfordshire, and positioned at the overgrown and neglected Maryland Pottery site at the western end of the island, fire breaks had been cut among the trees and bunkers installed to protect the naval personnel operating the blazing oil, delivered by the naval barge British Lustre. Banks of rhododendrons provided a natural camouflage for the fuel, guns and equipment. Believed developed at Brownsea, the opening of water taps once the oil-jets had been lit, produced a realistic fire-fighting steam to the eyes of the bomb-aimers circling above.

Two particularly heavy raids targeted the port in quick succession: that of 27 May thought to have involved over fifty German aircraft, the second, mounted on 3 June, lasting for an hour and a half. Bombs fell between Brownsea, Arne and the quayside. Homes were destroyed from Hamworthy to Upton and from Sandbanks to Rossmore. Sunk during the Whit Sunday raid, Sona was replaced by HMS Ladas, towed to Poole from Southampton. The German radio claimed the destruction of the 'Naval Base at Poole', though the number of bomb craters clearly visible across the mudflats of the harbour at low tide, revealed just how effective the 'Starfish' decoy fires had been. Bombs had landed close to the Parkstone Bay moorings and the Marine Terminal and had breached the harbour wall at the rear of the Blue Lagoon. Pre-war, the 'lido' style bathing facilities and smart white blazers of the attendants had been very much in vogue with the times. Positioned outside the harbour, the Examination Ship Rosa Arthur was attacked by a single bomber. As with *Maia*, the near miss claimed a single life and holed the trawler, which took two months to repair.

Prime Minister Winston Churchill chose to return to America by air and in June boarded a special train for the west coast of Scotland, embarking aboard *Bristol* moored in Loch Ryan just before midnight to avoid the long range Focke-Wulf 'Kurier' aircraft operated by the Luftwaffe over the Atlantic. Situated on the western shore of the loch, RAF Wig Bay had opened in 1940 and trained flying boat crews in anti-submarine warfare whilst maintaining and servicing Sunderlands and Catalinas. Flying a westerly course, Captain Kelly-Rogers landed on the Potomac River at nine o'clock in the evening after a flight of some twenty-seven hours. Nine days later, *Bristol* brought the Prime Minister home after secret discussions with President Roosevelt on the progress of the Manhattan Project (the atomic bomb), when both had been shocked to learn that Rommel had taken Tobruk, (21 June 1942) leaving Cairo and Alexandria threatened by the Afrika Corps.

At Poole meanwhile, the blockship Empire Sentinel had been moved nearer the harbour entrance, the main channel position taken over by the equally elderly warship HMS Flinders, towed from Portland Naval Base. Three purpose-built air-sea rescue launches (two named Commodore and Eve) had been delivered to the Navy Officer in charge. Operated in all weathers, their top speed of 12 knots was much slower than the two Speedlarks and Eve was stationed off Swanage to partly remedy the situation – always assuming the Luftwaffe would comply with the arrangement!

Among the more notable wartime VIPs seen at Poole were Lord Beaverbrook, Air Chief Marshal Sir Charles Portal, Sir Dudley Pound and Sir Samuel Hoare. The military included General Alan Brook (Chief of the Imperial General Staff) and Generals Auchinlek, Sikorski, Wavell – and Charles de Gaulle, whose own arrivals in Dorset were almost immediately followed by air raids. Eighteen year old Woman Seaman Eileen Wigg remembered ferrying the singer and 'Forces Sweetheart' Vera Lynn by launch to her flying boat. She also recalled General Montgomery bringing them back bananas, a luxury in food-rationed Britain.

Pan American Airways had dominated the pre-war Pacific and Atlantic routes, but America's entry into the war following the Japanese attack on the Hawaiian island bases during the morning of Sunday, 7 December 1941, had caused the airline to sell the Clippers to the American Government. Apart from *Honolulu Clipper*, which the airline continued to fly between San Francisco and Honolulu, they were operated by the U.S. Navy and Army Air Force as C-98 transports, together with the surviving Martin 130s *China Clipper* and *Philippine Clipper*. *Hawaii Clipper* had disappeared without trace between Guam and Manila in 1938. Used to fly medical supplies and personnel to Europe and the Far East, the return brought vital war materials, especially rubber, to America – while Sikorsky flying boats would go on to conquer the North Atlantic.

Excambian. © NEW ENGLAND AIR MUSEUM.

ATLANTIC NON- STOP

Having learnt to fly with the Ryan School of Flying in San Diego, Charles F. Blair Junior had been awarded a Bachelor of Science degree in mechanical engineering at the University of Vermont before entering the Naval Air Station at Pensacola and had subsequently joined VP-7F at San Diego. In 1933 he began a seven year stint with United Air Lines. The experience enabled him to become chief pilot for the new, American Export Airline, when he selected and trained all its pilots while remaining on the Naval Reserve. After proving flights with a PBY appropriately named 'Transatlantic', the airline bought three of the new four-engined Vought-Sikorsky (VS-44A) flying boats, designed specifically to cross the ocean in direct competition with the Clippers. Named after three of the parent company's four 'Flying Aces' passenger ships, *Excalibur*, *Excambian* and *Exeter* were of all metal construction; given a graceful high upward curve of the hull and 1,200 horsepower Pratt and Whitney Twin Wasp engines capable of propelling 25 tons non-stop across the Atlantic, at a comfortable 170 miles an hour.

A subsidiary of a successful steamship company, AEA knew how to look after its passengers. Provided with a steward and stewardess, they were given more individual space than with any other airline of the time, the luxuriously appointed cabins fitted with lush carpets and forty inch wide divan style seats and adjustable cushions, swiftly converted to full-size beds. There was also a lounge, smoker's room and spacious dressing rooms with hot and cold running water. The five man crew had a sleeping/rest room in the bow, with a separate cabin at the rear for the stewardess.

Juan Trippe knew all the right government connections to protect his airline, but in 1940 President Roosevelt approved a seven-year contract for AEA to fly to Lisbon. The neutral port had attracted a variety of refugees hoping to escape the war and begin a new life in America, a situation featured in the much-loved 1943 triple Academy Award winning film Casablanca, starring Humphrey Bogart, Ingrid Bergman and the song As Time Goes By. In January 1942 AEA was granted a temporary licence to fly between LaGuardia and Foynes for the U.S. Navy Air Transport Service, the politicians, entertainers and diplomats to be flown at night to avoid the Luftwaffe.

On 22 June Captain Blair took *Excalibur* away from the Shannon expecting to refuel at Newfoundland as normal. A strong tail-wind caused him to continue to New York however, where his calculations were justified by having over 90 gallons of fuel left in the tanks after flying non-stop for just under twenty-five and three quarter hours. He would make five consecutive record-breaking crossings during 1944. Military passengers were required to change into civilian clothes before landing at Foynes, while spies were also known to use the services to pass into Europe. Eleanor Roosevelt had herself arrived at the terminal as 'Mrs Smith', but *Excambian* had been trapped by the mud at low tide and the First Lady had had to spend an unscheduled two days in the little town. The record-breaking *Excalibur* fatally crashed while taking-off from Botwood on 3 October 1942, when landing flap is thought to have been run out causing the aircraft to stall. But by the end of the war in Europe, *Excambian* and *Exeter* would between them have made over four hundred Atlantic crossings.

THE FAR EAST

With Japanese intentions towards French Indo-China clearly apparent towards the end of 1940, BOAC had ended services to Hong Kong from Bangkok and transferred the flying boats to the trans-Africa service. To ease the crew situation, in October 1941 Qantas crews had begun taking over the Australia-bound flying boats at Karachi rather than Singapore. But on 8 December, the day after the Japanese attack on Pearl Harbour, land-based aircraft of the Imperial Japanese Navy sank the battleships Repulse and Prince of Wales in the South China Seas leaving Singapore virtually isolated. Caught out by the attacks, Captain Robert Ford decided to fly *Pacific Clipper* the long, westward route home from New Zealand rather than chance flying to Honolulu. Leaving Auckland on the 8th the Clipper eventually landed at LaGuardia on 6 January 1942, after an epic and dangerous journey of over 31,000 miles across Australia, the Dutch East Indies, India, Africa, the South Atlantic and the Caribbean, inadvertently becoming the first commercial airliner to circumnavigate the world.

Supplies and munitions continued to be delivered to Allied forces and increasing numbers of wounded and refugees, mainly women and children, flown out on the return. Plans to keep the Horseshoe Route open had been quietly surveyed in 1941, the first diversionary route from Rangoon avoiding Bangkok by hugging the western coastline of Burma as far as the island of Mergui, before re-joining the original route at Penang for Singapore. Should Lower Burma be invaded, a second route would pass deeper into the Bay of Bengal to Port Blair or Nancowry, in the Adaman Islands, and on to Sabang, on the western tip of Sumatra before heading for Penang.

Unarmed, overloaded, attacked by ground fire and fighter aircraft, seven civilian flying boats were lost in four months. Having flown in ammunition and fuel to an RAF staging post on Weh Island (to the north of Sumatra) for the hard-pressed Singapore garrison, at the end of December Captain Madge brought *Cassiopeia* down to refuel at Sabang. During the subsequent take-off run, the hull collided with an obstruction and capsized and despite heroic rescue attempts by the crew, all four passengers were drowned. With increasing air attacks on Malaya and Singapore, the third diversionary route was activated, which avoided Burma by continuing on from Sabang to Padang, off the southern coast of Sumatra, before re-joining the original route at Batavia, on the north-western tip of Java.

On 30 January 1942, the day British forces were withdrawn from the mainland to reinforce Singapore, Captain Aubrey Koch took *Corio* away from Darwin loaded with troops, intending to bring out Dutch refugees from Soerabaja, to the East of Batavia, on the return. Airways headquarters staff had already been sent from Singapore to Batavia, considered safe from Japanese fighters patrolling over Malaya and Sumatra. But while approaching Koepang and the Dutch port of Timor, *Corio* was intercepted by seven fighters. With the wings full of highly inflammable aviation fuel and nothing between the bullets than thin sheets of aluminum, you could only push the engines to the limit and try to out-run the opposition. But with fighters attacking on all sides, there was only going to be one outcome. Brought down low to the surface, *Corio* was turned towards each attack to lessen the profile. But with two engines streaming flame and most of the passengers killed or wounded, Captain Koch attempted a forced landing, when the punctured keel tumbled the flying boat nose-first into the water. Of the twenty-three aboard, only the two pilots, radio officer and three passengers survived. Though shot in an arm and a leg, 'Aub' Koch and one of the passengers decided to leave the barely floating wreckage to make for the shore, five miles away. It took them three hours. The others eventually joined them and when word reached Koepang, a flying boat was sent to retrieve them.

A shuttle service was flown from Batavia to Singapore but with increasing Japanese air activity, Captain Crowther made the last (Qantas) departure from the island during the early hours of 4 February 1942, when he took a heavily loaded *Corinna* off in moonlight without a flare path. Shelled, bombed and strafed, the island was invaded five days later. The garrison surrendered on 15 February. Having carried thousands of troops and hundreds of sick and wounded to safety, the ten Empire boats stranded in the Australian sector of the Horseshoe (*Clifton, Coogee, Coriolanus, Corinthian, Circe, Camilla, Coolangatta, Corinna, Centaurus* and *Calypso*) were either absorbed with their crews by Qantas – or by the Royal Australian Air Force. The Horseshoe Route now ended at Calcutta, from where the flying boats retraced their steps to Durban, but the marine bases on the islands of Sumatra, Java and Timor became easy targets for Japanese planes which extended their attacks to the north-west coast of Australia, bringing increased fears of invasion.

On 19 February, the Japanese First Air Fleet virtually destroyed the Naval Base at Darwin, ending support for the islanders of the Dutch East Indies. Partly concealed by smoke from a burning ammunition ship close by the mooring, *Camilla* survived the bombing. Leaving the relative safety of the Darwin Hotel, Captains Crowther and Hussey climbed aboard, started up, and taxied clear of the ship, when the sound of renewed bombing caused them to take-off immediately. The 11,000 ton ammunition ship exploded shortly afterwards. Flown to Groote Eylandt (Dutch for 'big island') over 600 miles away in the Gulf of Carpentaria, *Camilla* returned before nightfall and continued on to Sydney in the early morning, her cabins full of grateful passengers, including Aubrey Koch, who had been recovering in Darwin hospital.

Recalled to Broome, Qantas crews began operating a shuttle service of over a thousand miles across the Indian Ocean to Tjilatjap, on the southern shore of Java. But on 27 February (the day *Coogee* crashed on landing at Townsville) an Allied battle fleet of American, British, Dutch and Australian ships was defeated in the Java Sea. Java was invaded the very next day, when *Circe* and *Coriolanus* brought out the last refugees from Tjilitjap. Both crews were initially in radio contact, but only *Coriolanus* landed at Broome. Japanese fighters had air superiority in the area and nothing was ever found of the thirty-four evacuees and crew aboard *Circe*. *Clifton* was formally leased to the Australian Air Force in March (A18-14) to replace *Coogee* but three more were lost in the month.

Heavily involved in the island evacuations, sixteen Dornier Wals operated by the Dutch airline KLM were among a host of flying boats anchored in Roebuck Bay off Broome on 3 March , which included military PBYs and two former Empire boats. Some were crowded with refugees, some were being refuelled as the Zero fighters swept in and most were sunk, including *Centaurus* (A18-10) and *Corinna*, though their passengers were fortunately ashore. Over seventy others lost their lives. Nineteen days later

Corinthian sank after hitting debris on landing at Darwin in the early morning. A fourth was lost in August, when *Calypso* (A18-11) capsized after landing on high seas near Daru in New Guinea in an attempt to rescue the crew of a torpedoed merchantman, though the military crew scrambled aboard two life rafts and were rescued after making a safe landfall.

With half its remaining flying boats taken over by the Australian Government, Qantas postponed overseas passenger services until after the war, though continuing to fly supplies between Townsville, Groote Eylandt, Darwin and Port Moresby. Flights were also made to Milne Bay in New Guinea, joining military flying boats in dropping supplies to Australian forces fighting in the jungles of Papua and returning the wounded to mainland hospitals.

RAF Hamworthy

Having evaluated Short's four-engined Sarafand, in 1933 the Air Ministry had invited tenders for a new General Reconnaissance four engined flying boat and K4774 had left the Medway in October 1937, just over a year after *Canopus*. The Ministry had also asked Saunders-Roe to produce a prototype, but the A33 had taken a year longer to fly and was scrapped after suffering structural failure during high-speed water trials.

Though benefitting from the technology of the C-Class and similar in appearance, the S25 Sunderland was a purpose-built machine with even more improvements than the S23s. Powered by four, 1,010 horsepower Pegasus engines, rather than the 950 of the prototype, fed by over 2,000 gallons of petrol within six fuel tanks, loaded with military equipment, eight bombs, and a seven (later eleven) man crew supported by a visibly deeper hull, the flying boat had a range of nearly 3,000 miles, though the wing loading was the highest of any British military flying boat. As with the C-Class, the take-off and landing run was minimised by the flaps of Arthur Gouge, who had envisaged a single gun in the nose and tail. Production Mark 1s had four machine guns in the tail however and both positions had enclosed Fraser-Nash power-operated turrets, another first for British flying boats, the shift in weight to the tail resulting in a more swept-back wing and a distinct outward splay of the engines.

A former peacetime seaplane base dating from about 1913, RAF Station Mount Batten occupied the south side of Plymouth Sound, overlooked by Plymouth Hoe, where Sir Francis Drake is famously thought to have delayed fighting the Spanish Armada until ending his bowls match! Formed in Australia before the war and expected to fly the new Sunderlands home after training in Britain, No 10 Squadron RAAF had arrived at Pembroke Dock in August, but with the declaration of war had remained 'on loan' by the Australian Government. On 1 April 1940 the squadron had been relocated to Plymouth.

Remembered for the training of aircrew in the more hospitable climates of Canada, Australia, Southern Rhodesia and South Africa, the Empire Air Training Scheme also made provision for trained aircrew to be grouped within squadrons of national identity, controlled by the RAF, with an identifying 'flash' on the uniform shoulders. On 25 April 1942, No 461 Squadron RAAF was formed from a nucleus of personnel transferred from 10 Squadron, the date held in memory of over ten thousand Australian and New Zealand Army Corps troops who had died during the disastrous landing at Gallipoli in 1915. Known inevitably as the 'Anzac' Squadron, 461 received a crest showing a harpooned sharks head and the motto 'They Shall Not Pass Unseen'. Aircraft would be identified by the letters UT. Squadron Leader Reginald Burrage and Flight Lieutenant Ron Gillies, both of 10 Squadron, were respectively made temporary commanding officer and temporary flight commander.

Training commenced with three Mark 2 Sunderlands built by the Blackburn Aircraft factory at Dumbarton on the north bank of the Clyde. Produced from August 1941, forty-three were built (five at Dumbarton), fitted with more powerful, 1,065 horsepower engines, while the upgraded tail turret had twice the ammunition (4,000 rounds).The two beam gun positions would later be replaced by a two-gun dorsal turret, offset to the right to maintain stability, though the deflection of air caused by its rotation was immediately transmitted to the controls in the cockpit. From October, air to surface vessel (ASV) Mark 2 radar was fitted, the low frequency waveband requiring four antennae on the spine and a double row of aerials on both sides of the fuselage. A receiving aerial was fitted under both wings, outboard of the floats. All of which caused some U-boat crews to refer to them as fliegendes Stachelschwein (flying Porcupines), which was odd as the animal was unknown in Germany. 'Sticklebacks' might have been more appropriate.

With military flying boat bases in short supply it was decided that Poole could support one squadron. To later command 40 Squadron RAAF, the only Sunderland Squadron based in Australia, Vic Hodgkinson was nearing the end of an operational tour with 10 Squadron, prior to being posted back home to fly Catalinas. Tasked with carrying out a survey of Poole harbour, he arrived on 2 January 1942 to find that with the army and navy firmly ensconced since the start of the war, there was very little left to choose from. His report was hardly favourable. The area was vulnerable to enemy action and there were many submerged 'spider' anti-invasion obstacles. Their Lordships decided on a site at Hamworthy however, opposite Gold Heath Point, to the north of the Wareham Channel, though bereft of any facilities. A concrete slipway was begun in June. By then thirty year old Wing Commander Neville Halliday had taken over 461, with the more experienced Sunderland pilot Squadron Leader Lovelock as his flight commander. The squadron became operational in July when it began

John Witcomb RAFVR.
© JOHN WITCOMB.

receiving the longer-range Sunderland 3. Visibly deeper than the C-Class, the hull had a pronounced upward curve rather than the sharp V of its predecessors, while trials conducted by the Air Ministry's Marine Aircraft Experimental Establishment at Helensburgh, had resulted in a faired main step to counteract the air drag caused by the increased loading.

Commissioned as RAF Poole on the first day of August 1942, just seven days later the new flying boat base was renamed RAF Hamworthy. Station Commander Group Captain Wigglesworth arrived during the month and the station record book recorded two officers and one hundred and thirty other ranks under the command of Squadron Leader Lovelock arriving by special train on the first day of September. Twenty-three year old John Witcombe was among the advance party waiting at the Hamworthy Junction railhead to off-load the tons of equipment and stores onto a Queen Mary trailer.

John's parents lived in Wallisdown in Poole and in August 1930 he had watched Amy Johnson land her de Havilland Gipsy Moth 'Jason' in the large meadow at Talbot Village Farm. The first woman pilot to fly the 10,000 miles to Australia solo, 27 year old Amy had come to Bournemouth to open a hospital fête in Meyrick Park and he remembered seeing her deftly using the biplane's mirror to check her make-up on removing her leather flying helmet! An apprentice cabinet maker with Bobbys department store in Bournemouth, John, like many other 19 year-olds, had volunteered for the RAF in 1940, taking a day off to board the Hants and Dorset bus to Salisbury. The recruiting sergeant at St Edmunds Hall had torn up his papers after noting he was an 'improver', a reserved occupation, though both knew that only applied to 30 year olds. Undaunted, John had filled in another form with a change of job description, but had to again make the journey for a second medical. This time he was in. The photo taken of him in uniform in November giving no hint of the loss of two days pay, the cost of two return journeys, and luncheon expenses.

On completing his flight mechanics course at a factory making Wellington bombers at Squires Gate, Blackpool, John was posted to No 9

RAF Observer School at Penrhos, a pre-war RAF station, where navigation training was carried out in Avro Ansons and Bristol Blenheims used for the bomb-aiming. Ground crew were encouraged to fly whenever possible and the Blenheim gave John his very first flight in an aeroplane, clearly remembered for the rough ride back to base accompanied by gesticulations of despair from the Polish pilot, the 25 pounder practice bombs released by the trainee observer having missed the canvas targets bobbing on their buoys below by a considerable margin!

A competent flight mechanic, John was posted to 461 Squadron in June and at the end of August, the nine Sunderlands were flown to Poole. But without Neville Halliday, who had crashed aboard UT-B while attempting to rescue the crew of a ditched Wellington. Promoted to Wing Commander, Colin Lovelock faced the unenviable task of settling the squadron in at Hamworthy. With very little space left within the harbour, the Sunderlands were allocated moorings within the Wareham Channel. A guard room and sentry box were installed a short distance inland at Lake Drive, where the duty sentry would also guard two concrete fuel storage tanks built alongside a siding off the main railway line. A tanker would replenish the supply, using a 6 inch pipeline laid from a small jetty near the slipway, the aircraft refuelled by a cumbersome fuel barge motored slowly out to the moorings. Bungalows were requisitioned on the Lake Estate to provide navigation and technical sections, armoury, stores, workshops, offices and a pilot room.

Everything else was dispersed about Poole, some miles away, mostly in large requisitioned houses: the operations room at 51 Parkstone Road, station headquarters at No 43 and pay and accounts at No 45. The sergeant's mess occupied the three-storey Longfleet Hotel (now the Dolphin) which had a lounge, dining room and a small bar on the ground floor and a single bathroom on each of the floors above. Next door was a bicycle shop and a cinema. A NAAFI operated from Longfleet Road School with a canteen at St Josephs Roman Catholic Church. WAAF hostels were installed at Varenna Court in Springfield Road, Parkstone and at Merrion Court and Stretton Court on Castle Hill, the latter given messing facilities.

A keen member of his local cycling club, John had previously splashed out eight pounds on a Dawes racing bike, worth every penny when the billet at Castle Hill was unavailable and the sergeant allowed him to 'lodge' with his parents. And even more when the early morning cycle ride to Hamworthy along the virtually deserted Ringwood Road brought an unexpected meeting with another lone cyclist, a pretty brunette, arriving from the other direction. Emily worked at Fosters opticians in Wyndham Road and they would be married at Kinson church in 1946 following John's return from the Far East.

A former retired RAF officer and Imperial Airways flying boat pilot, Group Captain Wigglesworth pushed hard to lessen the dispersed nature of his command and was rewarded when 461 was allowed to conduct operations from the former Harbour Club premises at Lilliput.

Accommodation was sought in the area and an officers mess was installed in the Harbour Heights Hotel at Canford Cliffs (the mess staff lodged at Brudenell House) with further quarters at Harbour Court and the Haven Hotel at Sandbanks which had additional messing facilities. WAAF officers were quartered at Bransdene in Brudenell Avenue. The Blue Lagoon at Lilliput provided a dining room for other ranks, the airmens mess staff lodged in Napier Road. Station sick quarters was based at 22 Dorset Lake Avenue, a pleasant two-storey building with bay windows, French doors and a sun balcony overlooking a semi-sunken garden. The ground floor provided a large waiting room, pharmacy, kitchen, admin offices and store rooms. The first floor had wards for male and female patents considered well enough not to require hospital treatment. A medical officer and a dentist attended the needs of the station staff and squadron personnel, assisted by male and female medical assistants, identified by the gilt (caduceus) badge worn on the left lapel of the uniform tunic.

Buses and lorries transported the larger groups of service personnel to their various work stations about Poole while service-issue bicycles gave their owners a valued independence, particularly the aircrew. To command 10 Squadron RAAF, promoted to Wing Commander, and to retire as an airline captain with thousands of hours spent in flying boats, Ron Gillies and others at the time, failed to understand the decision to move 461 to Poole, where crews were faced with a limited take-off run from shallow waters beset with tidal mud flats, and channels barely wide enough to encompass both floats of a Sunderland. The harbour was not the easiest place to find at night in wartime and night flying had initially taken place from Plymouth. The concrete was too small for a hangar and allowed little space to work on aircraft perched on beaching gear.

Servicing and general maintenance was carried out at the moorings, when the broad expanse of the wing was accessed from the hatch above and to the rear of the navigator's position. Fold down panels either side of the engine nacelles were bridged with a plank to give a work platform, though not for the faint hearted, as the aircraft constantly moved in response to the wind and tide. As with BOAC, fitters soon learned to fasten tools about the waist with string rather than lose them in the water immediately beneath their feet, while trusting the launch crew to remember which mooring they were on and to pick them up on time. Major inspections required a flight to Pembroke Dock or to a maintenance unit in Scotland. Minor inspections took place on the 'hard' – once a machine had been brought ashore from the nearest mooring buoy.

Loaded with a pair of twin-wheeled wooden beams and a four-wheeled steerable tail trolley, a small dinghy would head for the buoy, trusting the wind not to take the long wooden lengths and the hapless airmen over the side. Wisely fitted with cork flotation gear, the beams were ballasted to drop wheel first into the water, and were fitted into slots on either side of the hull and beneath the wing centre sections: taking far longer to perform than to describe and usually with both aircraftsmen getting thoroughly wet. With a shoreward facing pinnace roped to the nose of the seaward facing flying boat, the mooring was slipped and a team of men on the slipway would begin pulling on ropes attached to both floats to guide the tail trolley into an electric cradle.

Clad in rubber suit and leaden boots, a partly immersed 'diver' chocked the trolley wheels on arrival to enable the whole contraption to mount the slipway. Roped to a metal eye on the under belly of the aircraft, a caterpillar tractor then pulled the Sunderland up onto the hard to become festooned with rickety looking timber work platforms. As far as John knew, this was the only occasion that a non-naval diver was officially allowed a rum ration, issued immediately afterwards by the duty sergeant within his bungalow office.

Bombing-up was also performed at a mooring, when the depth charges were winched up by a hand operated chain winch to racks run out on rails beneath both wings. In action, the pilot pushed a button to electrically open the pair of spring-loaded, inward opening, drop-down doors in the sides of the fuselage. The drive motor cut out when both carriages had reached full travel. In an emergency, the doors could be opened manually, using a nearby lever. On one occasion the 'bomb scow' had arrived flying the red warning flag denoting 'live' stores were aboard and was positioned alongside a Sunderland to allow the depth-charges to be loaded onto the racks. The 250 pound Torpex filled 'DCs' were normally winched up from the scow to be attached to the fuse-setting control link, but that day the duty armourers included a particularly 'ape-like' individual who preferred lifting each one in his burly arms.

Not a problem perhaps, but a passing seaplane tender chose to ignore the warning flag and went hurtling by, setting the attendant launches pitching and rolling alarmingly. Over the side went our muscular airman, still clutching a depth charge, to re-emerge without it. Panic ensued. With no aircrew aboard, an engine fitter started up the outboard engines and quickly moved the Sunderland out into the channel where a vacant buoy was eventually found and tied up to after some very wet and anxious moments. Years later, John was attending a Burma Star Association reunion within St. Clement Danes, the Central Church of the RAF in London (where he had rectified the omission of both 461 and 10 Squadron badges) when a person standing behind him enquired after his interest. The stranger turned out to be his former commanding officer at Poole (please call me Colin!) who recalled the incident, adding that he had had an 'interview' with the culprits at his office at Salterns Way shortly afterwards.

In July 1942 both G-Class flying boats were flown into Poole to reinforce the West Africa service, the twenty-hour endurance giving a comfortable margin on the long and dangerous Lisbon-Bathhurst sector. In August the pair were joined by *Guba* and *Catalina.* After all that had happened to her, the loss of *Clare*, a familiar sight at Poole, was a particular tragedy. Leaving Lagos early in the morning of 14 September with six crew, thirteen passengers and cargo, the flying boat had refuelled at Freetown and had changed crews at Bathhurst before departing for Lisbon. Sixty minutes later, three messages were received; the first reporting a return on three engines, followed by a request for flares (to light the approach) and then a terse SOS announcing a fire on board. Aircraft and launches were sent to the last reported position but it was only on the second day that floating wreckage was sighted by a Catalina, all that remained of a forced landing on high seas. *Champion* and *Cathay* were withdrawn from the route.

War was never far away at Hamworthy and John remembered hastily abandoning working within a canvas marquee on the hard for the solid surroundings of a bungalow workshop, when bullets started bouncing off the concrete as a low flying bomber roared overhead with bomb doors open, seconds away from delivering a mid-morning attack on the shipping at Poole. Pilots leaving the Naval Air Station at Sandbanks were obliged to inform the harbour defences well beforehand to avoid problems. But on one occasion John watched in fascination as a training floatplane was skidded desperately low about the harbour to avoid the shells and bullets put up by the local gun crews! The guns were certainly in evidence in October, when a strange sounding floatplane arrived overhead.

FLOAT SPITFIRE

The idea to fit floats on a Spitfire had first arisen during the Norwegian campaign when the lack of airfields had prompted use of the fjords. Trials using floats from a naval Blackburn Roc proved unsuccessful and were abandoned with the invasion, though the idea was revived for the war against Japan, possibly instigated by Churchill as a gesture of practical support for the Americans in the Pacific. The Folland Aircraft Company undertook the conversion of a Spitfire Vb using floats designed by Supermarine, with a shorter propeller, an extended air intake to avoid spray, and a ventral fin instead of a tail wheel. The first of the secret test flights was made by Jeffrey Quill from Southampton Water, though the organ-like sound produced by an open-ended tube, which located on the axle of the launch wheels, broadcast its presence for miles around. Though found to have a lack of directional stability, due to the increased side area of the floats producing a continuous yaw in flight, the need to complete the trials took precedence over increasing the fin area.

The next trials required flying at low speed between Southampton and

Poole. The local anti-aircraft headquarters arranged for flight times to be broadcast to the gun sites two hours in advance, while the 1,000 feet altitude would give the gunners a good look at the aircraft. Assistant test pilot Lieutenant Don Robertson had learned to fly at Brooklands before the war and had spent three years flying on skis and floats in the north of Canada, before becoming a wartime Fleet Air Arm pilot. His preliminary handling flight at Hamble had found there was so much power that the 'hump' of water was overcome with less than full throttle. Having begun the trial by flying low over Christchurch, the floatplane was circling over Poole when another Spitfire came alongside. After waving, the pilot flew off again. Now over the Royal Motor Yacht Club, the floatplane was targeted by red tracer shells from a Bofors gun emplacement.

From first thinking there must be enemy aircraft in the vicinity, the pilot quickly realised the shells were meant for him! Other guns joined in and after using the inherent sideways drift to confuse the gun layers (no radio was fitted), the Spitfire was dived to the water, below their trajectory, hurdling the Sandbanks chain ferry before heading back to Christchurch. Despite flying parallel to the coast a few times, more guns opened up as he headed inland, causing another dive, this time skimming the trees of the New Forest.

Seeing a squadron of Spitfires approaching, a vertical, five 'G' turn was made (with floats!) to show the famous elliptical wings, when the formation flew off. Landing at Hamble, a fast taxi was made to the slipway in case the floats had been hit. But with no evident damage, the pilot rang up the controller to report what had happened, only to be told by a high-pitched, excited voice to get off the line, there was an air raid on! Invited to a drinks party that evening at the local anti-aircraft regiment headquarters, the pilot was greeted by the commanding officer and was delighted when his wife Ella responded without hesitation to the contrary, when it was suggested her husband had been scared stiff by the 'unfortunate' experience, adding that he had realised that if they couldn't recognise a Spitfire after three years of war, there was little chance of them hitting him!

It was thought that the gunners (some of which were women) had fired some ninety Bofors shells, 400 machine gun bullets, and eight, four and a half inch shells and that the senior army officer in charge was removed from his post. Subsequent trials were flown on the same course, but between 15,000 and 20,000 feet, when the floatplane had to wait for the pair of escorting Spitfires from Tangmere to catch up. Three conversions were sent to Egypt in October 1943, armed with four machine guns and a pair of 20 millimeter cannon, though the invasion of the British held islands of Kos and Leros in the Agaen Sea ended their intended rôle against German transports and they were withdrawn to the Great Bitter Lake, in the Suez Canal region.

Both G-Class flying boats were withdrawn from the Africa service to operate a shuttle between Foynes and Lagos to simplify the Boeing winter service. In November they were replaced by two more Catalinas loaned by the RAF (FP221 and 224), the month German and Italian forces began retreating from the North African coastal town of El Alamein, 150 miles west of Cairo. On 8 November, American forces supported by British infantry and commandos landed at Casablanca, Oran and Algiers. Having waited for confirmation of both events, which would end Axis hopes of controlling Egypt, the Suez Canal, and the Middle East oil fields, Churchill issued his orders. Over 300 years ago, beacons had been prepared along the south coast of England to warn of the arrival of the Spanish Armada in the channel, and since June 1940, cathedral and church bells had lain silent to enable a clear warning of a German invasion. But on Sunday, 15 November 1942 the bells were heard ringing across all of England in celebration of the first really encouraging news of the war.

Chapter Six

Highs and Lows

Tagus Tragedies

Released from war service, *Golden Hind* and *Golden Horn* used their superior range and speed on flights to Gibraltar, while *Catalina* flew on to the besieged island of Malta, able to take up to six VIPs or military personnel considered vital to the war effort, along with a ton of mail, freight and essential spares.

As with both G-Class survivors, *Golden Hind* had been stripped of military equipment when returned from RAF service, though retaining bomb doors, a concealed (push button) escape hatch, and modified window panels for hand-held guns. The gun turrets were faired over. To return the interior to airline standard at minimal coast, BOAC had reduced the forty seats to thirty-eight in order to maintain the high standard expected of the airline. Slightly larger than the C-Class, the four cabins were given light grey, fabric covered, ceilings and upper walls, with the remainder a dark grey. The seats and carpets were light green. Though cost-effective, the use of fabric rather than panelling also reduced the noise levels. Smoking was now tolerated in three of the cabins, provided with fresh or heated air on demand. If less than thirty-two passengers were aboard, half the main cabin was used as a promenade and viewing area, for which a long handrail had been fitted. The steward's compartment and pantry were at the front of the aircraft, with two passenger toilets and wash rooms at the rear. The crew toilet adjoined the flight deck staircase. Four tons of freight and baggage could be carried

From 1943, Poole customs officers acting on behalf of the port medical officer were taken by launch to newly arrived flying boats at their moorings, and were authorised to allow everyone ashore on receiving a satisfactory declaration of the aircraft's health from the captain. Security and customs personnel were in attendance at the pottery building, where passengers were called by name in the lounge to be cleared through the various sections. A medical inspection room had been set up and after signing a declaration of health, with details of inoculations, vaccinations and their movements during the previous fourteen days, each received an official landing card and was advised to visit a doctor should they become ill during the next twenty-one days. No-one was considered to have landed until leaving the inspection room. The aircraft were also subject to health checks, performed without warning by the port sanitary inspector or his deputy. Unless specifically requested by a captain, when no-one was allowed off until the arrival of the medical officer, who looked for evidence of vermin or mosquitos if a return had been made from the Far East, together with a thorough examination of the galley and sanitary arrangements.

With so many famous names using the wartime flying boats, losses were brought much closer to the public consciousness. The 39 year old Duke of Kent had died in the Scottish highlands in August 1942 when the 228 Squadron Sunderland in which he was travelling had crashed in poor visibility, and the New Year brought tragedy for BOAC and Pan Am at Lisbon. Forced to return on 30 December with a faulty starboard outer engine, *Golden Horn* took off to test a replacement on 9 January . This time the starboard inner seized, and with flames streaming back to the tail, the aircraft landed heavily, porpoised, and crashed into the Tagus. Just two of the fifteen aboard survived. Examination of the wreckage found a cylinder had failed, wrecking another, while the opened roof hatch and co-pilot window suggested smoke had been sucked into the cockpit, partially obscuring the forward vision during the landing, made difficult by the fire ravaged tailplane. The disproportionate number of casualties also revealed that nine 'guests' had been allowed aboard for the test flight and had tragically paid with their lives.

On 22 February *Yankee Clipper* arrived over the Tagus as lightning flashes lit the darkened dusk sky and throttled back for the landing, made a fatal low turn when a wingtip touched the surface, causing the big aircraft to cartwheel over and over before collapsing into the river. Over half the passengers lost their lives, including the actress and singer Tamara Drasin, famous for introducing the jazz classic 'Smoke gets in your Eyes' to Broadway in 1933. In shock and on their own due to a lack of rescue boats, the survivors had to fend for themselves. Among them was 36 year old Jane Froman, voted America's top female vocalist in 1934, who headed the United Service Organisation entertainment party on their way to entertain American troops. With severe fractures to both legs and an arm, the singer was dragged aboard a makeshift raft by the co-pilot, whose back had been broken by the impact. When rescued, she bravely refused to let a surgeon amputate her right leg and began a long and painful convalescence, resigned to wearing a concealed leg brace for the rest of her life. Two years later, she duly entertained the troops, supported by a radio controlled electric pedestal. She married her rescuer and was portrayed by Susan Hayward in the 1952 Twentieth Century

Fox hit biographical movie *With a Song in My Heart*, when her voice was used for all the songs.

Unable to fly the Mediterranean and with increasing demand for air transport to support the land battles in North Africa, BOAC had turned to Short Brothers who in 1942 had begun converting six military Sunderland 3s for the airline and the RAF. Stripped of military equipment and given a blunt fairing over the tail turret, they retained the wartime camouflage and the retractable nose turret, which concealed the mooring bollard. Fitted with sixteen utilitarian canvas seats for priority passengers, the Transport Sunderlands were put on the Poole-Lagos West Africa service from March 1943 within the new RAF Transport Command, though the airline was allowed to retain its own identity. Having flown from Poole to Foynes, a crew waited for nightfall before leaving for Lisbon and continued by night to Bathurst, Freetown and Lagos. For the passengers, a draughty, austere and unheated journey in the dark (with no steward, sandwiches had to suffice), was followed by a welcome change to a camouflaged Empire flying boat for the connecting shuttle across Africa to Stanleyville, taking the Horseshoe Route north to Khartoum or the Far East as their mission demanded. Routed through military zones and neutral countries, air crews were awarded RAF Reserve rank and subject to the Air Force Act, though free to choose whether airline or service uniform would bring the greater advantages when ashore!

CHANGES AT HAMWORTHY

Twenty-five year old Wing Commander Desmond Douglas, a regular officer in the Royal Australian Air Force and former flight commander with 10 Squadron, had taken over 461 (Anzac) Squadron at Poole; the Australians supplemented with RAF aircrew and WAAF and RCAF personnel among the ground staff. On 18 March 1943 the Operations Record Book recorded an unusual and tragic accident, begun when a twin-engined Dakota arrived and began circling over the harbour with a Royal Artillery Officer suspended in his parachute below the fuselage. Surface craft from BOAC, the Royal Navy and Air Ministry were sent to the western end of the harbour, and though not acknowledging radio messages from Hamworthy, the Dakota duly flew to the west and began circling at under 1,000 feet. Joined by two more aircraft, the pilot finally descended to just a few feet above the surface and the soldier was seen to fall with a large splash into the water. Sadly, he did not survive his ordeal and the Dakota returned to its base at Broadwell.

Life went on, and having hopefully arrived at a Sunderland moored in the Wareham Channel without getting drenched in the launch, pilots entered the forward hatch on the port bow and climbed the short vertical ladder to the cockpit. The layout was much the same as the Empire boats, but with more military applications. Parachutes were not worn, as the seats were upholstered, rather than the 'bucket' variety, the captain's deposited in a metal frame on the back of the left hand seat and the co-pilots within a frame on the cockpit wall, which also stowed the Aldis signal lamp and spare glasses. Strapped into his adjustable seat, the 'skippers' hands dropped comfortably onto a three-spoke control wheel, the upper segment removed to give an unrestricted view of the instrument panel, with a flip-up bomb release button clamped to one of the arcs and firing and transmit buttons clamped to the other. Beneath the standard instrument panel, three switches controlled the mooring mast, downward identification, and navigation lamps. A whistle was usually hung from the panel. There was also an 'action station' klaxon button. On the floor by his left hand sat the main P4A compass, aft of which were the bomb selector switches, bomb carriage ready indicator lamps and fuse setting switches. At shoulder level on the cockpit wall were the switch and push buttons for the I.F.F (identification friend or foe) transponders.

Above, surrounded by an Emergency Use Only placard, was the release switch for the type J blow-out dinghy fitted within the starboard wing, given a break-out panel in the event of a ditching. An intercom socket was positioned at the front of the seat, with a Morse switchbox for the downward identification lamps and a landing lamp dipping lever just above the right knee. Above, on the cabin roof between both seats, were the rudder and elevator trim-wind handles with setting indicators, and four engine master cock levers; the intervening space to the windscreen taken up by four spring-loaded, slow running and cut-out levers and the fuel jettison control. Midway back were adjustable spotlights to illuminate the instrument panels, with dimming controlled by the captain. Immediately over his head, on the left hand side, push buttons operated the engine fire extinguisher system, while the window panel by both seats had a (break out) cutter for emergencies.

The top of the central instrument panel was fitted with a row of flap indicator lamps, meters and switches, two banks of ignition switches and a drogue signals switchbox. Underneath was a large compass repeater, switches for the air to air recognition lamps, the aircraft's clock, and two rows of four instruments to show the revolutions and boost of each engine. Cabin heating and ventilation relied on two pipes fitted to an air intake within the leading edge of the port wing. One supplied cold air to outlets in the hull, the other sent air heated by a steam unit in the wing centre section into the cockpit and crew stations. A boiler was fitted to the port inner's exhaust. Between the seats, a central console held the familiar quadruple sets of throttle and mixture levers, followed by the 'airscrew' speed control levers. The left hand side also had a landing lamps switch and a push-down hand pump to deliver de-icing fluid to the wiper-equipped windscreens. Nearer the stairs, metal containers protected the essential lead/acid accumulator batteries, topped up by the pull-start single cylinder engine and dynamotor within the starboard wing. Without the auxiliary 'trolley-ac' (accumulator trolley) available to landplanes, the batteries started all four engines, beginning with the starboard inner which activated the aircraft's generator. From 1943, extra metal boxes held centimetric Mark 3 radar, to counter the U-boats detection radar, with rotating dishes concealed in streamlined pods on the underside of both wings; the mesmeric rotating beam watched in an enclosed 'tent' by the gunners in half-hour shifts to avoid falling asleep.

As with his civilian counterpart, the co-pilot performed most of the external pre-flight checks but without the white overalls issued by the airline. More of a clamber-on than the 'walk-round' performed on landplanes, he carefully avoided slipping on the wet, sea-bird targeted surfaces while keeping a wary eye open for the crew 'joker' who might be lurking near a wing float, ready to tip an unsuspecting rookie into the 'drink'. Back inside, his seat was without the armour plate of the captain, the bomb release switch usually clamped on the right of his control wheel. Able to monitor all the switches and gauges on the central panel, he had his own height, speed, and turn and bank instruments, together with a thermometer style gauge showing the nose-down or nose-up (fore and aft) level of the aircraft. A signal pistol and cartridges were stowed behind the seat, the firing sleeve set in the roof behind the captain.

The starboard side of the flight deck also held the navigators table, astro-dome, and the flight engineer: sat facing rearwards with his array of levers and instruments giving the engine temperatures, pressures and fuel levels. To his right and forward of the wing spar, the wireless operator faced his own set of dials and (coloured) knobs, the Morse key to his right and a window port to his left. Everything close to hand and with practise, operated automatically, though pilots were not encouraged to land on the open sea. If circumstances demanded, a landing was made with 75 knots 'on the clock' – unlike the Americans, who preferred approaching with full flap and full power to achieve a fully stalled state along the swell to avoid bouncing off the wave-tops. Catalinas could get away with that, and were generally more flexible on the water. The more rigid, box-like structure of the C-Class and Sunderland hull was more prone to damage should it come off a wave and be thrown back onto the next, especially if at an angle.

In the extreme nose, the bomb aiming compartment contained the bomb sight and an outward opening, glazed viewing panel. Immediately behind, the spacious mooring compartment contained a sea anchor chained to a hand-operated winch, a spare canvas sea drogue, mooring bridles, boat hook, a lightweight ladder and even a fog bell. Above, the forward gun turret was wound backwards by a hand-operated winch in the roof, to allow the big sea anchor to be passed out and to access the small mooring deck and demountable bollard. Mooring and 'slipping' was performed by two of the air gunners. Approaching the 'trot', with an eye on the wind and tide which very rarely acted together, a pilot had to counteract the tendency for the nose to weathercock into wind, using the outer engines to control the speed before the tide ideally allowed the aircraft to float slowly in range of the floating hawsers. With the engines idling, one gunner stood in the space vacated by the nose turret armed with a long-handled boat-hook. The other stood precariously on a rung of the lightweight ladder clipped to the port side of the hull, holding on with his right hand while swiftly passing a floating loop of rope up for securing to the bollard, hopefully without need of the boat hook. A winch chain was then run out over the bows and shackled to a cable attached to the buoy. Another cable was shackled to a metal ring welded to the bows.

Moving aft along the lower deck, a step down on the starboard side led to a flushing porcelain toilet with wash basin and shaving mirror, the header tank topped up with seawater away from base. Once airborne, the toilet was discharged into the sea by a hand pump. Rounding the flight deck ladder, a luggage locker and rifle racks preceded a door to the (officers) wardroom, provided with a bunk on each side and a table.

Next came the all-important galley, fitted with a stainless steel sink and an oven with two kerosene pressure-stoves, the fresh water carried aboard in five, 5-gallon tanks with integral taps. A ladder passed directly up to the flight deck. On both sides, a metal container fitted beneath a hatch stored a canvas 'sea anchor', secured by wire hawser to a bulkhead before deployed by hand. Both hatches had been used as firing positions before Shorts had installed open gun ports. The floor had a water-tight cap to protect the tube holding the retractable aerial of the wireless operator. His high frequency transmissions relied on a fixed aerial fitted to the tail fin. Next was the tall bomb room which stored the bombs/depth charges, winched up to the under-wing rails. A door led into the first of two crew rooms. Both had two bunks, the first fitted with a table, while the second had a fixed ladder to the rear of the upper deck, used to stow smoke and flame floats and reconnaissance flares.

The remainder resembled some vast, reverberating metal cave, bulged outwards from the central walkway with row upon row of metal 'ribs'. On the right, a ladder led up to the gun positions, replaced by a dorsal turret on the later Mark 2s. The starboard side also had stowage for spare propeller blades, a maintenance platform and a fire extinguisher before reaching the rear entry hatch. Both entry hatches were secured from the outside by a Yale style lock, an emergency fit-all key secured in a slot in front of the astro hatch, fitted with a tear-off strip. A dinghy, long handled paddles, distress flares and emergency rations were stowed aft of the door, while a metal box held rubber plugs and plasticine for filling small holes in the hull, together with a few heavy coir-mats. The camera was also stowed here.

The port side held the master gyro-magnetic compass, generally known as the DR (dead reckoning-without wind) compass. Largely unaffected by localised magnetic influences, the readings were passed electrically to the cockpit repeater, with another in the navigators position. Shorts had provided a small workbench complete with vice and tool kit for in-flight repairs, used as a work station by ground armourers and fitters. The floor noticeably rose towards the narrowing tail and a handrail was fitted on the starboard side, across from which a rack held smoke and flame floats for the rear gunner to check drift or illuminate the sea. Clipped to the side was a flare chute, used in conjunction with the camera aperture in the floor, a short wooden pole clipped nearby to prevent jamming (and fire) in the tube. Stores could also be released electrically using push-button switches by the captain's compass and in the bomb-aiming compartment. Over 80 feet from the nose, the rear turret was reached via a narrow walkway and fabric draught screen fitted beneath the fin and rudder.

Salt-water corrosion was a constant problem and fitters routinely coated the gun barrels with a protective mixture of lanolin and white spirit. The exterior could only be cleared of marine growth when on the hard and John remembered brushing anti-fouling lanolin, or 'sozzle', the full length of the hulls using standard issue two pound tins, taking care to avoid turning against the non-drying 'light-primrose' smelling mixture. Major overhauls emptied the bilges and re-lanolised the hull. As with ships, the bilges were a gravity fed meeting place for all manner of liquids and solids (oil, fuel, grease and lubricants), the metal decking plates fitted with ring handles to enable frequent inspection. Water sloshing around in the hull easily upset the weight and balance (trim) of the aircraft and a hand-held and power pump were carried. Connected to an auxiliary power unit in the starboard wing root, the latter was more efficient, but was used only when the engines were shut down. And then only after clambering out onto the wing via the flight deck, to open the fireproof flap and pull-start the little petrol engine which sucked in air and passed fumes well outside the aircraft.

Beneath the metal decking, a bulkhead sealed each compartment from the next, aided by a pair of very visible, 3-foot high watertight 'swash' doors, almost always locked in position to prevent the spread of water or fire. The foul air emanating from the more obvious parts of the aircraft was ducted into the low-pressure area of the starboard wing, though cockpit windows and entrance doors were invariably left open at a mooring! The cockpit side windows were slid back to improve visibility, but in an unheated and uninsulated metal aircraft, only added to the noise, vibration and cold during a typical eleven-hour patrol. Named after the American actress, a 'Mae-West' life jacket was worn over the fur lined leather flying jacket, with a polo neck, heavy white woollen sweater, issue silk gloves under chamois leather outers, and long white socks tucked into fleece lined flying boots.

Three days after the Dakota and soldier incident, on 21 March 1943 Flight Lieutenant Manger prepared to leave Poole aboard Sunderland UT-C, the third of a second, seven strong batch of Mark 2s built at Dumbarton. The early 'command' training undertaken by Ron Gillies at Mount Batten had soloed a pair of pilots together, acting as captain and co-pilot, and Fred Manger and Colin Walker had been the first to complete the system. That Sunday, the pilot opened up his throttles for what would prove his shortest ever 'flight', for within seconds the operationally loaded Sunderland failed to take off and careered across a mud flat, stopping just short of a stone pier. The crew escaped with only minor injuries but T9111 was completely wrecked, having lost the port wing and starboard tail plane.

Unloaded after returning from Lagos two days later, *Catalina* was taken away for a training session by Captains Winn and Rotherham. But at a quarter to four in the afternoon, the flying boat collided with floating timber: the impact tearing open the hull and projecting the aircraft into the air before crashing back to the surface, when the mixture of hot engine parts and fuel ignited. Both pilots survived, but the engineer, two radio officers and their instructor were killed. The wreckage was left to burn itself out. In November, Woman Seaman Pamela Bates would receive a Certificate of Commendation for her conspicuous devotion to duty aboard Launch 39. Despite the water being covered with fire from burning fuel, and visibility down to 15 to 20 yards, she had shown 'great initiative and presence of mind' in assisting the rescue of Captain Winn and had insisted on carrying on in the launch for further duties.

With more and more demands made on resources, Coastal Command decided to equip flying boat squadrons with twelve machines rather than nine. There was no way the limited maintenance facilities at Hamworthy could cope with the increase, remembered by many as poor, primitive and inadequate, while the frequent withdrawal of aircraft for servicing had affected the sortie rate. A system of planned flying and maintenance would take care of that, with extensive overhaul and repair facilities well established at Mount Batten. The last squadron patrol from Poole was made on 21 April 1943, after which Flight Lieutenant Walker landed UT-N at Plymouth. The original intention had been for 461 to be equipped with the Catalina, rather than the Sunderland, but it fell to the replacement 210 Squadron to bring them into Poole.

Sold to the Air Ministry for evaluation, in July 1939 a Consolidated model 28-5 had been flown across the Atlantic to the Marine Aircraft

Experimental Establishment at Felixstowe. Fifty were subsequently delivered for RAF Coastal Command (some seven hundred would follow) and the jury remains undecided as to whether the RAF or Consolidated were first to name them after the island of Santa Catalina, to the north of the San Diego factory.

Unlike the first, they were all fitted with the distinguishing waist gun 'blisters'. Orders had also come from France (absorbed by Britain after the occupation), the Royal Australian Air Force (over 160 were flown out) and by the Dutch Government to patrol the East Indies (curtailed by the Japanese invasion), causing Consolidated to enlarge the factory premises. Production lines were also set up by Boeing Aircraft of Canada and by Canadian Vickers.

Thanks to Wing Commander Humphrey de Verd Leigh, who had privately developed his own solution to locating surfaced U-boats at night and had overcome all manner of officialdom and bureaucracy to see it accepted, the 210 Squadron Catalinas were fitted with the Leigh Light. Mounted within a nacelle beneath the starboard wing, in line with the pilot's eyes, the 20-inch (ninety million candlepower) searchlight had a range of 2 nautical miles, enabling a head-on attack instead of circling and dropping flares – by which time the enemy had submerged. A lens also gave a ten degree spread in the vertical and horizontal planes, but experienced operators were not prepared to accept the eighty percent reduction in illumination. Before switching on, direction and distance indicators were set in the cockpit, keeping the target in front and in the moonbeam on clear moonlit nights. Patrols were usually flown at less than 2,500 feet to enable a swift dive to around 500, preferably when a mile away from the target, to give time to level the wings for the run in. Used in conjunction with ASV radar from mid 1942, the light had helped reduce sinkings by U-boats in the Atlantic (some 600,000 tons a month) by two-thirds.

Apart from a detachment sent to Gibraltar to cover the landings in North Africa, 210 moved its aircraft and squadron headquarters to Hamworthy in April 1943. Able to remain airborne for some twenty hours, the elegant Catalina gave credence to the Squadron's Welsh motto *Yn y nwyfre yn hedfan* – 'Hovering in the Heavens'.

AIR TRANSPORT AUXILIARY

BOAC had taken over the administration of the Air Transport Auxiliary, a civilian organisation formed just before the outbreak of war to deliver aircraft from the factories to the squadrons in October 1941. The famous ring-bound pilot's notes had been created by flight engineer Bob Morgan, their quality and those of the ferry pilots judged by the fact that a factory-fresh machine would be safely taken away after no more than a twenty-minute perusal of the concise handling notes. From 1943 the ATA included flying boats on their deliveries. Chosen from those with multi-engine, preferably light flying boat (Walrus), or sailing experience, pilots were trained on Catalinas and Sunderlands by the RAF, initially at Alness (Invergordon) on the Cromarty Firth and then by 131 Operational Training Unit at RAF Killadeas in Northern Ireland (Lough Erne). They were then posted to one of the Ferry Pools: No. 6 based at Ratcliffe to clear Sunderlands from Rochester, No. 4 at Prestwick to clear the Blackburn and Lake Windemere factories and No. 8 Pool at Belfast to clear the Short and Harland factory on Queens Island.

The proximity of Cowes to the occupied French bases had caused the workforce of Saunders-Roe to be dispersed to the south-east coast of Anglesey, where a factory and slipway had been built on the deep and sheltered shore of the Menai Straits. Named after the nearest town, at the height of the Battle of Britain the Beaumaris factory had been awarded the contract to fit British equipment within the Catalinas arriving from America.

Landfall had initially been made at Largs on the west coast of Scotland, where civilian personnel from the Prestwick based Scottish Aviation Company performed the conversion work, in conjunction with a much larger factory at Greenock. But from the close of 1942, flights had routed direct from Bermuda to Anglesey, the ferry pilots including a London-born RCAF officer by the name of Hughie Green, who would rise to fame in post-war Britain as the host of the television talent show Opportunity Knocks.

Beaumaris was cleared by all three ferry pools, a typical crew made up of two pilots, a flight engineer and a couple of air training corps or sea cadets trained to assist with mooring etc. Over 400 Catalinas and over 500 Sunderlands would be delivered, though flying boats were the only type the women pilots (and engineers) were not involved with. Having fought a long uphill battle to be allowed to fly more than the basic training Tiger Moth, the women would ultimately ferry fighters, transport aircraft and heavy bombers, flown overseas in the harshest of conditions following the invasion of Europe. Only eleven women ever qualified to fly four-engined (Class 5) aircraft and even these were excluded from flying boats, due, it is said, to ferry crews often having to sleep aboard the aircraft. Perish the thought Carruthers! Such thinking would also delay women serving aboard ships of the Royal Navy until 1977.

The new rescue boats at Poole had certainly proved their worth, retrieving a Spitfire pilot from the bay in January, the crew of a Whitley bomber 5 miles off Christchurch in February and a Hurricane pilot from off Green Island in March. From April, BOAC Transport Sunderlands flown to Hythe for maintenance, returned to Plymouth rather than to

Poole for the Gibraltar flights, but the surrender of some 250,000 German and Italian troops in Tunisia in May 1943, ended the North African campaign and secured Egypt and the oilfields of the Middle East from invasion. The Mediterranean could now be flown in safety. But the Pacific was far from safe for unarmed civilian flying boats.

Returned to operations fifteen months after his last ordeal with *Corio*, Captain Koch had taken *Camilla* and twenty-six military personnel away from Townsville and headed north for Port Moresby, on the island of Papua, New Guinea. Encountering worsening weather during the six hour flight, he arrived just before 8 o'clock during the evening of 22 April to find Fairfax Harbour obscured by low cloud and driving rain. Though in radio contact with Port Moresby, the descent through cloud ended with a brief glimpse below before a heavy crash-landing on the sea, with the loss of the radio operator, purser and eleven passengers. The rest were eventually rescued. The pilot had had to swim for three hours when *Corio* was shot down. Having now given his life-belt to a passenger, he and three others, including his first officer, endured almost eighteen hours in the water until detected by the rescue boats.

India had become the hub of the war against the Japanese and the Transport Sunderlands were the means of supply. Leaving Poole for Lisbon or Gibraltar, they were refuelled on the island of Djerba off the east coast of Tunisia before flying on to Cairo and the former Horseshoe Route to Karachi. With the faster Mediterranean route to Egypt and India in operation, Empire boats were withdrawn from the Congo, able to assist the flow of combat aircraft to Burma by returning ferry pilots from Karachi to Cairo. Neutral Lisbon had continued to allow entry to Portugal and Spain, but in June, Britain mourned the death of an actor loved on both sides of the Atlantic.

LOSS OF A FILM STAR

Quintessentially English, though of Hungarian origin, Leslie Howard (Steiner) had risen to fame as a theatre and twice 'Oscar' nominated (Best Actor) matinee idol in Hollywood before starring in the 1939 star-studded film *Gone with the Wind*. Returning home a few days before war was declared, he had decided to stay and had helped the war effort by championing democracy and freedom on BBC radio. Anti-Nazi films had followed and in 1942 he had portrayed Reginald J Mitchell alongside David Niven and Rosamund Johns in the *First of the Few*, which he had directed and co-produced. Location filming was at RAF Ibsley, an active RAF Spitfire airfield in the New Forest near Ringwood, when he had stayed at the Kings Arms Hotel in Christchurch. Reluctant to accept a request by the British Council to tour Spain as well as Portugal to promote *The Lamp Still Burns*, which starred Stewart Granger and

Rosamund Johns (later to star in the classic *The Way to the Stars*), he was persuaded to do so by Foreign Secretary Anthony Eden and by his business manager Alfred Chenhalls, who had a passing resemblance to Prime Minister Winston Churchill. He also smoked cigars.

The neutrality of Portugal was acknowledged by all sides and the civilian aircrews of Britain, Germany and Italy generally knew each other and were able to mix freely about the airport. As did the spies, a fact Harry Pusey was well aware of, for there was a large German presence about Lisbon, which had become the headquarters for an international espionage network. Promoted to station operations officer and posted from Poole to Lisbon, he had watched in fascination as twinkling lights had appeared in the darkness as the Transport Sunderland (later named *Hampshire*) captained by Jack Davys approached at midnight on 6 March 1943. Situated within a bungalow on the hillside above Cabo Ruivo, the operations room gave an unobstructed view of the Tagus and the flying boat moorings, the main ops room situated within the Avenue da Liberdade, with another at Portela airport, between the offices of Lufthansa and Ala Littoria. The deep, clear glazed windows made briefings less than private, though the 20 year old contrived to have those attending his briefings stood with their backs to the windows. There was a war on, after all.

With the conclusion of the third Washington Conference (Trident) in May, Captain Gordon Store and *Bristol* had flown Churchill from the Potomac River to Botwood and on to Gibraltar, where *Ascalon*, a new Avro York of 24 Squadron's Northolt based VIP Flight, had taken him and his entourage (which included Foreign Secretary Anthony Eden, Generals Brooke, Alexander, Ismay and Air Marshal Tedder) on a tour of North Africa. Chenhalls and the famous film star had joined passengers climbing aboard the twin-engined DC-3 *Ibis* at Portela, on the outskirts of Lisbon, on the morning of Tuesday, 1 June 1943, about the time Churchill and Eden were due to return from meeting allied military leaders in Algiers.

Reserved by the British Government for diplomats, service and civilian VIPs and their families, the BOAC flights to Whitchurch (near Bristol) were operated four times a week by crews of the Dutch airline KLM who had escaped to Britain; flown in daylight and not above 3,000 feet in order to clearly identify the camouflaged airliner. The take off went smoothly just before ten in the morning. But just before mid-day, when the aircraft was well out in the Bay of Biscay and some 200 miles from the Spanish coast, Whitchurch received two brief radio transmissions: the first signifying the airliner was being followed, the second saying it was under attack. Nothing was ever found of the thirteen passengers, which included women and young children, or the four crew led by Captain Quirinus Tepas, awarded the OBE in February.

Known by German Intelligence to be used as 'home-runs' by escaping prisoners of war and by covert operatives, *Ibis* had been attacked twice before. The first made by a single Me110 twin-engined fighter in November, while in April, six enemy aircraft had arrived: Captain Koene Parmentier diving to sea-level and using the speed to reach cloud cover and escape to Lisbon, though the damage included a holed petrol tank. Captain Tepas had also dived down to skim the waves, but this time the aircraft had caught fire and crashed. After the war it was found that Berlin had received a copy of Flight 777s passenger list the previous day, while captured Luftwaffe documents confirmed that eight Junkers 88s from V/KG40 had been involved. Copy Luftwaffe photographs, showing the smoking wreckage on the water, were sent to the family, though the actor's son Ronald, believed his father, and not Churchill, was the intended victim – due to his public anti-Nazi comments, and his meeting with prominent anti-German activists during the promotional tour.

An unexpected sequel occurred at 7 o'clock the following evening, when the eleven–man crew of a 461 Squadron Sunderland 3 was attacked by eight Junkers 88s, having reached the exact location reported by the doomed airliner, with instructions to keep an eye open for a dinghy and survivors. Possibly a 'copycat' attack, the Germans broke their formation of four and two following pairs, to line up on both sides of the Sunderland before attacking in pairs from the beam. Dumping the bomb load, but with no time to reach a cloud layer higher up, Flight Lieutenant Colin Walker began throwing the big flying boat about the sky at full throttle, though taking hits which ignited the port outer engine and sent flaming alcohol from the smashed cockpit compass across him and co (First) pilot 'Bill' Dowling.

N Nuts sustained some twenty attacks during the ensuing forty-five minutes, when the navigator was wounded by shrapnel in the leg and the radio was smashed by a cannon shell. Another killed the starboard galley gunner. Though the intercom was out of action and the hull a mess of jagged holes, the top gunner sent a Junkers flaming into the sea after it had narrowly avoided colliding with his turret. The nose and port galley gunners combined their fire power to destroy another coming in from the left and though knocked unconscious by both pilots desperately heaving on the badly shot-up controls, the injured tail gunner came round in time to join the top gunner in shooting down a third, even though his turret was damaged. The nose gunner then flayed another, setting an engine on fire with smoke pouring from the cockpit. The five remaining fighter bombers had been badly damaged, the last pair breaking off to head back to the coast at a quarter to eight in the evening. The unrelenting and suicidal nature of the attacks would later question whether the Germans believed Churchill to have boarded the Sunderland, which had taken the same course as the airliner, or thought the crew had picked up survivors from the crash.

Stripped of everything possible to reduce weight, the battered Sunderland was turned for home on three engines, with Second Pilot Jim Amiss maintaining course on the co-pilot compass. Unlike the Catalina, Sunderland propellers at the time could not be prevented (feathered) from turning an engine and the propeller of the burnt-out port outer, which had given trouble long before the attack, had simply dropped off. Pembroke Dock was repeatedly called, using a radio from an emergency dinghy, and though unanswered, EJ134 was beached at dusk on Praa Sands below the Cornish village of Marazion. A fierce storm completed the destruction during the night. Thirty-eight years later, a dinghy paddle was handed in with other relics, after an appeal on Cornish local radio by John Witcomb on behalf of the 10 and 461 Squadron museum at the Cornwall Aero Park Helston.

For their part in one of the epic flying boat battles of the war, Colin Walker received the Distinguished Service Order and was rested from operations. The navigator, Flying Officer Ken Simpson, was awarded the Distinguished Flying Cross. First wireless operator/dorsal gunner Flight Sergeant Eric Fuller and wireless operator/tail gunner Flight Sergeant Ray Goode, both received Distinguished Flying Medals. RAF flight engineer/waist gunner Sergeant 'Ted' Miles was posthumously commissioned as a pilot officer. Awarded a Mention in Despatches, and with pilots in demand, Flying Officer Jim Amiss was posted to another Sunderland, while 'Bill' Dowling was given command of UT-M (which had sunk U-332 and had helped sink U-106) and returned to operations with the rest of the crew. Sadly, DV968 failed to return from the Bay on 13 August after a message had been sent saying they were under attack by six Ju88s (inevitably from V/KG40).

Churchill and his entourage returned to Gibraltar and the Prime Minister was safely flown to London during the night of 4/5 June . *Bristol* flew his chief military assistant General Sir Hastings Ismay, and his staff, to Poole on 6 June , when the sound of highly tuned engines announced the strong escort of RAF fighters. BOAC continued to operate the Lisbon-Whitchurch service, though the flights were re-routed and flown at night. In 2009 a plaque was unveiled at Lisbon (Portela) Airport, followed a year later, by a service and unveiling ceremony at Bristol Airport dedicated 'To Those Who Never Came Back' on that fateful day.

CATALINA TO INDIA

The long-range exploits of *Guba 11* had attracted the Australian Government, and in 1940 Captain Taylor, now with Qantas, was chosen to navigate the first of eighteen Catalinas (positioned at Honolulu to preserve American neutrality) flown by the airlines operations manager Captain Lester Brain, over 7,000 miles of the Pacific for service with the

Catalina departing RAF Kogalla circa 1944. AUTHOR COLLECTION

Royal Australian Air Force. Not over-fond of the names chosen by his parents (Patrick, Gordon), from being called 'Bill' in the British Royal Flying Corps, Captain Taylor had come to be known as 'PG'

The idea of re-establishing contact between Australia and London arose again in October 1943, when talks between Hudson Fysh and BOAC considered the possibility (calculated by Qantas pilot Captain Crowther) of using specially adapted Catalinas to fly non-stop between the Swan River at Perth, on the west coast of Australia, and Trincomalee, on the east coast of Ceylon. The diplomatic mail could then be forwarded overland to Karachi to be put aboard a BOAC flying boat about to return to the UK. The introduction of Transport Sunderlands to the West Africa service had freed BOACs two remaining Catalinas, and the Air Ministry would supply both to Qantas, selected as the agent for BOAC. Trial crossings would be carried out by RAF Catalina crews based in Ceylon, despite opposition and misgivings from senior RAF (Transport Command) officials for placing such an undertaking in the hands of a civilian organization – and an Australian one at that!

Crewed by BOAC and seen with RAF serials and the white and blue roundels of RAF South East Asia Command on the wings and fuselage,

G-AGFL and FM respectively left Poole on the 11 and 17 of April 1943 bound for Trincomalee. The arrival of the two Catalinas at Ceylon on 21 and 25 April enabled RAF Catalina crews from No 222 (General Reconnaissance) Group to begin proving flights to Western Australia with Qantas personnel as supernumerary aircrew.

One hundred and sixty-eight years earlier, an enthusiastic teenage midshipman serving aboard the twenty-four gun frigate HMS Seahorse had felt Trincomalee to be the ' best harbour in the world'. Seventeen year old Horatio Nelson had yet to acquire the knowledge and seamanship that would earn him the undying gratitude of a nation however, and in his wildest of dreams would have had no conception of the problems of unsticking a supremely overloaded flying machine from those waters. An inland freshwater lake on the south of the island proved far more suitable.

The largest natural lake in Ceylon, Kogalla was an extensive RAF flying boat base, the Sunderlands and Catalinas coming to share the sheltered waters with the Qantas flying boats. The eventual five-strong fleet would all be named after the stars, essential to the astro (and dead reckoning) navigation required by the crews who would have to fly in non-radio conditions to avoid Japanese fighters. Each Catalina would have the name and a star painted below the rim of the cockpit, followed by the name of the airline, with a large identifying numeral (1-5) beneath the high tailplane. Given charge of the airlines Western (Indian Ocean) Division, Captain 'Bill' Crowther opened an office in Saint George's Terrace, Perth, and acquired crew lodgings at a hotel on the Esplanade and within the New Oriental Hotel at Galle, an old Ceylon trading township, encircled by the crumbling walls of an ancient fort.

With two crews fully conversant with the Catalina, Qantas formally took over from the RAF on the first day of June. Stripped of all non-essential military equipment (no oxygen, no de-icing) and fitted with a large (eight sectioned) auxiliary fuel tank in the fuselage by the engineers at Rose Bay, Captain Russell Tapp carefully lifted an overloaded *Altair Star* away from Nedlands and the Swan River at four thirty in the morning assisted by senior first officer and navigator Rex Senior. Engineer Frank Furniss and radio officer Glen Mumford completed the crew. A little over twenty eight hours later, the much lighter Catalina was landed on Koggala Lake after a somewhat tense and lonely flight across the ocean. The first eastbound service to Perth was flown on 10 July 10, with Captain Thomas taking *Vega Star* away eleven days later.

The base at Nedlands had been something of a nightmare to begin with, due in part to the secret nature of the air service, and the lack of co-operation from the Department of Civil Aviation, which appeared to have taken a dim view of the proceedings, echoing the RAF view of the first Atlantic Ferry flights. Allotted a derelict site on a bank of the river,

Catalina '5' *Spica Star*, Nedlands, Western Australia.
AUTHOR COLLECTION

with no hangar and no slipway (as at Hamworthy), the initial maintenance was performed in the open or in an open ended shack. The aircraft had to be manhandled to and from the water. With no refuelling facilities, each had to be taxied some 3 miles upriver to Crawley Bay, the superbly equipped American base of Fleet Air Wing 10 that had operated Catalinas since March 1942, until the situation at Nedlands improved.

Though primarily directed at flying diplomatic mail to London, along with microfilmed mail for the armed forces, the restricted interior (due to the extra fuel tanks) could take up to three passengers, usually military officers travelling in 'mufti'. There was precious little in the way of comfort, for the three chairs designed by the engineers at Rose Bay practically filled the space between the side blisters. At just under 3,600 nautical miles, it was the longest passenger service in the world. Though adequate, the sandwiches and thermos drink was a far cry from the bar of an Empire flying boat. It was noisy. And you couldn't smoke. But the view of the starlit night skies was something else, provided you ignored the danger of having to cross Japanese held islands in strict blackout conditions.

It wasn't exactly a honey of a trip for the crews either. Filled with nearly 2,000 gallons (some 7 tons) of fuel and effectively exceeding the recommended all up weight by some 4 tons overall, the low-lying Catalina sat even deeper in the water during the longish take-off run, having to overcome a higher than usual bow wave before rising, with engines blaring, onto the step when the floats were retracted to coax it into the air. Pilots exercised individual ingenuity in leaving the surface during light or nil wind conditions, when the 4 mile run up to the bridge at Fremantle was barely adequate, the locals treated to a clear view of the faces inside as the Catalina skimmed the structure to begin a slow, climbing turn over Rottnest Island.

Maintaining 1,000 feet off the virtually deserted coastline of Western Australia, full use was made of the automatic pilot for the 683 miles to Exmouth Gulf, reached towards the end of the day, when the aircraft was turned out into the Indian Ocean for the long flight to Ceylon. Maintaining just under 100 knots at 2,000 feet over the water, the throttles were regularly pulled back to reduce power, and balance the airspeed, to give an economic flow of around 22 gallons per hour for each engine. It took ten hours for the weight to come down to normal. Designed for military use, the flying boats were uninsulated and cold, particularly at night, and uniforms were supplemented with the heavier and warm flying suits and fur-lined boots issued to their service counterparts. Brief and limited weather information was received around midnight, though the Morse could not be acknowledged, for the slightest carrier wave could be picked up by enemy radar.

Two bunks were fitted in the cabin for off duty crew, though everyone was aware of the atrocities meted out to downed aircrew, causing the ears to subconsciously register any change in engine note for the first seventeen hours or so, after which a forced landing would be just that, without added complications. The loading during those critical hours ruled out struggling along on a single engine and until fuel dumping valves were introduced, an unforeseen landing, even away from enemy occupied territory, was likely to seriously damage the hull. A safe arrival and rest at Galle, was followed by a steady climb to between 10,000 and 12,000 feet to contact the high-level winds for the return, a factor denied young military aircrew engaged on equally clandestine operations.

On 23 April 1943, the evening after Aub Koch's swim to safety, Australian Catalinas had begun a two year mine-laying campaign against Japanese held ports and sea-lanes: crewed typically by two pilots, navigator, first and second engineers, first and second wireless operators, a rigger and armourer. Each mission required celestial navigation during the hours of darkness, the final run-in made on a timed leg from a known landmark, sometimes in the face of searchlights and gunfire, though most involved one or two crews operating independently to confuse the enemy. Attached beneath both wings, the torpedo-shaped mines were set to explode at the first indication of a ship, or later, in the hope of destroying a convoy, and were carried into the target area just a few hundred feet above the sea to avoid enemy radar. The 'drop' had to be extremely precise to prevent the mine exploding on contact with the water. Based in the Darwin area, the crews of 76 Wing performed most of these operations, flying up to three missions each week, with more than one area targeted on the night, though the last thing you needed was to be setting off for home in daylight with the risk of running into fighters. Particularly the Zero, the design of which Howard Hughes claimed to have been copied from his record breaking H-1 monoplane racer.

Operated in complete secrecy, at night, on instruments, and without visual navigation checks, the black painted flying boats came to be known as 'Black Cats', though their achievements would not begin to be told until well after the end of the war.

As with the military crews, the Qantas personnel were unable to talk of their work in public and were subjected to mild abuse by those believing them to be too far south of the war zone, as Jim Peers had experienced in South Africa. Despite the efforts of Hudson Fysh, they received no recognition whatsoever for their long range operations. To

This is to certify that ______________________
has spent more than 24 hours continuously in the air on a regular air service, thus entitling him to membership of the rare and...

SECRET ORDER OF THE DOUBLE SUNRISE

Time taken on journey ____ *hrs.* ____ *mins.* ★ *Qantas Empire Airways, Long Range Operations*
Month __________ *Year, 19*____ ______________ *Commander*

Long-range passenger certificate. AUTHOR COLLECTION

rectify the situation, Captain Crowther awarded a brass star (the 'Crowther Cross') to each crew member on completion of four ocean crossings. The first had been presented to those making three Pacific crossings delivering the first PBYs to Australia.

For their part, passengers received a certificate for having uniquely witnessed two successive dawns during some twenty-seven hours aloft, though strong headwinds might have added another seven hours to the flight time. Edged in gold, the certificate began by declaring that the recipient, whose name had been entered by hand, had spent more than twenty-four hours continuously in the air on a regular service, thus entitling him to the rare and Secret Order of the Double Sunrise, the words framed by a banner supported by the smiling red faces of two suns rising above the ocean. Underneath, a Catalina was depicted over a wave flecked ocean surmounted by stars, the banked wing encroaching on a semi-circle of flying fish enclosing a pair of pilot wings and a single red star. The journey time was recorded in hours and minutes, together with the month, the year and the qualifying words Qantas Empire Airways Long Range Operations, personally signed by the 'Commander'.

Two more Catalinas left Poole for Australia in August, *Rigel Star* commencing services with Captain Ambrose on the fifteenth, followed by Captain Thomas and *Antares Star* on 27 September . Employed mainly in doping the fabric of the wartime civilian flying boats, Ruth Wiseman would fortunately retain a few snapshots of her time at a maintenance

Long-range Catalina *Rigel Star* at Rose Bay.
COURTESY CAPTAIN HENRY DE COURCIER.

base at Rose Bay, the shot of a moored *Rigel Star* clearly showing the identifying 3 on its fin, while on the back was written 'we put in extra fuel tanks to do the trip across the Indian Ocean, South Africa, to UK'. The weekly operations continued until October when there were sufficient trained crews to operate three times every fortnight, a third pilot (second officer) added to the existing complement of captain, first officer, navigating officer, radio officer and flight engineer. But having made the long and dangerous ocean crossing, it was found that it was taking another three days or so for the vital diplomatic mail (and passengers) to be forwarded overland to India. In November 1943, Captain Crowther completed the first extended service to Karachi, by flying an extra 1,500 miles up the eastern seaboard of India. A fifth Catalina, *Spica Star,* would arrive in May.

Chapter Seven

Thoughts of Peace

Poole Terminal

Dixie Clipper had carried President Roosevelt to the January 1943 meeting of Allied leaders at Casablanca, and the President had celebrated his birthday aboard on the way home. In August another conference was held at Quebec and while discussions centred on the future of Italy and France, and the invasion of Normandy, Churchill signed a secret agreement with Roosevelt that would lead to Britain sharing her nuclear technology with a nation more able to develop its potential. Accompanied by his wife and daughter aboard the RMS Queen Mary for the outward crossing, Churchill chose to return aboard the battleship HMS Renown. Captain Tony Loraine and *Bangor* brought the rest of the British contingent to Poole during the afternoon of 29 September . Escorted by the RAF, the party included Foreign Secretary Anthony Eden, Chief of Staff General Alan Brooke, First Lord of the Admiralty Sir Dudley Pound, Air Chief Marshal Sir Charles Portal and Lord Louis Mountbatten, Chief of Combined Operations.

Security was vital. In 1941, Rogers, the Warmwell airfield intelligence officer, a former professional golfer in Germany, had taken a call one night from the Wareham police asking him to interrogate a suspect. A survivor of the Battle of Britain, Pilot Officer Harold 'Birdie' Bird-Wilson, had gone along with him and on arrival at the police station they were told that soldiers stationed at Lulworth Cove had captured a suspected fifth columnist in one of the beach huts. When found, he was wearing just gym shorts and shoes with only a bus ticket and a ladies coat button in his possession. After considerable interrogation the man had confessed to being a German, planted in England a few years before the outbreak of war. A go-between from one of the aircraft factories and another contact, on this particular night he had been waiting to be picked up by an E-boat. The coat button, which had a blue cross on a white background, was his proof of identity.

The medical staff at the Carter Pottery premises were in as good a position as any to suspect anything unusual, though an Admiralty officer performed much the same function as Captain Carter at Airways House. On 16 July 1943 a passenger named Pierre Neukermans was among the arrivals from Lisbon, having declared he was a Belgian who had escaped the Germans. Though passed through the examination room, he continued to be watched by security officers. On the first of November, another arrival from Lisbon also declared he was a refugee from the Germans. Born to German parents, Oswald Job had lived in Paris for some thirty-two years, but suspicions were aroused and he was later found to have invisible ink concealed inside a key. Job would be executed at Pentonville Prison in March 1944. Neukermans would be executed at Wormwood Scrubs in June, some eight months after landing in Dorset.

In the meantime, a naval Walrus had unexpectedly given a young wartime Wren her first experience of a flying boat. Having requested a transfer from catering to the signals branch, on completing her training 20 year old June Bamford had been issued with a blue 'S' patch to sew on her sleeve and was posted out to Tanganyika (Tanzania) East Africa. To take almost three months, the journey began aboard a troopship at Goorock in Scotland, where 500 servicewomen and 6,000 men were packed aboard the American liner SS Argentina.

Allocated one of twelve bunks in a cabin intended for four peacetime passengers, June had her first taste of Coca-Cola during the convoys zigzagging, U-boat avoiding, passage to Durban. After three weeks ashore, she joined a British India Company liner which took another three zigzagging weeks to convey the contingent of Wrens and civilians up the coast to

Wrens and Walrus. MRS JUNE TOPHAM (NÉE BAMFORD).

Mombassa. Allowed to work at RNAS Tanga (HMS Kilele) rather than in Nairobi, June found she was one of seven Wrens and a handful of nurses who were to be flown, three at a time, by Walrus from Port Reitz. When her turn came, she was sat next to the pilot, who proceeded to fly at low level down the coast, though she was too busy watching to feel anxious, enjoying the sensation of speed and seeing frightened native African boys jumping out of their canoes as the noisy little biplane bore down on them.

On landing at the dusty grass airfield, which had apparently been carved from a former coconut plantation at a cost of £1 a tree, the girls were met by a party of officers which included a grinning 22 year old wearing dark glasses and an Observer brevet. Unknown to her at the time, Geoff Topham had served aboard the aircraft carrier Ark Royal since its commissioning and had survived the famous Swordfish attack that had crippled the battleship Bismark in May 1941. Billeted in a former hotel on the sea front, a couple of miles away from the malaria infested airfield, the girls enjoyed swimming, sailing and regular dancing in the Tanga club. In October 1943 June was chosen to be part of a publicity shoot featuring 'The War Effort and Wrens Overseas', when the girls were positioned about the Walrus (possibly L2664 of 788 Squadron) which regularly flew supplies, personnel and mail between Tanga, Mombasa and Nairobi. June and Geoff kept in touch and were married after the war, when they came to live just over the road from the former RNAS base at Sandbanks.

A further batch of six Mark 3 Sunderlands had been delivered to BOAC in March for the West Africa route. Twelve more had arrived by October, the month ML728 (later *Haslemere*) began a Poole-Cairo service, later extended to Karachi and then Rangoon, when the seating was increased to twenty-two day passengers. With the invasion of occupied Europe planned for 1944, the military Catalinas began leaving Poole at the end of December 1943, the 210 Squadron Headquarters disbanded to enable the Hamworthy slipway and hard-standing to be extended for exercises involving the loading of tanks and vehicles on to landing craft. From February, DC-3s began flying from Croydon to Shannon, ending the Poole shuttle operated by *Golden Hind* and the three Transport Sunderlands, two of which would be named *Hadfield* and *Hampshire.* The unnamed third would catch fire while refuelling at Calcutta in exactly two years time. By now RAF Hamworthy had been taken over by 116 Wing of RAF Transport Command to control the BOAC Sunderlands on the India service, the resultant ferrying of some 250 transport aircrew to Cairo maintaining a constant supply of military aircraft into Burma and India. Briefed by specialist officers at Hamworthy, the M Flight crews received instructions in the air from 44 Group as they flew out to Gibraltar, Tunisia, Cairo and Karachi, returning to Poole after an absence of some twelve to sixteen days.

Ivor Faulconer would have particular reason to remember the March of 1944. On completing his training at Lawrenny Ferry, in December 1941 he had begun a two year association with the battleship King George V which had helped sink the Bismark and was equipped with two Walrus flying boats.

22 year-old Sub-Lt. Faulconer.
© IVOR FAULCONER.

A typical crew comprised the pilot, observer and air gunner and to avoid sending all three to a watery grave in severe sea states, the gunnery officer in charge of catapult operations would launch as the ship began to roll, the slight delay in execution ensuring the little flying boat would be safely projected onto a horizontal path. Prior to the launch, the pilot's raised hand signified the crew were readying themselves and was dropped only when he was satisfied they were ready to go, when the 3 ton amphibian was propelled from rest to 65 miles an hour in just 50 feet. Pressing himself back into the padded seat, Ivor had learnt to curl the fingers of his left hand immediately above the throttle lever, rather than on it, to avoid them being jerked backwards by the acceleration (five times that of gravity), causing a disastrous loss of power. It was equally desirable to check that the camera hatch, set in the floor of the cockpit, had been closed before landing! Having accumulated some 500 hours on the Walrus, he was posted to No 784 Naval Air Squadron, a night fighter training unit based at Drem, to the south-east of Edinburgh, equipped with the long-range Fairey Fulmar.

The threat of the long-range Focke-Wulf Kuriers of 1/KG40 based at Bordeaux-Mérignac, subsequently prompted the Admiralty to draft three of the squadrons crews for duty aboard an escort carrier on the Gibraltar run, despite their inexperience. Ivor and his colleagues undertook a speedy refresher course of dummy deck landings at night at RNAS Crail, before making a few brief night landings in the Clyde on HMS Ravager, an Attacker-Class carrier built in America from the hull of a merchant ship. The Fulmars were then embarked aboard the equally newly commissioned HMS Nairana, a British built Vindex-Class escort carrier. Returning from a low level, aircraft interception exercise (LAI) in the Bay of Biscay on 3 March 1944, Ivor was unable to communicate with the carrier due to a failed r/t and hit the Rounddown (ships stern) as it was rising and falling in a 60 foot high corkscrewing motion. The impact broke the Fulmar in two and with nothing left behind the rear cockpit of the observer/radio operator, the front collapsed onto the propeller. Of no further use to anyone, the two halves of DR673 were unceremoniously heaved over the side. It could have been a lot, lot worse for both fliers.

As the summer of 1944 approached, the harbours from Felixstowe to Swansea became packed with over 4,000 craft and nearly a quarter of a million soldiers assembled for the channel crossing. Dorset received thousands of American troops, who would leave Poole and Weymouth as Force 'O' of the invasion. In the meantime, rocket-firing Typhoons and night-fighter Mosquitos left RAF Station Hurn to respectively attack German ground installations and defend the night skies over the packed south-western ports. Hundreds of locally built landing craft crammed Holes Bay, and with no room for flying boats in the congested harbour, RAF Hamworthy closed down at the end of April. BOAC's flying boats were moved to Pembroke Dock and with the staff of Airways House about to be flown to Neyland in South Wales, Bob Rayner had to provide another signed consent from his parents.

One of the best-kept secrets of the entire war, the landings were made on the beaches of Normandy during the early morning of 6 June rather than at Calais, the shortest and expected crossing. Held at bay from the invasion area by patrolling naval vessels, and low flying Sunderlands, the U-boats had retreated to bases in North Germany and Norway. The threat continued in the Atlantic however, where their increased armament caused them to fight it out on the surface if encountered by a lone flying boat, rather than crash dive as before.

On 23 August 1944, Flying Officer Duff of 210 Squadron left Poole a half hour or so before midnight to test his Leigh Light on the Helwick Lightship stationed in the Bristol Channel. Arriving back at the harbour in the early hours of Thursday morning, he circled overhead for nearly half an hour while the flare path was being laid and on given a green from the water controllers pinnace at four thirty, appeared to be making a normal approach. A burst of power announced the Catalina had overshot the alighting area however, and AD-E passed overhead the upwind pinnace at around 100 feet before disappearing into the darkness. A crash was reported a few minutes later. But the search parties were hampered by a sea mist and it was some time before the wreckage of FP287 was discovered close by a naval camp (part of HMS Turtle) on Long Island. Of the twelve aboard, only four survived the impact which destroyed both wings and the whole of the front of the flying boat. Among the casualties, 22 year old pilot Peter Rutherford Duff, RAFVR, is remembered by his former Boys High School at Umtali, Southern Rhodesia and at the Brookwood Military Cemetery.

Strangely quiet after so much invasion activity, Poole received the returning BOAC flying boats in September, the month the big Boeings were also returned.

BOAC BOEINGS

Victor Reginald Pitcher had served the local Home Guard on leaving Eastbourne Grammar School and in 1942 had volunteered his services to the RAF at the Long Room of Lords Cricket Ground. Subsequently passed to an Initial Training Wing at Cambridge University, he was taught to fly by the instructors and Tiger Moths of No 22 EFTS at Marshalls airfield. Shipped out to South Africa within the Empire Training Scheme, with his forage cap displaying the white flash of trainee aircrew, the perspex windows of the inevitable Anson navigation trainers clearly revealed just how many stars were visible in the southern skies. Well built and over 6 foot tall, he loved the climate and open air life, so different to war-starved Britain, and was chosen to represent the RAF as a welterweight boxer and as a cricketer for the Combined Services team. Boarding a Castle Ship for the return to Britain, the cadets were delayed at sea until an outbreak of smallpox was isolated, when they were landed at New York. Passed to an American base, they were issued with superb American uniforms and continued training in America. Enjoying the experience, Vic was in no hurry to return but on eventually boarding an American troopship was issued with leaflets detailing how to approach and deal with the English! Landed at Liverpool he found the RAF had lost his records and was sent home on leave before posted to 105 Operational Training Unit at RAF Bramcote (Warwickshire).

Specialist navigator at Baltimore.
© VIC PITCHER

Tasked with training crews for 44 Group RAF Transport Command, the unit was equipped with the twin engined Wellington bomber designed by Barnes Wallis, creator of the dam-buster bouncing bomb. Graded 'Exceptional' Vic was loaned to BOAC as a specialist navigator, and on completing the course at Croydon received a civilian licence and a passport signed by Anthony Eden classifying him as a 'government official' to avoid problems when landing in neutral countries. With excellent credentials, the 20 year-old had been posted to BOACs No 3 Line fleet of Boeing 314As at Baltimore, commanded by Flight Captain Kelly Rogers. Everything was impressive, from the sheer size of the flying boats and their modern equipment, to the appearance and calibre of the crews.

Irishman Kelly-Rogers would become director of Aer Lingus after the war, while traffic manager Ross Stainton would be appointed chairman of BOAC and receive a knighthood. Provided with a beautifully tailored uniform, the young navigator had no qualms about throwing his UK issue away. Five double crews were lodged at Baltimore where the Benjamin family went out of their way to make him feel at home.

Flying such long distances required a high standard of competence from everyone. Each aircraft carried a double shift of pilots, navigators, radio operators and engineers, with the purser given charge of two stewards, remembered by Vic for their dignified aura and for having trained in Switzerland. Designed to seat up to seventy-seven passengers, in BOAC service the Boeings normally accommodated twenty to ensure maximum comfort during the 3,500 mile Atlantic crossing, usually flown at an economical 110 knots. Vics first flight was made aboard *Berwick* on 19 July 1944, landing at Botwood nine and three quarter hours later and Foynes after a further thirteen and a half hours in the air. The return to Botwood aboard *Bristol* took twelve hours and as many minutes, the round trip ended at Baltimore on the 22nd after a further nine and a quarter hours. The stop at Foynes would at the very least have given the young navigator time to sample a rather special cup of coffee.

During an early visit to Foynes, Irish Prime Minister Éamonn de Valera had realised the restaurant needed to be upgraded to present a first class image of Ireland to the world. It would also need to offer the best of Irish food and drink. Born in County Clare, Brendan O'Regan had studied catering abroad before making a name for himself in Ireland. Offered the task, he had the interior redesigned to present a strong Irish theme, before employing well educated restaurant staff, but would have had no idea of the consequences of employing Joe Sheridan as his chef.

Bad weather had subsequently forced an American Clipper to return to Foynes after hours of battling strong winter headwinds. Realising the chilled passengers needed something more than hot coffee to warm them up, Joe had added brown sugar and a tot of whiskey, with freshly whipped cream floated across the top. Asked whether he was serving Brazilian coffee, he had said No, it was 'Irish Coffee'. The rest, as they say, is history.

Harry Pusey was also at Foynes. The previous August he had celebrated his twenty-first birthday with an appropriate number of well wishers, from the embassy and the other airlines, within the Avenue da Liberdade. The festivities in the Portuguese café had gone rather too well however and though he was easily the youngest there, some of the senior and more staid airline officials considered he was to blame for the 'conduct unbecoming of men of a nation at war'. He had also incurred the displeasure of a particular senior official for taking Launch 22 for a test run on the Tagus at

Christmas, following a double engine change, and had received a posting back to England! Given the choice of a landplane or a flying boat, he had had no hesitation in choosing the latter and in January 1944 had hitched a ride back with Captain Craig and *Berwick.*

Without todays sophistication, the wartime met. forecasts tended to suffer from the time factor, and at sunrise the crew found themselves on the wrong side of a frontal depression and the German-occupied port of Brest, having been blown much more to the east by unexpectedly strong north-westerly winds. Harry spent the rest of the flight within the astro dome watching for enemy fighters.

Landing at Foynes and looking forward to his forthcoming marriage at Beaulieu Abbey to Norma, a Cornish lass employed as a cost accountant with Imperial Airways at Hythe, he was surprised to be buttonholed by Captain Bailey who told him to wash and brush up before being shown around the base, ignoring Harry's protestations that he was far too tired and just wanted to go home. Unknown to him, the operations superintendent at Cairo had died and Captain Bailey was about to fly out to replace him. Harry was to hold the fort at Foynes, though this was the first he had heard of it.

They had met before. Naval launches had begun training at Poole while *Guba* was carrying out 'circuits and bumps', causing considerable frustration and annoyance to the senior pilot who had had to land on unnecessarily rough water every time around. After the final landing, he had climbed up onto his seat and shaken his fist at the offenders, when the hand had come into contact with the arc of the port propeller, just feet above the cockpit. Harry had met him as he had come ashore, with his r/t lead wrapped around the stump as a tourniquet. An artificial hand had eventually been fitted and Frank Bailey's favourite party piece was to slap an unsuspecting newcomer on the back, causing the previously loosened empennage to dramatically leave its owner – to the amusement of everyone else in the room!

Within a short time of settling in at Foynes, Harry had been intrigued to discover he was billeted next door to a German employed at the electricity station at Ardnacrusha – some 25 miles away! The flying boat terminal and main electricity generating plants had been protected by surrounding gun batteries since 1938 and with diplomatic mail and senior military personnel among the civilians arriving from America, fears for the security of the base had caused the Irish security services to suggest that BOAC replace virtually all their staff with Irish nationals. Given the remarkable distance the man had to travel to work, Harry thought he was obviously a spy, positioned to watch the comings and goings of the flying boats, but was more than likely under surveillance by the 'cloak and dagger' boys. As may have been the young acting operations superintendant, who remembers his stay with fondness and amusement and still possesses the blackthorne stick presented to him by IRA sympathizers at Listowel for joining in with their drunken renderings of anti-British ballads!

Incidents, some amusing, some less so, were inevitable during the long ocean crossings which taxed both the aircraft and their occupants. On one occasion, faulty bonding had caused the flight deck to be strangely lit by the discharge of electricity known as St Elmos Fire. On another, an imperious demand from a King's Messenger that they turn back to Foynes, after he had awoken to discover he had left his diplomatic bag behind, had been flatly refused! It was put on the next flight out. Of the many personalities seen aboard, Vic would particularly remember the comedienne Joyce Grenfell, the actor Charles Laughton – and Yehudi Menhuin. On the last day of August 1944, *Berwick* had suffered an engine failure and fire in the starboard inner engine after leaving Botwood, thought to have started in the feathering mechanism. The engineer had crawled into the wing with an extinguisher but had quickly used up the canisters on the flight deck. Sent below for another, Vic had found the violin virtuoso silently practising on a finger board on the lower of two bunks and could not help commenting that Nero had (also) fiddled while Rome burned!

With flames and smoke trailing from the wing, where both engines had been shut down, an S.O.S. had been sent and a dive made from 6,000 feet to sea-level in preparation for a 'ditching' and release of the emergency dinghies. In the event, the fire had been doused and they had made it back to Botwood, but the radio had packed up after the distress message was sent and they had been met by a relieved but tearful operations assistant, engaged to one of the engineers. Repairs were made overnight and leaving Botwood the very next morning they had landed, if a little late, at Foynes after a flight approaching twelve hours and twenty minutes.

With Poole added to the Boeing schedule from September 1944, a stopover might be made at Natal before crossing to Belém, with returning ferry crews dropped off at Nassau before continuing on to Bermuda. Without pressurised cabins, crews would normally fly below 10,000 feet, while a descent to 1,000 was often essential to avoid stronger winds, when the breaking surf was visible to everyone on board. Despite reports, the meteorological officers at Foynes refused to believe that such big flying boats could be forced to travel backwards by the winds. Departing for Botwood on 16 October , *Berwick* was forced to return to the Shannon almost fourteen hours later due to engine failure. Three days later they tried again, when the winds were estimated at 50 to 60 knots, the return ending a thirteen-hour battle with winds so severe that the flame floats (dropped to check drift) had reappeared in front of the aircraft! The westbound crossing was cancelled for the remainder of the winter. Swiftly re-charted to West Africa and the West Indies, *Berwick* reached Bathurst on the 22nd after virtually nineteen hours in the air, with half the time flown on three engines! The journey resumed six days later, and Trinidad was reached after twenty hours and twenty minutes. Two days later they began an eleven hour flight to Bermuda, followed by a seven hour, seven minute return to Baltimore. Crews had their own rest and dining area, but Vic was always delighted to be served a cooked breakfast, as only BOAC stewards knew how, at his bunk.

With most of the ocean uncharted, navigators had to be proficient in celestial navigation despite bumpy conditions, when Vic would be firmly held by an engineer as he took his star shots with a sextant from an opened hatch. Though glimpsed briefly between gaps in the clouds, he had come to recognise several by their (perceived) colour, such as the blue tinted Vega and yellow Capella, while the planets of Mars and Saturn appeared to respectively glow a distinctive red and yellow. Though associated with the C-Class flagship, Canopus was not the brightest star in the heavens, for the bluish white brilliance of Sirius, believed to have shone for three hundred, million, years, had marked climatic events for the Egyptians and Greeks and guided islanders about the Pacific. Vic had repeatedly found magnetic anomalies in compass readings when far from any land mass, caused by splits in the earth's crust deep below the ocean, but nothing was known about the phenomenon at the time and his observations had not been taken any further.

The winter Poole-Lisbon service averaged seven and a half hours, followed by a twelve-hour flight to Bathurst and an eleven-hour crossing of the South Atlantic to Belém, on the north-east coast of Brazil, before flying on to Trinidad, Bermuda and Baltimore. On two occasions Vic flew direct from Bathurst to Trinidad in twenty hours and twice flew the direct distance between Bermuda and Lisbon in nineteen. His flying career might well have come to a painful end at Belém however, where the Boeing mooring was on the Paré, part of the Amazon network of rivers, some 60 miles inland from the coast.

Navigators usually used the side hatch to give the radio operator a hand during mooring – though never intended to be taken literally. On one occasion the rope had caught around his arm and the 30 odd tons of flying boat had started to swing away in the strong current. With his arm providing the only contact with the shore and beginning to be pulled from the socket, Vic had screamed at the radio operator to cut it off! It seemed the only thing to do. But with great presence of mind, Paddy Nickell had flung himself head-first from the hatch clutching a machete and had severed the offending rope, though cutting Vic's wrist in the process. Visiting him in hospital, Captain Bill Craig had said "You OK Vic? Good. As you and Paddy each have one good arm we should be alright to take off. " Which they did!

Crews usually stayed overnight at the Montego Bay Hotel, Jamaica, and Vic remembers being invited on more than one occasion to accompany a steward to a soirée hosted by Noël Coward; his hillside Caribbean villa at

Blue Harbour, near Port Maria, frequented by some of the best loved celebrities of the period.

A less welcome, though intriguing, memory concerns a passenger flown to South America early in 1945. On landing at the neutral Lisbon, Vic had wandered into the Casino where an individual was displaying the airs of a wealthy millionaire. Back on board, a steward had told him that he was a senior official travelling under an alias to escape from Germany, and several people seemed aware he was on his way to Argentina. It is now known this was the primary route (to Spain and to Argentina) used by war criminals to escape from Europe. Me108 Taifuns and two Heinkel 111s (given long-range tanks and two bunks in the bomb bay) were expressly based at Schwerin airfield, south-east of Lübeck, to fly escapees to South America via Spain.

Wherever he went, the efficiency of the BOAC staff, in the air and on the ground, seemed quite remarkable. None more so than at Poole, where he had watched with interest the arrival of a launch carrying an attractive blue eyed blond with a slim station assistant stripe on the sleeve of her smart uniform. The vivacious 18 year-old had immediately claimed his heart. Having worked as a hotel receptionist, Patricia Kelly was used to dealing with people and had been selected to accompany the VIPs to London aboard the two special railway carriages. She also prepared the loading sheets for the flying boats and would sleep overnight, and alone, within the Carter warehouse as night watchman for the high value (bullion) cargoes. Flying in to Dorset just once a month, Vic knew he could not afford to waste any time and they became engaged on only their second meeting!

In March 1945, Captain Bernard Frost took *Berwick* away from Poole as a finalé for the Boeings, which after nearly 600 Atlantic crossings were about to be replaced by Lockheed Constellations. In April they began operating a thrice weekly service between Baltimore and Darell's Island Bermuda. On subsequently arriving at Baltimore for servicing, each was stripped of the drab wartime paint and furnished to accommodate up to fifty-five day passengers rather than the twenty or so carried across the Atlantic. Posted to Montreal for the new service, Vic married Pat at Saint Peters church in Parkstone, when the bride left BOAC to join her husband.

The services lasted until January 1948, when Captain John 'Oscar' Burgess finally returned *Bristol* to Baltimore. Bought by the General Phoenix Corporation, *Bristol*, *Berwick* and *Bangor* languished at their moorings until bought by World Airways, founded by Benjamin Pepper in March. The airline also bought *Dixie Clipper* and *American Clipper* (the last of the 314s) *Pacific Clipper* and *Anzac Clipper*, with the intention of operating unscheduled services between New York and San Juan, on the Caribbean island of Puerto Rico. *California* and *Dixie Clipper* would provide spares. But in 1950 the cash troubled airline was sold for 50,000 dollars. By then, *American Clipper* and *Anzac Clipper* had been scrapped (believed at San

Boeing 314A *Bangor* at Baltimore. VIC PITCHER.

Diego). *Berwick* and *Bangor* were broken up at Baltimore. Bought privately, *Bristol* remained moored for another year until sunk by a squall, and was later retrieved and broken up for scrap.

Posted to Dorval and then Whitchurch, on hearing that BOAC proposed to employ only pilot/navigators, Vic joined the Airways Aero Club, moving from the Tiger Moth to the delightful Miles Hawk. With fond memories of Poole, the family home was moved to Dorset and after navigating Constellations, Stratocruisers and Comets around the world, he retired in 1965 to take up executive positions with BP and Shell.

Retaining fond memories of the 'good people' met in his flying career, he was himself honoured by being elected to the chair of the International Airline Navigators Council. He also received a Master Air Navigator Certificate from the Court of the Guild of Air Pilots and Air Navigators in recognition of his 'skill, experience and service in the profession of aviation'. As chairman, he fulfilled the wish of the American council members by awarding the President of America with the Air Travellers Medal of Our Lady of Loretto, instigated in 1920 by Pope Benedict the Fifteenth. The letter of acknowledgement, personally signed by John F Kennedy, remains among his most treasured possessions.

HYTHE- CLASS

BOAC had lost two Transport Sunderlands in 1944: G-AGES crashing on Mount Bradon, Ireland, in bad weather while returning to Foynes from West Africa in July, and IB crashing at El Taurub, Tawaali on the Egyptian/Libyan border in November. Another five had been delivered and in preparation for the re-opening of the former 'Empire' services, the fleet had begun to be upgraded to airline standard. The stripping of the interiors and refitting took about six weeks to complete and though

Hythe *Harlequin*: nose turret retracted, metal skin exposed.

they would vary, the three basic configurations comprised the (H1) fitting of sixteen passenger seats, the (H2) addition of a C-Class promenade deck and the (H3) addition of a further eight seats to accommodate twenty-four passengers. Begun at Hythe in January 1945, the later named *Hamilton* was the first to be modified.

From March, black, four lettered RAF Transport Command codes were applied to the rear of the RAF roundels on the fuselage sides. The letters OQZM, for example, indicated that M (later named *Hythe*) was a Sunderland (Z) operated by (Q) BOAC. Each of the four, nine cylinder,

Hythe *Hailsham* partly submerged off Isle of Wight.
MRS MOLLIE HARMAN

Sunderland pilot Bob Harwood. CAPT. R.E. HARWOOD

engines was upgraded to Pegasus 38 standard (1,030 horsepower) to support up to forty-seven passengers and crew and 6,500 pounds of mail. Three extra dinghies were stowed aboard. The retractable nose turret remained, but not wishing to delay the return of fare-paying services, the rear turret position was simply faired-over rather than fit the streamlined tail cone that would identify the forthcoming Sandringham. The last to be converted, ZS (*Hanbury*) and ZP (*Halstead*) would be used for training.

The RAF codes were gradually replaced by black civil registration letters, outlined in silver with an underlining flash of red, white and blue. But with the end of the European War, the Sunderlands received an overall silver finish with uncluttered black civil registration letters on both sides of the hull, beneath the tailplane and across the wing, though the roundels were faintly discernible beneath the lighter paintwork. A Union Jack was painted forward of the rudder and the Speedbird logo positioned beneath the rim of the nose turret position. The Hythe-Class fleet comprised *Hadfield, Hampshire, Hailsham, Hanwell, Hamble, Hamilton, Harlequin, Hawkesbury, Haslemere, Henley, Howard, Hobart, Hythe, Hudson, Honduras, Huntingdon, Hotspur, Himalaya, Hungerford, Harwich, Hunter, Hanbury and Halstead*. Delivered in April 1946, the stripped out *Helmsdale* would be used to carry cargo.

On 18 July 1945, 24 year old Flight Lieutenant Harwood joined Captain Wynn aboard *Hadfield* for a return flight to Invergordon, and nine days later helped deliver the Sunderland to Hythe, the first of several twenty-minute shuttles.

For some, the turmoil of war had brought the substance of dreams to a reality, made all the more special to those given a modest start in life, their wartime experiences enabling post-war careers quite unthinkable before the conflict. Unaware of any such future, 14 year-old Robert Edmund Harwood had left school after an elementary education at Saint Mary Cray in Kent. Among his many childhood memories, he recalled the advice of his father, who had seen an awesome loss of life with the Machine Gun Corps in the First World War and whom he was to lose within the next two years. If war comes, he was told, do something for decent pay until you get killed, don't just be shot at for sixpence a day!

War was coming and there were notices advertising a RAF sergeant pilot's pay at thirteen shillings and sixpence, and that of a wireless operator or air gunner ten shillings and sixpence, when most could expect no more than two shillings a day. Unable to satisfy pilot training requirements due to his lack of higher education, 'Bob' had volunteered as a wireless operator/air gunner and was surprised when the so-called 'phoney war' period allowed six months deferment after recruit training. By then the RAF had become acutely short of pilots and as a measure of the times, a guiding spirit had emerged in the form of Group Captain Robinson, a kindly officer tasked to remedy the shortage by selecting suitable candidates for pilot training from those without the formal requirements. More than once he rescued Bob from difficult and searching questions posed by the Selection Board at RAF Uxbridge, inspiring and surprising him during a personal interview afterwards by saying he believed he possessed an inborn brightness and could succeed.

Aircraftman Second Class Harwood R.E applied himself to the task at No 2 Ground School of an RAF Initial Training Wing, though without the relaxations of the more academic. For him the future demanded study and more study, a readily given promise to write monthly of his progress ensuring only the best from the aspiring pilot. Sent to Canada within the Empire Air Training Scheme, he was taught to fly de Havilland Tiger Moth biplanes at No 20 EFTS at Oshawa, where many instructors were seasoned bush pilots. He and three others were then passed to No 16 Service Flying Training School at Hagersville, Ontario, for conversion to twin-engined Avro Ansons, where they were met with unreserved generosity from classmates and instructors alike. The long hours of study and the letters of progress home, all bore fruit, when after 216 flying hours he was awarded his wings and Sergeant stripes. Group Captain Robinson now left his young protégé, the newly fledged pilot aware of the debt he and many others owed this dedicated officer. Though disappointed with a posting to No 31 General Reconnaissance School at Charlottetown, the thought of failure helped renew the dedication to study. Navigation had to be of RAF Observer standard and at Anticosti Island, Bob was relieved to find a natural liking for the subject.

Having absorbed all that could be taught, he was returned to Britain and to No 4 Operational Training Unit at RAF Invergordon. Unimpressed at first sight by the Catalina and Sunderlands, he chose to fly Sunderlands, simply because 'they were our own'. The first flight dispelled any doubts however, bringing an unexpected thrill and the knowledge that he had at last arrived in the world of flying, while the choice of aircraft would not be regretted in the years to come.

After two months of bombing, air-firing and night exercises in Sunderland 3s, in April 1943 he was posted to Pembroke Dock as co-pilot to Flying Officer Silburn. Given a new Sunderland to fly exclusively for the next five months, their first flight delivered JM677 to No 95 Squadron at Bathhurst (West Africa) via Gibraltar and Fort Lyautey. The crew was mostly RAF volunteer aircrew and Bob considered himself fortunate to have a skipper who allowed him plenty of practice to pass his Day and Night pilot assessments. Commissioned into the RAF Volunteer Reserve in October, he returned to Invergordon for his Captain's Course, when he was assessed as Above Average, and posted to 302 Flying Training Unit at Oban. In May 1944 bad weather forced Flying Officer Brodie to land Sunderland EK593 south of Luing Island. Unable to take off again, the long overdue crew had eventually taxied into Oban after what Bob would log as 'a voyage through the Western Islands'. The experience would prove to be invaluable.

Posted to 204 Squadron in West Africa, he flew his own crew out to Bathurst via Gibraltar and Jui (Sierra Leone, West Africa), though having to dive DW104 into cloud on sighting a prowling Junkers 88 over the Bay of Biscay. The squadron operated from a creek in Freetown and Bob flew from Fishermans Lake, Lagos, Dakar and Fort Etienne that first year. Though short of spares with priorities directed towards the fighter squadrons, and despite the increased loading required of the capacious hulls, the Sunderlands were operated with a minimum of fuss: the spirit of the age bringing just a questioning glance from the waves to the co-pilot on encountering a reluctance to lift off, when a more powerful burst of throttle brought her on to the step and away. The lengthy patrols demanded a high crew spirit and accurate navigation. It could take up to three hours to locate a particular convoy in the Atlantic and another six to eight hours shadowing the ships as they steamed to Britain with their precious supplies. The next patrol frequently returned to the same convoy, tossed relentlessly by the dangerous seas which hid both U-boat and surface raider, until a blinking Aldis lamp signalled the return to the comfort of the mess in a few hours time . . .

On 18 December the pilot had lost an engine while taking part in Exercise Buzzard and had waited for darkness before bringing K-Katie down to the uncertainty of the ocean below. The safe landing saved a valuable aircraft and the lives of the nine crew and two passengers, though the

K-Katie down. Crew visible topside.

episode was far from over. Encouraged perhaps by that unscheduled taxi between the Scottish islands in May, it was now a matter of delicately juggling the throttles to pass between the ocean swells as the waves rolled beneath the floats to alarmingly pound the metal hull.A naval frigate appeared on the skyline and hove-to at a respectful distance before offering to take them all aboard before giving the gunners target practice on the flying boat. The offer was declined. The next to arrive was one of the squadron's fast boats, a measure of the accuracy of the 'fix' transmitted before ditching. The tow lasted twenty-seven hours, during which low flying squadron aircraft added encouragement. Back at base, they were

Met by 204 Squadron towing launch.

Crew by opened hatches and nose turret. COURTESY CAPT HARWOOD met by the commanding officer, resplendent in full khaki drill, who decided to give a personal hand after his brave lads' long ordeal, the gesture ending in hilarity when a mooring rope fouled his legs and sent him head-first into the water. His order that they convalesce with seven pints of beer a week, rather than the wartime issue of 7 pints a month, found a quick appreciation and his health was enthusiastically toasted for quite some time!

Bob would later be awarded a Mention in Despatches for distinguished service with the squadron, along with the 1939-43 Star, Atlantic and Defence Medals. Though returned to operations, the end of the war had been sharply brought into focus when the squadron had returned to England and was disbanded in June 1945. Amid the uncertainty of what lay ahead, the crew sadly watched K-Katie being slowly towed out to the centre of Wig Bay to be sunk, while an interview with another 'paternal officer' decided the fate of the pilot. Noting the 24 year old had completed two tours of operations with no wish to be posted to the Far East, he had suggested he be seconded to BOAC.

August 21st brought two sessions of circuit flying at Poole aboard *Halstead* with Flight Lieutenant Warrior and six days later the Sunderland settled back into the harbour after Senior Captain Rose had evaluated Flight Lieutenants Harwood and Hibberd for service with BOAC. Both were sent off together later in the day and again two days later, this time with *Hampshire*. Bob's first flight as a First Officer came on 4 September when Captain Rose (logged as a Squadron Leader) lifted *Huntingdon* away from Poole for France and Lake Marignane before flying on to Augusta and Cairo. Two days later they set off for Kallia, Lake Habbaniya and Basra, leaving the next day for Bahrein and Karachi and the day after for Gwalior, Allahabad and Calcutta. On the ninth, they landed at Raj Samand on the Nile before heading back to Karachi, returning to Poole after a thirteen-day absence with eight full days of flying – though for the next two months Bob was confined within Farnborough County Hospital with yellow jaundice!

Captain Rose. Marine Terminal Lilliput Poole.
© ROSE COLLECTION.

Captain H.J Rose personified the élan associated with the former Imperial Airways pilots. A boyhood spent about his father's farm at Fincham in Norfolk, listening to the sound of aircraft operated from RAF Marham, may have unconsciously attracted the young Harry James to flying and he had joined the Royal Air Force as an RAF apprentice, one of the original Halton 'Brats'. His love of sports and the open air had led to a place on No 12 Course at RAF Sealand, where he was sent solo on an Avro Lynx in October 1932. A year later he joined the Vickers Virginia equipped No 10 Bomber Squadron at RAF Boscombe Down, Wiltshire, and in September 1934 converted to the Handley Page Heyford, the last biplane bomber to serve the RAF. Assessed as Above Average in May, he flew in the July Royal Review watched by King George V and Queen Mary and exactly a year later was assessed as 'Exceptional'. Known as 'Sonny' by his family, he was inevitably known as 'Tommy' by his peers in the Air Force, after the famous Hampshire (Chilbolton) born former Royal Flying Corps fighter pilot Captain T. Rose, a well known racing pilot of the era. Reformed as 97 Squadron, B flight moved to Leconfield in February 1937 and in August, he had taken a months leave to fly Sir Donald Hall-Craine and Miss Naismith about the South of France and Corsica in a twin-engined BA (British Aircraft) Double Eagle monoplane.

War clouds were gathering in Europe, but Prime Minister Neville Chamberlain's 'Peace for our time' speech made on his return from Germany in 1938, encouraged him to join Imperial Airways. His RAF engineering apprenticeship would have stood him in good stead, for the airline required their first officers to be engineers in order to cope with whatever arose during the long service trips. For the same reason, a captain would not be appointed unless he had served as a first officer. Leaving the RAF in January 1939, he had been accepted as a supernumerary first officer with Imperial and in March had joined Captain Dennis Peacock aboard the long-range *Caledonia*.

On his second trip he had again flown out to Durban and *Challenger* had been handed over at Kisumu. It had subsequently crashed at Mosambique. In September he had joined Captain Brown aboard *Corio*, which had returned Prince Philip of Greece from Karachi, and in June 1940 flew out to Singapore aboard *Circe*. Unable to return after the fall of France closed the Mediterranean, he was based at Durban for the next two years: his first flight in command made in July 1941 when bringing *Cassiopeia* back from Lagos after Captain Finnegan had reported sick. With more and more military aircraft arriving at Newfoundland, ferry crews needed to be returned as quickly as possible and in September 1941 BOAC had assumed responsibility for the task, using stripped out long-range Consolidated Liberators. Transferred to the Atlantic Return Ferry Service in 1942, he had met his future wife while flying the converted four-engined bombers from Prestwick to Montreal. Among the first to volunteer for the Womens Auxiliary Air Force, Connie had become the personal assistant and cipher officer to the AOC Transport Command, Sir Frederick Bowhill, and would be awarded the MBE for her wartime service.

Posted to the West Africa flying boat service in January 1943, the pilot had found a number of familiar faces among the passengers using the Poole-Foynes shuttle. On 11 June the French film star Adolphe Menjou was aboard a Transport Sunderland (later named *Hampshire)* making a test flight to the Shannon. A return flight was made four days later and breakfasting early, Captain Rose was urging the Pan Am Clipper passengers to hurry along to their own before activity increased at Poole, when one face seemed familiar, prompting him to call 'I've seen you somewhere before!' On later checking the passenger list, he found the unmistakable profile belonged to Lester T, better known as 'Bob' Hope, the famous American comedian, making one of his many visits to wartime Britain. Connie and Tommy had tragically lost their partners earlier in the war, but were married in London at the beginning of 1944. Services had recommenced to Cairo in November and in August another celebrity had been added to the list after returning Noel Coward from Egypt, when the cargo had included 150 live frogs! Three months later he had been posted to Poole as the Training Captain.

The war with Japan officially came to an end on 15 August 1945. Of the C-Class trapped in the Far East, *Clifton* (33 Squadron) and *Coolangatta* (11 Squadron) had survived service with the Royal Australian Air Force, but were written off after rejoining Qantas at Rose Bay: *Clifton* as the result of a training landing accident in January 1944 and *Coolangatta* after an emergency landing in October. All four pilots had died. The sole surviving C-Class in that theatre, *Coriolanus* was the first transport aircraft to fly into a liberated Singapore, bringing the first of thousands of prisoners of war to Poole Quay on 18 September 1945 where they were welcomed by the mayor, the sheriff and town clerk. Thereafter the arrivals became a daily occurrence. Woman Seaman Eileen Wigg remembered the seriously injured were the first to be brought home and never forgot how a boy, practically a skeleton, was carried from the fuselage on a stretcher and laid on an engine cover, when he said 'Oh it's lovely to be home' – and died. Thank God he was home and on such a lovely sunny day, she thought.

Unlike Britain, America had developed transport rather than military aircraft during the war and in June 1945, the U.S Civil Aeronautics Board ended Pan Ams monopoly by allowing American Export Airlines (AEA) and Transcontinental and Western Airlines (TWA) to fly the North Atlantic.

Pan Am made the first crossing by a commercially equipped landplane in September, when a converted C54 Skymaster brought nine crew and ten observers from LaGuardia to Hurn, having spent just nine of the seventeen hours between Gander and Rineanna. The event was pipped on 23 October however when the first, fifteen, commercial passengers alighted at Hurn from an AEA Skymaster. Having taken *Excambian* away from Foynes for the very last time on 22 October, Charles Blair brought the first of the company DC4s in to Rineanna on the 24th. Five days later Captain Wallace

Culbertson, commander of the first Martin 'China' Clipper to operate the 900 mile service between San Francisco and Hong Kong, took Pan Ams 314A *Pacific Clipper* away from the Shannon for the last flying boat service to Lisbon.

On 17 February 1946 Captain Parker took *Hythe* and BOAC Chairman Lord Knollys, away from Poole on a 'flag flying' visit to Australia and New Zealand, becoming the first British civil flying boat to visit China (Shanghai) and Japan (Tokyo). Operated by BOAC and Qantas, Hythes opened the post-war service to Australia in May, though without two of their number. Encountering poor visibility on returning to Poole from Singapore on 4 March , *Hailsham* had damaged a float on landing and the engines were opened up to reach shallow water near Brownsea Island. None of the sixteen passengers and five crew were injured and all were taken off by an Air Ministry Fire-float before the tide returned. Though refloated, *Hailsham* was a write-off. Six days later a fierce sandstorm capsized *Hamble* at Rod-el-Farag on the Nile.

The wartime development of runways and long-range aircraft had overcome the unique ability of flying boats in using the existing natural waterways of the world and with the war now fully at an end, the demand from the military ceased abruptly. Many new Sunderland Vs were fitted as contractually required, before being towed out and sunk off Queens Island, though others would be modified for civil use rather than the war-weary C-Class survivors that had clocked up hundreds of thousands of air miles. With thirteen surviving Empire boats operating the Africa services and twenty-four Hythe-Class Sunderlands at Poole, BOAC was ready to consolidate and extend services under peaceful skies.

SANDRINGHAM

Commercial operations required more seats to be profitable however and Shorts began converting ML788, one of the penultimate batch of Sunderland 3s, as the prototype Sandringham. Unlike the blunt outline of the Hythe, caused by the faired nose and gun turrets, *Himalaya.* had a smoothly contoured nose concealing a C-Class style mooring compartment, while the tail ended in a graceful cone. The secondary structure was altered to seat twenty-four passengers on two decks, the first British flying boat to do so, though this and the provision of a dining saloon and bar would be optional on subsequent conversions.

The first Sandringham order had come early in 1945 from Alberto Alphonse Dodero, the youngest son of Captain Nicolas Dodero, an Italian who had emigrated to Uruguay from Genoa. Together with his brothers, Alberto had transformed his father's modest shipping business and had personally made a multi-million fortune through shipping contracts during the war, helped by his personal friendship and support for the political ambitions of retired Colonel Juan Domingo Perón.

While his fleet of ships catered for the post war migration to Latin America from war-torn Europe and Japan, 58 year old Alberto had begun planning his long-held ambition to operate his own flying boat service between Buenos Aires and Montevideo. Encouraged by talks with government officials, the initial order was for four Sunderland 3s to be converted to airline standard at Belfast, with two more to be delivered by the close of 1946. The first pair (Sandringhams 2s) would be flown on internal services, with seventeen of the forty-five passengers seated on an upper deck provided with a bar. The second pair (Sandringham 3s) would fly twenty-one passengers on longer, international, services, fitted with a bar and a dining saloon on the upper deck.

The order was finalised by Alberto in America, while buying replacement engines for the fleet; the latter pair to receive Pratt and Whitney Twin Wasps and Hamilton variable pitch propellers. Conversion kits were also purchased to later increase the seating to that of the domestic services. The Pegasus engines and de Havilland propellers were to be sold at Belfast to offset some of the expenditure. Formed at the close of the year by Captain Lamplugh and Air Commodore Powell, to ferry American airliners to buyers in Europe, British Aviation Services (Britavia) was appointed technical adviser to Alberto's Compañía Argentina de Aeronavegación and would deliver the flying boats to Argentina. Former RAF aircrew would be hired on a temporary basis with the intention for Argentine crews to be trained to replace them. BOAC received the training contract and a leased Sunderland V (SZ573) was flown into Poole on 9 November 1945.

Completed on 26 November, two days later *Himalaya* gave a demonstration flight from the Medway for Minister of Aviation Lord Winster, despite lowering visibility and a falling tide, with Hudson Fysh among the VIPs. BOAC would take delivery of nine Sandringham 5s in 1947, but TEAL would beat them to it by a year, having decided to replace the faithful *Aotearoa* and *Awarua* with longer-range thirty-seat Sandringham 4s. BOAC was again without a trainer, but on 2 May another Sunderland V (SZ584) arrived at Poole from Belfast. Dudley Travers flew *Tasman* out to Sydney in July and Captain Jury took over for the crossing to Auckland. Between them, *Tasman, Australia, New Zealand* and *Auckland* would reduce the Tasman Sea crossing to eight hours.

CHAPTER EIGHT

Post-War Years

CIVIL SEAFORD / SOLENT

Intended to replace the Sunderland 3, the first of two Mark 4 prototypes had left the Medway at the end of August 1944. Heavier and more powerful, it had a redesigned planing bottom, strengthened wings to take four 1,700 horsepower Bristol Hercules engines, and a visibly larger fin and rudder to maintain control if both engines failed on one wing. Even as the Seaford prototypes had begun trials, production had commenced for thirty for the RAF in the Pacific, for the Sunderland V was already in squadron service. Both trial aircraft were destroyed by fire however and of eight built for Coastal Command, the first two had been returned to the MAEE at Felixstowe after evaluation by the RAF – and fortunately by BOAC, who alone ordered twelve airliner versions of the 'Civil Seaford'.

Known as the Solent, following trials at the close of 1945 with the second production aircraft, the new flying boat was evaluated by BOAC from April 1946 to June 1947. In May, Bob Harwood joined Captains Davy and Travers on test and training flights with G-OZZA between Hythe and Poole, when the high tail and distinctive curving fillet (which added extra area to the leading edge of the fin to avoid rudder lock) demonstrably set it apart from previous Sunderland variants. In many ways Dudley Travers resembled the popular 'Biggles' created by Captain W.E. Johns. Having qualified as an 'ace' twice over by shooting down twelve enemy aircraft for the Royal Flying Corps, and decorated by Britain and France, he had joined Imperial Airways and had transferred to the C-Class from open cockpit airliners. One of the few to hold a Master Pilot Certificate, he was the second to command *Canopus* and had flown many celebrities before taking over *Golden Hind*, BOACs biggest flying boat. By the time he retired his log book would show some 20,000 flying hours.

On 25 July 1946, Solent Flight Captain J.C Parker took the new flying boat away from Poole on a proving flight to the Far East, though Bob Harwood had to wait until October for his first 'service' flight to Singapore. Before then, he was able to sample two of the C-Class with Captain Stone: *Cathay* flown to Hythe in July followed by *Champion* in August. Both would

SHE FLIES ON WHEELS!

Marguerite Wilson of the British Overseas Airways traffic section is used to speed. She has won sixteen world cycling titles, and any cycle race from 25 to 1000 miles is right up her street. Here she is at the Poole Dorset flying boat base giving a lift to BOAC pilot Captain R.F. Stone, while a Karachi bound flying boat passes overhead.

Tandem Duo. Capt. Stone and champion cyclist Marguerite Wilson
IVOR COLEMAN & BOAC BRATS NEWSLETTERS

be scrapped within a few days of each other in March 1947.

The Hythes began flying to Hong Kong and Australia in August. The following month Dudley Travers brought *Golden Hind* into Poole. Captain Mollard had flown it out to Kisumu in July 1944 and in October Captain Travers had made a proving flight to Kogalla Lake via the Seychelles. Based at Kisumu, it subsequently flew from Kogalla to Mombasa via Addu Atoll (in the Maldive Islands) and to Lake Victoria, mostly occupied by RAF personnel and frequently by Catalina crews flying the Indian Ocean. A shuttle had also been flown between Lake Victoria and Diego Suarez (Madagascar). Delivered to Belfast at the end of 1945, it had received Hercules XIV sleeve valve engines and a streamlined tail cone to replace the faired rear turret. Furnished for twenty-four day passengers, the big flying boat took over the weekly Poole-Cairo service at the close of September 1946.

In the early days, the crews of Imperial Airways were associated with a particular flying boat, but times had changed. Joining Captain Staples aboard *Harwich* on 20 October, Bob Harwood left Poole at half-past six in the morning and landed on Lake Marignane at a quarter past eleven. After supervising refuelling, a one o'clock take-off ended at Augusta at a quarter to six in the evening after an identical second sector leg of four hours and forty-two minutes. A change to *Hudson,* leaving for Cairo just after four thirty the following afternoon and arriving a few minutes before eleven, the entire six hours and eighteen minutes qualifying for entry in the Night Flying column of his logbook.

Not much time for sleep, departing for Bahrein at twelve minutes past two in the morning and arriving just before ten, when he was given the landing: able to take an hour from the seven hours and forty-two minutes to add to his 'Night' total. A change to *Hobart*, leaving before seven in the evening and arriving at Karachi at one o'clock in the morning after six and a quarter hours of night flying. Forty-seven minutes later they were off again, landing at Calcutta at a quarter to ten and ready for breakfast after virtually eight hours in the air. Departing at eight thirty in the evening, he was given the landing at Rangoon at a quarter to one in the morning. No time to admire the scenery, taking off an hour later and ready for another breakfast on landing at Singapore after seven and a half hours in the air.

Begun at seven minutes past midnight aboard *Hunter*, the return service brought the longest sector time of almost eight and a quarter hours between Calcutta and Karachi. A change to *Hotspur* followed, given the landing at Bahrein and the take-off for Basra, before commencing a six and a half hour flight to Cairo. A days respite before boarding *Hobart* for a seven hour flight to Augusta, followed by a change to *Huntingdon*: Captain Staples giving his first officer the final take-off from Marignane and arriving at Poole at midday on 11 November . A trip to remember for Bob, having flown six Hythe-Class Sunderlands during eleven days and nights, with seventy-six hours added to the 'Day' total and over twenty-three to the 'Night'.

In their absence, *Canopus* had been broken up at Hythe in October after the councillors of Poole had declined an offer for it to be presented to the borough free of charge for display purposes. *Cleopatra*, the last of the C-Class to be delivered, was scrapped in November. The survivors had all been refitted with Pegasus 22 engines towards the end of the war, easing the spares situation and giving 1,010 horsepower for take off, as had production Sunderlands. But with *Castor* completing the final Karachi-Cairo Horseshoe Route shuttle on 15 January 1947, the sad procession of returning 'Empire' flying boats continued. By the close of March, *Cameronian, Cambria, Carpentaria, Corsair, Cooee, Castor, Cordelia, Coorong, Cathay* and *Champion* had all been scrapped. *Caledonia* began the final Horseshoe service from Durban on 12 March and on 17 April was flown from Poole to Hythe by Captain Alington and Bob Harwood.

Cathay was offered to the Science Museum at Kensington, though bomb damage had left insufficient space to house such a large exhibit. The problem was certainly not unique and I remember my mother taking my twin brother and myself, both Air Training Corps cadets with No 85 (Southgate) Squadron, to join our father at Borehamwood to see the castle erected in a field near Elstree Film Studios for the 1952, triple Academy Award nominated film *Ivanhoe*, which featured a young Elizabeth Taylor. Rounding a bend at the rear of the extensive barbed wire enclosure, we were confronted by the fuselages and stacked wings of Lancaster bombers! All three had been taken out of storage to fly the sequences for the classic film *The Dam Busters*, Britain's biggest box-office success in 1955, for which Richard Todd would forever be remembered for his portrayal of 25 year old Wing Commander Guy Gibson VC. As with the flying boats, there appears to have been no real effort to preserve any of them afterwards. Not so much Sic transit Gloria as, perhaps, where on earth are we going to put an aircraft that size?

In addition to the celebrities met during the war, in May 1946 Senior Captain Rose had taken *Hungerford* away from Poole to enable Derek McCulloch, 'Uncle Mac' of the much loved BBCs Childrens Hour programm*e ('Goodnight children, everywhere'), to* make a special broadcast from over the pyramids. A number of local flights were made before leaving and First Officer Norman Tebbit had occupied the right hand seat for the first of two 'jollys' the previous day, later to become chairman of the Conservative Party and the Lord Tebbitt of Chingford. In June, a routine stop at Bahrein with *Howard* had revealed the loss of eighty-six wrist watches from the 'precious cargo' compartment! *Champion* was flown to Hythe for the very last time on 4 April 1947 and en route to Karachi with *Haslemere* in May, the pilot had experienced some of the worst 'bumps' in his career, the strength of the thermals confirmed by vultures circling at 8,500 feet!

BOAC SANDRINGHAMS

BOAC had received the first of the new Plymouth-Class Sandringham 5s in March 1947; *Portsmouth* leaving Poole for Karachi in May and *Portsea* departing for Hong Kong in June. The nine-strong fleet comprised *Portsmouth, Penzance, Portland, Pembroke, Portmarnock, Portsea, Poole, Pevensey* and *Perth*. The wartime residents of Bridport, Beaminster and District had clubbed together to buy a Spitfire for the RAF (The Brit), while the more numerous residents of Bournemouth had bought two (Bournemouth and Bournemouth 11 Crest). Poole had also financed a fighter in 1941, but along with the Bridport Spitfire, Villae de Poole had been written off during the final month of the year. Named after the port and flying boat terminal, the former Dumbarton-built Sunderland 3 (NJ188) had served 330 (Norwegian) Squadron before refitted as a Mark 5, and had been sold back to Shorts for conversion to airline standard in May 1946. Sound-proofed and with much less vibration than in military service, the airframe comfortably accommodated twenty two day passengers. Sixteen were flown by night, when a steward raised the backs of the facing pairs of window seats to form a top bunk, supported by a metal framework, while the cushions formed the lower. The dining saloon could sleep another four.

Just three months after its own conversion at Belfast, on 23 August 1947 *Portland* crashed after a heavy landing at Bahrain Marine Air Base while en route to Poole, with the loss of almost half the passengers and crew. Most of the mail bags were retrieved, though the contents had to be individually hand stamped in violet ink with a thought provoking Damaged By Sea Water. It would prove the only casualty to the Sandringham fleet. In September, Captain Rose saw half a ton of vaccine loaded aboard *Henley* at Basrah to combat a cholera outbreak in Cairo. Sandringhams had replaced the Hythes on the Australia and Hong Kong routes and in October, *Penzance* inaugurated the Poole-Bahrain service, though landplane Lancastrians would soon fly faster to Sydney from the new terminal at London Airport. The final Sandringham 4 would ultimately be preserved at Southampton. *Bermuda Sky Queen* and *Hamilton* would not be so fortunate.

Parkstone Yacht Club Dolphin One designs 'broad-reaching' 1947. Hythe *Harlequin*, Sandringham *Portmarnock*. © AUTHOR COLLECTION.

SKY QUEEN AFFAIR

China Clipper, the last of the Martin M-130 flying boats, had crashed on landing at Port of Spain, Trinidad, in January 1945 and with Pan Am declining the American Government's offer to buy back the Boeings after the war, in 1946 *American, Pacific, Anzac* and *Capetown Clipper* were moored and put up for sale at San Diego harbour. Though bought by Universal Airlines, the company closed down within a year and *Anzac* and *Capetown Clipper* went to American International Airways, another unscheduled carrier based at New York.

Overhauled and renamed *Bermuda Sky Queen*, NC-18612 (the former *Capetown Clipper*) ended a three day flight to Poole on 11 October 1947. The following afternoon, sixty-two passengers and over one and a half tons of baggage were loaded aboard before the Clipper departed in hazy conditions for the return to New York. Landed at Foynes later in the afternoon, passengers had to remain overnight due to heavy weather reported in the North Atlantic, though the lone steward could only offer them soft drinks. They eventually left Ireland at twenty minutes to four during the afternoon of 13 October when some of the nine seamen returning to America had to sit on the floor at the rear, as there just were not enough seats to go round.

Encountering strong headwinds and icing over the Atlantic, the aircraft was taken down through the clouds just after midnight, and 600 miles short of Gander was turned back with only enough fuel in the tanks for another two and a half hours in the air. Having contacted the U.S. Coast Guard Cutter and weather ship Bibb of the North Atlantic Ocean Patrol, on station within the 10-mile-square range of Station Charley, 1,400 miles from Foynes, the big Boeing was landed between 30-foot high waves generated by the stormy ocean. But while attempting to take aboard a towing line, a collision with the ships stern punched in the nose which

The only known photograph of Boeing 314 Bermuda Sky Queen passing the Fire Launch prior to turning to leave Poole during the hazy morning of October 12 1947. PETER DAVIDSON.

began taking in water. Moved apart by waves, three of the merchant seamen bravely volunteered to be passed by line in a small rubber raft to the cutter. Others followed, and all but twenty-four were rescued by nightfall. The rest were retrieved in the morning, when the seas had abated. Sent from the Coast Guard Air Detachment at Argentia in Newfoundland, Catalina 48335 had circled above throughout the rescue, ready to drop life-jackets and supplies, but had to fight the same headwinds on the return and lost all power from one fuel starved engine while taxiing off the runway.

The abandoned flying boat was an obvious hazard to shipping and was raked by the cutter's 40 millimeter cannon until catching fire and sinking, smoking, beneath the waves. The same fate had been dealt to *Honolulu Clipper* in November 1945 after force landing on the Pacific, when the wing and nose had collided with the seaplane tender USS San Pablo. Allowed to leave Station Charley, Bibb landed the crew and sixty-nine passengers, including twelve children, to a massive public welcome at Boston, which included fireboats and a fly-past. Together with the rescuers, the pilot was hailed as a hero – until November, when the findings of a four-day public hearing were made known. Passengers had confirmed the aircraft was overloaded, while the Civil Aeronautics Board determined the aircraft had been 5,000 pounds over the certificated gross weight on leaving Foynes and that the 26 year old former navy pilot had disregarded the basics of long distance planning. He was fined 200 dollars for violating civil air regulations. The licence of the airline was suspended indefinitely.

Three days after the departure of *Bermuda Sky Queen*, Captain Rose took

Sandringham *Auckland* Mechanics Bay Oct 1947. © ROSE COLLECTION.

the Sandringham 4 *Auckland* away from Poole on the first leg of a delivery flight to New Zealand. By now Nora Bevis had become the last Woman Seaman at Poole. No stranger to boating, she raced her own 14 foot yacht and unlike the majority of the girls, had risen to Coxswain 1st Class, chosen to handle the special launch that had taken Crown Prince Saudi and his entourage out to a Hythe-Class Sunderland waiting to return him to Cairo.

On 11 November 1947, *Hamilton* left Hythe to operate the eleven o'clock Poole-Singapore service. The date was significant, known in Britain and the Commonwealth as Remembrance Day, held in memory to the dead of both World Wars. Encountering fog, the flying boat crashed on the lower slope of Brighstone Down on the Isle of Wight, with the loss of the first officer. Twenty-four hours later, the skies cleared as the country celebrated the marriage of Princess Elizabeth to the Duke of Edinburgh. Mindful of the uneconomic and costly use of launches at Poole and the detached maintenance base at Hythe, a government commission of enquiry had evaluated post-war flying boat operations and changes were already under way. In America a colossus had finally become airborne.

SPRUCE GOOSE

Five years earlier, Henry Kaiser, builder of the wartime Liberty Ships, had seen over three quarters of a million tons of shipping lost to German U-boats and had approached millionaire Howard Hughes with an idea to build giant transport aircraft capable of flying nonstop over the Atlantic to Europe. Awarded an eighteen million dollar government contract to build three giant flying boats, each capable of carrying 750 troops, work had begun on the prototype using strips of laminated birch sealed with plastic glue (Duramold) rather than deplete vital stocks of steel and aluminium. But it all took time and in 1944 Kaiser had withdrawn his interest, prompting Hughes to change the name from HK1 (Hughes Kaiser One) to H4 (Hughes aircraft number Four) Hercules, though it would always be known as the 'Spruce Goose' as applied by its critics. The giant had still not flown by the end of the war, when the order was reduced to one, and Hughes had injected seven million dollars of his own money to complete the work by 1946.

Accused of fraud and misuse of government funds, he was ordered to appear before a committee of the United States Senate, but had the flying boat assembled in his absence at a dry dock at Long Beach Harbour, California. Having acquitted himself well, he returned from Washington and on 2 November 1947 began a series of fast taxi trials across the harbour. On the third run he applied take off flap to the 320 foot wing and opening up the eight, 3,000 horsepower engines, remained airborne for perhaps a minute before safely landing the 150 tons just over a mile away. Returned to the air conditioned hangar, the giant was patrolled by armed guards for

'Spruce Goose' H4 (Hughes) Hercules.
© EVERGREEN AVIATION & SPACE MUSEUM, OREGON.

over thirty years (at an estimated million dollars per year) until the death of the 70 year old millionaire in 1976.

Donated to the Aero Club of Southern California and displayed within a purpose-built dome of the Wrather Corporation in 1983, the 'Goose' resides today within a massive glass fronted hangar at Delford Smith's Evergreen Aviation and Space Museum at McMinnville, Oregon.

BOAC Solents

The luxury associated with the C-Class had ended with the war, but the Solents would recapture some of the spirit of the Imperial Airways services, though thoughts of 'Empire' were fast becoming out of touch in the emerging new world. *Salisbury*, the first of the Solent 2 fleet, was completed in November 1946, and was followed by *Scarborough, Southampton, Somerset, Sark, Scapa, Severn, Solway, Salcombe, Stornoway, Sussex* – and *Southsea*, launched in April 1948, after which the Rochester factory closed down. All other flying boats would be built at the Queens Island, Belfast, factory jointly owned by Harland and Wolff.

Unlike the Sandringham, the thirty passengers would enter from a separate door on the starboard side, to be faced by the cocktail bar of the promenade cabin. To the left, a luxurious ladies powder room preceded a mail, freight and baggage compartment. The attractive peach coloured décor of the cabin blended nicely with the light blue cloth of the seats, a thème continued throughout the air conditioned aircraft. At the end of the cabin, a spiral staircase led up into the 'servery' or buffet bar, behind which the galley was equipped with the mandatory stainless steel sink, racks and fittings, together with a refrigerator and a steam oven. A service lift connected with the lower deck, while a flashing button on a wall panel would direct a steward to the flight deck or the requisite passenger cabin. The buffet led directly to the dining saloon and top cabin, the extreme rear of which provided stowage for baggage, bunks and bedding. If more than twenty-four passengers were aboard, both upper cabins would join those below in seating six and sleeping four.

Back downstairs, a cloaks room was provided for outer travelling clothes and preceded the gentleman's dressing room, fitted with two wash basins, hot and cold running water and electric shaver points. Two separate toilets were on the right of the passageway. Next came the first forward cabin, given a pair of double seats and table on the right and a matching arrangement of single seats opposite. The extra 4 feet or so of the Solent allowed a second cabin forward of the front spar, the rest of the nose taken up by two mail and freight compartments: the smaller on the left due to the space taken up by the loading and crew entrance hatch. Wide, non-inflammable plastic windows greatly improved the views and the natural light throughout the aircraft, while the dressing rooms and toilets were noticeably more spacious than in the Sandringham. The flight time to Africa would be shortened, but two stewards and a stewardess would be carried and in December, Solent Flight Captain Parker departed on a proving flight with a young stewardess whose new career had already introduced her to her future husband.

A volunteer member of the wartime Womens Auxiliary Air Force, 22 year old Marjory Joan Godber had helped guide Beaufighter night fighters to their prey as an operations assistant at the GCI (Ground Controlled Interception) radar station at Treleaver Cornwall, when she was lodged at the requisitioned Headland Hotel. The end of the war had left her determined to find a job involved with flying. Interested in people and with airlines employing the first stewardesses, Joan wrote to every company she could think of, at home and abroad, knowing it was not going to be that easy.

BOAC had responded with an interview however, and one of the questions asked of her by the all-male selection board was whether she could fillet a fish – completely out of context, she thought, with the job in mind. Naturally she had said 'Yes' though she had never had to do it. She also implied her French was quite fluent, which fortunately for her, was also not put to the test.

Intelligent, slim, blonde, and with a classic profile, she fitted the bill for the forthcoming Solent Africa service and was sent to the No 1 Catering Course at Aldermaston. A more enjoyable aspect of the course, almost a week was spent at the Elizabeth Arden headquarters in the Regent Street area of London, where the girls learned how to make the best of their appearance, and use of the products: part of the free beauty treatment to be available in a Solent powder room, when Blue Grass perfume would permeate the cabin interiors! Due to a delay in the Solents coming into service, they were sent to the Victoria Terminal to be trained as waitresses in the restaurant. The 'Maitre d' appeared to resent their presence, causing a few tears, and it was a relief to be posted to Heathrow, which was losing its image as a muddy, tented encampment. Joan had to be inoculated before flying, but the jabs were all administered at the same time, bringing considerable embarrassment during the train journey to visit her mother at the family home in Whitstable, Kent, when she began breaking out in virulent red spots!

Equipped with twin-engined Dakota aircraft, the crews of BOAC No 1 Line flew out to Tehran, Cairo and Nairobi, each stewardess given fourteen lunch boxes for the passengers and provided with an enamel bowl in the back of the aircraft for the washing up. The girls looked smart in the wartime style uniform, though Joan disliked the black 'granny' lace-up shoes, and the stiff starched shirt that had to be fastened to a collar. Some found it hard to accept a woman within the crew, more noticeably the older, senior captains that had started with Imperial Airways, but behind the glamour the girls had to know their stuff during those early post-war years. The return would often be made with a different crew and on one not to be forgotten day, Joan had landed at Cairo and was told by a fellow stewardess that she would be joining a Captain Mills, adding, you're lucky, he's nice!

A storm had blown up as the Dakota approached El Adem, a small RAF Station in the African Desert near Tobruk, and with no improvement during the routine refuelling, Joan heard the captain say they would 'go and have a look at it' which, even in her inexperience did not seem a good idea at all. The aircraft's ceiling was around 16,000 feet, for which you would need oxygen, which meant they would be flying through the weather, rather than above it. Forced to return to the isolated outpost with engine trouble, they were faced with having to look after the passengers until spares were flown out from England. On landing, the first ever words spoken to her by Harry Mills were 'Miss Godber, will you help me carry the bar box off the aeroplane?' Not particularly romantic perhaps, but it was a start. The contents had duly provided a little comfort for all of them during the enforced stay in the desert, during which time Joan had come to know her future husband, who it turned out, was just a year older than herself. Later, she would find he had received an immediate Distinguished Flying Cross for destroying a petrol supply ship at Benghazi, having set off well behind the squadron's eight Wellington bombers due to engine trouble, and survived the hornets' nest aroused by them.

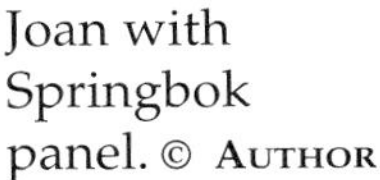
Joan with Springbok panel. © AUTHOR

A full load of reporters and staff had joined *Severn* for the proving flight to Africa. But things had not gone entirely to plan and at twilight on 5 December, Joe Parker had to make an emergency landing at Port Bell with a damaged wing float. Almost crushed to death by the rush of male bodies scrambling to the escape hatch to balance the other wing, Joan was quickly hauled up to join the others grouped high on the slippery metal as launches headed out to them in the dusk...

Plymouth-Class Sandringhams had begun flying to Japan in March, while the delivery of the three Bermuda-Class Mark 7s between April and May, brought the fleet to the required twelve. By then, Lockheed Constellations had taken over the Bermuda service and the thirty-seat *Saint George, Saint David* and *Saint Andrew* were instead used on services to Johannesburg, Hong Kong and Japan. With Qantas introducing Constellations on the eastern sector of the Australian service at the end of 1947 and Boeing Stratocruisers flying the North Atlantic, the landplane hand was writing strongly on the wall – though the Solent was about to enter service with BOAC.

SPRINGBOK SERVICE

Bob Harwood last flew from Poole on 26 March 1948, crewed with Captain Hallam as supernumerary first officer aboard *Stornoway,* on a proving flight to South Africa. The eighteen days provided fourteen full days of flying and introduced him to Luxor, Port Bell, Victoria Falls and Valdaam on the outward journey and Mwanza and Malaka on the return. The third day out had seen a return to Khartoum on three engines, while a three day stopover at the vast lake created by the Vaalbank dam across the Zambesi, some 50 miles south of Johannesburg, had seen five take offs and landings with Captain Rotherham. Another four take offs and landings were carried out at Augusta with Captain Lawrence Glover, after which *Stornaway* was returned to Southampton, and not Poole, on 13 April.

The majority of staff and equipment had left Lilliput aboard two coaches and eight furniture vans on the Easter Monday of 29 March , the very last flying boat arrival and departure handled by a skeleton staff the following day. The remaining equipment had been packed aboard the fleet of launches heading off for Southampton. During the eight and a half years of operations, over 34,000 passengers had flown in to Poole, rising from the first fifteen movements recorded in 1939 to a peak of 463 in 1945. The final three months of 1948 had seen forty-two arrivals from Sydney, thirty-eight from Bahrein, twenty-eight from Hong Kong and two each from Durban and Marseilles. Throughout, not a single passenger had been injured and only *Maia* was lost to enemy action. Shipping had been unaffected, the lack of industrial pollution had assisted operations, and the natural enthusiasm of everyone involved with the services had ensured their success.

Built for BOAC by Southern Railways, the owner of Southampton Docks, the new Marine Air Terminal was officially opened by Minister of Civil Aviation Lord Nathan of Churt on 14 April 1948, with Harold Fysh (Qantas) and James Greenland (TEAL) among the distinguished guests.

Harbour Club post-war. BOAC Marine Terminal to right.

Mayoress Mrs Dibben named G-AHIN *Southampton* and her husband the Mayor presented the aircraft with a ships clock, though the enthusiasm surrounding the ceremony was in marked contrast to his Lordships opening address, when he had stated that Britain was the only country employing flying boats on an extensive scale and faced a particular problem if it was not to be placed at a disadvantage with competitors using landplanes! Just one of the two floating pontoons was in place, but the facility had already coped with sixteen services a week, divided equally between arrivals and departures, expected to rise to twenty-two a week in May with the start of the Solent services to Africa.

The new terminal was certainly impressive. On arrival, passengers waited in the reception lounge to be called by name to separate rooms to complete the formalities required by health, immigration and customs, when their luggage awaited them in the customs hall. Each section was duplicated to avoid incoming and outgoing passengers meeting head-on. They were then passed to the departure lounge. With echoes of the pottery premises on Poole quay, the restaurant and lounge bar was on the first floor and took up the entire 110 feet. Waiting friends and relatives could use the facility, the chic deep mushroom upholstery comfortably seating sixty-eight and the lounge bar sixty-five, with large windows overlooking Southampton Water.

The rest of the upper floor was arranged as offices for the Ministry of Civil Aviation, the airport commandant, the airline's station superintendent and the signals, teleprinter and telephone exchange supervisor. Flying control was run by Ministry of Aviation staff from a tower at the end of the building. On completion of the formalities, passengers were escorted to a covered gangway which led down to the waiting flying boat, rather than having to embark from a bobbing launch as at Poole, where the staff had been almost exactly halved to 167 for the move to Southampton. BOAC was proudly advertising new overnight accommodation for the long-distance passengers. Each room would have a radio, and each bedroom would be air conditioned, with extra large divan beds, dressing and bedside tables, recessed lighting, and sliding doors to 'its own' shower and toilet.

Loaded with representatives from travel agencies and the popular press, in May 1948 *Southampton* took off in advance of the first scheduled service to Africa. But only on the second attempt, as Captains Rotherham and Peers had been forced to return after a faulty magneto had caused a drop in revolutions in one of the Hercules engines. Having clocked over a million air miles with Imperial Airways and BOAC, and received the King's Commendation for Valuable Services in the Air the previous year, 'Teddy' Rotherham had insisted on a seasoned co-pilot for the important 'flag waving' trip.

Jim Peers had made his first flight as a captain aboard *Cleopatra* in 1944,

Solent *Southampton* Lake Nyasa. © DAVID ROSE.

the year *Golden Hind* was put on the Africa service. Formerly with Imperial Airways, the Swiss-born, No 4 Line Manager, Captain Roger Mollard had needed an experienced pilot in the second seat for the repositioning flight, rather than a recent graduate from Vaaldam, and had chosen Jim. His first return home since war was declared, Jim had found the Solent cluttered with invasion craft and the qualifying landings were completed at Pembroke Dock before departing for Foynes and Lisbon. An engine had been 'lost' between Lagos and Leopoldville, and six days were spent fitting a spare that just happened to be aboard. Thereafter *Golden Hind* had become the exclusive preserve of Dudley Travers. The closure of Durban had seen Jim return *Corsair* and many of the staff to Poole. Turning in over Sandbanks on 13 January 1947 the 29 year old had encountered the first flakes of a snow storm for only the second time in his career. They were grounded for three days. He had then flown Hythe-Class Sunderlands, including a night flight with Captain Rose, and while at Southampton had been saddened to see *Corsair* being chopped up by workmen using long handled axes . . .

With no need to refuel at Lake Marignane, *Southampton* ended the first day with a night landing at Augusta, some 1,280 miles from Southampton. In the morning, the distinctive chequer board lighthouse with its tall mast and windsock was left behind as they headed off for Cairo, where refreshments were taken aboard the houseboat Puritan before flying on to Luxor, a new refuelling station on a distinctive bend of the Nile, the night spent within the Luxor Palace Hotel. In the morning, the bright sun lit the ancient temple ruins on the river bank as they taxied into wind, without the need for the flare path lights mounted on barges in the river. Refuelled at Khartoum, over 700 miles further on, the longest sector of over 1,000 miles ended with an evening landing at Port Bell at the northern end of Lake

Victoria, where a new jetty and reception building had been built by East African Airways. The presence of so many hills had discouraged night operations and passengers spent the night in the bungalow style accommodation of Silver Springs, rented by BOAC five miles inland.

A noticeably longer take-off run was needed in the morning due to the heat and lower pressure (4,000 feet above sea level) giving less bite to the propellers. Just under an hour later, the Equator was crossed while still over the lake and the permanent cloud of spray marking Victoria Falls sighted a good 50 miles from descending to the Zambesi for lunch. The final landing was made on the calm expanse of Vaaldam Lake, some 640 miles further on, followed by a two and a half hour coach drive back to Johannesburg. The return flight passed the in-bound *Severn* and at Augusta found *Salcombe* en route with the second of the scheduled passenger services which would regularly complete the journey in four and a half days.

Joe Parker was not the only pilot to experience problems with the wing floats however. On subsequently taking a Solent away from Khartoum, Jim saw the starboard float work loose, but with fuel transferred to the port wing tanks, landed safely at Port Bell, if a little left wing low. On finding a support rod had disintegrated, he submitted a report with suggestions for solving the problem. Nothing was done at the time, presumably with the emphasis on getting the new service up and running, while it was difficult to see the cause with the amount of spray thrown up while taking off and

Solent *Salcombe* Lake Nyasa Nov 1949. © DAVID ROSE

landing. But about a month later, Captain Rotherham had just left Southampton on a clearance flight to South Africa for the second pilot, when another rod failed, causing the float to fold against the underside of the wing, perilously close to the aileron. With a full load of passengers, there was no question of continuing and the experienced hands pulled off a safe landing without incident.

The entire Solent fleet was grounded in June 1948 and Jim was sent to Belfast to test his original suggestions. He had taken up photography in South Africa, and his use of 16 millimeter film proved very useful during the trials, when he positioned himself in the mooring hatch to distance the lens from the spray as Shorts chief test pilot Tom Brook-Smith began a series of tests in a nearby loch. The film would clearly show that the wave generated on the take-off run (displacement to planing) caused rapid vertical movements of the floats, though this had quickly become of less importance when 'Brookie' inadvertently pulled back too hard on the wheel and left the surface, leaving Jim exposed to a 90 mile an hour gale with nothing to hold on to but the camera! Jim and the all important film subsequently accompanied Captain Algar to GKN House, after which Jim completed a series of trial flights to South Africa with a crowd of technicians aboard.

As a consequence, the floats were refitted further out and more forward of the wing to give more support, particularly in choppy conditions. Services were resumed in October, the month a new marine airport opened to the south of Alexandria. Reclaimed from marshland, Fuad Airport featured four intersecting runways and the artificial Lake Mariut, the average depth of ten and a half feet almost twice the displacement of a Solent. BOAC had installed workshops, stores and a marine office, together with a kitchen to prepare the in-flight meals. Passengers were provided with a modern restaurant and a rest room for the routine immigration and health checks, with customs completed within the control

Cecil Hotel, Alexandria © ROSE COLLECTION.

tower building between the lake and landplane runways. Overnight accommodation was provided by the Hotel Cecil, some 3 miles away on the seafront. Rod Faraq on the Nile had had its day.

Retired in September 1947, *Golden Hind* was eventually flown away from Poole by Chris Blackburn who in 1948 had applied to join Fleet Airway, a new company, whose two directors had combined their RAF gratuities to buy the big flying boat. Invited to join the repositioning flight, he had arrived to find the Airwork ferry pilot had not turned up and agreed to take his place, though his total experience was six circuits as co-pilot of an RAF Sunderland. A somewhat 'shaky' take off followed. But a safe landing was made on the winding Medway, and a mooring made in Tower Reach near Rochester Bridge, in sight of the old Shorts factory. And there the giant had remained. The certificate of airworthiness duly expired and in February 1953 Shorts confirmed there were no longer any spares, tools or jigs available. Towed down river to a new mooring near Sheerness Dockyard early in 1954, a wingtip had caught the central span of the bridge causing severe damage to the metal, while at low tide, the stony river bottom began to damage the planing bottom.

Another mooring was found some 2 miles away at Harty Ferry on the Swale, but a combination of spring tides and strong winds dragged the anchor, allowing the hull to weathercock against a concrete causeway. Pierced by stones and gravel at low tide and ground afresh across the rough concrete at each high tide, mud and slime soon filled the once pristine interior. Reports were made and Kent County Council engineers arrived to inspect the damage, though confining their attention to the concrete! Further storm damage caused irrevocable damage however and the once proud flying boat was finally broken up for scrap – though a few of the metal tables could be seen at the Ferry Inn where a wooden wall plaque featured a painting of the G-Class flagship powering away from the river.

BOAC received the first of the former Seafords in March 1949. Converted to airline standard at Belfast, the thirty-six seat Solent 3s had been sold to the Ministry of Supply, which in turn leased them to the airline. *City of London*, *City of Cardiff*, *City of Belfast* and *City of Liverpool* were joined by *City of Salisbury*, *City of York*, *City of Edinburgh* and *City of Southsea* following conversion of the former Mark 2s Salisbury, Scapa, Sussex and Southsea. Determined to promote the new 'Springbok' service to the full, BOAC arranged a promotional outing in London and on 5 May journalists from leading London newspapers arrived by coach at Southampton after spending the night at the Grand Hotel at Lyndhurst in the New Forest, for the new rail terminal had yet to be completed. Ushered aboard an immaculately prepared G-AKNO, they were landed on the Thames by Captain Davys, Flight Captain of No 4 Line, having circled low over London to give those below a good view of the new flying boat and those aboard a birds-

Solent *Scapa* at Southampton. Bob Rayner

eye view of the Tower of London, Buckingham Palace and the airline's headquarters.

One of five captains to have helped evacuate British troops from Crete in unarmed Transport Sunderlands, in 1943 John Davys had been chosen to fly out Viscount Wavell, the new Viceroy to India: the special 'Executive' version given two cabins, furnished with grey hide ceilings and walls, with pile carpets, together with a state room and attendant steward. The following year he had received the Kings Commendation for Valuable Services in the Air.

With echoes of Alan Cobham, waving crowds greeted them as they taxied along the river and under a raised Tower Bridge to be met at Tower Pier by BOAC deputy chairman Sir Miles Thomas. The Solent was then opened to the public, for which two extra stewardesses had been taken aboard, and on Tuesday 10 May was named *City of London* by Sir George Aylwen, the Lord Mayor of London and Admiral of the Port, who promptly poured South African champagne over the nose from a 200 year old silver chalice. Oswald Short and John Lankester Parker were among the watching senior airline officials and VIPs. Throughout the stay, the crew were wined and dined at a top class restaurant courtesy of a London evening paper. Over 10,000 people came aboard and when questioned by the media, stewardesses Joan Godber and Enid Davies revealed that the ladies powder room was what most women wanted to see. Enclosed by dove-grey walls with mock marble flooring, the interior featured a wide vanity shelf with illuminated mirror, real flowers, and a bow-fronted nest of drawers, together with a pair of padded stools and a couch provided with the latest glossy magazines. The men were more interested in the cocktail bar in the promenade cabin, overlooked by a glazed panel etched with a Springbok antelope. Young boys were given a view of the flight deck from the galley hatch. Most women had said they would feel safer crossing the sea in a flying boat rather than an 'ordinary plane' – which must have encouraged Sir Miles.

Joan came to love her job, seeing new places and meeting new people, with most evenings ending in a party with the passengers. She would often take charge of the bar, a popular meeting place once airborne, when she would find it difficult to persuade passengers to take their seats for lunch. As with the pioneering C-Class, the Solents descended to give a closer look at things, though circling over Victoria Falls after a four course lunch usually ended with the inevitable. On one particular departure from Victoria Falls, the Zambesi was unusually low and Joan was on the upper deck when the Solent hit a rock, normally much deeper in the water. Asked by Captain Majendie to let passengers know the hull was being checked for damage, she descended the stairs to find those below already sat knee-deep in water! Typically, there was no panic and they were taken on by landplane the following day as the crew flew on to Johannesburg with a temporary patch over the damage.

Joan was never apprehensive, for most trips passed off without incident, though a lady had held on to her hand after a particularly bumpy take off

Solent passenger. © ROSE COLLECTION.

BOAC Solent stewardesses Enid Davies and Joan Godber. COURTESY MRS JOAN MILLS

from Southampton and had told her she was a very, very, brave girl! After a ten-day break, the Johannesburg service allowed a full week to be re-acquainted with the sights and sounds of Africa. Other flights included the 'Dragon' service to Hong Kong aboard a Sandringham, and the last trips of the Hythes, one remembered for being devoted entirely to children flying out to visit their parents during the boarding school holidays. The return took about three weeks which allowed plenty of time to become acquainted with the Orient.

In June 1949, after a year as deputy chairman, Sir Miles Thomas was appointed chairman of BOAC and moved into the palatial Stratton House, the airline's Mayfair headquarters. Though years before economy flights for the masses, flying was no longer a preserve of the rich and passengers found the longer flying boat services could not compare to being cosseted within a pressurised cabin, high above a threatening weather system. For many the romance would never fade, but the practicalities, demonstrated by the move to Southampton, had to outweigh the cost. Airmail was reaching destinations faster and more frequently by landplane, helped by the acres of concrete laid during the war. Having barely taken over from the Hythes, the Sandringhams were replaced by Canadair C-4 Argonaut airliners. *Saint Andrew* ended the Yokohama- Iwakuni- Hong Kong flying boat service in August and *Portsea* returned the last Sandringham passengers to Southampton at the end of September. *Saint David* brought home the staffs and families while *Helmsdale* returned the spare engines and equipment. All eleven Sandringhams were returned to the Air Ministry.

On 4 October 1949 Tommy Rose flew *Salcombe* out to Johannesburg, with Sir Geoffrey Colby, the governor of Nyasaland, alighting at Lake Nyasa. Eleven days later, the return to Southampton with *Southsea* brought his time on flying boats to a close. Perhaps typical of his experiences, on New Year's Day the rudder of *Southampton* had jammed on landing at Khartoum, January had seen him make the first landing (with *Scapa*) at Hartebeaste Port, selected as an alternate for Vaaldam in bad weather, and five months later he had had to return *Southsea* to Southampton with a jammed aileron! The next fourteen years would be spent aboard Hermes, Comet jet airliners, Constellations and Britannias, his last command brought from Montreal to London in December 1963.

Bob Harwood also went on to landplanes, after returning *City of Cardiff* with Captain Denis Briggs (famous for sighting the Bismark from a 209 Squadron Catalina in 1941) after nine days on the Africa service. Initially posted to No 2 Line at Hurn Airport, he went on to fly Argonauts, Hermes, Constellations, Comets and then VC-10s as a Senior Captain with British Airways, before finally unbuckling the seat straps for retirement in September 1973. Argonauts had begun leaving London for the Middle East in November 1949, the month a new flying boat station had opened in East Africa.

LAKE NYASA

Demobbed from the Royal Navy in 1946, 'David' Rose had returned to Poole and was swiftly promoted to Coxswain 1st Class of the passenger launches. Having requested an overseas ('contract') posting, he was flown out from London Airport by an Avro York, but not being a fare-paying passenger, was offloaded at Cairo. After a few months operating passenger launches at Karangi Creek, Karachi, he was posted to Calcutta, on the Hooghli river, and then Rangoon, on the Irrawadi, where passengers and crews stayed overnight at the Strand Hotel. He had then joined the Africa service at Khartoum on the Nile, followed by eighteen months on the Zambesi at Victoria Falls, before finally posted to Cape Maclear, Lake Nyasa, where preparations were in hand for the forthcoming Solent service.

David and Charles Livingstone had arrived at the Cape in 1861 and had named it after Sir Thomas Maclear, the Astronomer Royal at the Cape of Good Hope. In 1928 Sir Alan Cobham had landed the Singapore flying boat on the long Rift Valley lake during his extensive survey of Africa, but was unable to persuade the then governor of Nyasaland to invest in air travel. Twenty-one years later, events had conspired otherwise.

Born of the post-war demand in food-rationed Britain for vegetable (cooking) oil, and orchestrated by the (Labour) Government's Overseas Food Corporation from 1948, the Ground Nut Scheme had attracted one hundred thousand British ex-servicemen: employed in clearing large areas of dense scrubland to commercially grow peanuts at Kongwa, in the central province of the British protectorate of Tanganyika, rather than the tree covered Southern District.

The scheme proved disastrous. The exposed top soils had blown away and there was insufficient rainfall to soften the hardened sand and clay beneath. In 1949 *Helmsdale* flew over 100 tons of salvaged agricultural equipment from Lindi to Nkhata Bay on Lake Nyasa, for use in another oil-producing scheme involving the cultivation of Tung trees. By then, Solents had taken over the Sandringham services to Dar-es Salaam, Karachi and Nairobi, and were flying due south from Lake Naivasha to Victoria Falls rather than follow the longer 'Horseshoe' route along the East African coast. Aware of the presence of *Helmsdale*, the new governor of Nyasaland persuaded BOAC to make a trial landing on the southern tip of the lake at Cape Maclear, where a luxurious hotel had just been completed, featuring a swimming pool and an airstrip, essential to avoid the rocky dirt 'road' through the hills, virtually impassable during the rainy season. BOAC and Central African Airways both subsequently applied to operate the diversion to Nyasaland (between Johannesburg and Nairobi) and after a long period of deliberation, the African Central Air Authority had agreed in favour of BOAC.

Flown from Victoria Falls to Harare (Salisbury) to pick up a Land Rover for the long drive to Blantyre, the capital of Nyasaland, and on to the Cape, David expected to arrive at Monkey Bay about ten o'clock in the evening. Coming across two local boys going that way he gave them a lift. But at nightfall, with just a few miles left, he took a bend too fast and ended up in the 'Bundu'. Nobody was hurt, only shaken, so he suggested the boys might like to go on to the hotel for help, which drew a swift 'No- too dark and leopards around!' The night was spent aboard the Land Rover waiting for the sun to rise. A lorry chanced by at daylight and though the roof and sides were packed with humanity, they were all able to squeeze aboard. Returning later with some crew members, David found the Land Rover was undamaged and pulling it back onto the road, continued on to the Cape as planned.

On arrival, he met up with station manager Gordon Davidson, engineer Bert Baker and radio operator John Harrop, whose 'radio shack' had been built a short distance from the shore, adjacent to the hotel. The sensitive ground to air radio equipment had been sent by lorry from Blantyre, some 50 miles away. As yet there was no mooring and no means of bringing passengers ashore, other than a 12 foot open launch owned by the hotel, though a BOAC passenger launch was on its way by rail from Durban. Given charge of four native boys, David began building a jetty, using the hotel launch to lay a mooring buoy fashioned from an old girder and chain link. The first landing was made on 3 November 1949 when a Solent was diverted during a return flight from Johannesburg. Flown by Captain Alastair Majendie, the flying boat emerged from the spray to find David standing in the little open launch and waving a flag to guide him to the buoy, hoping he would not be swamped in the process!

Ferried ashore in the launch, the passengers had their documents scrutinised by a doctor and by Peter Green of the Nyasaland Police, who had driven 150 miles from Fort Johnson (now Mangochi), before allowed to continue by road to their various destinations. Seven days later, the first of the full diversionary services left Southampton. From then on, one of the thrice-weekly Solent services to Vaaldam was diverted to Nyasa on Tuesday, followed on Thursday by a crew flying a reciprocal course. The Zambesi terminus had also been updated and the Rhodesian Government had financed a new, 6 mile road to the luxurious and elegant Victoria Falls Hotel.

The BOAC launch duly arrived at the railhead at Chipoka, some 12 miles round the lake, where David found it perched in a cradle on a flat-top railcar. With his head boy Gideon as interpreter, he organized a large number of local people into laying a line of old railway sleepers to the shore. Exposure to the open air had opened up the seams however and the launch was left in the shallows for twenty-four hours, where it was constantly bailed until 'plimmed up'. Both Power Meadow engines were untested and a tow was organised back to the flying boat station. A 16 foot launch eventually arrived at the railhead, this time accompanied by a crane! With two passenger launches available, passengers were taken the more direct route to Monkey Bay to continue on by car. The smaller hotel launch was retained for water control, for apart from the odd floating branch, a wary eye had to be kept open for basking hippos – and for crocodiles, all too visible on the rocks in the clear waters below. The permanent staff lodged in an annexe of the hotel. Then as now, it was a lovely spot for off-duty hours and having had a word with the aircrew, a few golf clubs were kindly flown in, enabling David to 'tee-off' across the baked earth of the airstrip, when he was usually joined by radio operator Johnny Harrop.

Having already filled a teaching post at the Field End Road Primary School at Eastcote, Middlesex, and known by her mother to have 'itchy feet', 22 year old Kathleen (Margaret) Lenham was advised by her second cousin, on leave from Tanganyika, to write to the Overseas Food Corporation to see whether they had a vacancy for an 'Infant Teacher'. Surprised to receive an answering letter and to find there was a vacancy, she had presented herself at the Hospital for Tropical Diseases in London, where she was subjected to the same inoculating jabs experienced by Joan Godber, and with her travelling expenses paid by her employer, had left the Pinner family home for the Victoria terminal and an expected three year absence abroad. On reflection, boyfriend David Gurney had taken it all rather calmly.

A former wartime RAF pilot, David had been taught to fly in the peaceful skies of eastern America as part of the (1941-43) Arnold Scheme, instigated by the uniquely five star, commanding general of the United States Army Air Forces, Henry H. Arnold. As a 24 year-old Army

Kathleen Lenham.
© MRS K GURNEY

Lieutenant, 'Hap' Arnold had himself been taught to fly at the Wright Brothers School of Aviation at Huffman Prairie, Ohio, in 1911! Despite the urgency for pilots, over fifty per cent of the British cadets had been 'washed-out', but David had gained his American wings and had politely declined an offer to become an instructor. A childhood friend of the husband of her older sister Doris, he had met Kathleen at a local tennis club and most of their courting had been done at the RAF hospital at Halton, where the reservist was under observation for suspected tuberculosis.

On 26 December 1949 Kathleen was driven by coach to Lyndhurst in the New Forest for an overnight stay, and in the morning was taken on to the Southampton terminal where the BOAC baggage department had stamped the tags of her two items of luggage with the destination of Nairobi, and overwritten both with 'Kongwa'. The flying boat appeared rather welcoming, gently rocking in the pontoon with the cabin lights ablaze, and with so much to take in, time and the conscious memory of the early morning departure passed all too quickly. She had however been given a card that informed her that for 'purposes of take off and alighting' she had been allocated seat number six in cabin E (on the top deck). To retain the seat at 'transit stops' she was to write her name on the reverse (though her name had already been typed in) and to leave the card on the seat, blue side uppermost- when all and sundry would be aware that it was Occupied (in bold letters) by Miss K. Lenham. Should she subsequently wish to change her seat, she was to please consult the steward. Of more importance perhaps at this stage of her journey into the unknown, was the slip of typed paper given to her which said that a telegram had been handed in at North London at thirty-three minutes past five and had been phoned through to Berth 50 at ten minutes past seven that morning. Addressed to Miss Lenham, BOAC Flight 155, it read 'Safe Voyage. Love and Best Wishes. Mum, Dad, Doris and Heather'.

At half past eight she received a carbon copied Flight Information flimsy that revealed the captain's name as Rotherham, and informed her that at 09.30 local time, the RMA *City of Belfast* was 20 miles north, north-west of Barfleur and 9,500 feet above sea level. She was also informed that 'in

Solent 2 *Salisbury* believed flown by Captain Baker.
COURTESY BOB RAYNER

about' fifteen minutes, they would pass the French coast to port ('left' added in brackets) when they would be 10 miles east of Caen. Equally helpful, the Remarks section advised her that 'Local time' required adding another hour to G.M.T. and the reader was asked to please pass the flimsy to other passengers, though later joining other mementoes within the rather stylish map case cum stationery folder presented to her and her fellow travellers.

Inscribed 'Your Speedbird Companion', the stiff-backed folder was decorated with colourful sketches of the sights associated with the routes: a smiling captain about to shake your hand, an efficient looking stewardess, a speeding passenger launch, a double decked passenger coach, an elephant, crouching tiger and leaping antelope, and an eagle eyed customs official rummaging through the contents of a suitcase – framed by evocative prose such as Tennyson's 'Close to the sun in lovely lands' and Masefield's ' Dipping through the tropics by the palm green shores'.

Inside, a large protective flap was decorated with a blue sky and white clouds overwritten by four lines of prose attributed to Kenneth Gandar-Dower and Amateur Adventure: 'To feel the engines power, Their brave strong purr, to reach at last the crest, Of my lone island in the sunset hour, And dipping down the dusk to come to rest'. The remainder featured a double row of bright cascading waterfalls either side of a sky-blue panel superimposed with summer clouds, the side panels devoted to the stars and planets.

The front of the double map pocket declared that BOAC aimed to make Speedbird travel the most enjoyable as well as the most efficient way of 'getting about' the world, a high ambition, but not beyond achievement. The reader was asked to help by finding time to complete a comment card issued by the steward towards the end of the flight, and to tell, 'quite frankly', just where and how the service could be improved, for which the airline would be sincerely grateful. Beneath, in much smaller print, Kathleen was informed that the steward had magazines, playing cards, books and other amenities available if she required them, the remaining space filled by (in bold print) 'British Overseas Airways Corporation In Association With Qantas Empire Airways, South African Airways (and) Tasman Empire Airways Limited'.

The maps were something else, the inside page taken up by an eye-catching advertisement for the Dunlop company, before the start of interesting information regarding the peoples, geography and economic growth of the regions concerned. Opened out, the pages formed a large double sided map of the outward and return passage from Britain to the Middle East, with coloured high ground, lakes and seas. Bold red lines showed the main routes and the mileage between refuelling stops, with a guide to converting miles to kilometres and feet to metres. There were also coloured illustrations of cloud formations. Refolded, the back page explained that because you would often be flying above cloud, or too high to see details on the ground (neither of which applied to flying boats) the airline did not provide an hour by hour description of the countries below, but hoped that the route map would help to form a mental picture of the lands and people over which you were flying. The remaining two thirds of the page was headed 'For Your Personal Notes'. Other mementoes tucked within the map pocket included a small oblong of blank notepaper, a colourful BOAC sticker – and a safety leaflet headed 'We Can't Be Too Careful' in large black letters; fronted by a photograph of passengers reading, chatting and applying make-up while secured by seat straps, superimposed by an overlarge 'No Smoking, Fasten Seat Belts' sign.

You were told that 'On ships you have boat drill, on cars you have bumpers and on trains communication cords- so please don't let this leaflet alarm you: rather let it reassure you that your care is our foremost consideration whilst you are travelling with us.' A fold-down section revealed six photographs of a stewardess attaching a lifebelt, with a reminder not to inflate it until well clear of the aircraft cabin and to use the whistle provided in a pocket in the battery case to summon assistance! Six explanatory paragraphs were headed Seat Belt, Life Jacket, Emergency Exits, Dinghies, Rations and First Aid Packs, while the lower half of the page, headed Aircraft Maintenance, detailed the servicing, inspection and

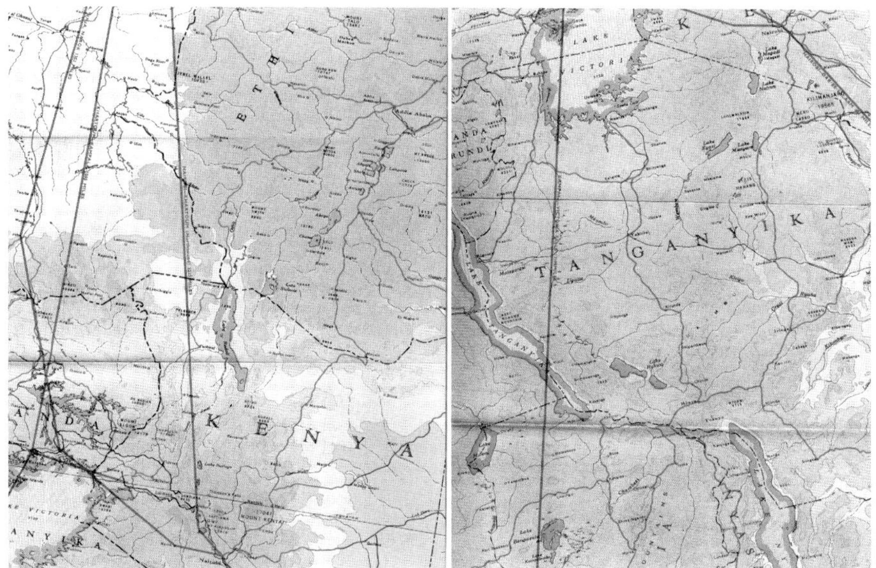

BOAC Africa Route Maps. © MRS KATHLEEN GURNEY

checks carried out on company aircraft. A thoughtful aside warned that after dark, a red glow might be observed coming from the engine exhaust outlets: the glow was there all the time and was quite normal, but was only visible after darkness.

As flying boat passengers were normally flown during the hours of daylight, they may have felt cheated, or perhaps relieved, at not seeing the phenomenon. The reverse of the little leaflet was taken up by three paragraphs headed Pressurisation, Oxygen Masks – and Your Ears, the only subject of interest in a Solent, as it explained how to relieve the 'fullness' in your head when descending or ascending in 'non-pressurised Speedbirds' Due to varying pressure at different heights, it could be quickly relieved by yawning, holding your nose and blowing with your mouth shut, chewing 'something', or just swallowing until you felt a

BRITISH OVERSEAS AIRWAYS CORPORATION

MARINE AIRPORT, BERTH 50, CANUTE ROAD, SOUTHAMPTON.

Telephone: Southampton 3811 Telegrams: Speedbird, Southampton,

B·O·A·C

BOAC Letterhead. COURTESY BOB RAYNER.

clicking sensation in your ears. Any slight earache you might feel was rare and would quickly pass – but again, it was unlikely that anyone aboard the relatively low flying Solent would have need of any of these remedies.

At Khartoum, a rather bemused Kathleen was served breakfast by an impossibly tall, white robed and red-belted ebony skinned waiter, complete with fez, the first African she had ever seen, though the heat had begun to affect her. At home, most would only just be getting over Christmas! On subsequently crossing the Equator ('the Line') she received a certificate, beautifully illustrated by Gordon Davey with mythological creatures and flying machines, which confirmed that Miss Kathleen Margaret Lenham of Hampstead had joined the Winged Order of 'Line Shooters'. The printers had obviously not anticipated female passengers as the certificate confirmed that 'he' was henceforth entitled to all privileges of Line-Shooters wherever 'he' may be. Filled in with ball point, the time, date and aircraft sections confirmed that the *City of Belfast* had crossed the Equator at exactly 11.45 GMT on 29 December 1949.

All good fun – but the long hours in the air, the heat, engine noise, and buffeting by thermals had taken their toll on Kathleen whose instinctive reaction on seeing Lake Naivasha was 'Oh boy- we've arrived!' A mini-bus took her to the Norfolk Hotel at Nairobi where she decided to stay for a couple of nights to recover, begun with a nice long drink of – milk! Despite the advertisements back home, there was no en suite here, the native 'boys' hanging about the landing waiting to be told (ideally in Swahili) to run her a bath! A DC-3 completed the journey to the school.

Kongwa was not far from a single track rail connection to the port of Dar Es Salaam and a township had sprung up complete with a hospital and a school, which provided education for the children of the employees, who joined one of the four 'Houses' of Curie, Livingstone, Nightingale and Wilberforce. Kathleen was given a single room, among a line of single storey mud 'huts' which, after the traditional gift of a blanket, would be looked after by her own 'house-boy'. The room had a bath, but the water had to be heated outside by the tall and utterly reliable young native. The early evenings were spent back in the class room, though there was no teacher, just sheets of typed Swahili to help newcomers communicate with the African staff. Fortunately, Kathleen had a natural 'ear' for languages.

At great cost to the British taxpayers, the forty-nine million-pound Ground Nut Scheme was abandoned in 1951 (the Tung Oil scheme was overtaken by a synthetic oil) and after just eighteen months, Kathleen was given the choice of returning by air or by ocean liner. Having 'done the one', she enjoyed a rather more stable trip from Dar Es Salaam to Tilbury. But not before giving her locally crafted safari boots to her faithful house-boy (they just didn't fit in the wooden travelling box), who insisted she provide a chitty to confirm they really were 'a gift'. Back home again, a letter soon arrived from the Crown Agents offering her a job elsewhere,

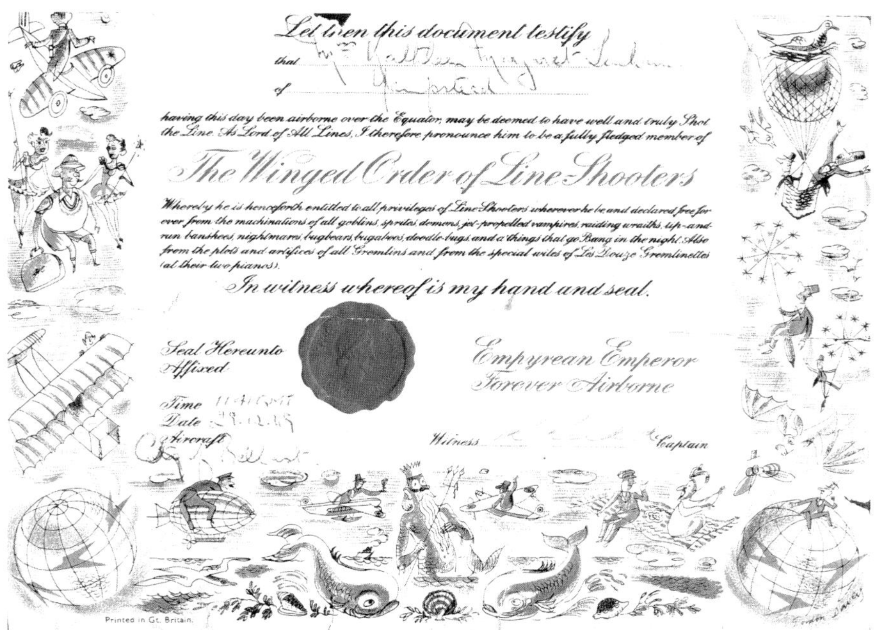

Let then this document testify

that

of

having this day been airborne over the Equator, may be deemed to have well and truly Shot the Line. As Lord of All Lines, I therefore pronounce him to be a fully fledged member of

The Winged Order of Line-Shooters

Whereby he is henceforth entitled to all privileges of Line-Shooters wherever he be and declared free for ever from the machinations of all goblins, sprites, demons, jet-propelled vampires, raiding wraiths, tip-and-run banshees, nightmares, bugbears, bugaboos, doodle-bugs and a' things that go Bang in the night. Also from the plots and artifices of all Gremlins and from the special wiles of Les Douze Gremlinettes (at their two pianos).

In witness whereof is my hand and seal.

Seal Hereunto Affixed

Empyrean Emperor Forever Airborne

Time

Date

Aircraft

Witness

Captain

Printed in Gt. Britain.

Crossing the Line Certificate. COURTESY MRS KATHLEEN GURNEY

which was rather nice, but she had already decided to marry the patient and understanding David. Called up to instruct on Chipmunks at Inverness during the Korean conflict, he had later bought a little blue and white, two-seat open cockpit Tipsy Trainer (G-AFWT) and Kathleen had spent happy weekends helping the instructional flights from Denham airfield.

By the late 1950s there was a shortage of former military pilots for the airlines and in 1960 the Ministry of Aviation, BOAC and BEA jointly opened a College of Air Training in Hampshire. Fifteen year-old Richard Gurney had written to British Airways expressing his interest in becoming a pilot and though interviewed at school (the Royal Grammar, High Wycombe), there was no place available until he was 19. In the meantime, he had joined the Combined Cadet Force, won his gliding wings with No 662 Gliding School at Arbroath and was awarded a Flying Scholarship: taught to fly Cessna 150 and 152s at Luton Airport. A graduate of the airline college, he now captains Boeing 747-400 long haul airliners, with memories of performing aerobatics in Chipmunks while training at the grass airfield at Hamble – just across the water from where his mother had set out for Africa. The site of the Kongwa school is now occupied by pupils

Capt. Rose at bar of BOAC Solent. © ROSE COLLECTION

and staff of Mnyakongo Primary School.

With BOAC yet to make a surplus, drastic changes had to be made. Director fees were halved and over eighty executives persuaded to leave. The longer-range landplanes enabled maintenance bases to be cut from eight to two, staffs were reduced by one third, and the airline recorded its first net profit at the end of the 1951/52 financial year. By then the flying boats had gone. Returned from Johannesburg on November 14 1950, *Somerset* had trailed a 20-foot long 'paying-off' pennant as she taxied across Southampton Water, ending all BOAC flying boat operations. Three days later she was returned to Belfast.

Despite her globe-trotting lifestyle, Joan had kept in touch with Harry, one of the first pilots seconded to Aden Airways, a subsidiary of BOAC at Asmara Airport, and was able to join him when her Solent landed at Alexandria. They were married in December, when after two and a half years of flying, her last passengers had loaded her with champagne and gifts. The DC-3s spent much of their time ferrying pilgrims to Jeddah, the nearest airport to Mecca, and almost constantly in the air, Harry had acquired a bushy black beard. Having risen to company chief pilot, he returned to BOAC in 1958 and when presenting him with an MBE for his services to civil aviation, the Duke of Edinburgh had said 'Don't let them make you take it off!'

The manager of No 4 Line at Poole and Southampton, awarded a Commendation for Valuable Services in the Air in the 1943 Birthday

Launch coxswain David Rose
Lake Nyasa.
© DAVID ROSE

Honours List and the 1951 Brackley Memorial Trophy for outstanding work in flying boat operations, Captain 'Jim' Alger had become general manager of Aden Airways. On retiring to Ringwood in Dorset, he presented Joan with a glazed panel rescued from behind the cocktail bar of a retired Solent and the 'Springbok' received pride of place behind the bar of the family home at Ashley in the New Forest.

Having remained with flying boats until the end, David Rose became a senior steward on BOAC long-haul services and married Hazel, a stewardess, whom he had met at an afternoon tea dance at Bournemouth Pavilion. Those were the days! Lake Nyasa now forms part of a National Park, where tourists still soak up the sun – though without the Cape Maclear Hotel. The short-lived revival of fortunes with the flying boats had caused the owners to move the hotel brick by brick to the lakeside beach of Senga Bay (Salima) in 1951, where the renamed Sunbird Livingstonia Beach Hotel retains the colonial style arched colonnade and aperitifs are sipped on the beach or beside the pool.

Unlike the ten years of the C-Class, the Solents had only been flying since 1948 – but only Aquila or Australia offered a chance of them avoiding the inevitable axe and blow torch.

Chapter Nine

A Closing Door

Hamworthy Breakers

With no buyers prepared to take on the retired BOAC Sandringhams, in March 1954 *Portsmouth*, *Penzance*, *Pembroke*, *Portsea* and *Perth* were sold for disposal. But with Aquila operating from Southampton, were moored by the slipway at Hamworthy, before languishing on beaching gear about the 'hard' until broken up. Notices and barriers warned off the curious, but the site continued to interest the locals. Earlier in the war, John Newell had seen the soldier dangling beneath the Dakota from his perch among the branches of a tree in the family garden. 'Demobbed' from RAF Benson, where he had been a librarian for the photographic unit, the 22 year old had joined his friend Derek Alton for a Sunday afternoon stroll along the shore. After parking Derek's car, they came to the hard and keeping a wary eye open, slipped in between the silent Sandringhams in the bright sunlight, before resuming their stroll, keenly anticipating the results of their 'photo-shoot'. They would not be disappointed. The Bermuda-Class

Retired Sandringhams Hamworthy. © John Newall.

Aerial view of Hamworthy and retired Sandringhams.
COURTESY HARRY ASHLEY.

trio were more fortunate however, *Saint Andrew* and *Saint David* leaving the forlorn weed infested concrete for new careers in Uruguay and *Saint George* later departing for Australia.

Leased from the Ministry of Civil Aviation, the retired Solents also began making their way to Dorset. With the exception of *Singapore* and *Southampton,* they were all scrapped: ending the sound, borne on the prevailing winds, of the regular engine 'run ups', even on a Sunday, that had so plagued the locals, though the residents of West Parley, close to Hurn Airport, probably wondered what all the fuss was about! The natural beach at Lower Hamworthy (near todays Ferry Terminal) had reverted to a weekend retreat for young families, with some having no qualms whatsoever in leaving the small family dinghy drawn up on the sand during the week, where the only other 'occupant' was the metal tank of the local oyster fisherman. That all changed with the arrival of *City of Salisbury,* moored off-shore before dragged tail first onto the sand, where the words Keep Off were emphatically chalked on the corroding metal. Had you avoided the fisherman, the natural choice of watchman, and slipped inside, you would have found a disappointing jumble of exposed cabling and sharp-edged metal, though the seat frames in the cockpit would have drawn you forward to imagine the far-off sights and sounds viewed during a relatively short career. For some, a more unique memory came

Solents *Solway & City of Liverpool* at Hamworthy.
Abandoned coffee bar project. AUTHOR COLLECTION

with the arrival of the Solent 2 *Solway* and the Solent 3 *City of Liverpool*, following the failure of a scheme to join the airframes to provide a novel coffee bar on the Thames. Moved from Lake to Lower Hamworthy, the removal of the engines and wing sections left the two fuselages precariously heeled over in the shallows, respectively supported by a stub of a port and starboard tailplane. An unmissable attraction for young boys, prepared to scramble up the steeply angled interiors to be 'snapped' topside on emerging from the mooring compartment!

The ancient tribes had utilised the harbour resources: fashioning the mud into black burnished pottery, leaving sea water in pots to be sun-dried to salt, and harvesting the oyster beds. The presence of so much metal at Hamworthy now attracted metal workers into the area to create new goods after the austere years of wartime. The scrapping of the last of the relics during the mid 1960s ended any tangible connection with flying boats however and another fifty years or so would pass before a group of residents decided to do something about it.

PRINCESS

Having failed to build the first jet fighter flying boats, due mainly to the prototype taking four years to emerge for a maiden flight in 1947, by which time the war in the Pacific had been won by carrier-based aircraft, Saunders-Roe had gone on to produce a radically new airliner. Born of

BOAC's interest in operating three giant flying boats across the Atlantic to New York, on 22 August 1952, six years after work had begun, when costs had risen from an estimated three million to ten million, Geoffrey Tyson slipped the giant Princess flying boat smoothly into the sky above Cowes.

Designed to seat 105 passengers and a crew of six for up to fifteen hours, the 150 tons were supported by a 148 foot wing fitted with ten Bristol Proteus propeller-driven turbine engines rated at 3,500 horsepower, capable of cruising at nearly 400 miles an hour for over 5,000 miles. The four inner engines comprised eight paired units driving a double set of four bladed propellers, the rearmost contra-rotating. Though demonstrated at the 1952 and 1953 Farnborough Air Shows, the advance of jet-engined landplanes effectively ended the project and with it, all hopes of a new British flying boat service. The sole flying example was cocooned at Calshot in 1954, along with a second airframe. The third was cocooned on the slipway at West Cowes, and I remember TV personality Hughie Green appealing on the radio for them to be preserved as an example of British technology. A plan to convert them into landplane freighters also failed to attract sufficient interest and they were broken up in 1967. Another design featured a seventy-four seat flying boat powered by six de Havilland Goblin jet engines concealed within an immaculately contoured swept-wing, but the Duchess never progressed beyond the drawing board. In the meantime, an enterprising former Sunderland pilot and squadron commander had found a niche for some of the survivors.

AQUILA

Barry Thomson Aikman had learnt to fly while at Oxford University and had become a regular RAF officer (RAFRO) with 210 Squadron. As a young Flying Officer, he was the first squadron pilot to encounter a long-range 'Kurier' during a convoy protection patrol in April 1941. Diving his Sunderland close to the surface, his gunners were told to withhold fire to draw the enemy closer, though the rear gunner was wounded in the legs as a shell exploded in the turret. But with all four Sunderland engines smartly throttled back, the German pilot was forced to overshoot and drew the full force of its guns, led by the four in the rear turret. With both port engines damaged and the inner stopped, the KG40 crew broke away and were thought by British Intelligence not to have reached the French coast. Able to return to Oban, Barry Aikman was recommended for the Distinguished Flying Cross. A Distinguished Flying Medal was also recommended for his wounded rear gunner Reg Williamson, who had joined the squadron a few days earlier as a trainee and earned one of the quickest medals for bravery of the war. By the July investiture, the pilot was flying Catalinas as an acting Flight Lieutenant. Command of the squadron and Wing Commander rank had followed before leaving the service and becoming a director of the Lancashire Aircraft Corporation. But with a number of retired Hythe-Class Sunderlands available, in May 1948 he had formed Aikman Airways Limited, though trading as Aquila Airways. Two Sunderlands were bought for twenty thousand pounds with an option to purchase another six for twenty-four thousand.

In June, the Soviet Union closed all road and rail links to the areas of Berlin controlled by America, Britain and France, in an attempt to control the supply of food and fuel and ultimately the whole city. Along with many post-war flying concerns, Aquila Airways owed its survival to the government decision to include civilian charter companies within the airlift of supplies: known as Operation Vittles by the Americans flying in to Templehof and Operation Plainfare by the British routed to Gatow. *Haslemere* and *Halstead* arrived at the company's base at Hamble in July and in agreement with British European Airways (tasked with organising the civil operation) joined the Berlin Airlift in August, supplementing the ten Sunderland Vs jointly provided by 201 and 230 RAF Squadrons.

Flying up to three sorties a day along a narrow air corridor between Finkenwerder on the Elbe to Lake Havel (which adjoined Gatow), helping to load 5 tons of supplies, and assisting the refuelling, meant long, tiring, days for the aircrew. The landplanes reeked of coal dust and inevitable seepages. But the flying boats were maintained against corrosion and the roof mounted control systems proved ideal for the task. Dispensing with exposed pulleys and wires, Shorts had provided the C-Class and Sunderlands with a hydraulic system to control the engines and propellers, whereby small pistons fitted to each engine reacted to the movement of matching pistons attached by fluid-filled pipes to the throttle and pitch levers in the cockpit. Together with their military counterparts, the Aquila Sunderlands flew in block (cooking) salt and brought out manufactured goods to keep the economy going. They also rescued hundreds of hungry young evacuees. Bought with *Hungerford* in December, *Hadfield* completed the trio of civilian flying boats in the airlift until ice floes closed the Havel River.

Acquired in January 1949, *Hunter, Hampshire, Hawkesbury* and *Henley* were joined by *Howard, Hobart, Hythe* and *Hudson* in February. *Himalaya,* the prototype Sandringham, arrived in May. As in Australia, holiday destinations as yet without runways in the vicinity provided a lifeline for the remaining flying boat operators and in March, Aquila began a weekly service to Lisbon and to Funchal Bay in Madeira. Operations doubled in the summer, when a new service opened between Falmouth and the Scilly Isles. Revenue also came from charters to deliver ships crews to the Middle East and bring seamen to their ports of departure in Britain. Though refused permission to take over BOACs 'Springbok' service, due to end in October, in June the company completed proving flights for an 'inter-city' service between Southampton, Edinburgh and Glasgow. *Helmsdale* was

Aquila Hythe-Class *Hampshire.* © José Carvalho.

bought in October, the month *Hungerford* ended a series of airborne pilgrimages from Foynes to Fátima in Portugal, where the Virgin Mary is said to have appeared to three young children. By December 1951 *Hadfield, Hudson* and *Hungerford* were the last Hythes in service. Denis and Margaret Thatcher were among the honeymooners heading off to the warmer climes of Madeira that December. Unthinkable to most politicians of the time, the 26 year old bride would become the first woman to lead a political party in Britain and the first to be elected prime minister. Lord and Lady Thatcher would return to the island for their golden wedding anniversary, though not by flying boat.

The fleet was updated in 1952 when Solent 3 *Sydney* took over the Southampton-Madeira service. But the loss of *Hudson,* which struck a rock at Funchal harbour in January 1953, and *Hungerford,* which sank while on tow between Fawley and Calshot following a disastrous night take off near Cowes seven days later, marked the end of the Hythes. *Hadfield* was held purely as a reserve.

A three million pound offer for the Princess flying boats stored at Calshot was refused, but *City of Funchal* (BOACs training Solent 3) arrived in 1954, the year the company was absorbed by the Britavia Group. Barry Aikman would remain chairman for another two years. Capri was added to the services and having made the proving flight to Madeira, chief pilot Captain Douglas Pearson brought *City of Funchal* in to Grande Marina Harbour on 21 May after a non-stop flight of less than six hours. Among

Aquila Solent 3 *City of Funchal* at Madeira. © JOSÉ CARVALHO.

the delighted passengers to step ashore was Gracie Fields, whose home, La Canzone del Mare (Song of the Sea), overlooked the bay of Marina Piccola. Scheduled flights would thereafter take around eight and three quarter hours, with a refuelling stop at Lake Marignane.

In 1955 Aquila purchased the Solent 4s *Aotearoa 11* and *Awatere* from TEAL, the four-strong Solent fleet bringing a return to the luxury associated with Imperial Airways and BOAC. Well-heeled passengers were flown on summer schedules to the Canary Islands, Madeira, Las Palmas, Genoa, Capri, Majorca and Montreux. Valuable military contracts took British troops out to Cyprus and in 1956, the year of the Suez Crisis, Solents landed on Egypt's Great Bitter Lake to evacuate hundreds of British civilians from Fanara. September gales wrecked *City of Funchal* at Santa Margherita harbour near Genoa however and to replace the loss, *Southampton* was retrieved from open storage at Hamworthy and prepared for service. The company recorded a surplus of over ninety thousand pounds in 1957. But just before eleven o'clock in the evening of 15 November, *Sydney* crashed on the wooded slopes of a disused chalk pit near Chessel on the Isle of Wight, having lost power from both starboard engines at the start of the flight to Lisbon. Thirteen ultimately survived the inferno. Public confidence was shaken and with parts increasingly difficult to find for the sleeve-valve engines, Aquila closed down following the return of *Awateri* from Madeira on 30 September 1958 – ending all British commercial flying boat operations.

A long and difficult enquiry subsequently cleared both deceased pilots of the ill fated *Sydney* of blame. Fifty years later, a memorial service was held at the parish church of Saint Mary the Virgin in the nearby village of Brook, and in 2008 the church on the grassy hill received a plaque in remembrance of the eight crew and thirty-seven passengers who lost their lives.

Sealand

The Grumman Aircraft Engineering Corporation had virtually cornered the light flying boat market, having evolved a workable combination of floats and retractable wheels way back in 1929. Many places were still reliant on rivers, lakes and small airstrips to communicate with the world however and Shorts final throw of the flying boat dice had been revealed at the first Farnborough Air Show held in June 1948. The sleek Sealand amphibian was powered by two de Havilland Gipsy Queen, 340 horsepower, inverted engines driving three bladed propellers. Crewed by a single pilot, or pilot and navigator (using the fold down second seat), seven passengers could be flown at a comfortable 150 knots for over 570 nautical miles, the 42 foot long fuselage given oblong windows either side of an angled recess for the main wheels. The tail wheel neatly retracted up and behind the fuselage. Shorts retained the prototype and though the demonstrator fatally crashed in Norway, the amphibian would be sold to a clientèle as diverse and as varied as their use.

By the close of 1952, two had been sold to the Yugoslav airline

Short Sealand. First of three for Shell. Author Collection.

Jogoslovenski Aerotransport; another was based at Cairo for the business tycoon Ahmed Abboud Pasha, who had rescued the ailing British shipping company Khedivial Mail Line among his other achievements; and two had gone to Shell Petroleum, based at Singapore and Borneo. The Norwegian Vestlandske Luftfartselskap had taken two (without wheels) to operate scheduled flying boat services from Bergen to Trondheim via Alesund, and three were based at Dacca: one owned by Ralli Brothers, a Pakistan jute company, and two by the Transport Commission of the East Bengal Government. Another had gone to the Christian and Missionary Alliance.

The third, pre-war, expedition of Richard Archbold had been surprised to find a hitherto unknown yet cultivated valley of the Baliem River while making an airborne reconnaissance of the western interior of New Guinea. Enclosed by steep mountain ranges cloaked by clouds and mist, home to 'stone-age' tribes of warrior farmers untroubled by disease or severe climate change, the valley was likened to the timeless Tibetan 'Shangri-La' created by English writer James Hilton in his 1933 book *The Lost Horizon*, later made into an intriguing Hollywood film. Able to deliver missionaries and supplies to the area from an airstrip or river, a Sealand had been flown out to CAMA, though a punctured fuel tank caused an emergency descent off the Central Java coast and the aircraft had to be abandoned. A second, named *Gospel Messenger* at Belfast, arrived safely and entered service. But on 28 April 1955, an hour after leaving the runway at Sentani, the aircraft struck the unseen face of the mountain range, 1,000 feet above the cloud covered 9,500 foot pass that led into the valley. A devoted missionary pilot, Albert Lewis had been reconciled to the possibility of one day not returning from the dangerous flights into the interior and four years would pass before a ground party was able to reach the scattered wreckage.

The Sealand had also interested the Indian Navy, which received ten modified versions during 1953, almost fifty years after Eustace and Oswald had supplied the Indian Army with three observation balloons! Delivered to the country's first Naval Air Station at Cochin on Willingdon Island, a wartime Royal Navy base within Lake Vembanad, the SB7s featured extended wings, long range fuel tanks, uprated Gypsy Queen engines giving more cruising power, increased rudder area and a strengthened hull. Dual controls allowed two-pilot operations, with room for an observer and three passengers. A toilet compartment had also been fitted. Production ended with the departure of a third amphibian for Shell from Sydenham Airport, the former airstrip that had served the wartime Belfast factory, to be re-named after footballer George Best in 2006. Of the twenty-four built, three Sealands are known to have survived: displayed by the Indian Naval Museum at Bogmalo, the Museum of Aviation at Belgrade, and the Ulster Folk and Transport Museum at Cultra, Northern Ireland.

The last flying boat built by Shorts, it was also the last to be built in

Britain, where the achievements of the three brothers, irresistibly drawn into aviation after watching a balloon float serenely over the family home in Stanton by Dale, Derbyshire, had few reminders.

But thanks to the efforts of the Short Brothers Commemorative Society, in 2008 a plaque was unveiled at Rochester Esplanade by Lord Brabazon of Tara. Dedicated to Horace, Eustace, Oswald and their workforce, it serves as a tribute to their founding of Britain's aircraft, seaplane and flying boat industry, both on the Isle of Sheppey and at Rochester. For some years however, a stretch of the West Dorset Downs had displayed an unintentional memento of their most famous military flying boat.

BLOT ON THE LANDSCAPE

Formed at Calshot at the end of July 1947 to train aircrew on Sunderlands, No 235 Operational Conversion Unit had used the Chesil Beach bombing range near Abbotsbury to drop small white practice bombs on targets at the eastern end of the range; the puff of smoke revealing the accuracy or otherwise of a particular crew to the watching observers.

On the moonless night of 4 June 1951, the familiar sound of a Sunderland was heard droning towards the range, the novice crew briefed to make their first solo night bombing practise at the western end (the east was unserviceable) which would be lit for them. Having identified the Clear to Bomb signal on the shore below, the bomb racks were run out, followed by a descending turn over the land and a final turn towards the target lights, confirmed to those further back in the dark fuselage by the pilot's warning klaxon. Held in a long attacking dive towards the imaginary submarine, the airframe was suddenly shaken by a series of hard, uneven vibrations, which ended as the captain instinctively regained height.

When everyone had recovered, the aircraft was put into a gentle test dive from much higher up. But nothing happened. Taking flashlights, the crew began checking the interior and the wings for evidence of a bird strike, or worse, but with no result – until the ring-pull of a metal bilge cover in the galley floor revealed a mass of earth, grass and gorse. Had the dive been too early? Should they have checked the wind? Or was it pilot error? The truth was much simpler and in context with the times. Charts, not maps, were carried by flying boat crews, which gave little land detail other than prominent landmarks visible from sea level. This and the customary use of the eastern range had meant that no one was aware of a spur in the hills that reached closer to the sea to the west of Abbotsbury, fortunately in a downslope. A couple of feet lower...

Arriving back at base, the pilot was told to remain airborne until daylight, when the extent of the damage could be seen. Ordered back to the range, where any problems caused by the impact could be resolved away from a populated area, the continuous drone in the sky between

Portland and Lyme Regis was accompanied by red, green and white lights as a pair of air-sea rescue launches began churning the surface of the sea into luminous phosphorescence. Come the dawn, the launches sped away and the Sunderland headed back for a low pass over the 'tower at Calshot Castle. The long gashes and creases revealed the hull to be battered, but not holed, enabling the skipper to beach the aircraft in the shallows to the west of Southampton Water, rather than bale the crew, who had spent most of the night with a parachute clipped over the 'Mae West'. Though settled deeper in the mud than the makers intended, the ten aircrew were able to step onto a squadron launch as dry as when they had set out.

Returned to service (and the range) six months later, EJ153 became known as 'The Ploughman', while the 500 yard scar across the chalk downs gradually became covered by the inevitable grass and gorse. Five years later, in October 1956, the ill-fated Sunderland hit another unseen obstruction, this time a submerged rock, while taxiing off Castle Archdale and was finally written off.

SEAPLANE CLUB OF GREAT BRITAIN

In 1927, the December issue of Flight had bemoaned the lack of a seaplane club in Britain. Singapore had equipped two de Havilland Moths with floats and it was suggested the Air Ministry should subsidise a similar scheme. A few years later, two Tiger Moths had been fitted with floats by Short Brothers for evaluation at Rochester and Felixstowe as a possible seaplane trainer for the RAF. Nothing had come of it, though most Queen Bee pilotless, radio controlled versions were fitted with floats for target practice by naval gunners! In 1943, de Havilland produced yet another Tiger Moth basic trainer for the RAF, T5370 surviving the war and winning the 1958 Kings Cup Air Race before subsequently purchased by Norman Jones, owner of the Croydon based Rollason Aircraft and Engine Company. He also chaired the Tiger Club of Great Britain, formed by him at Croydon to primarily race Tiger Moths.

With the closure of Croydon, the club moved to Redhill Aerodrome in Surrey where, during the course of repairs following a heavy landing, Rollason converted the Moth to a floatplane using archive drawings supplied by de Havilland and a pair of American Edo floats from an Aeronca Sedan. Painted yellow overall, G-AIVW first took off from water on 20 July 1963, when Air Commodore Christopher Paul made a twenty minute flight from Lee-on-the-Solent. Official certification followed and on 29 September the Seaplane Club of Great Britain was inaugurated during a small ceremony at the Naval Air Station, when the 'Sea Tiger' (donated by Norman Jones) was named after Oswald Short, whose generous gift of five hundred pounds had enabled the club to get started. After a winter spent on wheels at Redhill, the Moth was refitted with floats in time to

Tom Brooke-Smith & Ivor Faulconer landing off Fishbourne Isle of Wight.
© IVOR FAULCONER

begin the first full season of flying during the 1964 Whit Sunday, within the auspices of the Tiger Club. On 16 August , Tom Brooke-Smith flew it to Shoreham for a first public showing during the Tiger Club Air Display. The longest cross-country to date, the drag of the floats was not helped by a strong headwind, but all went well and the return to Lee saw Beryl Saunders become the first lady member to fly the Moth solo. Tom also demonstrated the Sea Tiger at a large air display at Rochester, when the former Sunderland test pilot made yet another landing on the Medway.

Club members had formed a roster and flying usually began at Lee at ten thirty on a Sunday morning, depending on the tide. Ralph Toms and Sid Parker had been cleared to instruct and having paid four pounds membership plus ten shillings entry fee, members could train for a seaplane rating at a cost of five pounds an hour. With the retirement of Lord Douglas of Kirtleside, the presidency passed rather appropriately to John Lankester Parker. Within a short time, the experience gained by members encouraged the Ministry of Aviation to replace the lengthy qualifying seamanship exam with a much shorter set of practical questions. A qualified pilot from any flying club in Britain could have a dual check flight with a club instructor, for which he or she was required to pay just five bob a day on top of the hourly rate- with hopes that the membership, looked after by secretary, manager and instructor Nepean Bishop, would grow accordingly.

Returned to civilian life after the war, Lieutenant Faulconer, RNVR, had

found there was no naval equivalent of the RAF Reserve Flying Schools and had transferred his allegiance to the Tiger Moths of No 15 RFS at Redhill, until the advent of jet aircraft ended the Reserve Training Programme. The airfield had reopened in 1959 with the arrival of the Tiger Club, and the Seaplane Club enabled Ivor to again fly a British floatplane,

Wooton Creek. © IVOR FAULCONER.

some twenty-six years after flying the Seafox and Swordfish at Sandbanks, when he had been assessed as Above Average. Now living in a cottage with direct access to Wootton Creek, a sheltered estuary just over a mile inland from the Solent, he was kindly loaned the Sea Tiger by Norman Jones, and with a cement-filled toilet cistern as a mooring buoy, had no trouble at all in flying from the harbour during summer holidays spent in company of his delighted family and friends!

To avoid the corrosive salt water at Lee, the Sea Tiger was operated from Normans' own lake at Castle Water near Rye and then a flooded gravel pit at Dungeness, conveniently situated north-west of Lydd power station. Seen at air displays, on the Thames and even in Scotland (over 1,000 miles return), in 1973, ten years after first leaving the water, a crash-landing believed caused by insufficient speed during the final turn, ended with the Moth upside down but afloat. The wreckage was eventually salvaged and restored to full flying condition, though flying was curtailed in 1977 for modifications to enable wheels or floats to be fitted to eliminate the arduous journey by road for maintenance and the annual inspection. Flying resumed in 1978 when among other excursions, pilots visited Banbury Sailing Club at Boddington Reservoir in Northamptonshire. Repeat visits were made in 1979 and 1980. But on 27 August 1982, the Sea Tiger fell into the sea off Silver Sands near Rye after performing a low, steep turn. Both occupants survived the crash and were rescued by lifeboat. Washed ashore, the aircraft was inevitably written off, though the cockpit now forms part of the Robertsbridge Aviation Museum at Bush Barn, East Sussex, where many of the artefacts have also been retrieved from the sea.

Madeira Mariners

Aquila had begun winding down in January 1958, the month the Lisbon-Madeira service was closed, leaving the island economy of Madeira faced with a return to much longer connections by sea with the outside world. Thoughts had turned toward the stocks of retired military flying boats quietly awaiting their fate in various yards and in July, two gull-winged, long-range former U.S Navy, Martin Mariner 5s were purchased by Commandants Cancio Ferreira and Durval Mergulhäo on behalf of Aero-Topográfica SA which proposed operating three flights a week (including Sundays) from Cabo Ruivo, Lisbon. To save time and money, the Mariners would be converted to airline standard in Portugal rather than America.

Ferried out in August and September, the nose and tail turrets were removed and faired over, while the internal secondary structure was stripped to fit two double rows of forward-facing seats either side of a narrow aisle; for the average flight time was expected to last less than three and a half hours. Not a problem considering the hulls had supported some

Retired U.S. Navy Mariner on arrival at Lisbon. © José Mergulhão.

25 tons of military fittings and equipment for up to eighteen hours.

Further soundproofing was added and the windows enlarged or modified to open in an emergency. With everything completed to the express requirements of the Aeronáutica Civil, two former Aquila captains and co-pilots were contracted and with scheduled flights expected to start in October, a rather famous pilot had been taken on as training captain.

Aquila cockpit. Capt. Andrew Evans on left. © José Carvalho

Born in London, Harry Frank Gibbs had been educated at Wychwood (Preparatory) School in Bournemouth and on moving to Australia, where his mother had remarried, had adopted the name of 'Jim' Broadbent. Two years after gaining a private pilots licence, in 1931 the 21 year old had taken just a day to fly between Melbourne and Adelaide. He had then flown around Australia in seven days and less than eight and a half hours. Caught up in the enthusiasm for long-distance flying, he had vied with Jean Batten (New Zealand's answer to Amy Johnson) in shortening the time between Australia and England, taking just over four days to reach England in April 1938. Subsequently employed by Qantas Empire Airways and RAF Ferry Command, he had moved to England after the war and had flown for

Cabin interior ARTOP Mariner. © JOSÉ MERGULHÃO

Porto Santo at Funchal Madeira. © José Carvalho.

Silver City Airways before renewing his acquaintance with flying boats at Aquila.

No stranger to the Lisbon-Madeira shuttle, he had joined ARTOP in September 1958, and on 1 October took *Madeira* and the first eighteen passengers to Funchal in three and a quarter hours. On Sunday 9 November he and Tom Rowell climbed aboard *Porto Santo* to fly the first of the scheduled services to Funchal. But an hour after their departure from Cabo Ruivo, a radio message announced an emergency landing was about to be made in the Atlantic. Nothing more was heard or ever found of the flying boat, despite an intensive search by the Air Forces of Portugal, Spain, Britain and America, and by *Madeira*. The enquiry into the first commercial airline accident in Portugal proved inconclusive, but *Madeira* was dismantled and the former Aquila Solents *Southampton, Awateri* and *Aotearoa,* thought to have been bought in December, were towed to the Tagus riverbank for storage.

As in Dorset, the trio patiently awaited a buyer. Unlike Hamworthy, there was no 'false-dawn' of engine run ups to keep hopes alive, and after thirteen years exposure to the elements, all three were broken up in 1971 without, it seems, any wish to preserve any of them for posterity. After a six-year wait, communication by air had been restored on 18 July 1964 when a Constellation of Transportes Aéreos Portugueses deposited eighteen passengers on a runway built above the east coast of the island. Concerned to show the families and friends that those taking that fateful flight aboard *Porto Santo* had not been forgotten however, in June 2010 former Aquila traffic officer Norman Hull presented a plaque to the Aquila Airways Lounge of the Madeira Story Centre Museum at Funchal, in lasting memory of the six crew and thirty passengers. Over 1,360 Mariners were built, the sole complete example preserved at the Pima Air and Space Museum at Tucson, Arizona, on permanent loan from the National Museum of Naval Aviation at Pensacola.

France

With Germany taking an active commercial interest in flying the Atlantic, in 1938 the French Air Ministry had issued a specification for an aircraft capable of flying forty passengers and mail for over 3,700 miles against a 60 mile an hour headwind. The Latécoère 631 had taken shape in the Toulouse factory and Flight Refuelling had sent advisers over the channel to assist with equipping the flying boat and a Farman bomber. But with the sudden collapse of France, company chief designer Harry Smith and chief engineer Percy Allinson were fortunate to find room aboard one of the last boats to leave Le Havre. Work continued under the Vichy French government and 01 flew from Lake Marignane in November 1942. Confiscated by the Germans as a potential long-range transport, 63+11 was flown to Friedrichshaven on Lake Constance but was destroyed by allied aircraft in 1944.

A second 631 had been completed in 1943, the year Pierre died, but was dismantled and hidden to enable the Resistance to blow up the factory! Toulouse was liberated in August 1944, the factory was rebuilt, and with the parts retrieved and assembled, the fuselage and wings were transported to Lake Biscarosse. After three months of re-fitting, 02 had taken to

Latécoère L631 *Lionel de Marmier*.

the air on 6 March 1945, fitted with 14 cylinder, 1600 horsepower Wright Cyclone engines, rather than the 12 cylinder, 920 horsepower Hispano-Suiza's of the first. Named after the ace French fighter pilot Lionel de Marmier by Ministre de l'air Charles Tillon, a former Resistance leader, it was flown to Dakar before displayed at Paris and in South America.The third aircraft, named after Henri Guillaumet, a famous aviator and former director of Air France, would begin the trans-Atlantic service to the French West Indies on 26 July and be joined by the unnamed F-BDRA and RC. In the meantime, RA was flown from Biscarosse to Hythe on behalf of the Office d'Exportation Francais, to promote the Air France Atlantic service, delayed by five long years of war.

The largest commercial flying boat in the world arrived at Hythe on Monday 14 July 1947, where visitors found the slim 144 foot long fuselage moored partly within a pontoon dwarfed by the tailplane and twin rudders. Unlike the more compact Empire flying boats moored across the water, the wings extended to over 188 feet and supported six, 1,600 horsepower Wright Cyclone engines. The two outer engine nacelles supported the floats which retracted to beyond the trailing edge of the wing.

Guided inside, they were shown the large kitchen, toilets and washrooms aft of the entrance and moving forward, found the first eight 'sleeper' cabins fitted with comfortable leather seats enclosed by expensive wood panelling. The high wing allowed unrestricted views, though the curtained windows appeared small and dated compared to the British and American flying boats. The passageway led to the restaurant and bar, where a fixed ladder provided the sole access to the flight deck. In flight, the restaurant suffered a noticeable increase in vibration and noise due to the proximity of the engines, though the metal interior of the fuselage had been sprayed with asbestos to reduce the overall noise levels. Beyond, the long nose contained a luggage compartment, (crew) toilet, and a pair of eight and four seat cabins, ending with a single pair of seats below a large window giving a clear view ahead.

Within the bow, the mooring compartment featured a long curving hatch which slid upwards and rearwards to allow a crew member to walk comfortably out onto a pontoon. A crew of three pilots, two navigators, two radio operators and two flight mechanics would fly the Atlantic. Unlike the C-Class cockpit, the space between the pilots was largely taken up by a metal 'capstan' with protruding metal wheels, which with the mast, directly ahead on the 23 foot sloping nose, gave an impression of being on a luxury sea going yacht. Forty-six passengers could be carried, but just over fifty seconds was required to lift sixty visitors away from Hythe. Trips went as far as the outskirts of London and in the evening an equally low-level excursion took in Calshot, the Saunders-Roe factory at Cowes, Bournemouth Airport and Poole, the passengers including Captains Travers and Algar – and Geoffrey Tyson, due to test the Saro A-1

Porte des Hourtiquets.

jet fighter flying boat on Wednesday evening.

Old-style seamen had regarded a vessel with caution had there been a fatality during construction or the early career, and the death of two passengers in October 1945, when the blades of a propeller sheared during the promotional visit of NT to South America, would certainly have aroused such suspicions. Operated every fifteen days, the Caribbean services proved popular however and featured in articles and photo shoots. Parisians began their Caribbean holiday at the Air France rail platform at La Gare des Invalides and ended the ten-hour journey at the Port des Hourtiquets. Opened in 1937 on the opposite shore to the Latècoère factory, the pine forest had been cleared for a broad hardstanding and slipway, with a two- storey control building and a hangar each end of the concrete expanse. Oil was piped in. A refuelling launch ferried drums of petrol out to a moored 631, where the contents were pumped by hand into tanks in the bottom of the hull and inside the wings. Compartments in the wings and rear fuselage held mail and freight, hauled up from below by the aircraft's collapsible manual winch.

Floodlit departures were made late at night from a T-shaped floating dock positioned just along the shore, at the foot of a hotel set higher up amongst the pines. The first leg to Port Etienne, French West Africa, took eleven hours, with a four-hour refuelling stop. The ocean crossing could take up to eighteen hours, depending on the winds, with position transmissions sent every thirty minutes and the mechanics checking the engines from catwalks inside the wings, as with the Boeing Clippers. As a consequence, the beige leather seats had to be twice made up as bunks and twice reinstated as seats. Fussed over by three stewards and a commissioner, though without a promenade facility, travellers made full use of the bar and restaurant, which delivered two servings of breakfast, lunch and dinner. They also had the use of a small TSF (transceiver sans feuilles) 'wireless' radio cabin. On arrival at Fort de France, on the west coast of Martinique Island, they found an Air France PBY (F-BBCB) available to take them on to Guadeloupe.

Encountering bad weather during the delivery to Biscarosse on 21 February 1948, RD was seen flying low over Sainte-Mere-l'Eglise amid snow showers before crashing into the sea east of the Cotentin peninsula, known as les Isles Saint-Marcouf. But on Saturday 12 June, Commandant Corentin Kersual took RC on a promotional three-day visit to Lake Geneva.

Timed to coincide with the annual meeting of the International Civil Aviation Organisation, the quayside and shore was crowded with people eager to see the giant flying boat, and commemorative franked mail was taken aboard for the return to Biscarosse. Seven weeks later, during the morning of 1 August, the flying boat disappeared en route to Fort Etienne with fifty-two on board, having last been reported some 1,200 miles from Dakar. Grounded by Air France, NU and RA were subsequently sold to the Société d'Exploitation du Materiel Aerien Francaise (SEMAF), when they were operated as freighters.

Two years passed without incident. But on 28 March 1950, *Guillaumet* crashed off the peninsular of Cap-Ferrat, bringing a second grounding and mandatory modifications to the fins and control systems of the others. Little wreckage was found from the crashes, though the vibration imparted to the ailerons was thought to have caused flutter, mechanical failure and a loss of control. With the close of SEMAF, France- Hydro took an interest in the remaining six aircraft, more immediately intending RA, RB and NT to extend the operations of RE, converted to fly 24 tons of cotton from Lake Leré to Douala in the Africa Cameroons. Modifications were made to NT (used for pilot training) during 1955. But having safely completed 2,000 flying hours, on 10 September a tropical storm completely destroyed RE while en-route to Biscarosse for servicing.

The stored 631s were banned from ever flying again. Of the eleven built, ten were registered and the last was unfinished. Stripped of their engines, the survivors awaited their fate parked inside the Latécoère hangar and on the hardstanding, slipway and mooring. In February 1956 heavy snowfall partially collapsed the hangar roof, which crushed RB and two others, including the incomplete aircraft. The very last were left to rot in the open until finally broken up for scrap, though the second production aircraft, *Lionel de Marmier*, survived at Hourtiquets until 1963 when it was dismantled to free up the hangar space.

Visitors to the Lac de Biscarrosse will find a fascinating museum amongst the pines at 332 Avenue Louis Breguet, on the site of the Latécoère hangar. Opened in 1980 by Marie-Paule Vié-Klaze, founder of the Association des Amis du Musée de l'Hydravation (Friends of the Seaplane Museum), the premises of the Musée de l'Hydraviation are devoted to the world-wide history of seaplanes. A guided tour of the 'pavilions' will reveal a host of artefacts, photos, and scale models, full size and restored flying boats, together with preserved relics found in the area. Even the restaurant is created in the style of the era. Marie-Paule is remembered by an engraved tablet and naming of the first gallery of the museum, and every two years the vast expanse of water attracts enthusiasts and sight-seers, treated to the sight and sound of every conceivable form of 'hydravion' from the recent past to the present.

Mister Blue

Production of the final GR Mark 5 Sunderland had begun with ML796, the first of an initial batch of six at the Rochester factory. Passed to No 4 OTU Invergordon, it was delivered (with thirteen others) to the Aéronavale (French Navy) on 4 August 1951 as part of the Western Union Defence Organisation, the forerunner to NATO.

One of the last pair of an eventual nineteen operated by France, 50.S3 had finally been demilitarised, bought by a dealer, and put on show before passing to the Bertin family, when as *Mister Blue* it became a distinctive venue alongside the Guérande road at La Baule in Brittany. Positioned on a concrete expanse just off the road, supported by a pair of angled blocks with airline boarding ramps positioned on the port side of the nose and starboard rear, the 'Night Club Européan' was an instant hit for those seeking something different. Faced by a well stocked cocktail bar before passing to the 'discotèque', patrons found the Carte des boissons offered a choice of five Les Whiskies, three Les Champagnes and seven Les Cocktails. Upstairs, each table had an intercom to the airline headset of the barman and a balustraded landing overlooked the proceedings. The cockpit was intact. After some years, when the metal had taken a severe pounding, plans for a motorway caused owner Monsieur Bertin to offer the aircraft to anyone prepared to take it away, taken up in 1975 by the Imperial War Museum.

Pieter Kroon was given the responsibility of organizing the move to Britain, having helped acquire a B17 for the American Museum at Duxford two years earlier. Aside from the routine dismantling of component parts, the hull was horizontally sliced in half to fit aboard a lorry, while considerable patience was needed to obtain an export licence and permits of passage from each of the districts between La Baule and Dunkirk for the 'convoi exceptionnel'. All went well, and the arrival in Cambridge on

Mister Blue La Baulle Brittany. COURTESY JOHN EVANS.

Friday 9 July 1976 was followed by a much needed restoration by museum staff and Duxford Aviation Society volunteers. Today, the Sunderland can be viewed in all its glory within the twenty-five million pound Air Space hangar, opened in July 2008, though to the dismay of the French, without Aéronavale markings and as NS-F of 201 Squadron.

NORWAY

Norway was liberated in May 1945 and in June, King Haakon and his family had been returned to Oslo aboard HMS Norfolk, exactly five years after their evacuation from Tromsø, when the British First Cruiser Squadron was given an ecstatic welcome by crowds lining the shore. *Najaden* and *Faulken* had both survived the war. But *Ternen* had been withdrawn in 1940 after an explosion had destroyed a petrol tank, and three years later *Hauken* (re-named *Hans Berr*, a First World War fighter pilot) had sunk after landing in bad weather at Hommelvik.

Re-formed as a national airline, Det Norske Luftfartselskap A/S, began operations in April 1946, with DC3s flying international services and five former Luftwaffe Ju52 floatplanes expected to join the re-named *Hans* and *Askeladden* on domestic services. In July the Board decided to invest in three modern flying boats, the Sandringham 6 to be equipped with radar and seat 37 passengers on two decks – though the envisaged higher operating costs caused some to question the decision. Delivered between April and June 1947, *Kvitbjørn* (White Bear), *Bukken Bruse* (Billy-Goat Gruff) and *Bamse Brakar* (Teddy-Bear Brakar) maintained a summer service between Oslo/Fornebu and Tromsø, the nine-hour flight time broken by intermediate stops at Hommelvik, Bodø and Harstad. Flown at less than 500 feet above the water, they were soon known as 'Flying Steamers'.

Seen at Ilsvika and Lake Jonsvatn (near Trondheim) before the war, the Junkers floatplanes now flew to Hommelvik, a former Luftwaffe base, some 10 nautical miles to the east, where passengers joined a Sandringham for the longer service and vice-versa. The smallish quayside meant that a third arrival was obliged to moor within the fjord.

All over the world, young men had struggled to come to terms with the uncertainty that peace had brought and how best to use the talents gained from the years of military service. There was certainly no lack of aircraft left from the mighty American war effort. In 1947, a small independent company named Vingtor Luftveier began a none too easy task, given the post-war economy, to establish a charter service using a pair of former RAF Catalinas bought from the Ministry of Supply. Delivered to Horten from 57 Maintenance Unit Wig Bay in May, on 30 June *Vingtor* became the first Catalina to land at Sunderland, on the north-east coast of Britain; delighting thousands who had come to watch the evening arrival from Gothenburg with fifteen seamen for the inaugural sailing of a Swedish steamership. It was certainly colourful: the wings and fuselage painted a deep red, with cream side flashes and an eagles head; cream floats, lower hull and registration letters; and a winged Viking ship and star high on the tail. The following day nine seamen were flown on to Wear.

At eleven o'clock in the morning of 5 August, *Vingtor* departed Fornebu/Oslo bound for Tromsø via Trondheim, Bodø and Svolvaer in the Lofoten islands, yet to have a land airport. On board were fifteen passengers including two children, a wireless operator, an engineer, and a double team of pilots led by Captain Mikkelsen. Five passengers left at Trondheim and another at Bodø. Arriving at Svolvaer shortly before 4:30 in the afternoon and faced with a heavy swell, the approach was made with senior pilots Captains Mikkelsen and Didoot at the controls. The first contact was light, but the second was considerably harder, a rapid nose-up stall ending in an impact which split open the hull from the bow to the radio compartment. Shaken and hurt, the crew had difficulty evacuating the fast sinking aircraft until the wings contacted the water. Seven passengers escaped without too much trouble however and just two needed help from Captain Mikkelsen and second pilot Hauge. *Vingtor* was written off.

Twenty-three days later, *Kvitbjørn* arrived at Harstad from Tromsø and left for Bodø just before nine in the morning. Shortly after the hour, Bodø sent a weather actual as requested, but contact was then lost. An eye witness later reported seeing the aircraft flying low above the Tjeldsundet, a long strip of water separating the island of Honnoya from the mainland, before climbing into the surrounding fog – followed by a loud explosion. The noise was also heard in Lødingen on the island, but the difficult conditions and terrain hampered searching villagers and soldiers until wreckage was discovered nearly 300 metres up on the mountain side. There were no survivors. A simple inscription was left at the wreck site. Sixty years later, eighty people gathered beside the fjord to hear the names of the twenty-eight passengers and seven crew read aloud during a moving ceremony conducted by the mayor of Lødingen, when a wreath was laid at a Kvitbjørn memorial information board.

Named after a mythical cave dwelling 'troll' or giant, *Jutulen* replaced the loss in May 1948 and *Polar Bjørn* (Polar Bear) arrived in June, the last of the Sandringhams built expressly for the airline. Four months later, on Saturday 2 October, *Bukken Bruse* arrived over Hommelvik Bay to find a strong crosswind whipping up foaming white waves.

At the point of alighting, a severe gust punched the left wing into the air and the right float broke away on impacting with the surface, rolling the fuselage onto its side as the nose pitched down and flooded. Thirty-six of the forty-five aboard escaped, including 76 year-old Bertrand Russell, the third Earl Russell of Kingston Russell (near Weymouth in Dorset), due to present a series of lectures to the local student society. Most survivors were towards the rear of the aircraft, where the earl had emerged from a kicked out window. Able to swim clear, he was picked up by a rescue boat, warmed by coffee and a glass of cognac, and taken with others to a hospital in Trondheim. Later, he revealed he had asked a friend in Oslo to reserve a seat for him in the smoking compartment (right at the back) and had said if I can't smoke I will die! He would receive the Nobel Prize for Literature and live until just two years short of his one hundredth birthday.

Vingtor Airways was declared bankrupt during the year and together with the landplane fleet, the remaining Catalina was put up for sale. They might have had more of a chance had the authorities granted a repeated request to fly scheduled air services. DNL was itself merged with the Danish Danske Luftfartselskab (DDL) and the Swedish Aerotransport (ABA) in 1949 to form the Scandinavian Airline System (SAS), when the fins of *Bamse Brakar, Jutulen* and *Polar Bjørn* were adorned with a Viking longboat and the flags of all three countries.

After almost three, trouble-free years, on 15 May 1950 powerful engines reverberated about Hastad as *Bamse Brakar* began leaving for the Narvik-Tromsø service. Almost immediately the noise dramatically halved as both port engines stopped. With all the power coming from the right, the left wing flicked down, wrenching off the float and outer engine as the fuselage cartwheeled into the water. All thirty-three aboard were fortunately rescued and the wreckage submerged an hour later. The engines of the Sandringhams had been found to suffer erratic 'burbling' due to air bubbles forming in the fuel supply and it was later thought the left tank may have been underfilled, and with fuel being fed from the inner tanks, air would have been drawn into the carburettors of both port engines. The almost complete wreckage required a large crane to retrieve it from the water and the one brought in for the job had been used to break up the

Bamse Brakar recovery in progress. © NORSK LUFTFARTSMUSEUM, BODØ.

battleship Tirpitz, sunk by RAF bombs in Tromsø fjord six years earlier.

Two years later *Jutulen* was leased to France-Hydro. But on 16 November 1952 the 'giant' was damaged by the mooring buoy at Bangui, Nigeria, sprang a leak, and despite the arrival of a barge with a pump, slowly sank from sight forty-five minutes later. The last of the Junkers floatplanes, *Veslefrikk* and *Boots* (the latter given the entire fuselage from another wartime survivor) were retired in 1956. Shipped to Ecuador for airline service with TAO, *Boots* would be rescued from dereliction and go on to delight the crowds at American air shows as *Iron Annie*, until returned to Germany for complete restoration and operation by Deutsche Lufthansa AG as *Tempelhof*. *Polar Bjorn* was also a survivor, going on to complete six years with SAS before being sold to Aerolineas Argentinas in May 1955.

Chapter Ten

End of an Era

Latin America

The use of flying boats had never made more sense than in Latin America, where the 30 mile wide confluence of the Uruguay and Paraná rivers formed the Rio de la Plata, the widest river in the world. The expanse effectively separated Uruguay and Argentina and ended, some 180 miles later, in a 137 mile wide estuary bordering the Atlantic. In 1938 lucrative passenger services between the two capital cities of Montevideo and Buenos Aires had been started by the Sociedad Argentina de Navegación Aérea (a Commodore and Sikorsky previously operated by NYRBA) – and by the Corporación Sudamericana de Servicios Aéreos and the Compania Aeronautica Uruguayana (CAUSA).

Named at Belfast on 1 November 1945 by Dodero's second wife Betty, the result of a classic millionaire/showgirl encounter at the Monte Carlo Follies, the Sandringham 2 *Argentina*, had been flown out from Poole on 25 November by Senior Captain Dudley Travers (on loan by BOAC) and Wing Commander Norman Littlejohn, under the overall command of Air Commodore Powell. The eleven passengers included Señor Dodero and Geoffrey Tyson, chief test pilot to Shorts. The flight lasted four days, with stops at Lisbon, Bathurst, Natal and Rio de Janeiro. Approaching Buenos Aires from the east, the flying boat slowly circled over the city and the estuary of the river Plata where over 30,000 people had gathered to watch the arrival. Named at Hythe by Señora Dulcia Pereira Cortinas de MacEachan, the wife of the Uruguay Ambassador in London, on 20 December sister Sandringham *Uruguay* was flown out from Poole by Captain Moreton: the eight crew and sixteen passengers arriving at Rio de Janeiro four days later, Montevideo the day after, and Puerto Neuvo on the 26th. The 20th had also seen *Argentina* take twenty-five passengers on a trial flight to the coastal resort of Mar del Plata, some 250 miles away.

Though encouraged (by the aviation secretary) to spend considerable amounts of his time and money in preparing the way for post-war commercial aviation in the Argentine, visiting aircraft manufacturers in Britain and America and organizing the million and one things necessary

Sandringham 2 *Uruguay*. COURTESY CARLOS MEY.

for flying boat operations, from spare engines, propellers and parts, radio equipment, autopilot systems, night landing buoys, beacons, and launches, to pontoons, workshops, offices and ticket machines – the authorities had made it increasingly difficult for Alberto to actually begin operations. Permission had only been given for 'trial' and 'experimental' flights, which could be stopped at any time, and the authorities were in no hurry to re-register the flying boats. As a result, the Sandringham 3 *Brazil* arrived without publicity in January 1946, the month the government announced that companies and shareholders having a major interest in other forms of transport were excluded from joining the merging of the existing airlines within regional 'joint venture' companies. International services would be flown by the Sociedad Mixta Flota Aerea Mercante Argentina (FAMA). In February just such an agreement was made with the Corporación Sudamericana, which had acquired Macchi M.C.94 flying boats from its financial partner Ala Italia and extended services to Rosario and Corrientes, respectively on the western and eastern shore of the Paraná River, and to Asunción, the ancient capital city of Paraguay.

Having commenced services with a pair of Junkers floatplanes, appropriately named *El Uruguayo* and *El Argentino*, at the end of the war CAUSA had ordered two Sunderland 3s to be converted to airline standard at Belfast to outdo the rival operations of the Corporación Sudamericana. Fitted with forty seats arranged on two decks but with the nose and tail turrets simply faired over to save cost, unlike the fully streamlined Sandringhams, the civil Sunderlands G-AGWW and WX were allocated to CAUSA in February.

In March WX was re-allocated to the Argentine airline as part of an agreement between the two companies to pool their resources. The transaction was bitterly opposed by Alberto, who in December had seen advertisements proclaiming that from January the 'Pullman seat' flying boat would begin flying four flights a day between the two cities, rising to six on Saturdays and Mondays. On learning the Corporation Sudamericana had joined the government scheme, he decided to bring his considerable efforts to a halt, which meant parting with staff recruited specifically for the flying boat services, though taking *Brazil* to America where C-54 Skymasters were being modified for the company. In his absence, Juan Péron won the presidential elections and meetings had resumed with the aviation secretary.

Named at Hythe by Lady Hildred, wife of the Director General of the British Civil Aviation Authority, *Inglaterra* arrived in March 1946. In April, the restrictive provisos governing entry to the government scheme were removed, enabling the Dodero family to acquire a controlling interest in the rival Corporación Sudamericana! The merger of the 'coastal aviation companies' began in May. Alberto's Compañía Argentina de Aeronavegación and the Sociedad Argentina de Navegación Aérea would form the Sociedad Mixta Aviacon del Litoralt Fluvial Argentina (ALFA), but until ALFA took full control of the flying boats, the Dodero company continued to receive public acclaim for each new achievement.

On 4 June 1946, the day Juan Péron took over the Presidency, *Inglaterra* inaugurated an international service to London for FAMA, part of a year-long lease with *Brazil*. Having taken eight hours to reach Rio from Puerto Nuevo, Captain Charles MacDonald and his passengers rose early the following morning for the nine hour leg to Natal. The following day they spent thirteen hours in the air before reaching Bathurst, the last night stop-over, followed by a two hour flight to Lisbon and a five hour flight to Poole. A coach drive completed the service to London, with presumably no one complaining about thrombosis in the legs!

By contrast, on 3 July Alberto accompanied the famous aviator Guillermo Hillcoat on a test flight aboard *Argentina* to the provincial capital city of Corrientes, some 490 miles away. A fabulously wealthy man, with mansions in Buenos Aires and Montevideo and second homes in London, Paris and America, Alberto was accustomed to spending summer holidays on the French Riviera in the company of the rich and famous, for whom he gave sumptuous weekly parties (costing two million francs a time) graced by tables piled high with lobsters and other delicacies. Virtually a permanent house guest at the presidential palace, in August he and Betty were the sole companions for Señora Maria Eva Duarte de Péron as *Argentina* flew her from Buenos Aires to Rio, returning in a company DC-3.

Inglaterra and *Brazil* had each made six return flights to Poole by October, when Avro Yorks acquired by FAMA took over the service. By then both flying boats had logged over 600 hours and Britavia had them ferried to Belfast to increase the seating and replace the engines. FAMA had shown interest in leasing a third converted Sunderland and the forty-seat *Paraguy* arrived in November, after time and money had been saved by simply fairing over the former gun turrets. Shortly afterwards *Inglaterra* returned from Belfast. But the work on *Brazil* had started late and then stalled, due to the difficulty in acquiring American engines this side of the Atlantic. Britavia was instructed to sell the aircraft. Only Norway showed any real interest, though the offer fell short of expectations due to having to cost the radar fit to match their exisiting Sandringhams. *Brazil* was returned to Argentina in December.

With ALFA yet to control the Dodero flying boat operations, in February *Rio de la Plata* (owned by Corporación Sudamericana) took 'the boss' on a return flight to Montevideo, repeated by *Argentina* four days later and by *Paraguay* in March.

Acquired from the Corporación Sudamericana in March 1948, *Rio de La Plata* was renamed *General San Martin* (another national hero) and joined *General Artigas* and *Capitan Boiso Lanza* of La Compañía Aeronáutica Uruguaya at Montevideo. Sandringham 7 *Saint Andrew* arrived from Hamworthy in December 1950 and was joined by *Saint David* in March, completing a fleet of three civil Sunderlands and two Sandringhams. But after five virtual trouble free years, a two-year spate of accidents (begun with *Saint Andrew* in October 1955), diminished the public preference for flying boats. Four Curtiss C-46 airliners were bought in 1961 and with the retirement of *General San Martin*, the Uruguay flying boat services came to a close: the last believed flown from the Laguna del Sauce, a lake to the east of Montevideo, in May 1962

They would last a little longer in Argentina, where the May of 1949 had seen the administration of Juan Perón amalgamate the four regional civilian airlines. Part of a country-wide nationalisation programme, Aerolineas Argentinas inherited some fifty aircraft including the ALFA flying boats formerly operated by Dodero. But not *Uruguay*. Arriving from Rosario on 29 July 1948, the crew were warned that the Buenos Aires hidropuerto was shrouded in fog. A slight change in heading was made to land outside the harbour, but a collision 'at engine height' with a dredger moored about a mile out from the shore, had ended the lives of eighteen of the twenty-two aboard. The salvaged remains were destroyed by a hangar fire in December 1949.

Seen with Aerolineas Argentinas painted in large letters beneath the cabin windows, *Argentina*, *Inglaterra*, *Brasil* and *Paraguay* were joined by the civil Sunderlands *Uruguay* and *Rio de la Plata* in 1951, the year Alberto retired to Montevideo having had his shipping and airline interests absorbed by the state. The regular river flights constituted the sole connection by air between the more remote townships, though the environment inevitably created problems. In March 1952 *Rio de la Plata* went a little off track preparing to leave Concordia and ran aground. Almost exactly two years later *Paraguay* was damaged by stones during a February landing at Villa de Concepcion and in October *Argentina* force landed over 70 kilometres from Posados. But in 1955 the fleet was joined by *Polar Bjørn*, the last of the Norwegian Sandringhams, which was renamed *Almirante Zar.*

Two years later, on the very last day of 1957, *Brazil* left Buenos Aires for Asuncion via Rosario, Corrientes and Formoso. Experiencing unusual oscillations, it was immediately turned back, only to have the landing area invaded by a small boat, when the engines just had to be opened up to full climbing power. After circling to the left, the channel was again seen to be blocked, this time by a cargo ship towed by two tugs, in front and behind the vessel. Four more circuits were made during the ensuing thirty minutes, at the end of which the captain informed the tower that with the wind and waves visibly getting stronger, he would have to make an immediate landing outside the harbour. Though seen to make a gentle descent, *Brazil* encountered the full force of a rolling wave and rose to some 60 feet before porpoising across the surface, losing an engine and wingfloat before pitching nose-down into the water. Forty-one of the fifty passengers and crew escaped the partly submerged aircraft.

No-one could have foreseen the series of accidents inflicted the following year: *Uruguay* hitting a buoy at Montevideo in February, *Rio de la Plata* and *Almirante Zar* damaged on two successive days in June, and *Uruguay* retired after yet more damage in August. By 1960 the company was flying Comet 4 jet airliners. That might have spelt the end for the stored flying boats, but in July 1963 all five were leased to the Cooperativa Argentina de Aeronavegantes, formed by the redundant flying boat personnel to carry cargo up the rivers. *Rio Aguilero* (the former Argentina) was retired before the year was out, leaving *Provincia de Formosa* (the former Inglaterra) *Paraguay, Almirante Zar* and *Rio de la Plata* to compete with increasing cash-flow problems until around June 1964, when the company closed down. *Rio Aguilero* was scrapped, but the rest remained at Basin F, Puerto Neuvo, until finally broken up, possibly during January 1967. It had been a good innings, with most of the survivors completing over twenty years service since emerging as military flying boats onto the factory slipways in England, Scotland and Ireland.

New Zealand

Manned almost entirely by tour expired members of 490 Squadron, in 1944 a flight of four Transport Sunderland 3s (ML792-5), had left Oban for New Zealand, landing intact at Waitemata harbour after flying to West Africa, across the South Atlantic to America, and across the Pacific. Modified to seat up to thirty passengers *Tainui, Tokomaru, Mataatua* and *Takitimu* were used by the Flying Boat Transport Flight of the RNZAF to carry personnel and equipment between Auckland and the South Pacific Islands of Fiji,

Noumea and Espiritu-Santos. Sold to the National Airways Corporation in 1947, they were operated on international services to the South Pacific Islands until May 1950 when *Takitimu* returned to Auckland from Suva. The surviving trio (*Tanui* was scrapped in 1949) were returned to the Air Force in 1951 and broken up.

In the meantime, New Zealanders in the Mission Bay area of Auckland harbour had been given a unique 'seaside attraction'. Respectively retired from the Tasman Sea Service in June and October 1947, *Awarua* and *Aotearoa* had rested on beaching gear at Hobsonville until June 1948 when they were sold by tender to Messrs Carter and Mabee. Stripped of engines and useful equipment *Awarua* was towed to the industrial Penmure area of the harbour at the end of the year and broken up. Intact save for her (starter) batteries, *Aotearoa* was towed to Mission Bay, brought ashore on beaching gear, and positioned within a secure waterfront enclosure where a large notice board announced the 'unique opportunity' to inspect the 'Pioneer Flying Boat of the Tasman Service'. Timber steps led up and inside the aircraft to view the passenger accommodation, the flight deck, the engineer's room, and the 'observer's chart room with the chart still on the table after the last Tasman crossing'. You could sit in the pilot's cockpit and actually handle the controls, an experience you would 'never forget' and a chance you would 'never have again'. The last sentiment was confirmed around October 1950 with the arrival of metal cutting equipment to clear the site for redevelopment, which included the adjacent miniature golf course provided for less air-minded souls.

In 1949 TEAL ordered four Solents to replace *Tasman, Australia, New Zealand* and *Auckland.* Found to be underpowered and prone to engine overheating during the long Tasman Sea service, the Sandringhams had been withdrawn from February to June 1948, when Douglas DC-4s had been chartered from Trans Australia Airlines. Built to the airlines specific requirements, the Solent 4 would be the heaviest and last of the type, able to lift 36 tons from the water, over a ton more than the Solent 3. Fitted parallel with the centre line of the aircraft to avoid the drag of previous marks, the 2,050 horsepower, sleeve-valve Bristol Hercules engines would drive four bladed, fully feathering, de Havilland propellers capable of supporting up to nine crew and forty-five passengers, at a comfortable 200 knots for over 2,000 nautical miles.

Launched by Princess Elizabeth in May 1949, *Aotearoa 11* was followed by *Ararangi, Awatere* and *Aranui.* In no time at all, the Auckland-Sydney crossing was reduced to five and a half hours. Former BOAC Solent 3 *City of Belfast* joined the company as *Aparimu* in 1950, the year the fleet took over the weekly Auckland-Suva (Fiji) service formerly operated by *Mataatua* and *Takitumu.* They also visited the Cook Islands, Tahiti, Western Samoa and Tonga, aptly known as the 'Coral Route'. In April the Sandringhams were sold off to Australian operators: *Tasman* and *Australia* going to Qantas

Aotearoa at Mission Bay waterfront New Zealand
© MARCUS BRIDLE/PETER LEWIS.

and *New Zealand* and *Auckland* to Barrier Reef Airways.

In 1953, the year the British Government sold its twenty per cent stake in TEAL to leave New Zealand and Australia joint and equal share holders, *Aotearoa 11* was chosen to carry the newly crowned Queen Elizabeth II and her husband the Duke of Edinburgh on a Royal Tour of New Zealand. Four years earlier the former princess had christened the new Solent at Belfast. In May 1954 *Ararangi* became the sole flying boat to be written off by the company after an engine caught fire during maintenance at Mechanics Bay, and with Douglas DC-6 airliners taking over the Wellington-Sydney service, *Aotearoa 11* and *Awateri* were sold to Aquila the following year. *Aparimu* was broken up in 1957, the Catalina service between Port Moresby and Sydney came to an end in August 1958, and *Aranui* ended the last Solent service between Tahiti and Auckland in September 1960.

A lovely example of the last mark of Solent built at Belfast, *Aranui* (Maori for 'The Great Highway') can be seen in pristine condition within the Museum of Transport, Technology and Social History (MOTAT) at Western Springs, Auckland, thanks to the efforts of the Solent Flying Boat Preservation Society. Here too can be seen a replica of possibly the world's first successful powered aeroplane with creator Richard Pearse at the controls. The last of his aeroplanes were discovered in a garage at Christchurch, where he had come to live, while the remains of some of his early engines were unearthed from the farm rubbish dump exactly sixty years after that first brief flight in 1903.

Solent 4 *Aranui.* IMAGE © MOTAT LIBRARY.

AUSTRALIA

By July 1945, over 270 crossings of the Indian Ocean had been made by the Qantas Catalinas, with not one engine failure, accident or injury to the aircrew or to some six hundred and fifty 'Double Sunrise' passengers. The only known incident involving the enemy had come in February 1944, when Russell Tapp had been diverted to Cocos Island to pick up a naval officer. With their captain ashore, the crew had begun topping up the wing tanks by hand, using four gallon fuel drums, when they were spotted and attacked by a single twin-engined bomber. The bombs had missed, the refuelling had been resumed, and *Vega Star* had arrived safely at Ceylon.

Liberators had begun to supplement the Catalina service in 1944, flying a more direct course from RAAF Learmouth (near Exmouth) to Ratmalana, a civil airport 100 miles or so north-east of Columbo. The shorter crossing took some seventeen hours, though the fuelled up return trip had to start from the longer runway at Minneriya until Ratmalana was extended during 1945. The payload of the landplane 'Kangaroo Service' quickly rose to two and a half tons, with each of the fifteen passengers receiving a certificate admitting them to 'The Order of the Longest Hop'. But in June 1945 BOAC Lancastrian conversions of the famous Lancaster bomber began flying a sixty-three hour passenger service from Hurn Airport near Bournemouth, with Qantas crews taking over at Karachi. The American Lend-Lease agreement stipulated that equipment of value could not be used for other purposes after the war and in November, the pioneering *Vega Star*, *Altair Star*, *Rigel Star* and *Antares Star* were towed down river and scuttled some 8 miles (13 km) south-west of Rottnest Island. Having made six crossings before fuel leaks caused her to be retired, *Spica Star* was dealt the same fate outside Sydney harbour in March 1946. In September 1972 a plaque was unveiled at Rathmines, dedicated to those who had served at the Royal Australian Air Force base and to all those associated with 'flying boats and seaplanes' between 1939 and 1960.

Situated some 370 miles off the eastern seaboard of Australia, the six-mile crescent of Lord Howe Island had been discovered in 1788 by 32 year old Lieutenant Henry Lidgbird Ball, captain of the 175 ton HMS Supply, while delivering settlers to Norfolk Island. The site of an extinct volcano, by the 1930s the sheltered coral reef and lagoon, backed by rugged terrain and virgin forest, had become a popular tourist resort, untroubled by (daytime) sharks or venomous snakes, insects or plants. As yet without an airstrip at the end of 1945 and with the Australian Government restricting post-war flying boat operations to island charters, to avoid unnecessary competition with landplanes, the island had attracted the attention of two companies.

Trans-Oceanic Airways

Formed by former RAAF Squadron Leader Bryan Monkton, who had flown Hawker Hurricane fighters and 'Black Cat' PBYs during the war, Trans-Oceanic Airways (TOA) had begun three-hour commercial passenger services to Lord Howe Island from Rose Bay in May 1947, using three former RNZAF Sunderland 3s (stored at Rathmines, converted to Hythe standard at Rose Bay) complete with steward and stewardess. Captain Taylor was a pilot and director for the company. Commissioned into the Royal Australian Air Force, he had transferred to the RAF as a civilian captain and in 1943 had ferried military aircraft over the Atlantic to Britain. A year earlier, he had suggested a Pacific route as an alternative connection between Australia and Britain for military and ultimately civilian aircraft, though a survey was delayed due to protective issues raised by the four major countries involved.

Commissioned by the Australian Government, in September 1944 he had taken the RAF Catalina JX275 away from Bermuda to find which of the host of islands could support a runway or a marine base. He had named the aircraft *Frigate Bird*, after the non-swimming sea-birds whose 2 metre wingspan could support them for nearly a week over the ocean. Typical of the islands was Clipperton, a remote three and a half square mile coral atoll in the Eastern Pacific, used in the early 18th century as a hideout and arsenal for raids on Spanish shipping by the British (Great Yarmouth) born buccaneer John Clipperton – three centuries after Harry Paye had made Poole his own base for raids against the Spanish and French! *Frigate Bird* had returned to Bermuda in November, but another fourteen years would elapse before the mid-Pacific route connected Australia with London, when the Qantas Boeing 707 jet airliners would appear as specks, miles above the earth...

Though an established tourist attraction, Lord Howe Island was without refuelling facilities and *Australis, Tahiti Star* and *Pacific Star* were obliged to carry sufficient fuel to complete the seven-hour round trip. In agreement with Qantas, TOA eventually took sole control of the service and went on to fly commercial services to New Caledonia, the Solomon Islands and the New Hebrides. *Australis* was retired in November 1950 and the BOAC Solents *Salcombe* (renamed *Star of Hobart*), *City of London* and *City of Cardiff* (renamed *Star of Papua*) were bought from the Belfast factory, though 'London' lost a float at Malta while en route on 28 January and was written off.

Squadron Leader Bryan Monkton.
© AUSTRALIAN AVIATION MUSEUM, NEW SOUTH WALES.

In March 1951 Captains Taylor and Purvis took *Frigate Bird II*, a former RAAF Catalina, away from Rose Bay to survey a route to South America via the Pacific Islands. Landed on the Clarence River at Grafton, New South Wales, the aptly registered VH-ASA (Australia-South America) headed out across the ocean for Noumea Island (New Caledonia), Lauthala Bay (Fiji), Satapuala Bay (Samoa), Aituaki (Cook Islands), Papeete Harbour (Tahiti) and Mangareva (French Gambier Islands). Refuelling was carried out on the turbulent water surrounding Easter Island, the overloaded take-off assisted by rocket packs fitted by the RAAF, after Captain Taylor had taxied at length to the leeward side of

Captain (Sir) P.G.Taylor.
© COLLECTION: POWERHOUSE MUSEUM, SYDNEY.

Solent 3 *City of Cardiff*. © JOSEPH MAY.

the island 'blipping' the engines against the wind! The crew were fêted and honoured at Valparaiso for having surveyed well over 7,000 nautical miles, and on returning to Sydney in April, the pilot was gifted the Catalina during a civic reception by the Australian Government. He also received the Oswald Watt gold medal and the Johnson Memorial Trophy of the London Guild of Air Pilots and Air Navigators.

Sunderland *Pacific Star* was retired in the month, while on 28 October *Star of Hobart* hit an unlit dredger on leaving Brisbane. Despite losing a large chunk of the right wing (7 metres!) it was skilfully beached, but had to be scrapped when a replacement wing could not be found. Solent 2 *Somerset* arrived in November, but having suffered a number of unfortunate accidents in a relatively short existence, TOA was finally dissolved in April 1953. *Tahiti Star*, the surviving Sunderland, was sold to Ansett. Undaunted, Bryan Monkton flew out to Hawaii and formed a new airline.

SOUTH PACIFIC AIRLINES

Solent 3 *Star of Papua* was renamed *Isle of Tahiti* and with Solent 2 *Somerset* and Solent 3 *Singapore* (bought from storage at Belfast) was flown to Alameda, California, to be rebuilt to comply with U.S regulations prior to operating a twice-weekly Honolulu-Tahiti service via Christmas Island.

Painted with a long orange 'cheat line', with the company name beneath the upper deck windows and an identifying SPAL high on the tail, *Isle of*

Sandringham 7 'Le Bermuda' Papeete 1964. © Ron Cuskelly Collection.

Tahiti was test flown from Oakland in November 1958 prior to making a route-proving flight to Papeete – but the British government's intention to use Christmas Island as an atomic test site ended everything. Returned to Oakland, in July 1958 *Isle of Tahiti* made one last flight and was beached at San Francisco Airport. Bought by the Howard Hughes Organisation a year later, all three Solents were maintained under armed guard at Oakland. Towed to Richmond for storage, the Solents were sold for scrap as a complete lot for 1,500 dollars. The richest man in the world and fascinated by flight, Howard Hughes died in the aeroplane taking him to hospital in April 1976.

The best of the trio, *Isle of Tahiti*, was subsequently advertised in *Trade A Plane*. Bought in November 1976 by the brothers Rick and Randy Grant, the owners of Seaflite Oceanographic, the Solent was named *Halcyon* and stripped to the metal by a company restoration group assisted by 'Friends of Halcyon'. Returned to an overall white colour scheme, it briefly featured as a Boeing Clipper in the 1981 film *Raiders of the Lost Ark*, when Harrison Ford enters and takes a window seat. The cost of restoration to full flying condition for oceanographic research, with local flights for enthusiasts, proved prohibitive however and in 1992 the aircraft was loaned to the Western Aerospace Museum at Oakland International Airport. Today the Solent is displayed outside the Earhart Road building of the renamed Oakland Aviation Museum. A firm attraction, visitors can choose between three guided tours a day – or take a BOAC style Silver Service dinner aboard on the second Saturday of each month!

Retired by BOAC with just 2,000 hours in the log, *Saint George* had perched on beaching gear at Hamworthy until bought by Captain Taylor for £20,000 from aircraft brokers W.S.Shackleton Ltd of Piccadilly, London.

City of Cardiff cabin. © OAKLAND AVIATION MUSEUM.

Refitted by Saunders-Roe at Cowes, *Frigate Bird III* departed for Australia in November 1954, the year 'PG' was knighted and thereafter known as Sir Gordon, when VH-APG (clever) was personally flown by him on 'air cruise' charters to the Western Pacific islands – until 1958, when it was sold to Transports Aeriens Intercontinentaux (TAI) for use as a shuttle between Papeete and Bora Bora to connect with the DC-6 service to Paris.

In 1961 Sir Gordon presented *Frigate Bird II* to the Powerhouse Museum, Sydney. Two years later TAI was merged with Union de Transports Aeriens but continued to fly from Papeete as Reseau Aeriens Interinsulaire (RAI). Fitted with forty-five seats, *Frigate Bird III* operated services to the islands of French Polynesia, which included Bora-Bora, Ranguora, Huahine and Raiatea. Known by locals as 'Le Bermuda', the Sandringham was mostly flown by chief pilot Douglas Pearson, a bearded likeness to the famous British film star James Robertson Justice. His 'star turns' included deliberately lining the flying boat up for the newly completed runway at Tahiti's Faa'a Airport – and shaping up a company DC-4 for a 'landing' on the nearby lagoon! The runway signified the end of the flying boat's career however and it was latterly used to fly sick and wounded islanders from the smaller lagoons to a hospital on the mainland. Commander Pearson made the last flight in September 1970. A heavy swell made the trip out to the flying boat rather unpleasant for the Governor and local dignitaries however, who once seated began to feel the inevitable symptoms of sea-sickness. Even worse befell the television crew, given a ducking when their

© OAKLAND AVIATION MUSEUM.

launch was overturned in the middle of the Manihi lagoon, when the cameras and equipment of the Office de Radiodiffusion-Télévision Française made their irretrievable ways to the bottom.

Approached by the Polynesian civil aviation authority in June 1971, the Musée de l' Air had to decline an offer to acquire the flying boat, as there was simply nowhere to display it. Interest was expressed by the London Science Museum and by the Aviation Historical Society of Australia, but the logistics of moving such a large aircraft was insurmountable at the time. Amid threats of being broken up and sunk in the lagoon, the Sandringham was eventually bought in 1975 by Douglas Pearson Junior, who subsequently contacted the Queensland Air Museum. But after considerable work by museum members to protect the aircraft from further vandalism, and the elements, the cost of removal again halted proceedings. Renewed threats of dismantling and sinking followed and the French museum was again contacted, having recently moved to larger premises. Now able to help, in 1978 the component parts were dismantled and shipped to Brest by the French Navy. Stripped of wings and tail, the unmistakeable fuselage was towed through streets at night and accompanied by police outriders to Le Bourget, where it was re-assembled and stored to await its future.

Sir Patrick Gordon Taylor, GC, MC, had died in December 1966 and was buried, as he had wished, in Hawaii. In 1985 his Catalina *Frigate Bird II* was restored by Hawker Pacific and hoisted over 30 feet above the floor of the Boiler Hall of the Powerhouse Museum, in time for the 1988 opening of the Transport Exhibition. In October 2008 his Sandringham, the former *Frigate Bird III,* was moved into a newly opened hangar at Le Bourget, fitted with workshops and classrooms for students to receive professional training in restoration work.

QANTAS

Nationalised in 1947, when the iconic Constellation was introduced on the Australia-London service, Qantas continued to operate *Tasman* between Sydney and Noumea in New Caledonia and from Port Vila Harbour to Santo in the New Hebrides. But in April 1951 the starboard wingfloat was lost while landing at Rose Bay. Returned to service, in June an outboard-powered dugout canoe suddenly crossed its path while powering away from the Inner Harbour of Port Vila. Turned sharply to avoid a collision, the hull was holed by coral and the engines kept at full power to drive the damaged metal up and onto the sandy beach of a nearby island. Considered uneconomic to repair, the Sandringham was abandoned after removal of the engines, instruments, seats and other useful equipment. At the time, the New Hebrides was jointly administered by the British and French who, once the novelty wore off, had the hulk towed into deep water and sunk.

The Sandringhams *Portmarnock* and *Pevensey* arrived from Britain in July and were joined by *Poole* in December. Fitted with twenty seats on the lower deck, rather than the thirty of the Plymouth-Class, they joined *Pacific Chieftan* (the former *Australia*) as *Pacific Warrior, Pacific Explorer* and *Pacific Voyager,* replacing the Catalinas that had maintained the Lord Howe Island services since 1946. Both had been written off in mysterious circumstances, VH-EAX blown ashore after the mooring broke in June 1949 and AW exploding after refuelling at Rose Bay in August. Competitor TOA was suspected, but nothing was proven.

The Sandringhams also flew to Fiji. But with landplanes taking over the routes, *Pacific Chieftan* went to Ansett in 1954 and *Pacific Warrior, Pacific Explorer and Pacific Voyager* were retired in 1955. Three years later, *Tasman* was located by the scuba-diving family of Denny and Merryl Smith, using echo sounding equipment to detect the large amount of metal lurking 40 metres beneath the surface behind Iririki Island, where it had settled after a long and ghostly gliding descent. Since then the wreck has attracted countless dive enthusiasts.

BARRIER REEF AIRWAYS

Barrier Reef Airways had been formed in October 1946 by Danish businessman Christian Poulson, who owned the lease of Heron Island, and former wartime Catalina pilot Captain Middlemiss, who began operating *Beachcomber,* a twenty-two seat converted military Catalina, on weekly services from the Brisbane river to Heron and other Great Barrier Reef resort islands. A second Catalina, *Buccaneer,* was purchased in February 1947 (four others provided spares), the year Christian was presumed drowned when his dinghy was found empty. Stewart Middlemiss took sole control of the company, assisted by his wife Hope and by Captain Frank Kelly. In 1950 he gave a majority share interest to Ansett Transport Industries to enable purchase of the former TEAL Sandringham 4s *Auckland* and *New Zealand*. Renamed *Beachcomber* and *Princess of Cairns,* they extended the charter and scheduled services and were also loaned to Trans-Oceanic. But in September 1952 *Princess of Cairns* was hit by a launch at its nightly mooring on the Brisbane river. Refloated and towed to the maintenance base at Colmslie Island it was written off and in 1953 was sold to become a floating restaurant at Coolangatta. By then, both Catalinas had been retired and the airline had been absorbed by Ansett, with Stewart Middlemiss appointed operations manager. *Princess of Cairns* finally sank off the coast while on tow to its new home in February 1954.

ANSETT FLYING BOAT SERVICES

Ansett Airways had been formed in 1935 by Reginald Myles Ansett, a pilot and entrepreneur who later bought the lease to Hayman Island and was knighted for his achievements. Fitted with sixteen seats on the upper deck to increase the seating to forty-one; the overheating engine problem solved by moving the carburettor air intakes from between the cylinders to above the cowlings, and with baffle plates directing air around all the cylinders, *Beachcomber* began services between Brisbane and Townsville, Cairns and Hayman Island, now a luxurious tourist resort. Bought from Qantas to replace *Princess of Cairns, Pacific Chieftan* joined *Beachcomber* on the subsidised Lord Howe Island services (taken over from TOA in 1953) until July 1963, when a storm broke the mooring. Beyond repair, it was stripped of anything useful and sunk in deep water outside the lagoon.

The search for a replacement included visiting Argentina and the Cooperativa Argentina de Aeronavegantes. None were considered suitable however and after approaching the RNZAF, a retired Sunderland V

(NZ4108) was converted at Rose Bay to seat forty-two passengers (though sat facing forwards), the nose turret replaced by a Hythe-style fairing and the tail by a Sandringham-style cone. Named *Islander*, the civil Sunderland joined the Lord Howe Island services and also flew charters to Tahiti and to Hayman Island. Hired by the Department of Environment and Conservation to explore the possible effects an airstrip would have on the natural attractions of Lord Howe Island, *Beachcomber* flew out a party of officials in June 1974, but ended up on the beach with the starboard wing damaged and without the float after a severe gale broke the mooring in the night. Repaired sufficiently for a return to Rose Bay, the departure was followed by the arrival of *Islander* to retrieve the stranded officials. With the end of the government subsidy and completion of an airport in September, Ansett Flying Boat Services closed down after the final visit of *Beachcomber*, when both flying boats were bought by Captain Charles Blair.

Antilles Air Boats

Having tested Grumman naval fighters and the giant Martin Mars in between record-breaking wartime Atlantic crossings between Foynes and New York (the best taking just over fourteen and a quarter hours), Captain Charles Francis Blair (Junior) had made the first postwar Atlantic crossings for American Overseas Airlines, and in 1947 had taken the Dublin-born actress Maureen (FitzSimons) O'Hara to Ireland. The company was merged with Pan Am in 1950 and the next ten years had only added to his achievements.

In January 1951 he utilised the little known high altitude 'jet stream' winds to fly his modified Mustang fighter *Excalibur III* from New York to

Beachcomber & *Islander* moored off Lord Howe Island.
© Frank Stamford.

London in less than eight hours. The record still stands. In May, he used advanced navigation techniques to become the first to fly solo from Norway to Alaska via the Arctic, for which he received the Harmon International Award from President Truman as the world's 'outstanding aviator'. Exchanging his Navy Reserve commission for that of the Air Force while working with Strategic Air Command during the Cold War period, he helped develop tactical navigation and missile systems for jet fighters and flew front-line supersonic jets of the era. In 1956 he led three Thunderstreak jets on the first non-stop crossing of the Atlantic, using in-flight refuelling, and in 1959 led a pair of Super Sabres from Britain to Alaska via the North Pole. Awarded the Thurlow International Award for his outstanding contribution to navigation, and the American Distinguished Flying Cross, he was promoted Brigadier-General on the Reserve.

Throughout, he had continued to fly as chief pilot for Pan Am, which had introduced the Boeing 707 on its Round the World service. His magazine articles were read on both sides of the Atlantic and in 1960 the airline drama *Beyond the Curtain,* starring Richard Greene and Eva Bartok, opened in Britain, based on the novel *Thunder Above* co-authored by the pilot and A.J.Wallis of the Hawker-Siddeley Group. Aware of the continued isolation of the Caribbean islanders, in 1964 he bought a surplus military

Charles and Maureen O'Hara Blair at Rhein-Main July 12 1969 during the pilot's round the world retirement flight for Pan Am.

PHOTO BY JIM COLE. USED WITH PERMISSION FROM THE STARS AND STRIPES.

Grumman Goose amphibian and formed Antilles Air Boats to operate virtually a taxi service about the American Virgin Islands. The second of such ventures, he had owned Associated Air Transport after the war, and when 'off duty' from Pan Am and the Air Force had enjoyed flying a long-range Super Commando on private charters! In 1968 he married the famous red-haired Hollywood star Maureen O'Hara, having grown accustomed to visiting her brother, television producer Charles FitzSimons, at the family home when flying into Los Angeles. The following year he retired from Pan Am to personally lead his airline, based at Christiansted St Croix, though the company was about to lose its first large flying boat.

Returned to civilian service after their Naval Air Transport duties, *Excambian* and *Exeter* had been retired in October 1945. Sold by the War Assets Corporation and briefly owned by financially troubled concerns, on 15 August 1947 an overloaded *Exeter*, operated by the Montevideo based Transporte Aéreo de Carga Internacional and believed returned from flying arms to rebels in the Amazon jungle, fatally crashed in total darkness on the River Plata. Subsequently purchased by the Aviation Exchange Corporation, a Baltimore based consortium, in 1950 *Excambian* was converted to carry freight up-river to the native communities. Considered impracticable however, the sole surviving VS-44A was abandoned in Ancón Harbour, Peru, where it attracted the attention of Captain 'Dick' Probert, the founding director of Avalon Air Transport. Restored to flying condition and ferried to Long Beach, California in 1957, the flight engineer controls were moved into the cockpit, the navigation and radio positions removed and the seating increased for forty-seven passengers.

Given an attractive blue and white livery, for ten years the Sikorsky had flown summer tourists between Long Beach and Catalina Island, known as 'Mother Goose' due to the rest of the fleet comprising the smaller Grumman amphibians. Purchased by Antilles in January 1968, a year later the Sikorsky was seriously damaged by rocks while taxiing in the harbour of Charlotte Amalie. Faced with prohibitive repair costs, it performed a heroic service as a 'hot dog stand' until donated to the Naval Air Museum at Pensacola, Florida, in 1976. Seven years later it would be transferred on long term loan to the New England Air Museum at Bradley International Airport, Connecticut, for it had always been a civilian aircraft.

In the meantime, 1969 had seen publication of *Red Ball in the Sky*, a personal account of the flying experiences of 'Charles F. Blair' and by 1970 Antilles was carrying over a quarter of a million passengers a year: over 120 flights a day linking 'downtown' St. Croix with St. Thomas, St. John, Tortola, Fajardo, St. Marteen and San Juan. Advertised as the world's largest seaplane airline with the world's most experienced seaplane pilots, and the major air carrier in the Virgin Islands, the fleet of nineteen Grumman Goose and two Mallards was joined by two four-engined flying boats in 1974 – the departure of Captain Blair and *Excalibur VIII* (the former

Islander) from Rose Bay in September and *Southern Cross* (the former *Beachcomber*) in November, effectively ending commercial flying boat services in Australia. Both retained their Ansett livery, but with Antilles Air Boats stenciled across the fuselage, and a 'flying eagle' on the fin after the bald eagle on the national flag of the American Virgin Islands. *Excalibur* was refused a certificate of airworthiness however, as the civil conversion had been made by Ansett and not by Shorts (evident by the upward bulge of the nose fairing) and was left on beaching gear in an empty steel hangar of the former American Naval Air Station San Juan (Isla Grande) on the island of Puerto Rico. Joining the busy fleet of amphibians, the larger capacity of *Southern Cross* was employed on a variety of charters until 1976 when it was decided to make a nostalgic return to Foynes – and ultimately Dorset.

Return to Poole

While staying at their home in the village of Glengarriff, County Cork, that Easter, where the grounds overlooked the shore of Bantry Bay, the famous couple had driven to Foynes where they found the flying boat mooring and pontoon were still in position. Plans were formulated and on 6 July 1976, *Southern Cross* left Christiansted with special guests joining family members of the crew, which included Captains Nick Castruccio and Ron

Southern Cross taxying past Sandbanks chain ferry August 1976.
© Bob Rayner.

Gillies and flight engineer Noel Holle. Ron and Noel were from the original TEAL flight crew while Noel had also been with Sir Gordon Taylor's *Frigate Bird III* in the Pacific. A temporary seat had been fitted behind the left hand seat to enable Maureen to be close to her husband when flying together, but for the longer ocean crossing, a regular passenger seat had been fitted further back, in front of the wing spar. Two days later, the flying boat broke cloud cover over Foynes and after making a pass across Shannon Airport, made two more over Foynes before landing on the Shannon – thirty-one years after the pilot had taken *Excambian* away from Ireland for the very last time. Forewarned, the schools were closed and the quayside crammed with thousands of well-wishers.

Foynes Yacht Club had organised the proceedings and a launch conveyed the two celebrities ashore to a magnificent reception attended by special guests from the wartime era. Having become the catering comptroller at Foynes and later Shannon Airport, where he had opened the very first Duty Free Shop, Brendan O' Regan performed a highlight of the evening by presenting the club with a sculptured head of the Irish God of the Sea and Wind inscribed 'Captain Charles Blair, the last to leave, the first to return'. Based at Killaloe on Lough Derg for the summer, *Southern Cross* flew a number of tourist flights within the auspices of Aer Árann, with the beautiful actress very much in evidence. During which time it was suggested by Michael Coghlan of Charlton Marshall in Dorset, that a nostalgic return might also be made to Poole.

Phone calls were made and on Monday 23 August the Purbeck hills

800 gallons pumped aboard in thirty minutes. © AUTHOR COLLECTION.

View to Brownsea Island.

View to Haven Hotel across sandbank. © Author Collection.

again reverberated to the sound of an approaching flying boat. Poole Harbour Master Captain Allinson had laid a mooring buoy, with additional buoys positioned by Michael Coghlan to mark a landing area between the west of the Training Bank and the Old Harry Rocks adjoining Studland Bay. Strong easterly winds had generated a heavy swell across the open sea however and after circling, the flying boat disappeared from the view of some forty disappointed enthusiasts, eagerly awaiting the arrival at Studland.

Bob Kent had come a long way since watching the moonlit arrival of the German bomber thirty-five years ago. On completing his apprenticeship, he had been called up for the RAF and had served as a wireless operator aboard the Dakotas operated by 246 Squadron from the New Forest airfield of Holmsley South. Both his elder brothers had been killed in the war and the RAF had kept him in Britain rather than send him to the Middle East. After the war he had become a shipwright at Lake Shipyard, where he had first begun testing craft after a refit, including the lifeboats of the RNLI, and had subsequently become skipper of the pleasure boat Maid of the Isles.

With a full load of passengers aboard and the only pleasure craft out that August day, the sound of engines had alerted first mate Les de l'Argy who, on seeing the aircraft coming round to the west of Brownsea Island, had qualified it as a Hercules about to drop another load of service parachutists into Studland Bay. 'No' said Bob – 'it's a flying boat!' An unexpected treat for everyone aboard, the aircraft could clearly be seen approaching over Arne to head into the easterly wind blowing along the former BOAC main runway. It was a 'wonderful' sight for Bob, who could make out the name as it came closer, and closer between the moorings, to the surprise and shock of the boat owners, to settle just 100 yards or so from the Maid at ten minutes past two in the afternoon- ending a round the world journey begun as *Auckland* with Tommy Rose twenty-nine years earlier.

In contrast to the excitement on board the pleasure boat, the aircraft was speedily targeted by the harbour master aboard the aptly named police launch Alarm, and by launches carrying customs and excise personnel and the police port squad, who all wanted to know exactly what it was doing there! More especially, the pilot was faced with an immediate order to fly out the way he had come, with the threat of imprisonment if he failed to comply. But when everything was explained, an overnight mooring was made at Pottery Pier to the west of Brownsea, courtesy of Poole Harbour Commissioners.

The following morning Bob was approached by a gentleman from Birmingham, armed with all the latest photographical equipment, who promptly hired the Maid of the Isles for a photo-shoot at some considerable cost! The local media had a ball. And with headlines announcing the pilot was in all sorts of trouble, Bob approached Captain Blair as he came ashore at the Fish Shambles steps to meet up with the harbour master,

Antilles Goose Charlotte Amalies harbour. © MICK BAJCAR.

prepared to offer his moral support by confirming the weather conditions at the time. On entering Captain Allinson's office, the pilot was told to forget all about it, it was only newspaper talk, and at half-past nine that Tuesday morning, *Southern Cross* was taxied round to Studland Bay.

The storm had abated but it was not until late afternoon that the swell allowed the mooring to be left for just a few flights, despite some having travelled from as far as Aberdeen and Germany. The first saw reporters from BBC television and the press joining several former BOAC personnel, including Captain Craig, believed to have taken the last BOAC flying boat from Poole, the engine starts awakening long-forgotten echoes from the chalk cliffs, now framed by a clear and sunny sky. Airborne within thirty seconds and settled at 125 knots, the flying boat passed off Bournemouth and Boscombe piers at 500 feet, causing holidaymakers to stand and stare on the beaches from Sandbanks to Hengistbury Head. A slight gain in height, and returned to a bygone era, passengers watched in fascination as the beach at Peacehaven was crossed to turn towards Yarmouth on the Isle of Wight. Another graceful bank and a little more height to pass over Gurnard Head before the nose dipped in salute to the former Saunders-Roe factory at Cowes. On past Ryde Pier and out to the Nab Tower, where another turn brought them beneath the line of Culver Cliffs to head towards Saint Catherines Point and Freshwater Bay, crossing back to Yarmouth before flying a reciprocal course over Bournemouth Bay for a textbook landing back at Studland – though an oft repeated anecdote suggested the valiant reporters had all rushed upstairs when spray covered the windows, fearing the worst!

The following morning, Bob again met up with Charles Blair on the quayside. Invited to 'come and meet the wife', he was guided towards the

Nearly a tragedy. Studland Bay August 24 1976. © AUTHOR COLLECTION.

Mercedes that had driven down from London and was rendered almost speechless when the rear door was opened to reveal the famous Hollywood actress sat inside. Faced with the dazzling smile and expressive eyes of the star of over sixty films, considered one of the most beautiful women in the world, all he could think of saying was 'I wish I was John Wayne!' Her husband had joined the rest of the crew amongst the peace and seclusion of the Bankes Arms Hotel at Studland and had remained unruffled by the enthusiasm generated by the press. As he had explained to a reporter, piloting a flying boat was entirely different from other forms of flight, you fussed and worried even when ashore, concerned for its safety, and permanently alert to changes in weather conditions. With launches carrying passengers out from the Ferry Steps at Sandbanks, nine flights were completed by Thursday evening, when Lilliput resident Jack Harris joined the proceedings.

Grandfather Sam had been a doyen of the British Film Industry, his promotion of the early cinematograph industry through his daily trade newspaper *Todays Cinema* bringing trips to the Hollywood studios during the 1920s through to the fifties. International celebrities and film moguls had visited the family home at Caterham in Surrey where a very young Jack had been dangled on the knee of 'Harry' (Hirsch) Warner of Warner Brothers. Living nearby, Sir Alan Cobham was also a friend of the family. Sam Harris had founded the Croydon Flying Club and at the age of 60 passed his 'A' pilot certificate and bought his own de Havilland Leopard Moth and a Rapide.

With a family move to Bournemouth after the war, aside from the family business Jack had also found a passion for flying, awarded a private pilot licence when 21 and winning some seventy pounds prize money after finishing fifth in the Kings Cup Air Race. Having met a host of international stars such as James Stewart, Cary Grant, Diana Dors, Dirk Bogarde,

Jack Harris back at the controls.
© AUTHOR.

Marilyn Monroe and Lawrence Olivier, his knowledge of the film industry had led him to join Film Aviation Services, formed by former BEA Captain, John Crewdson. Aircraft were provided for films such as *I was Montys Double* starring John Mills; which brought drama away from filming, when a pneumatic de-icing boot peeled away from a wing and began wrapping itself around an aileron of the four-engined Avro York; and the *Inn of the Sixth Happiness* starring Ingrid Bergman; the twin-engined Airspeed Oxfords painted to resemble Chinese bombers for the 'bombing' scenes enacted over Snowdonia in Wales. They had also located three de Havilland Mosquitos in Israel, one of which had been fitted with dual controls, for the 1964 film *633 Squadron*, based on the book by Bournemouth author Frederick E Smith.

Now with Flight Refuelling in Dorset, former Shorts test pilot Tom Brooke-Smith had rung Jack to see whether he knew about the flying boat at Studland. Would he like a flight? Phone calls were made, and climbing aboard for the last trip that Thursday, Jack was unexpectedly greeted by Charles Blair, shown up to the flight deck, and installed in the left hand seat as *Southern Cross* began filling up with passengers. Remembered for his charming and natural personality, the famous pilot talked Jack through the starting procedures. With everyone aboard, the port and starboard outer engines were fired up, followed by the two inners on leaving the buoy. Taxiing into wind and completing the final pre-flight checks, Jack was told 'It's All Yours!' and was surprised by how effortlessly they left the surface. Encouraged to stay at the controls for the following twenty-five minutes or so, he was guided into lining her up to the left of the Old Harry Rocks and holding the attitude, without the 'flair' required by a landplane, pulled off an equally smooth landing. The experience would be even more cherished in the light of future events, which virtually ensured his landing would be the last of any flying boat in the area.

The major fuel companies had long since scrapped the last of their launches. But on Friday morning, an open catamaran freely loaned by Stephen Willis headed out to the mooring. On board were eight drums of aviation fuel and an electric pump borrowed from Flight Refuelling by retired technical director Peter Procter, who was invited aboard the first flight. On arrival, the refuelling party was shocked to find that vandals, possibly from among those who had seen their small craft alarmingly tossed by the wash of the unexpected landing in Poole, had removed the aft bilge cap of the starboard wing float.

It was already one third full of seawater, while a strengthening wind not only prevented taking on fuel at the exposed mooring but was rising beyond landing limits, supposing a take-off was possible in the circumstances. Faced with the entire event ending in tragedy, Ron Gillies scrambled aboard and started up the inner engines as the catamaran departed in search of pumping equipment. In the midst of a lot of yelling and waving of arms in the wind, Ron noticed a cross-channel ferry was about to enter Poole and promptly tucked *Southern Cross* behind the stern, praying no one would stop the engines. As he would tell me later, in all his time on Sunderlands and Sandringhams he had never had to taxi broadside on to a wind sending such strong sheets of spray over the propellers, threatening to send the damaged float and aircraft beneath the waves. Approaching the chain-ferry steps at Sandbanks they were met by Alarm, which led the way past the conflicting sea and harbour currents between the North and South Havens, providing a rare sight for the few braving the elements to watch from the shore.

At twenty minutes past two in the afternoon a mooring was made at Buoy 50, south-west of Brownsea Island, in the calmer waters of the inner harbour. South Western Marine Factors generously provided an electrical stack pump and hose and the catamaran was carefully positioned to allow the fourteen volt battery to power the pump and clear the float; sealed with madapolam and wing fabric dope to allow a flight to Belfast for repairs. Using a funnel and chamois leather 'filter', 800 gallons of high octane petrol was passed into the wing tanks in thirty minutes. The wind continued to churn the waves outside, while strong sunlight lit the pine-clad slopes of Brownsea from a deceptively clear blue sky: the presence of the flying boat accentuating the natural beauty of the ancient harbour – as if a missing piece of some forgotten and treasured puzzle had been found and restored to its rightful place.

On Saturday, goodbyes were made and the mooring slipped to follow Alarm across the harbour. At two minutes past two, a booming roar shattered the silence surrounding the cliffs and Old Harry Rocks as *Southern Cross* fought free of the high tide that had cancelled the Regatta at

Approaching the Havens. © Author Collection.

Studland, turning low over the sea and coming back to circle overhead in a last salute. Then she was gone: the sound of the fading engines lingering about the hills as her wake dissolved into glistening fragments. She would never come again.

The following summer Charles Blair repeated the experience with Aer Árann at Killaloe, though issues raised by the Poole bird-watching and sailing communities prevented a return to Dorset. Obliged to operate from Calshot, similar objections restricted movements to the mouth of the Beaulieu River, some 4 miles away, though the presence of his beautiful wife undoubtedly boosted the sale of T-shirts. His untimely death in September 1978, when the Grumman Goose he was flying crashed into the sea near St Thomas Island, irrevocably ended the link with Poole, and the distinguished pilot was buried with full military honours at Arlington National Cemetery. Though ten of the happiest years of her life had abruptly come to an end, Maureen O'Hara-Blair assumed control of the company and was subsequently elected America's first woman president of a scheduled airline, a position held until September 1981, when the new owners, Resorts International, left the Virgin Islands.

By then the fleet was entirely made up of Mallard amphibians which in March began operations for Virgin Islands Seaplane Shuttle, formed by Antilles former general manager Nicholas Castruccio. The two big flying boats had also found new owners.

Preserved for the Nation

Abandoned after the death of Charles Blair, the Sunderland and Sandringham had suffered unwanted attention from the curious and from

Safely moored to Buoy 50. © AUTHOR COLLECTION.

souvenir hunters. Threatened with scrapping to pay for their 'tenancy', both were taken over by former chief pilot Ron Gillies in order to find a buyer. In far the best condition, though not for much longer, the Sandringham became the subject of fundraising by a Dorset consortium to pay for the purchase and overhaul required for a return to Britain, where it was hoped to complete a few seasons of pleasure flying before putting the aircraft on permanent display. The Science Museum in London had agreed in principle to a purchase for the nation, provided the aircraft was delivered to Britain. Ron finally took *Southern Cross* away in October 1980, landing at Killaloe after an Atlantic crossing of some fifteen hours, only to find they had to remain there until the authorities made up their minds to allow entry to Britain! In January, Maureen unveiled a large scale replica of her husband's record-breaking Mustang at London Airport, funded by friends and former employees of Pan Am, while on 2 February the flying boat in which they had flown so many happy hours together made the very last landing of its career at Calshot.

Driving up from Bournemouth, I spent an interesting evening with Ron and Noreen Gillies within their temporary home, a former coastguard cottage, where I learned of some of the difficulties in operating *Southern Cross* in Britain and of the ferry flight home. Times had so obviously changed, the attitude of some of the controllers during the last season of pleasure-flying from Hampshire, disappointing to say the least, particularly when remembering how many flying boats had regularly filled the same airspace in wartime. Serious consideration had been given to making a commemorative flight on the fiftieth anniversary of the 1934 London-Melbourne Air Race as a pretext to finding a permanent home 'down under', but a close scrutiny of the hull brought the realisation that all thoughts of keeping her flying were financially out of the question.

Unable to remain at Calshot, now an activities centre and lifeboat station, a berth was kindly provided by HMS Daedalus, the inboard engines performing the taxi to Lee where *Southern Cross* was finally hauled from the water on beaching gear on 7 July 1981. The following year, the National Aeronautical Collection of the Science Museum, secured ownership for the sum of £85,000, made up of £40,000 from the museum and £45,000 from the National Heritage Memorial Trust. Despite thoughts of storage within the museum's hangar at Wroughton, Wiltshire, and understandable competition from Rochester, Southampton City Council were given the opportunity to build a new museum centred, literally, around the flying boat: conveyed to Southampton Eastern Docks on 2 March 1982 aboard a large twin-engined barge supplied by the 17th Port Regiment. Dismantled, the components were restored and repainted within a large disused customs shed and in August entered the incomplete museum premises in Albert Road South.

Previous attempts to open a museum dedicated to Reginald J. Mitchell had all foundered due to the cost of acquiring suitable premises. But following the suggestion of Squadron Leader Alan Jones, MBE, the Commanding Officer of No 424 (Southampton) Squadron of the Air Training Corps, together with his promised assistance of everyone connected with the squadron, a dilapidated former NAAFI canteen and dance hall next to the squadron headquarters in Havelock Road had been released by the council, and to the credit of everyone concerned, the

Moored off Studland Beach. © AUTHOR COLLECTION.

Mitchell Museum had opened to the public in 1976.

Constructed to primarily house *Southern Cross* and the Mitchell Museum, together with memorabilia from the numerous historic aviation concerns of the region, the Southampton Hall of Aviation would also provide a new headquarters for the hard working A.T.C. Squadron. Positioned a short distance from where liners and flying boats had once docked, and just over the road from the former South Western Hotel, the museum was completed at a cost of over four hundred thousand pounds. Formally opened on 26 May 1984, in due course the museum would be renamed Solent Sky.

Costly Acquisition

Abandoned at Isla Grande, at best retained for spares, *Excalibur VIII* was saved from scrapping by Charles Edward Hulton, the millionaire grandson of Sir Edward George Hulton, remembered for his pioneering photojournalism and hugely successful *Picture Post* magazine of the 1930s and 40s. Purchased from Resorts International in May 1979 by his American based company Juliet Flying Boats (Inc), and restored to airworthy condition within the echoing hangar by a Miami based

Beachcomber Solent Sky Aviation Museum.
© Author collection.

company, N158J was renamed *Juliet* by Maureen O'Hara Blair before returned to Saint Croix. The Federal Aviation Authority again refused a commercial licence however, causing the new owner to move his flying boat to Lake Marignane, where marine facilities continued to support flying boat operations, though now by faintly Catalina look-alike Canadair CL-215 'Scooper' water bombers, owned and operated by the Sécurité Civile.

The lake was also within easy reach of the millionaires home at Monaco. Long-range tanks were fitted and a ferry crew led by Bryan Monkton finally landed on the lake in May 1981 to enable further restoration to begin. The journey had taken seven months rather than an intended seven days, due to a variety of problems with the 37 year old aircraft. Completed at Belfast in the spring of 1944, the eighth machine of a twenty-five strong, eighth batch of Sunderland 3s, ML814 had served 201, 461 (RAAF) and 422 (RCAF) Squadrons before returned to Belfast to be virtually rebuilt as a General Reconnaissance Mark V prior to serving No 330 (Norwegian) Squadron.

In August 1982 the re-registered G-BJHS was met and escorted to overhead the Port of London by a Nimrod of 201 Squadron, where the landing on the Thames by Ron Gillies was the first by a flying boat for thirty years. Moored near Tower Bridge to raise money for the Falklands Fund, the stay lasted until October when a return was made to Calshot. Essential work ended hopes for the 1983 air display season however and was followed by notice to quit Calshot,

The councillors were unwilling to renew the lease at Rochester, but supported by the Medway Branch of the Royal Aeronautical Society and by GEC Electronics, a major employer since the closure of the Shorts factory and naval dockyard, Medway City Council offered a berth at Chatham. Water trials were completed by Ken Emmott and on 17 November, the renamed *Sir Arthur Gouge* was flown out by Reg Young, who had temporarily forsaken the even larger Martin Mars water bombers in Canada to help out: the arrival marked by low passes over the city and the former Seaplane Works. Welcomed by the City Council and by the Chatham Historic Dockyard Trust, a mooring was made in bright sunshine off the dockyard; the clean white lines broken by a royal blue flash between the windscreen and the nose, with matching cheat line and registration letters. High on the tail, a blue disc positioned by her owner featured a large white 'tusker' in defiance of the opinion expressed in print by a member of the Fleet Street fraternity!

Hauled up within the covered Slipway 7 (next to the former submarine berth), work was begun by resident Australian engineer Peter Smith (taken on in France) and by volunteer former Sunderland technicians, in order to pass the licensing requirements for passenger flights. In 1985, the Sunderland was filmed on the water in the livery of a Pan Am Clipper for the BBC production *Mr and Mrs Edgehill* and was filmed internally. It was also seen flying and was filmed internally for the 1985 sequel to the television drama *Tenko (Tenko Reunion)*. But having spent nearly three million on his flying boat, Edward Hulton experienced a crippling setback in October 1987. With the work virtually complete, a hurricane struck the south-west: forcing the hull off the tail trolley and seriously damaging the float and starboard outer wing on which the weight now rested, as at Lord Howe Island twenty-two years earlier. Prepared to restore the damaged metal to display standard, the Imperial War Museum at Duxford exchanged it for an airworthy outer wing from ML796 (*Mister Blue)*, but another two years work would be required before the aircraft was ready to fly again.

Chapter Eleven

Last of the Breed

Foynes Clipper

In 1987 members of the Foynes community council had approached the county development team with the idea of establishing a museum within the original terminal building. By the close of 1988, a limited company had been set up, various experts had been consulted, and an all important lease agreed with the harbour trustees for part of the building. Work had begun that November. On 9 July 1989, the fiftieth anniversary of the arrival of *Yankee Clipper* with the first regular passengers from America, Maureen O'Hara Blair formally opened the Foynes Flying Boat Museum before over eight hundred people, many of them former Pan Am employees.

The Sunderland at Chatham was of obvious interest. But her owner had had enough and had offered her for sale, though refusing two hundred thousand pounds to keep her there as the agents thought she was worth around a million in flying condition. Hopeful of operating pleasure flights around Ireland in conjunction with Foynes Museum however, Ryanair financed restoration to full flying status. Granted the hallowed U.K certificate of airworthiness in August 1989, the renamed *Spirit of Foynes* was flown to Ireland: the cheat line now broken by the name of the airline, repeated on the wing floats (a new twist), with a stylised logo on the fin. The lease and option to purchase were to be signed at Foynes. But two days later Edward Hulton changed his mind and had the aircraft returned to Calshot.

Returned to its former name *Islander,* brief appearances of the sole airworthy Sunderland in the world (thanks to Ryanair) had begun with a surprise appearance at the 1990 Great Warbirds Air Show at West Malling in Kent, featuring the United Kingdom's sole airworthy Flying Fortress *Sally B* operated by Elly Sallingboe. The 1991 Sotheby's auction failed to reach the reserve however and it wasn't until February 1993 that a sale was concluded to Kermit Weeks, an aviation engineer and world-class aerobatic pilot, whose Miami museum had been devastated by Hurricane Andrew.

As a larger, 300 acre site was cleared in Florida, work continued at

Last Sunderland capable of flying.
© KERMIT WEEKS FANTASY OF FLIGHT MUSEUM FLORIDA.

Calshot where yet another change of name, *Fantasy of Flight* (the new museum), was painted in crescent form beneath the cockpit with an identifying 'Polk City USA' above the port entry hatch. Kermit and a five man crew finally departed for Killaloe in July and after a second landing at Skerjafyordur (Iceland), arrived overhead Wittman Regional Airport in

Goodbye Calshot. © COLIN LEE.

Wisconsin during the world famous Oshkoss Fly-In. A prolonged stay ended with the completion of a concrete ramp in Florida and the re-registered N814ML flew to her new home in August 1994. The museum opened in 1995 and the following year the Sunderland uniquely carried the Olympic Torch from Sarasota to Miami on the celebrated Fourth of July. Protected within a hangar of 'the greatest private aircraft collection in the world', the Sunderland may now be viewed with other interesting exhibits such as the Paraguay Air Force Catalina that flew Juan Perón into exile in October 1955, ongoing restorations, 'Splash-Ins' on the museum lake, biplane and balloon flights – with 'Spitfire' sandwiches available in the pre-war / Art Deco styled Compass Rose Diner!

Three years after the opening of Fantasy of Flight, in November 1998 Maureen was the guest speaker during a ceremony held at the New England Air Museum dedicated to the beautifully restored *Excambian*. The damaged hull and six years exposure on the beach had meant a virtual re-skinning of the aluminium before restoring the interior to the standard seen in its heyday with American Export Airlines. For ten years, the work had been freely undertaken within a temporary hangar at the Sikorsky Memorial Airport in Stratford by former pilots and mechanics and by technical schools in tribute to her husband. Reassembly and completion had taken another year at New England, after a 71 mile journey and closure of two lanes of two major interstate highways, with State Police keeping the convoy clear of highly curious traffic!

In 2002, the Foynes museum was able to buy the entire terminal building. The exhibition space was enlarged the following year, and an even bigger, one point six million euro, revamp completed by 2006 featuring a unique full-size replica of the Boeing 314 *Yankee Clipper*. Founder and managing director Margaret O'Shaugnessy had seen the need to portray a physical presence of the Clipper flying boats, and thoughts of assembling a single full-size cabin had moved to a complete fuselage due to the expertise of television and film set designer Bill Fallover. With funding approved by Minister for Tourism John O'Donoghue, the project had taken less than a year and was unveiled during the official re-opening ceremony on 3 July. In a moving address by museum Patron Maureen O'Hara Blair, the assembly was told that her husband's heart was in Foynes and that she had followed his heart there and would continue to do so to keep his memory alive, for as long as she lived. The following year 40,000 people passed through the same entrance as the wartime VIPs, in contrast to the 3,000 recorded in 1989. Maureen returned in September 2009 for the opening of the newly rebuilt air traffic control tower on top of the museum building.

Today, tourists are surprised and delighted to find such a fine museum, unheralded now by wartime engines and bustle. On arrival you are faced by an impressive bronze and limestone 'Clipper fountain' created by the

Worlds sole Boeing 314 Clipper replica.
© FOYNES FLYING BOAT MUSEUM.

renowned sculptor Jim Connolly, whose father James was among the first radio technicians sent to Ireland, and by the triple fins and rear fuselage of NC18603. Inside, the reception hall pays tribute to Brendan O'Regan and chef Joe Sheridan within the story of Irish Coffee, while an arresting head and shoulders bronze, sculpted by Jim Connolly and presented to Maureen by the museum during her eightieth birthday party at the Dunraven Arms Hotel, adjoins a display dedicated to the internationally famous actress.

A cosy 1940's style cinema leads to an exhibition room dedicated to the early Atlantic flyers, which includes the airline uniform, medals, 'bone-dome' and flying overalls of Charles Blair donated by Maureen. The radio and weather room contains some of the original equipment, while the war room features a model of the Shannon estuary and lit alighting area as would be seen by an approaching Clipper pilot. Simulators are provided within the children and pilot training rooms, while the treasure room has a fascinating collection of Pan Am artefacts and trinkets donated by the public.

Refreshments, including the inevitable Irish Coffee, are available in the new Brendan O'Regan Restaurant, while the exhibition hall has large models of a Catalina and Sunderland beneath the high translucent roof. There is also a Sikorsky floor mosaic. More Pan Am artefacts are displayed within the departure room, which leads outside to the 'moored' *Yankee Clipper.* Approached from beneath the port engine and wing section, a companion way leads across the sponson to an open entrance hatch, the fully furnished interior including the rear 'bridal' suite, galley, dressing rooms, and seats converted to curtained overnight bunks, with full instrumentation replicated on the flight deck. A fine tribute to Margaret O'Shaugnessy and her team, the museum continues to surprise thousands of visitors each year and has a vital rôle within the local tourist economy.

AFRICA SAFARI

However hard we try, most aviation museums can never really recapture the sights, sounds and smells associated with the life of its grounded inhabitants, particularly flying boats. Such a chance, perhaps the very last, had come in 1988 with the formation of the Catalina Safari Company in Harare, Zimbabwe, by Pierre and Antoinette Jaunet.

En route to a new life in Australia after working for a well known structural engineer in England, Pierre had become fascinated by Africa and had bought a Land Rover to explore the Kalahari Desert. Inclined to see more of the country, he had subsequently led a six-month tourist trip from Johannesburg aboard the Land Rover, followed by a trip to the Kalahari for some Americans and a four-month tour across Africa for four English tourists. Having crossed the Sahara a few times, he then ran a number of safaris for a small French company: the February 1975 trip remembered for meeting his future wife, who decided not to return to Paris to finish her studies in interior decoration! The following winters were spent running desert safaris, with summers spent in Botswana, northern Kenya, Pakistan and Libya, now with a brand new Land Rover. Moving to the Sudan, they came to love North Africa and the Nile, and Pierre became fluent in Arabic and Italian in addition to his native French.

The idea for an 'airborne safari' had come in 1985 when he had noticed the landing pontoon was still in place at Victoria Falls and heard that a PBY5A was available at a storage yard at Reno, Nevada. He subsequently spent three weeks with Bob Schlaefli of Moses Lake, Washington, who owned six such water bombers, possibly the first to use them after the war, who on realising he could not talk Pierre out of using his hard earned profits on the venture, did all he could to help – entirely without charge. For three days Bob flew Pierre in his Beechcraft Bonanza on inspection trips to Reno, Los Angeles and British Columbia; the Reno prospect considered the best due to the relatively low hours and the fact that it had been licensed to carry passengers. Guided by Bob and his friend Harry O'Hara, who had flown flying boats as a wartime Squadron Leader and postwar director of Alaska Airlines, C-FJCV was purchased over two years later – but for less than half the sum quoted in the first *Trade-A-Plane* advert!

Built by Canadian Vickers for the Royal Canadian Air Force, the flying boat was a Canso (technically a CansoA for amphibian) for the Canadians never adopted the name Catalina, preferring instead to name the licence-built PBYs after the Strait that separates the island of Cape Breton from Nova Scotia. Civilianised after the war, when the nose turret was replaced by a mooring hatch, it was latterly used to transport fishermen about British Columbia.

Prepared for its new life by Russ Popel, another of Bob's friends, whose company Victoria Air Maintenance specialised in rebuilding wartime aircraft at Vancouver Island, the austere metal hatches were removed to give an unrestricted floor to ceiling walkway, and the interior refitted to provide a pair of eight-seat cabins with comfortable padded seats, a proper toilet, and a galley with sink, stove, fridge and freezer. The intact side blisters were incorporated into a lounge area provided with a small library and bar. A luggage compartment was fitted behind the captain's seat, where the weight would help trim the aircraft in flight, while the tail would stow an inflatable dinghy to transfer passengers and luggage ashore in the absence of a boat. A 5 horsepower outboard engine would be stored above the galley within the pylon, the engineer's instrument panel transferred to the cockpit. Both engine cowlings retained the deep red paint scheme seen during the years with Austin Airways (among others), when the colour was repeated on the wingtips, lower fuselage and tailplane. The hull and floats were now slate blue. Below the cockpit, on both sides of the white fuselage, a large colourful disc portrayed the identifying logo of the Africa Safari Company.

Pierre had also secured the services of Bushbuck Safaris as managing agents. The family business had started in 1985, as he had begun acquiring permits to follow the tracks of the 'Empire' flying boats through Africa to the Zambesi, and had established a personalised wildlife operation using the best camp sites and guides within Botswana and Zimbabwe. Providing full-time employment for Booh Shirley-Beavan, with her retired father Mike regularly popping in, and his wife Jennifer helping out in a part-time capacity, the company had just begun attracting important clients from America.

Following an eleven-hour Atlantic crossing from Gander to the Azores by Jim Ledergard, an experienced water bomber pilot recommended by Bob, with Oliver Evans in the second seat, the October 1988 route proving flight was accompanied by a BBC film unit and in December, the first safari passengers climbed aboard for the return flight to the Nile. With others, I couldn't resist watching the fascinating BBC television documentary that went out on a well scheduled Sunday, early in January 1990. Enticingly entitled *The Last African Flying Boat,* the film portrayed the journey of London-based journalist Alexander Frater from Cairo to Mozambique, attracting over four million viewers and a British Academy Film Award. Not altogether surprising when remembering the BBCs highly successful broadcasts of the 1950s and 60s, featuring the Oscar winning underwater adventures of Hans and Lotte Hass and the African safaris of Armand and Michaela Denis. The company couldn't have wished for a better start. Within a very short time the Shirley-Beavan family was working flat out to satisfy the demands of a business rapidly approaching an annual turnover of one million (American) dollars.

In keeping with those pre-war flights of Imperial Airways, the safaris were somewhat of a preserve for the rich. Seventeen thousand dollars bought you a place on the complete, three week, itinerary, though soon supplemented by a choice of a half-safari in either direction, ending at Nairobi. Each was personally hosted by Pierre and Antoinette, who aside from leading the overland excursions, served excellent refreshments on board the aircraft. Up front, the former RCAF cockpit was occupied by a seasonally employed captain and co-pilot, whose accents were invariably Canadian. Having taken flying lessons at Maun Airport in Botswana, Pierre spent hours seated atop the luggage compartment watching the cockpit procedures from a small window behind the left hand seat.

The appearance of the graceful flying boat could not be said to be a true reminder of the past however, for though used to patrol the oceans on either side of the continent, PBYs had never flown passengers (or anything else) over the inland waterways of central Africa. But as with Imperial, the low altitude brought memorable images of the pyramids and temples of the Nile, now in contrast to the spreading ramparts of the Aswan High Dam: the alighting on Lake Nassar on the Egyptian sector of the reservoir, utilising the ability to lower the main wheels as 'sea anchors', independent of the nose wheel, reflected by the essential 'isolation valves closed' pre-flight check in the cockpit! The bulbous 'blisters' gave incredible views, the ridges of the Ndoto mountains surpassed by the snow-capped, volcanic peak of Mount Kenya, known as Kirinyaga, a sacred 'place of light' by the Kikuyu people, before the approach was begun for Wilson Airport in Nairobi.

In the autumn of 1990 photographer Tim Spearman joined the safari at Nairobi. An avid fan of piston-engined aeroplanes, with most of his holidays spent seeking them out to photograph and hopefully take a flight, Jim had left the UK aboard a British Airways Boeing 747 accompanied by younger sister Philippa. Though arriving late in the day, they were in time to meet the rest of the group over dinner at the Norfolk Hotel. The next day was free, enabling them to explore the locality, and on the last Sunday in October, the sixteen British, Dutch, Swiss and American enthusiasts climbed aboard the re-registered Z-CAT.

With the luggage stowed and everyone in their seats, the 'pwhee' of the starter motors, slow-turning propellers, and metallic 'chuffing' of

American engines might have come from a classic film of wartime Flying Fortresses. Until the compressed fuel ignited, turning the props into a blur and settling the airframe to a steady vibration – the taxi to the runway and steady climb out watched by virtually everyone it seemed. A comparatively short flight gave impressive views of the snow-clad volcanic peak of Mount Kilimanjaro, Africa's highest mountain, before landing at Arusha (Tanzania), the 'safari capital' of East Africa, to clear customs; with Pierre ensuring everyone's paperwork was in order following a particularly unhelpful experience with officials as they had passed through the Sudan. Off again, and not the first to have felt 'unsettled' by the vibration of piston engines, Philippa was now enjoying the experience, as brother Tim watched the unfolding panorama from 'within' the blisters in the lounge, where Pierre had thoughtfully provided a small library of vintage aviation books in addition to the maps and magazines on Africa.

The next landing was on an airstrip beside Lake Manyara, beneath the Rift Valley Escarpment. An area of unbelievable beauty, teeming with wildlife, the stay provided an overland safari aboard 'four by fours' to the Ngorongoro Crater. Thought to have once towered 15,000 feet above sea-level, over two million years ago the volcano had imploded after a subterranean lake of molten magma had drained away, leaving a vast bowl enclosed by cloud-topped rims over 2,000 metres high. Driven down from the rim in the late afternoon, the light dramatically highlighted the awe inspiring landscape. The night was spent within a luxurious tented encampment, though Tim was awoken in the pitch black early morning by the sound of hippos appearing deceptively close! The next morning the vehicles took them within the crater itself. Irrigated by two rivers, the fertile grasslands, swamps and lush forests of the valley floor attract a variety of grazing animals (and their hunters) and there is always something to see. To their surprise, the party came across mating lions, which they were told was an extremely rare sight.

The return to Arusha for refuelling was followed by a brief stop at Dar Es Salaam to clear customs before alighting at Zanzibar: the arrival opposite Stone House delighting the crowds that had gathered on the harbour wall to watch the proceedings in the warmth of the late afternoon sun. While awaiting the arrival of a small boat to ferry them across to the immigration office, some of the party soaked up the atmosphere sat on the wing with a cool drink. The crew then took the vacated 'Cat' to the airport. Having spent the night at the 'Spice Inn' and hearing that Pierre had arranged for some 'action filming' off Mnemba Island for a building society television advert, Tim was delighted to be allowed aboard for the sequence of take-offs and landings, undertaken in gin clear weather in one of the most perfect locations on earth! They were then returned to Dar Es Salaam before crossing the Kipengere Mountains to Lilongwe, where customs were again cleared before landing off the south-western shore of Lake

Catalina Safari Lake Malawi 1990. © TIM SPEARMAN.

Malawi. Tim's natural instincts, that sunny first day of November, resulted in an evocative shot of Z-CAT as the dinghy headed back over the invitingly clear blue water, with Pierre stood in front of Antoinette, seated amongst the luggage. The Canadian captain and Zimbabwean co-pilot then flew on to nearby Salima to moor for the night as their charges began exploring the amenities of the Livingstonia Beach Hotel.

In the morning Tim and Philippa left to head home via Harare, having enjoyed what for Tim has remained one of the most exciting journeys of his life. The rest of the group were flown to Maun in Botswana, where a Cessna 206 took them to the cottage-style Delta Camp set amid the Great Okavango swamplands; able to explore the nearby Chiefs Island or take a canoe trip along the waterways. In their absence, the crew had watched as the hull was sprayed with the obligatory Perakwat to protect the waters of the region from parasitic aquatic plants, though the chemical was highly corrosive to aluminium. It did however enable a landing on the Chobe River to experience the authentic cottages of Chilwero Camp amid an abundance of migrating bird life, before a final, short flight, to the Zambesi, where the old flying boat jetty had inspired Pierre to start it all.

Of the more famous names involved with the Catalina Safaris, Pierre remembered the private charter booked by 'Bill' Gates, co-founder of the Microsoft Corporation, to see the mountain gorillas living amongst the tropical forest of Kauzi-Biega National Park. The group of twelve friends and special guests included his future wife Belinda and the anthropologist

Perhaps a flying boat . .
© PIERRE AND ANTOINETTE JAUNET

Don Johanson, famous for his 1974 discovery in Ethiopia of the remains of one of our earliest upright walking female ancestors. Flown from Lake Tanzania to Lake Kivu, they were then landed on the crystal clear Lake Tanganyika to view the chimpanzees living among the mist shrouded hills of Mahale National Park, though not a single chimp put in an appearance, despite a two night stop-over within the luxurious tented camp.

Remembered as the best of the 'repeat' clients by Mike Shirley-Beavan, in 1991 Arnold von Bohlen und Halbachglobe booked a trip to Egypt and Jordan for a group of twelve friends, all vintage aircraft enthusiasts, followed by a second to East Africa the following year, and a third to Ethiopia and Yemen in 1993 – the year of the much publicised Peter Stuyvesant Travel *Odyssey*. Intended to give young people a true sense of adventure, rather than the 'packaged' variety available on the tourist market, the *Odyssey* allowed competition winners from three European countries to 'Discover The World' in successive stages as the flying boat

U.S. Navy Martin Mariner.
© GLENN L. MARTIN MARYLAND AVIATION MUSEUM COLLECTION.

circumnavigated the North Atlantic. Filming of the event would be shown in each of their respective countries.

Flown to Eindhoven, Holland, to be given the blue and red livery of the Dutch cigarette company, with large identifying logos above the cabin windows and on the tail, Z-CAT departed Schiphol Airport just after mid-day on the last day of May 1993. Between then and the final splash down at Lelystad Marine Harbour on 17 July, veteran Australian pilot Brian McCook, American co-pilot Mike Terryl, and Zimbabwean flight engineer Harry Holdcroft, guided their charge across the changing landscapes of France, West Africa, the Cape Verde Islands, Brazil, the Virgin Islands, the Cayman Islands, Mexico, America (New Orleans, Georgia and New York), Newfoundland, Greenland, Iceland and the Shetland Isles. The fourteen and a half hour Atlantic crossing to Brazil had prompted Pierre to uncork a celebratory bottle of champagne, while the arrival at Belém after another six hours had brought a reminder of the PBYs operated about the Amazon by the Força Aérea Brasileira, featured among the exhibits at the Belém Air

Base Museum at Pará – and by the Museu Aeroespacial da FAB at the Afonsos Air Base, Rio de Janeiro.

July 25th 1943 had been a day to remember, begun with the detection of U-199, 19 miles off Rio by the radar of an American flying boat. Intended as a long-range successor to the Consolidated PBY, the PBM (Patrol Boat built by Martin) Mariner featured a gull-wing with bomb bays unusually within the nacelles of both engines and a prominent 'radome' housing search for ASV radar above and behind the cockpit. Having sunk U-153 twelve days earlier, the Rio-based Mariner '7' of VP-74 was now in the hands of Lieutenant Walter Smith, tasked to sweep the harbour approaches east of the Trinidad-bound convoy JT3, which had left Rio protected by aircraft of the American Navy and the Brazilian Air Force.

Twenty-eight year old Hans-Werner Krauss had had a successful war, awarded the Iron Cross First Class and the coveted Knights Cross, with promotion to Kapitänleutnant. Returned from the Mediterranean to attend the building of the 1,200 ton U-199 at Bremen, he and his hand-picked crew had left Kiel on 13 May with his customary Viking ship painted on the conning tower. Refuelled in Norway and ordered to an area off the coast of Brazil thought to be a major shipping lane, Krauss had sighted only fishing vessels. Patrolling more to the south of Rio de Janeiro and closer inshore, he had torpedoed an armed Brazilian merchant ship and sunk an unfortunate fishing vessel which had also chanced across him while surfaced at night. He had then sunk a British ship, but six days later had been 'scanned' by the Mariner while heading in to submerge and lie in wait in the shallows.

Though a haze hung over the water, the submarine was visibly sighted when 15 miles away and at 5 miles the flying boat was targeted by guns mounted on the casing and conning tower. The Mariner 3c had been specifically improved to counter the increasing fire-power of the U-boats however, with extra armour plating for the eleven-man crew and a pair of .5 calibre machine guns in the nose and dorsal turrets. Two hundred and eighty feet long and 22 feet wide, the submarine presented a slim but lethal target. Attacked from the beam just after seven fifteen in the morning, six depth charges exploded in a welter of spray as the Mariner banked hard left to drop the remaining pair between the bow and the stern. Smoking, with ruptured oil tanks, and the stern awash, Kraus proceeded slowly inshore on the surface, intending to submerge for repairs. But having reached the shallows, a Força Aérea Brasileira Hudson alerted by the Mariner's radio, delivered a single attack across the bow. Both bombs fell short.

Tasked to sweep ahead of JT3, Second Lieutenant Alberto Martins Torres was also alerted, and at nine o'clock brought his Brazilian PBY '2' in to attack as the Mariner bore in again. His first pair of depth charges exploded off the port casing. By now U-199 was well down by the stern and Krauss gave the order to abandon ship. Turning to port, Torres dropped a second pair of depth charges directly over the stern, forcing the bow clear out of the water before disappearing from sight. Both aircraft dropped life rafts and of the sixty-one Kriegsmarine personnel that had left Germany, just twelve, including Kapitän Krauss, were retrieved by an American seaplane tender. By then the Mariner had landed at Rio, despite a damaged engine caused by drawing fire away from the Hudson and PBY.

Alberto had the name *Arará* painted across the nose of the PBY, in memory of the crew of the Brazilian ship torpedoed by U-507 while rescuing survivors of four other Brazilian ships sunk by the submarine during two infamous days in August 1942. Brazil had declared war with Germany five days later, on the 22nd. In 1943 the pilot exchanged the slow flying PBY for a single-seat Thunderbolt of the First Brazilian Fighter Group and survived ninety-nine gruelling missions in support of the United States Fifth Army in Italy. After the war he bought a pair of PBYs and founded his own airline Transportes Aéreos Bandeirantes. Krauss was among 25 prisoners who had escaped their Arizona POW camp in December 1943. The severe cold caused most to surrender, but the U-boat Kapitän had covered over 40 miles before an injury to his companion forced him to give up. He died in 1990, seven years after the PBY had been retired by the Brazilian Air Force.

The *Odyssey* had gone well. But passing Aberdeen with expectations of a comfortable five-hour crossing to Amsterdam, the port engine lost power. A Mayday was sent and Pierre was asked to open the tap at the bottom of the port fuel tank to reduce the weight and rate of descent. With so many oil rigs in the North Sea, they were soon surrounded by yellow rescue helicopters, causing Mike Terryl to abandon normal radio phraseology to tell them to rapidly clear the back of the aircraft (not exactly the words used) unless they wanted to inhale 3,000 litres of Avgas! Costly. As was the replacement engine and special propeller spanner, boxed and documented with foresight by Pierre. Flown from Harare to London by British Airways the next morning, they were transported by road to Aberdeen Airport. Now practised in wearing life jackets, the Peter Stuyvesent contingent was flown on to Amsterdam where filming was completed in less than a week.

The problems of operating a 50 year old aircraft were not getting any better however and Pierre had already begun looking for a buyer. The engines used up to 2 gallons of oil an hour and the Odyssey had required a flight to Paris to buy 200 litres of the stuff. Keeping the engines serviceable after the return to Africa had proved a constant drain on resources. Two more had needed replacing, faster than Field Aircraft Services at Harare could rebuild them, and with another going 'tech' in early 1994 an expensive hiring of a de Havilland Otter floatplane was necessary to keep fourteen Americans on track with their safari. A new engine had to be air freighted from Seattle to Entebbe in Uganda. Added to which, the irritating problems encountered with paperwork and officialdom, particularly while en route with passengers, had climaxed with a new directive which indicated that foreign registered aircraft could only enter Tanzania from international airports. Bob Schlaefli must have known something. But in June, Pierre was contacted by two members of a New Zealand syndicate, looking to find a flying boat licenced to carry passengers.

A previous attempt to acquire an airworthy Canso by the New Zealand War Birds syndicate had failed that January. Featured in the 1970 film *Tora Tora Tora* and once hired by Jacques Cousteau, another famous underwater explorer featured on BBC television during the 1960s and 70s, N5404J had been purchased from retired TWA Captain Hank Hancock, but had lost an engine while crossing the Pacific en route to New Zealand. Having reached the point of no return, it had crash landed on the ocean, at night, and was finally abandoned after attempts at bailing the damaged hull. Alerted by the Mayday relayed from Hawaii, a U.S Coast Guard Hercules had dropped supplies to the yellow life raft and had guided a diverted giant container ship to their position. Led by Captain Kirkland Broeder, whose reactions had kept the wings level during the life-threatening bounces caused by the impact, the seven occupants, which included Doctor Ross Ewing, who headed the thirty strong syndicate, and Peta Carey, who had joined them in Texas to record the flight for TVNZ, began the steep climb to the deck of *Direct Kookaburra* after eleven hours afloat on the ocean.

Reformed as the Catalina Club of New Zealand, and helped by the (British) insurance payout, a price was agreed with Pierre following an inspection by trustee Chris Snelson: though the deal required Z-CAT to be flown out in the existing company name, by a company crew, with company insurance. Watched by Pierre, Z-CAT left Africa in October: the

Catalina Club of New Zealand XX-T. © PHILLIP TREWEEK.

rising sun brightening runway 05 of Harare International Airport as Bob Dycke and co-pilot David Andrews took her away for the journey to New Zealand. Also aboard were engineer Harry Holdcroft, assistant engineer/third pilot John Howroyd, Chris Snelson – and for the first time in 14,000 hours, professional air hostess Vicki Hollings, who would look after them until rejoining Singapore Airlines at Colombo. Almost 10,000 nautical miles, the journey would require 90 flying hours spread over fourteen days, the crossing of the Indian Ocean taking eleven and a quarter hours, though without having to worry about the occupants of the islands below, as had the Double Sunrise crews. The crossing of the South Pacific made use of the runway built on the hardened lava of Norfolk Island, followed by a five-hour leg to Cape Reinga on the tip of North Island – the landing at New Plymouth on 26 October greeted by some 400 enthusiasts. The apt re-registering to ZK-PBY was followed by a move to Ardmore Airport, from where club members visit air shows and the occasional freshwater lake. Given the call sign 'Warbirds Catalina', the object of their affection now wears the wartime paint scheme of XX-T (NZ4017) of 6 Squadron RNZAF.

Canada

The use of former military aircraft as water bombers was the thême for the 1989 film *Always* directed by Stephen Spielberg: the hilarious opening sequence depicting a sleepy pair of rod fishers on a tranquil lake who have to dive overboard to avoid being run down by a water-scooping Catalina! The need to drop as much as possible in a single load was dramatically underlined by a series of severe fires during the late 1950's and in 1959, guided by 'tanker' pioneer Dan McIvor, a consortium of British Columbian forest companies acquired four Martin Mars heavy-lift flying boats retired three years earlier by the United States Navy – despite their having already passed to a scrap dealer!

Each weighed 38 tons, the 200 foot wings fitted with four, 3,000 horsepower, eighteen cylinder Wright Duplex Cyclone engines driving sixteen-foot, four bladed, propellers, with reversible pitch to both inners. Stripped out and fitted with a 7,000 gallon tank and a pair of retractable scoops by Fairey Aviation of Canada, *Caroline Mars* entered service with Forest Industries Flying Tankers in 1960, but a year later fatally collided with a tree line during a firefighting operation. *Marianas Mars* was destroyed at her mooring by Typhoon Freda in 1962. *Philippine Mars* and *Hawaii Mars* were then converted, and with an additional tank for a thickening agent (Gelgard), entered service in 1963. Sold in 2007 to Coulson Forest Products, evolved from the 1930 company of Cliff Coulson and run by his son Wayne, the much photographed, gloriously red and white painted water bombers are based at Sproat Lake, near Port Alberni on Vancouver Island.

Hawaii Mars California Fires 2004. © COULSON GROUP.

Seen with the identifying Coulson Flying Tankers across the tail fin, the float struts, and beneath the cockpit, with the name of the aircraft aft of the cabin windows, each is crewed by two pilots and two engineers. Operated from the nearest (3 mile minimum) expanse of water to a fire, over a ton of water a second is drawn into the lowered scoops during a thirty-five second, full upload, when the aircraft is held on the step at between 60 to 70 knots. Foam concentrate can be injected once airborne, the familiar 'tumbling' over a drop zone turning the mixture into foam by expansion. Thermo-gel can also be injected during a 'scooping', the encapsulated water producing a more lasting layer over the ground: a 7,000 gallon load able to take some 21 gallons of foam or 70 gallons of gel. To the keen eyed, there is a difference in technique however, the red-tailed *Hawaii Mars* deploying its load from twenty-four doors in the bottom of the hull, formerly occupied by fuel tanks, while the white-tailed *Philippine Mars* offloads from two doors on each side of the fuselage, adjacent to the former cargo hold.

Previously confined to the areas of their owners, the pair now respond to any emergency. In May 2011, *Hawaii Mars* and a 'lead' Sikorsky helicopter spent twenty days in Mexico after soaring temperatures and lightning strikes ignited conflagrations across vast areas of forest and grassland in northern Coahuilai. A condition of the 2007 purchase, on retirement at least one of these 'big birds' has to be left at Port Alberni for preservation and display for the community, while in Britain, the continued presence of an airworthy flying boat relies solely on a determined group of enthusiasts based at a preserved World War Two fighter airfield.

PLANE SAILING

Built by the Consolidated New Orleans factory in 1944, PBY-5A 46633 had also been retired by the U.S Navy in 1956, but four years later was converted to Super Canso standard: principally by having the bow turret removed, the fitting of more powerful 1,700 horsepower Wright Cyclone engines, a larger and redesigned rudder, and twenty-two passenger seats. Retired again, this time after survey operations in South Africa, in 1984 the aircraft was bought by RAF (Harrier) instructor Paul Warren Wilson, fellow RAF (Tornado) pilot John Watts and the well known (Red Arrows) aviation photographer Arthur Gibson, who more usually flew Piper Aztec

Plane Sailing Catalina Lake Biscarrosse 2010.
© DAVID BARRIE.

G-FOTO. Ferried to the UK in 1985 the 'Super Cat' was based at Duxford and seen at air shows under the auspices of Plane Sailing Air Displays Ltd, initially as the camouflaged 'Y' of Flying Officer John Cruickshank.

No 210 Squadron had reformed on the first of January 1944, when 190 Squadron had been renumbered at Sullom Voe in the Shetland Islands, and it had taken sixteen months and forty-eight operational flights for Flying Officer John Alexander Cruickshank RAFVR, a Scot from Aberdeen, to finally encounter an enemy submarine. Flying through fog to the west of Narvik on 17 July, a surfaced U-boat was spotted through a small gap in the clouds which helped conceal the approach. The depth charges failed to release however, prompting the 24 year old pilot to turn back for a second attack. This time DA-Y was met by an intense barrage of shells and machine gun bullets, an explosive direct hit puncturing the pilot's lungs and legs. It also killed his navigator/bomb aimer and wounded three others, including co-pilot Flight Sergeant Jack Garnett. Though bleeding profusely from over seventy wounds, the pilot released the depth charges himself, which straddled and sank the submarine with all fifty-two aboard, later identified as U-361. Only then did he allow himself to be taken to the rear of the aircraft, though refusing morphine in a determined effort to remain conscious.

Five hours later, the shattered Catalina arrived back over Sullom Voe, when he insisted on being helped back into his seat. In acute pain, barely able to breathe, he resumed control and circled until the morning light and sea state allowed a descent to be made in safety. Handing control back to his co-pilot, he supervised the landing to ensure the punctured hull of JV928 would skim the shallows and end up on the shore. Unaware of what had happened beforehand, station medical officer Patrick O'Connor (later Air Vice-Marshal O'Connor CBE, OBE) rushed to the beach and with the barest of equipment, performed an immediate blood transfusion to give the young pilot a chance of surviving the ambulance drive to a hospital in Lerwick. For conspicuous bravery in sinking the submarine, and for saving his aircraft and the lives of the surviving crew, John Cruickshank was awarded the Victoria Cross, the British Commonwealth's highest award for valour in the face of the enemy. Of four presented to Coastal Command during the war, his was the only one not to be awarded posthumously. Jack Garnet received the Distinguished Flying Medal.

The Super Cat had then been repainted in the overall white of Flight Lieutenant David Hornell's 'P' of 162 RCAF Squadron, which eighteen days after the Normandy landings, had come across a surfaced U-boat to the north-west of Bergen, over 100 miles north of the Shetland Isles, while returning to RAF Wick at the end of a twelve-hour patrol.

The last to escape from Lorient (during an air raid), the double hulled, long-range U-1225 had been seriously damaged by mines while negotiating anti-submarine nets placed across the estuary, but had avoided

Allied vessels and escaped into the Bay of Biscay. Fitted with the new Schnorkel breathing apparatus that April, it had sunk seven vessels while heading for Bergen, but had sustained more damage when spotted by Liberators from Iceland.

Though met by withering fire, which set the starboard engine and wing alight and damaged the radio, preventing a sighting report, and with one of the nose guns jammed, the pilot continued his attack; which blew the prow of the submarine clear from the water before falling back beneath the waves. Struggling to gain height, he saw the fiercely burning engine fall from the wing, which had been punched open by the shell fire, but managed to keep control to make a textbook into-wind landing on the remaining engine. Left with a single, four-man, rubber raft when the second exploded, the eight crew paddled clear and watched the burning Catalina settle into the heavy swell.

Alerted by their flares, another Catalina circled their position. But no communication was possible and over twenty hours elapsed before a high speed rescue launch arrived. During that time they had taken turns to slip into the icy water to enable the rubber to be bailed, though all had been tossed overboard by a particularly mountainous wave. An airborne lifeboat had been dropped, but was too far away and the pilot had had to be restrained from attempting to swim to it. Unprotected, cold and wet, two died from exposure.

Every effort was made by the launch crew, but the exhausted 34 year old pilot, blinded by the ordeal which had lasted throughout the night and into the morning, slipped into a coma and never regained consciousness. For his unfailing courage and leadership, in the air and on the water, David Hornell was awarded a posthumous Victoria Cross. A clutch of medals (a DSO, DFC and two DFMs) was awarded to the surviving members of his crew. A Royal Canadian Air Cadet Squadron in Toronto is named after him, while 'P' is replicated by the Catalina displayed by the Canadian Warplane Heritage Museum at Hamilton International Airport, Ontario.

The Plane Sailing team had worked hard to ensure the vintage Catalina had every support, both in the air and on the ground. But in 1988 John Watts was tragically killed in a flying accident. Arthur Gibson died in 1992 and though in the midst of a career change after sixteen years with the RAF, Paul assumed overall responsibility. In 1994 the flying boat was re-registered in Bermuda (VR-BPS) and the company name changed to Plane Sailing Bermuda Ltd, to allow full use of the sixteen newly fitted and (FAA) approved passenger seats (rather than the six deemed acceptable by the British Civil Aviation Authority) for a second Peter Stuyvesant Odyssey. Accompanied by journalists and television crews, another four sets of six competition winners exchanged the muffled sound of the jet airliner that had brought them across the Atlantic for the more immediate vibrations of the twin radials: either of which could cope with a fully loaded Super Cat, unlike those of the original PBYs and the ill-fated NJ. Global positioning system receivers and transponders had been installed, together with portable oxygen equipment to cross the Andes Mountains in comfort (the engines had fuel-booster pumps). There was even a modern toilet.

By contrast, July and August 1995 saw landings off the sunny beaches of every major Italian resort to promote the bottled beer Peroni/Nastro Azzurro, when free samples were handed from the 'blisters' by attractive young Italian hostesses. A distinct advertising vehicle, the fuselage had been painted a deeper blue with the corporate name in bold white letters across the nose and rear, repeated in red across the white floats and undersides of both wings. A second 'Peroni' tour was made in 1996. But on Monday, 27 July 1998, while performing a second 'touch and go' on Southampton Water for VIP passengers, part of a promotion by Southampton City Council for a Seawings 2000 air show to celebrate the millennium, the port nose wheel door slightly opened under the 60-knot impact of water, bringing the flying boat to a stop and flooding the inner nose bay. Of the eighteen aboard, two of the passengers tragically lost their lives after helping others to escape: which included the mayor, a non-swimmer. In future, the torque tube mechanism would be the subject of regular inspection for signs of corrosion.

The insurance pay out was a good fifty thousand pounds short of the cost of restoring the aircraft however and required thought on how best to proceed from Paul, who had just begun flying Boeing 747 Classic Freighters for Cathay Pacific. Armed with the knowledge that running costs far outweigh the initial capital outlay, a business plan was formulated and shares offered for part ownership of a replacement Catalina. Part ownership also would embody the right to fly as a pilot (subject to qualification) or as a passenger: though those responding were far more concerned for the success of the project than a hard-nosed business investment. As with Pierre Jaunet, the search for another Catalina centred on finding a solid airframe suitable for passenger carrying, preferably with the 'blisters' still in place.

In 1981 the Canadian Province of Saskatchewan had purchased three Canso water bombers from Northern Air Operations and C-FNJF (tanker 7) and JB (tanker 9), were finally retired in 1996. Sold to another Harare-based tourist operation, they were flown over the Rocky Mountains to Vancouver Island, where JF was stripped of firefighting equipment and given passenger seats, a hydraulic entry staircase, and a pair of hydraulic smoked blisters to replace the originals removed after the war. The enduring instability in Africa cancelled the project however and both were re-advertised at the close of 1999. After a three-year stint in the open, in August 2002 JF was sold to the Plane Sailing shareholders and overhauled and refitted by Catalina Aero Services. On 1 March 2004, Paul, retired British Airways Boeing 747 pilot Rod Brooking, and engineer Gary Short, took the bright yellow, green-striped Catalina away from Nanaimo. Delayed en route, twenty-nine days later they were greeted at Duxford by a host of media representatives. Left behind, JB would deteriorate and suffer from mindless vandalism.

With the Air Show season imminent, the water bomber was seen at several venues, still sporting the red nose and prominent green '7' on the tail from its days at Lac La Ronge, Saskatchewan, while a visit to Biscarosse enabled the hull to perform its true function during several water landings. Re-registered in November, G-PBYA (clever) was flown to Marshalls of Cambridge in the New Year and repainted as a PBY of the 5th Emergency Rescue Squadron of the U.S. 8th Army Air Force based at Air Station 365, Halesworth, Suffolk. The white overall paint scheme made temporary concealment of the all important sponsor logos much simpler for film work, while the tail now had an identifying 433915.

Towards the end of the war, General Spaatz had wanted to use his own, Army Air Force, PBYs for air-sea rescue in the North Sea, rather than continue to rely on the RAF, and in January 1945, six had been ferried across the South Atlantic to Air Station 112, Bovingdon, Hertfordshire. Known as OA-10s, they were considerably modified for the task by the 3rd Strategic Air Depot at Neaton in Norfolk (RAF Watton). Delivered to Halesworth towards the close of March, the armour plating had all been removed and heaters fitted to improve the recovery rate of those plucked from the water.

Tasked to lend assistance to the crew of 44-33917 which had been forced to land on high seas on Friday 30 March, 2nd Lieutenant John Lapenas had been diverted from circling overhead to locate a Mustang pilot forced to abandon his fighter off the Dutch coast. Escorted by a pair of the fighters during the darkening evening, he had landed 33915 *Sophisticat* within 100 feet of the small dinghy, some 4 miles from the island of Schiermonnikoog. Almost immediately the starboard engine seized due to a ruptured oil line. Unable to manoeuvre, despite deploying a drogue, with no hope of leaving the 6 foot swell on a single engine, 915 was taxied out to sea as the current carried the fighter pilot towards a brief captivity. The European war would end in May. On Saturday morning a lifeboat was dropped from a pair of circling RAF Warwicks with American fighter escort, but the worsening sea caused the craft to break up after making contact with the metal hull.

Born on the Isle of Wight, Uffa Fox had been apprenticed to Samuel Saunders at Cowes, had started his own business when 21, and by the outbreak of the Second World War was a leading designer of racing dinghies and sailing canoes. Determined to improve the chances of downed airmen following the capture of his own grandson, in 1943 he had completed the first lifeboat capable of being dropped by parachute from an aircraft. Twenty-three foot long, the light, canoe-shaped, wooden craft was fitted with a pair of 6 knot engines, a mast and sail, watertight compartments, radio transmitter, sea anchor, clothes and medical supplies. The crew of a Halifax bomber had been the first to be rescued by an 'airborne lifeboat' that May, the end of their sixteen-hour ordeal bringing founder membership of the Goldfish Club.

Fighter cover was maintained over the stricken *Sophisticat*, but at midday a pair of Me 262 jet fighters made two low-level attacks which tore away the tail and severed the port wing float. With the wing beginning to slip beneath the surface, the six crew paddled away in three rubber dinghies which were then lashed together. A second lifeboat impacted heavily when the parachute failed to open, but in the evening the crew scrambled aboard a prototype lifeboat dropped by a hastily converted B17 bomber. Designed by Andrew Higgins, whose landing craft had played a vital rôle during the Normandy landings, the laminated mahogany and birch was more durable than the 'Fox' lifeboat, though Sunday brought rain, numbing cold, and 20 foot high rolling waves driven by 30 knot winds. Both engines stopped during the early hours of Monday morning and a particularly heavy wave tossed the co-pilot and wireless operator overboard. Both were retrieved, though the craft required constant bailing.

Two more British lifeboats were dropped with supplies during Tuesday, but with similar hang-ups, and another night was endured until the arrival of two Royal Navy motor torpedo boats during Wednesday morning: the thirty hour ordeal and the onset of frostbite requiring four of the crew to be carefully lifted from the lifeboat. Given warm clothes, hot food, drink and medical attention, they reached Great Yarmouth the following morning.

Improved for use in the Pacific, in the '50s the final, aluminium, version of the Fox lifeboat, built by Saunders-Roe at Anglesey, was capable of propelling ten survivors over 1,000 miles of ocean, clad in protective suits with sleeping bags and medical supplies. By then, Uffa was seen sailing in company of the Duke of Edinburgh and the younger members of the Royal Family. Awarded a CBE, he considered the lifeboat the most worthwhile of his achievements: an image of which, suspended beneath a cluster of parachutes, was carved into his headstone within the churchyard of St Mildreds at Whippingham, near East Cowes. Twenty-eight years later, the millennium year of 2000 saw a much restored and rare example of the first wooden airborne lifeboat put on show by the Classic Boat Museum at Newport.

In its first year of display as an American air-sea rescue PBY, '433915' was invited to join the RAFs Battle of Britain Memorial Flight Lancaster, the B17 Flying Fortress *Sally B,* and a clutch of DC3s and B25 Mitchell bombers in flying over Buckingham Palace to celebrate the sixtieth anniversary of the ending of the Second World War. Since then, venues have included Norway and Sweden, France (Lake Biscarosse), Belgium, Austria (Lake Wolfgangsee), Poland, the Czech Republic, Slovakia,

Switzerland (Lake Geneva) and Spain. With well over 1,000 hours on type, Paul is chief training pilot and assisted by public support at air shows and displays, and membership subscriptions from The Catalina Society, he and his colleagues continue to keep the sole airworthy Catalina in Britain flying.

City Centre Seaplanes

The very last commercial flying boat service in the United Kingdom had ended at Southampton in September 1958. But in 2004, after years of flying passenger jets, Captain David West took his amphibious six seat (five plus pilot) Cessna 206 Turbo Stationair floatplane away from Loch Lomond to inaugurate Loch Lomond Seaplanes, the sole commercial seaplane tour service within the U.K, and in 2007 moved onto the Clyde with a ten seat (nine plus pilot) Cessna 208 Caravan to become the sole City-Centre based seaplane company in Europe. Born and bred in Alexandria in West Dumbartonshire, there could be no better 'guide' for the airborne Discovery Tours of the west coast, with its castles, lochs and 'remote' five star hotels and restaurants, while others have a fascinating commute to work. Over 30,000 passengers, including a host of celebrities from the world of TV, sport and international stardom, have been acquainted with the joys experienced by those early Imperial Airways passengers. The company also features in an International Scottish Tourism television advert, though the views from today's comfortable leather seats are even more 'immediate'.

Dornier Dream

Coincidentally, the year 2004 had also seen the start of a world tour by the sole Dornier Do-24ATT owned and operated by Captain Irén P. Dornier, the grandson of Professor Claudius Dornier and co-founder of the Philippine based South East Asia Airlines.

The most successful German flying boat, nearly 280 Do-24s were built following the 1937 inaugural flight: the three, 1,000 horsepower Wright Cyclone engines capable of supporting a three-man crew for over 1,600 nautical miles. Unlike most, it could safely take off and land in rough seas. Two years earlier the company had loaned its first amphibious flying boat, the single-engined, all metal Do-12 Libelle (Dragonfly*)*, to act as a tug for trials on Lake Bodensee with the See Adler (Sea Eagle) glider. But though achieving many firsts for women in aviation, Hanna Reitsch was not the first to pilot a glider flying boat. In September 1922, Glenn Curtiss had been towed aloft behind a launch at Manhasset Bay (near Port Washington) to test his 'stepped' hull design on a delightful biplane glider flying boat constructed from duralumin, with silk covered wings supported by spruce

Dornier 24 piloted by owner Irén Dornier over Bavarian Alps.
© DR. ANDREAS ZEITLER.

struts – though his dream of emulating the Albatross by somehow soaring above the waves had failed miserably!

Intended to replace the Wal flying boats operated by the Dutch Navy, the Do-24 order had increased with the threat from Japan. Production had been set up in the Netherlands under licence and was greatly developed under German occupation for the Luftwaffe (using BMW Bramo engines) as was the case in occupied France. The Royal Australian Air Force operated six survivors of the Japanese invasion of the Dutch East Indies while in 1944, a dozen had been sent from France to neutral Spain to rescue downed airmen, whatever their nationality.

First flown in 1943 as a Do-24T-3, the flying boat had ended its Spanish air-sea rescue missions in 1971, when it was returned to the Immenstaad factory on the Bodensee. Between 1979 and 1983 it was rebuilt as an experimental, amphibious technology, (Amphibischer Technologie Träger) ATT variant. Fashioned from a single sheet of aluminium, the 30 metre wing was fitted with three Pratt and Witney (Canada), 1,070 (equivalent shaft) horsepower turbo-prop engines driving five bladed Hartzell propellers, the sponsons widened to take a double pair of main wheels for a retractable, tri-cycle, undercarriage. Unable to secure an order in the aviation market however, D-CATD was loaned to the Deutsches Museum at Schleissheim.

Having founded SEAIR with his friend and fellow pilot Captain Nikos Gitsis seventeen years earlier, in December 2002 Irén had wandered into the museum and was confronted by his favourite flying boat. Prepared to buy it, instead it was gifted to him by the owner. The following year, the unique amphibian was shipped out to the Philippines where it was beau-

Glenn Curtiss aboard his flying boat glider. Manhasset Bay 1922.

tifully restored by the airlines engineers at Diosdado Macapagal International Airport (Manila) at a cost of six million dollars.

Intended to raise additional funds for the United Nations International Childrens Emergency Fund (UNICEF) and in particular help young disadvantaged Philippino children to achieve their dreams, the extensive world tour was known appropriately as Kayang–Kara or We can do it! By partly retracing the route taken by the Do-X, the 'Flight of Dreams' paid tribute to the achievements of the pilot's grandfather, while promoting the Philippines as a tourist resort. It was certainly a dream come true for Irén, who had been sat in the cockpit of a Dornier 24 when he was 12 and had determined that one day he would actually fly one.

Approaching the wide sponsons, the low-lying 'Latina' appears partly submerged and at one with the surface. Up front, the bright blue cockpit has a pair of Catalina-style oval control wheels: though these are rosewood rimmed, with 'Dornier' inscribed in white on both left hand yokes, the captain's fitted with a trim button, with the aircraft's clock bolted to the centre. The space between the high-backed leather seats is taken up by a horizontal, knee-high virtual flight engineers panel, swung upwards for access. Aside from the white flap control, the eye is inevitably drawn to the red flip-up switch guards and gauges of the power panel; the left hand hydraulic panel and fuel panel, nearest at the bottom. In between are over sixty switches and knobs within clearly defined sections: which include de-icing, water pump (wiper, windshield), exterior lighting (anti-collision, strobe, navigation, landing, taxi, at anchor and towing) and interior lighting (dimmer, cockpit, cabin, exit, no smoking and seat belt). Triple lighting dimming knobs are fitted to both sides.

Immediately above are twenty-four gauges of the main instrument panel: inevitably arranged in triple rows to indicate torque, temperature, rpm, fuel flow, fuel quantity, oil temperature and pressure; surmounted by the central emergency cut-off switches and right hand fuel feed switches. On the captain's side, the roof mounted throttles are positioned at shoulder height in front of a projecting panel of communication boxes immediately beneath the windscreen. Overhead, a warning red and white zone at the rear of the throttle track denotes reverse pitch, with matching zone on the right for the three (white) propeller feathering/stop levers. Beyond, above the windscreen, the engine start switches are zoned by black and yellow diagonals, with projecting compass mount immediately below. Blue tinted visors are clipped to both side windscreens, the rearward sliding roof panels enabling both pilots to directly access the cockpit, which has a cooling fan positioned above the left hand seat.

Aside from individual airspeed, altitude, vertical speed, gyro compass and blind flying instruments, each pilot has a side panel with a seven-deep row of avionic, lighting and engine buttons, the captain with additional aileron, hydraulic, landing gear and fuel sections, with a sliding elevator trim indicator over. In front of his right knee, above the rudder pedal, an undercarriage control box is surmounted by a reassuring green light. A plastic cover groups the (triple) undercarriage levers. On the right, the gear safety (sea/land) switch is zoned by black and yellow diagonals, as are those of the lower gear select panel, protected by a red flip-up switch guard. Above, a screen can monitor each of the undercarriage doors.

Moving back across the 'bar-bell' connecting the wood-rimmed trimmer wheels between both seats, and passing the metal rack on the inside of the door for flight manuals, a step over the crimson painted curve of the metal bulkhead brings you into the 'navigators' cabin. On the port side, beneath square curtained windows and a clear vision panel to the captain, a smooth rosewood table is inlaid with 'compass' stars and a 'wings over globe' Dornier logo, together with a pair of slim drawers. The space underneath is taken up by a microwave oven! There is also a fully stocked mini refrigerator on board. A high backed, cream leather seat takes up the remaining space with a pair of matching seats across the aisle.

Passing through the white painted, unlined, 'engineers' compartment, with utility mattress-style double 'seat' for crew members, and stepping over the crimson curve of the second bulkhead, you enter the first passenger cabin to find the inside of the watertight metal door fitted with a sculpture of a long-haired, well-endowed native woman entirely au naturel! Throughout the aircraft, positioned by wood inlaid viewing ports, luxury reclining leather seats with bright cushions have an adjacent, roll-topped, rosewood fitting provided with a pair of cut outs for drinks bottles and a little lidded compartment. Facing seats have a matching fold down table. The concave metal sides are covered by tangential floral silk panels and the floor is carpeted. Both this and the subsequent cabin is accessed from the cambered, strutted, sponson by a short ladder slotted beneath an upward opening hatch, with a pair of grab handles between the portholes. Both cabins have a television screen attached to the bulkhead: the front with a flashlight clipped to one side, the second with a fire extinguisher clipped above the door (the co-pilot has another). The very last compartment is used to stow baggage or equipment, frequently a spare tyre, while two steps take you up to a double leather 'love seat' below the clear observation 'bubble', where a fabulous view can be had while cruising at a comfortable 140 knots.

The first half of the world tour raised over 60,000 U.S dollars alone to the cause of the children. Resumed in the following years until 2007, the immaculate, glossy flying boat attracted thousands at air shows and historic fly-ins along the way, including Oshkoss, when the experienced landplane, floatplane and helicopter pilot and owner Harrison Ford of Indiana Jones fame, donned a headset to fly the aircraft with Irén. Since then the ATT has continued to delight the crowds and is available for special charter.

A CELEBRATION

Town Clerk Ian Andrews had ensured that a series of pictorial tiles installed about the exterior of the Poole Civic Centre building, opposite Poole Park, during the late 1980s included a dedication to the flying boats. Designed by former Poole College lecturer and Poole Maritime Trust secretary Frank Turland, and crafted into stone by the Dorchester based firm of Richard Grassby, the images also recalled the Vikings, for Kanute assembled his fleet in the harbour prior to seizing the throne of England, and we still use many of their words, including *ský*.

Concerned for the lack of public awareness of those momentous years of flying boat operations however, a group of friends normally involved with promoting and protecting the environment and associated history of the area, decided that something had to be done about it: the first meeting in June 2006 coincidentally held a few days prior to the reopening of the Flying Boat Museum at Foynes. Many things were discussed during that evening at Sandbanks, with hopes for at least some form of reminder to be installed close to the harbour shore. Five founder trustees were appointed and the first of a series of fundraising talks and suppers held within the appropriate surroundings of the Harbour Heights Hotel and Royal Motor Yacht Club, courtesy of John Butterworth of FJB Hotels and other sponsors, when Bob Harwood was welcomed as the first Honorary Life Member of Poole Flying Boats Celebration.

In June 2008 a floral tribute to the flying boats was arranged by members and bedded out in Poole Park, while in April 2009 three storyboards were commissioned and ceremoniously unveiled atop three Purbeck stone

2009 plinth. David Rose, Vic Pitcher, John Witcomb. © AUTHOR.

plinths along a popular harbour side tourist pathway. Since then, PFBC has achieved charity status with Lady Nadine Cobham welcomed as Patron. A supporting Friends association helps to keep members in touch via a regular newsletter, a website has been set up, an office has opened above the historic Parkstone Library building and there is an ever increasing public-access archive. Volunteers also host presentations at the highly successful annual air display at Bournemouth. A lot of time and effort has brought an idea into fruition and perhaps Poole too will someday offer visitors a more tangible reminder of the time when the harbour was once the hub of flying boat operations in this country.

FESTIVALE

The biannual Bournemouth Air Show held at 'Hurn' Airport, which latterly featured a slow pass from Concorde and a message to the crowds from the captain, has virtually passed from public memory – though I clearly recall the commentator diving from the little caravan in front of the crowd to avoid being decapitated by the wingtip of *Sally B* piloted by the exuberant Ted White. In its wake, summer visitors flocked in their thousands to the seafront to watch the annual display of formation flying by the Red Arrows, highlighted by the two 'singletons' swooping low across the sea to perform a last minute head-on break in front of a capacity filled Bournemouth pier.

In August 2008 the town hosted a new and free four-day Air Festival within the natural amphitheatre of Bournemouth Bay, the Pier filled to

PFBC storyboard Poole harbourside. © AUTHOR.

capacity. The cliff-top hotels joined in the fun by providing barbeques and refreshments within the grounds. Saturday was the only real sunny day, but 75,000 people lined the cliffs and promenades between Boscombe and Bournemouth Piers to watch the variety of piston-engined and jet aircraft, helicopters, wing walkers and parachutists as Royal Marines stormed the beaches. Though coinciding with British Tourism Week, the event proved to be no fluke and continues to attract even greater crowds who annually generate a considerable sum towards the local economy.

Jack had phoned to say he really didn't feel up to joining a group booked to leave Poole on the last day of the second annual Air Festival and had kindly sent me his tickets. The weather that Sunday wasn't expected to be that bright, but a boat trip would be interesting in itself I thought, and anyway, I much prefer the unplanned. Finding the pleasure boat almost ready to leave the quayside, I slipped upstairs and onto one of the rear-most seats. Surprised as usual by how long it takes to reach the harbour entrance, it was fun watching the variety of small craft also going our way, and rounding the Havens we headed towards the vague outline of Bournemouth Pier. On arrival, we joined an assorted armada of craft assembled under the protective eye of the Royal Fleet Auxiliary ship Mounts Bay, our skipper giving the engines periodic busts of power to maintain position on the swell.

Saturday had experienced a contrast in sounds: from the comforting drone of the Battle of Britain Memorial Flight to the blasting arrival of the

Eurofighter Typhoon, culminating in an evening of illuminated hot-air balloons, laser show and fireworks. Today had an end of the week feel about it however. As the afternoon wore on, the clouds lowered and darkened, with most of us buttoned up against an intermittent drizzle or drying off below while taking a drink and a sandwich or two. The shoreline to Christchurch and Poole had disappeared in the murk. With no programme amongst us, we were taking guesses as to what was holding the crowd's attention, when we became aware of an approaching aircraft which began a series of manoeuvres immediately above us it seemed: the engines sounding hollow and unfamiliar compared to the deeper note of vintage Merlins.

Questions were asked, the boat's little microphone was offered, and I distinctly remember the shock as my eyes dropped from describing the interior of a wartime Catalina, timed in sequence with a particularly long and slow right-banked pass, to be met by a momentarily forgotten mass of damp, upturned faces hanging on to every word. Then she was gone, swallowed up in the gloom prior to heading back to Duxford, leaving a ponderous silence: for there was no chattering public address system out here. The Red Arrow display was cut short and the fleet began to disperse and to head back to Poole. An estimated and record, one and a third million people had filled the town over the four days. Though no large passenger flying boat remains in service, for a moment we had admired a unique form of flying that had once graced the waterways of the world: from the grey, heaving Atlantic to the dry heat of Africa and the idyllic sun drenched islands of the Pacific.

I hope you have enjoyed the journey.

The Author.

Appendix

Listed in chronological order of events to portray the real time history.

British Marine Air Navigation Company
Supermarine Sea Eagle

	G- EBFK	crashed	1924	
	BGS	Imp.Airways	sunk	1927
	BGR	Imp.Airways	retired	1928

Imperial Airways
Calcutta-Class

City of Rome	G- AADN	lost	1929	
City of Khartoum	ASJ	crashed	1935	
City of Alexandria	EBVG	sunk	1936	
City of Athens	VH	retired Hamble	1937	*City of Stonehaven*
City of Salonika	AATZ	retired Hamble	1939	*City of Swanage*

Kent-Class

Sylvanus	G- ABFB	fire	1935
Scipio	BFA	crashed	1936
Satyrus	BFC	scrapped	1938

Imperial Airways / BOAC
C-Class 'Empire'

Capricornus	G- ADVA	crashed France	1937
Courtier	DVC	cr. Athens	1937
Cygnus	DUZ	cr. Brindisi	1937
Calpurnia	ETW	cr. Iraq	1938
Coogee	EUG	to Qantas	1938
Coolangatta	FBK	to Qantas	1938
Cavalier	DUU	cr. Atlantic	1939
Capella	DUY	cr. Batavia	1939
Challenger	DVD	cr. Africa	1939
Centurion	DVE	cr. India	1939
Centaurus	DUT	to QEA	1939
Calypso	EUA	to QEA	1939
Connnemara S30	FCW	burnt Hythe	1939

C-Class 'Empire'

Aotearoa S30	G- AFCY	to TEAL	1940
Awarua SS0	FDA	TEAL	1940
Cabot S30	FCU	to RAF destroyed	1940 V3137
Caribou S30	FCV	to RAF destr.	1940 V3138
Clyde S30	FCX	destr. Lisbon	1941
Clio	ETY	to RAF crashed	1941 AX659
Cassiopeia	DUX	crashed Sabang	1941
Corio	EUH	from QEA lost	1942 VH-ABD
Coorong	EUI	from QEA lost	1942 VH-ABE
Coriolanus	ETV	absorbed QEA	1942
Circe	ETZ	abs.QEA	1942
Camilla	EUB	abs.QEA	1942
Corinna	EUC	abs.QEA	1942
Corinthian	EUF	abs.QEA	1942
Clifton S33	FPZ	abs.QEA	1942
Australia S30	FCZ	lost off Bathurst	1942 Claire
Ceres	ETX	burnt Durban	1942
Canopus	DHL	scrapped Hythe	1946 First C-Class
Cleopatra S33	FRA	scr. Hythe	1946 Last C-Class.
Cameronian	EUE	scr. Hythe	1947
Caledonia	DHM	scr. Hythe	1947
Cambria	DUV	scr. Hythe	1947
Carpentaria	FBJ	scr. Hythe	1947 from QEA1942 VH-ABA
Corsair	DVB	scr. Hythe	1947
Cooee	FBL	scr. Hythe	1947 from QEA 1942 VH-ABF
Castor	DUW	scr. Hythe	1947
Cathay S30	FKZ	scr. Hythe	1947
Champion	FCT	scr. Hythe	1947
Cordelia	EUD	scr. Hythe	1947

Imperial Airways / BOAC
G-Class

Golden Fleece	G- AFCJ	to RAF – lost	1941 X8274
Golden Horn	FCK	to RAF – crashed	1943 X8273
Golden Hind	FCI	to RAF-BOAC scr.	1954 X8275

BOAC
Model 28/Catalina

Catalina	G- AGDA	crashed Poole	1943
Vega Star	GFL	to Qantas	1943
Altair Star	GFM	Qantas	1943
Rigel Star	GID	Qantas	1943
Antares Star	GIE	Qantas	1943
Spica Star	GKS	Qantas	1944
Guba	GBJ	to RAF SM706	1944

Hythe-Class Transport Sunderland 3

unnamed	ML729		G- AGIB	crashed	1943
unnamed	788OQZF		GKX	**sold** Shorts	1945
unnamed	JM662	ZT	GET	fire	1946
Hailsham	664	ZV	GEV	written off	1946
Hamble	JM722	ZB	GHV	sunk	1946
Hanbury	DD860	ZS	HEP	to RAF	1947
Hamilton	ML725	ZC	GHW	crashed	1947
Haslemere	728	ZA	GIA	**sold** Aquila	1948
Halstead	JM716	ZP	HEO	Aquila	1948
Hanwell	665	ZW	GEW	written off	1948
Harlequin	ML726	ZX	GHX	scrapped Hythe	1948
Hungerford	789	ZG	GKY	**sold** Aquila	1948
Hadfield	JM660	ZR	GER	Aquila	1948
Hawkesbury	ML727	ZZ	GHZ	Aquila	1949
Henley	751	ZJ	GJJ	Aquila	1949
Hunter	791	ZI	GLA	Aquila	1949
Hampshire	JM 663	ZU	GEU	Aquila	1949
Hudson	ML755	ZN	GJN	Aquila	1949
Honduras	756	ZQ	GJO	written off	1949
Howard	752	ZK	GJK	**sold** Aquila	1949
Hobart	753	ZL	GJL	Aquila	1949
Hythe	754	ZM	GJM	Aquila	1949
Harwich	790	ZH	GKZ	scrapped Hythe	1949
Helmsdale	PP142		HER	**sold** Aquila	1949
Huntingdon	ML786	ZD	GKV	**sold** Belfast retired	1951
Hotspur	787	ZE	GKW	**sold** Belfast retired	1951

Sunderland/ Sandringham 1

Himilaya	ML788	G- AGKX	**sold** Aquila	1949

Remainder built at Belfast.

Plymouth-Class Sandringham 5

Portland	NJ171	G- AHZB	crashed	1947
Portsmouth	ML838	HYY	scrapped Hamworthy	1949
Penzance	783	HZA	scr. Hamworthy	1949
Portsea	818	HZE	scr. Hamworthy	1949
Pembroke	NJ253	HZC	scr. Hamworthy	1949
Perth	JM 681	JMZ	scr. Hamworthy	1949
Pevensey	ML828	HZG	**sold** Qantas	1951
Portmarnock	NJ 257	HZD	Qantas	1951
Poole	188	HZF	Qantas	1951

Bermuda-Class
Sandringham 7

Saint Andrew	ML840	G- AKCR	**sold** CAUSA
Saint David	EJ 172	KCP	**sold** CAUSA
Saint George	JM719	KCO	**sold** P.G.Taylor **to** RAI

***Musée de l'Air et d'espace Le Bourget.**

Solent 2

Severn	G- AHIT	returned Min.Supply 1949		scrapped Belfast
Solway	HIU	retd. MoS	1949	scr. Hamworthy
Stornoway	HIW	retd. MoS	1949	scr. Belfast
Sark	HIR	retd. MoS	1950	scr. Belfast
Scarborough	HIM	retd. MoS	1950	scr. Belfast
Salcombe	HIV	retd. MoS	1950	**sold** TOA
Southampton	HIN	retd. MoS	1950	**sold** Aquila
Somerset	HIO	retd. MoS	1950	**sold** TOA
Salisbury	HIL	converted to Mk 3 renamed		
Sussex	HIX	Mk 3 renamed		
Scapa	HIS	Mk 3 renamed		
Southsea	HIY	Mk 3		

Solent 3

City of Edinburgh		G- AHIX	capsized	1950	
City of Salisbury		HIL	returned MoS	1950	scrapped Hamworthy
City of York		HIS	retd. MoS	1950	scr.Belfast
City of Liverpool					
Seaford	NJ205	KNS	to MAEE	1950	scr. Hamworthy
Southsea		HIY	retd. MoS	1950	scr. Belfast
City of Belfast					
Seaford	NJ204	KNR	retd. MoS	1950	**sold** TEAL
City of London	202	KNO	retd. MoS	1950	**sold** TOA
City of *Cardiff*	203	KNP	retd. MoS	1950	**sold** TOA
Singapore	206	KNT	retd. MoS	1950	**sold** SPAL
(trainer)	NJ201	GWU	retd. MoS	1950	**sold** Aquila (ANAJ)

Boeing 314A

Berwick	G- AGCA	**sold** World Airways	scrapped 1950
Bangor	CB	**sold** World Airways	scrapped 1950
Bristol	BZ	**sold** World Airways	**sold** /scr. 1951

AQUILA
Hythe-Class Transport Sunderland 3

Hunter	G- AGLA	scrapped Hamble	1949
Halstead	HEO	scr. Hamble	1949
Hawkesbury	GHZ	scr. Hamble	1952
Henley	AGJJ	scr. Hamble	1952
Howard	GJK	scr. Hamble	1952
Hobart	GJL	scr. Hamble	1952

Hythe	GJM	scr. Hamble	1952
Helmsdale	GER	scr. Hamble	1952
Haslemere	GIA	scr. Hamble	1952
Hudson	GJN	crashed Madeira	1953
Hungerford	GKY	sunk Calshot	1953
Hampshire	GEU	scr. Hamble	1953
Hadfield	GER	scr. Hamble	1956

AQUILA

Sunderland 3s replaced by

Himalaya	G- AGKX	Sandringham	scr. Hamble	1952
City of Funchal	NAJ	Solent 3	written off	1956
Sydney	KNU	Solent 3	crashed	1957
Southampton	HIN	Solent 2	scr. Lisbon	1971
Awatere	NYI	Solent 4	scr. Lisbon	1971
Aotearoa II	OBL	Solent 4	scr. Lisbon	1971

Return of Awatere September 30 1958 ended UK passenger services.

Sealand

G- AIVX	Shorts company aircraft	scrapped Belfast	1955
KLM	Shorts demonstrator	crashed Norway	1949
LN	Vestlandske Luftfartselskap	LN-SUF	
LO	Shell Brunei register	VR-SDS	
LP	Shell Brunei register	VR-UDV	
LR	Jogoslovenski Aerotransport	YU-CFJ	
LS	Jogoslovenski Aerotransport	YU-CFK	
LT	Christian Missionaries CAMA	PK-CMA	
LU	Vestlandske Luftfartselskap	LN-SUH	
LV	Ralli Bros	AP-AFM	
LW	Abboud/Khedivial Line	SU-AHY **Ulster Museum**	
LX	E.Bengal Transp. Comm	AP-AGB	
LZ	Indian Navy	INS101	
MA	Indian Navy	INS102	
	Indian Navy direct	INS103- 110	
	CAMA direct Gospel Messenger	JZ-PTA crashed 1955	
	Shell direct Venezuela register	YV-P-AEG (P for Privada)	

Production closed down Nov 1953

PORTUGAL

Aero-Topográfica SA (ARTOP)

Martin Mariner 5

Porto Santo	N7824C	CS-THB	lost	1958
Madeira	N10162	HA	scrapped	1958

FRANCE
Aéromaritime

Sikorsky S38	F-AOUC
Sikorsky S43	UK, UL, UM, HY
Valkyrien	REX

Ceased operations 1944/45

Air France
Lioré et Olivier LeO H242

Ville de Cannes	F-ANQH	crashed 1937
de Bone	NPB	crashed 1938

remainder **retired 1942**

Ville de Tunis	F-AMOU
d'Algiers	MUL
d'Oran	NPA
de Marseille	PCNA
d'Ajaccio	ANPD
de Tripoli	NPE
de Beyrouth	NPM
de Toulon	NQF
de Nice	NQG
de Bizerte	NQI
de Casablanca	APKJ
de Rabat	PKK

Latécoère L300
Croix du Sud F- AKGF lost 1936

Latécoère L521

Lieutenant de Vaisseau Paris	F- NORD	to Aeronavale	destroyed 1944
Ville de Saint Pierre	F- ARAP	to Aeronavale	destroyed 1944

Latécoère L631

01	F-BAHG	Latécoère	Luftwaffe 63+11	destroyed	1944
07	BDRD	Latécoère		crashed	1948
06	DRC	Air France		lost	1948
03	ANU	Air France	*Henry Guillaumet* SeMAF	crashed	1950
08	DRE	Air France	France-Hydro	crashed	1955
11	unfinished/ stored			crushed	1956
04	DRA	Air France	SeMAF France- Hydro	crushed ?	
05	DRB	Air France	France- Hydro	crushed ?	
09	WDRF	stored		scrapped	
10	WDRG	stored		scrapped	
02	BANT	Air France	*Lionel de Marmier* France-Hydro	dismantled	1963

GERMANY
Deutsche Luft Hansa AG
Stettin/Lubeck to 0slo 1927-1934
Dornier Wal

Hai D-861	*Sägefisch* 862	*Thunfisch* 863	*Hecht* 864
1213 unnamed	*Lübeck* 1397	1488 unnamed	*Flensburg* 1626
1647 *Bremerhaven*		1648 *Helgoland*	

SuperWal
Narwal D-1255 *Graf Zeppelin* 1447 *Hugo Eckener* 1500
Junkers G24a-See floatplane
Dyonysos D-949 *Donar* 954

Rohrbach Ro V trainer
Rocco D-1261 loaned May/June 1928
Ju52/3m-See floatplanes
Kurt Wolf D-ABIS *Paul Bäumer* D-2725 *Otto von Parschau* D-3127

NORWAY
Det Norske Luftfartsrederi A/S
Supermarine Channel 1
N-9 **sold** N-10 spares N-11 **sold**
Friedrichshafen FF49C
N-6 withdrawn N-8 written off N-3 **sold**
Ceased operating Oct 1920

Det Norske Luftfartselskap A/S Fred. Olsen & Bergenske

Havørn	LN-DAE	Ju52-3/m-See		crashed	1936
Valkyrien	AG	Sikorsky S43		**sold**	1938
Ternen	AB	Junkers W34Hi		withdrawn	1940
Hauken	AI	Ju52/3m-See	*Hans Berr*	sunk	1943
Najaden	AF	Ju52/3mg2e	*Hans*	**to** DNL *Veslefrikk*	
Falken	AH	Ju52/3mge	*Askeladden*	**to** DNL *Boots*	

Vingtor Luftveier Catalinas

Vingtor	JX419	LN-OAR	crashed Aug 1947
unnamed	JX381	AP	**sold** RNoAF

Det Norske Luftfartselskap (DNL) merged SAS 1949
captured Luftwaffe Ju52 floatplanes post-war

unnamed	N9+DA	LN-LAB	scrapped	1946
Tyrihans		KAB	scr.	1948
Peik	8A+AK	KAI	scr.	1948
Pãl		KAE / KAL	scr.	1950
Per		KAD	scr.	1950
joining	*Veslefrikk*	KAG	retired	1956
	Boots	DAH	**sold**	**1956**

***owned / operated Deutche Lufthansa AG as *Tempelhof*.**

Sandringham 6

Kvitbjørn	LN-IAV	'White Bear'	ML809	crashed	1947
Bukken Bruse	AW	'Billy goat gruff'	JM720	cr.	1948
Bamse Brakar	AU	'Teddy Brakar'	ML807	cr.	1950
Jutulen	AI	'Troll'	W4037	sunk	1952
Polar Bjørn	LAK	'Polar bear'	JM 714	**sold** Aer.Arg.	1955

ITALY
Ala Littoria
Macchi MC-94
I-NEPI retired 1937?
I-ARNO, ENZA, LIRI, NARO, NETO, SILE, TORE **absorbed** Luftwaffe
I-ANIO, LATO, NEVA **sold** Corporation Sudamericana 1939

Savoia-Marchetti S55
Jahú **I-BAUQ** 1927 Private South Atlantic crossing
***Displayed Museu Transportes Aéreos del Mercosur, São Paulo, Brazil**

Savoia-Marchetti Sm66

I-LIDO, NAVE	destroyed	1935	NEMI, REDI	destroyed	1935
MIRA	destroyed	1936	PRUA, ALGA	written off	1937
RIVA	crashed	1937	VELA, ALTE	cancelled	1938
AABF	retired	1939	EGEO	retired	1939
FBAA	crashed	1939	VALE	retired	1939
SOLA	retired	1939	BLEO	written off	1940

Societè Aerea Mediterranea
Savoia-Marchetti S55

I-AABE	retired	1928	TACO	crashed	1929	OLCO	destr.	1930
AABG	destr.	1931	AABC	military	1933	NDRA	destr.	1935
RZIO	destr.	1935	SILI	destr.	1935	STRO	destr.	1935
OLAO	destr.	1936	AABF	retired	1939			

URUGUAY
La Compañía Aeronáutica Uruguaya S.A. (CAUSA) Montevideo

El Uruguayo	CX-ABA	Ju 52/3m * **Museo Aeronautico**			
El Argentino	BB	Ju 52/3m			
unnamed	NA	Sandringham 7	*(Saint Andrew)*	written off	1955
General Artigas	FA	Civ.Sunderland	*(Rio de la Plata)*	w/o	1956
Capitan Boiso Lanza	KR	Civ.Sunderland	DP195	w/o	1956
General San Martin	KF	Civ.Sunderland	ML876	retired	1962
Unnamed	NI	Sandringham 7	*(Saint David)*	retired	1962

Flying boat services ended May 1962

ARGENTINA

Corporación Sudamericana de Servicios Aéreos

Rio de la Plata	LV-LAB/AAD	MC.94	I-ANIO	**sold** Dodero /ALFA	1946
Rio Parana	MAB/AAE	MC.94	I-NEVA	**sold** ALFA	1946
unnamed	NAB/AAF	MC.94	I-LATO	**sold** ALFA	1946
Rio de la Plata	AAS	Civ.Sunderland ML876		**sold** CAUSA	1948

Compañía Argentina de Aeronavegación Dodero SA

Rio de la Plata	LV-AAD	MC.94	hangar fire		1948
Rio Parana	AE	MC.94	fire		1948
unnamed	AF	MC.94	fire		1948
Uruguay	AP	Sandringham 2	DD834	crashed	1948
Argentina	AO	Sandringham 2	DV964	**sold** Aerol. Arg.	1949
Brasil	AR	Sandringham 3	DD841	Aerol. Arg.	1950
Inglaterra	AQ	Sandringham 3	EJ170	Aerol. Arg.	1950
Paraguay	CT	Sandringham 2	ML843	Aerol. Arg.	1950

Aerolineas Argentinas

Brasil	LV- AAR	Sandringham 3	DD841	crashed	1957
Uruguay	HG	Civ.Sunderland	EK579	scrapped	1961
Rio de la Plata	HH	Civ.Sunderland	EJ171	Coop. Arg.	1963
Argentina	AO	Sandringham 2	DV964	Coop. Arg.	1963
Inglaterra	AQ	Sandringham 3	EJ170	Coop. Arg.	1963
Paraguay	CT	Sandringham 2	ML843	Coop. Arg.	1963
Polar Bjørn / renamed Almirante Zar	PAE/AHM	Sandringham 6	JM714	Coop. Arg.	1963

Cooperativa Argentina de Aeronavegantes

Rio Aguilero	LV-AAO	Sandringham 2	*Argentina*	retired 1963 scrapped 1964
Provincia de Formoza	AQ	Sandringham 3	*Inglaterra*	retd. 1964 scr. 1967
Paraguay	CT	Sandringham 2		retd. 1964 scr. 1967
Almirante Zar	HM	Sandringham 6		retd. 1964 scr. 1967
Rio de la Plata	HH	Civ.Sunderland		retd. 1964 scr. 1967

BRAZIL

Transportes Aéreos Bandeirantes.

(initially Transportes Aéreos da Bacia Amazônica)

PP-BLA	(ex PP-SDA)	PBY-5A	dismantled
PP-BLB	(ex PP-SDB)	PBY-5A	crashed 1949

AUSTRALIA

Qantas /QEA

Bought six C-Class to operate Singapore-Sydney route.

Corio	VH-ABD	to Imperial Airways 1939	
Coorong	BE	to Imperial Airways 1939	
Carpentaria	BA	stranded / BOAC 1942	
Cooee	BF	stranded / BOAC 1942	
Coogee	BC	RAAF A18-12	crashed 1942
Circe	G-AETZ	absorbed after fall of Singapore	lost 1942
Corinna	UC	abs. after Singapore	destroyed 1942
Corinthian	UF	abs. after Singapore	crashed 1942
Centaurus	DUT	exchanged '39 to RAAF A18-10	destroyed 1942
Calypso	EUA	exchanged '39 to RAAF A18-11	sunk 1942
Camilla	EUB	abs. after Singapore VH-ADU	crashed 1943
Clifton S33	FPZ	RAAF bought 1943 VH-ACD	cr. 1944
Coolangatta	VH-ABB	RAAF A18-13 to '43 VH-FBK	cr. 1944
Coriolanus	G-AETV	abs. after Singapore VH-ABG	**retired 1947**

Long Range 'Double Sunrise' Catalina fleet.

Vega Star	FP221	G-AGFL	'1'	scuttled	Nov 1945
Altair Star	FP224	FM	'2'		Nov 1945
Rigel Star	JX575	ID	'3'		Nov 1945
Antares Sta	JX577	IE	'4'		Nov 1945
Spica Star	JX287	KS	'5'		Mar 1946

Lord Howe Island Catalina Service

JX635	VH-EAX	written off	June 1949
JX662	AW	burnt out	Aug 1949

Sandringham

unnamed	Mk 4	VH-EBW	*(Tasman)*	written off	1951
Pacific Chieftan	Mk 4	BX	*(Australia)*	**sold** Ansett	1954
Pacific Warrior	Mk 5	BV	*(Portmarnock)*	retired	1955
Pacific Explorer	Mk 5	BZ	*(Pevensey)*	retired	1955
Pacific Voyager	Mk 5	BY	*(Poole)*	retired	1955

Barrier Reef Airways

Princess of Cairns	VH-BRD	Sandringham 4	*(New Zealand)*	sunk	1952
Beachcomber	RA	Catalina	JZ834	retired	1953
Buccaneer	RB	Catalina	JZ838	retired	1953
Beachcomber	RC	Sandringham 4	*(Aucklamd)*	**to** Ansett	

Sir Gordon Taylor Air Cruises

Frigate Bird 111	VH-APG	Sandringham 7	*Saint George*	**to** TAI.

Transports Aeriens Intercontineaux (TAI)

unnamed	VH-APG	Sandringham 7		**to** RAI.

Resaau Aeriens Interinsulaire (RAI)

'Le Bermuda'	VH-APG	Sandringham 7	retired 1970.

*** 1978 Musée de l'Air et d'espace Le Bourget**

Trans-Oceanic Airways

Australis	VH-AKO	Sunderland 3	ML733	retired	1950
unnamed	TOA	Solent 3	*(City of London)*	written off	1951
Pacific Star	BKQ	Sunderland 3	ML731	retired	1951
Star of Hobart	TOC	Solent 2	*(Salcombe)*	crashed	1951
Tahiti Star	AKP	Sunderland 3	ML734	to Ansett	1953
unnamed	TOD	Solent 2	*(Somerset)*	to SPAL	1953
Star of Papua	TOB	Solent 3	*(City of Cardiff)*	to SPAL	1954

Ansett Flying Boat Services

Tahiti Star	VH- AKP	Sunderland 3	ML734	retired	1954
Pacific Chieftan	BRE	Sandringham 4		written off	1963
Beachcomber	RC	Sandringham 4		**sold** Antilles	1974
Islander	RF	Sunderland V		**sold** Antilles	1974

NEW ZEALAND

TEAL Tasman Sea Service

Aotearoa	S30	ZK-AMA	(G-AFCY *Cumberland*)	retired	1947
Awarua	S30	MC	(G-AFDA *Captain Cook*)	retired	1947

Training / route proving Catalinas

NZ4038	ZK-AMI	returned RNZAF
NZ4035	ZK-AMP	returned RNZAF

Replaced 1946/7 by

Tasman-class Sandringham 4

Tasman	ZK-AMB	ML761	**sold** Qantas	1950
Australia	MD	NJ 255	**sold** Qantas	1950
New Zealand	ME	NJ 179	**sold** Barrier Reef	1950
Auckland	MH	JM 175	**sold** Barrier Reef	1950

Solent 4

4 delivered 1949

Ararangi	ZK-AMM		fire	1954
Aotearoa II	ML		**sold** Aquila	1955
Awatere	MN		**sold** Aquila	1955
Aparimu	MQ	(Mk 3 *City of Belfast* bought 1950)	retired	1956
Aranui	MO		retired	1960

*** Museum of Transport & Technology, Auckland**

USA
New York, Rio, and Buenos Aires Line (NYRBA)

Consolidated Commodore		**Sikorsky S38**	
Rio de Janeiro	NC658M	38A	NC5933
Havana	659M	38B	73K
Cuba	660M		113M
New York	661M		301N
Uruguay	662M		302N
Trinidad	663M		308N
Puerto Rico	664M		943M
Argentina	665M		944M
Miami	666M		946M
unnamed	667M		

absorbed Pan American Airways

PAN AMERICAN AIRWAYS
Consolidated Commodore
NYRBA fleet + NC669M, NC670M

Sikorsky S38
38A NC8000, 020, 044
38B NC3V,16-19, 21, 22-40V
73K, 113M, 142-146M, 197H,
300 - 302M, 304-6-8-9, 943-946M,
9107, 37-51, 9775, 776.

Douglas Dolphin
NC-14239 '21' retired circa 1941
240 '22' retired circa 1941

Sikorsky Clippers
S40

American	NC-80V	to U.S.N.	retired circa 1943
Caribbean	81V	to U.S.N.	retired circa 1943
Southern	752V	to U.S.N.	retired circa 1943

S42

unnamed	NC-824M		crashed	1935
West Indies	823M	*Pan American/ Hong Kong*	sunk	1944
Brazilian	822M	*Columbia*	scrapped	1946

S42A

Dominican	NC-15376	crashed	1941
Jamaica	373	scrapped	1946
Antilles	374	scrapped	1946
Brazilian	375	scrapped	1946

S42B

Pan American 11	NC-16734	*Samoan*	crashed	1938
Bermuda	735	*Alaska / Hong Kong 11*	sunk	1941
Pan American 111	736	*Bermuda*	burnt	1943

Martin 130 Clippers

Hawaii	NC-14714	lost	1938
Philippine	715	crashed	1943
China	716	crashed	1945

Boeing B 314 Clippers

Yankee	NC18603	operated for U.S.N.	crashed	1943
Honolulu	601		sunk	1945
Atlantic	604	operated for U.S.N.	scrapped	1946
California	602	to U.S.N.	**sold** World Airways scr.	1950
Dixie	605	operated for U.S.N.	**sold** World Airways scr.	1950
American	606	to U.S.N.	**sold** World Airways scr.	1950

314A Clippers

Pacific	NC18609	to U.S.N.	**sold** Universal Airlines	scrapped after	1946
Capetown	612	to U.S.N.	**sold** American Intn.	sunk	1947
Anzac	611	to U.S.N.	**sold** Am.Intn-World Airways	destroyed	1951

American Export / Overseas Airlines
Sikorsky VS-44A

Excalibur	NC41880		crashed	1942
Exeter	882	**sold** later acquired TAI (CX-AIR)	crashed	1947
Excambian	881	**sold** Avalon Air Transport 1957	**to Antilles**	1968

South Pacific Air Lines

unnamed	N9947F	Solent 3	*(Singapore)*	scrapped	1973?	
unnamed	45F	Solent 2	*(Somerset)*	scrapped	1974	
Isle of Tahiti	46F	Solent 3	*(City of Cardiff)*	**sold**	1976	Grant Bros *Halcyon.*

***displayed as *City of Cardiff* Oakland Aviation Museum**

Private
Douglas Dolphin 117 amphibion N-26K *Rover* William (Bill) Boeing 1934
***U.S. National Museum of Naval Aviation, Pensacola, Florida.**

Lockheed
Model 8 floatplane NR-211 Sirius. Charles (& Anne) Lindbergh converted 1931
*** (Smithsonian Institution) N.A.S.A Museum, Washington, DC.**

Sikorsky

S38 BS	NC29V	*Osas Ark*	10 seat amphibion	Martin & Osa Johnson 1932	written off 1945
S39CS	NC52V	*Spirit of Africa*	5 seat	Martin & Osa Johnson 1932	lost Gulf of Mexico 1942

***S38 replica NC28V Fantasy of Flight Museum Florida**
***S39 replica NC50V Fantasy of Flight Museum Florida**

CANADA
U.S. Navy Martin JRM long range transports

Hawaii Mars	76819	sank	1945
Marshall Mars	822	burnt	1950

Philippine Mars 76820, *Marianas Mars* 821,*Hawaii Mars 11* 823, *Caroline Mars* 824

Forest Industries Flying Tankers 1959

Marianas Mars	CF-LYJ	crashed	1961
Caroline Mars	YM	Typhoon Freda	1962

Coulson Forest Products 2007

Philippine Mars	C-FLYK	**Sproat Lake, Vancouver Island**
Hawaii Mars	YL	**Sproat Lake, Vancouver Island**

VIRGIN ISLES
Antilles Air Boats
Excambian N41881 Sikorsky VS44A damaged 1968
Gifted Naval Aviation Museum 1976
***New England Air Museum**

Southern Cross Sandringham 4 N158C VP-LVE
bought Science Museum 1981
* **Solent Sky Museum Southampton as *Beachcomber***

Excalibur V111 Civil Sunderland N158J *(Islander)* stored.
sold Edward Hulton 1979
* **sold** Kermit Weeks 1991 N814ML. (ML814/G-BJHS)

Index

Pilots, Planes, Personalities

Paths Through Grief

Paths Through Grief

Helen Jaeger

A LION BOOK

A Lion Book
an imprint of
Lion Hudson plc
Mayfield House, 256 Banbury Road,
Oxford OX2 7DH, England
www.lionhudson.com
ISBN 978 0 7459 5209 3
ISBN 0 7459 5209 7

First edition 2006
10 9 8 7 6 5 4 3 2 1 0

Picture acknowledgments

All photographs copyright © Digital Vision, except as noted below.

pp 8, 30–31, 38–39, 40–41, 48–49, 53, 74–75, 80–81, 83, 94, 97, 105 copyright © Alamy Ltd.
pp. 58–59, 61, 64, 71, 77, copyright © Getty Images.
p. 91 copyright © Jonathan Roberts.

A catalogue record for this book is available
from the British Library

Typeset in 9/12 Americana BT
Printed and bound in China

Even though I walk
through the valley
  of the shadow of death,
I will fear no evil,
for you are with me;
your rod and your staff,
they comfort me.

Psalm 23:4

Contents

Introduction

When grief struck my life, I was little prepared for it. But then, who is prepared for suffering? Like a violent storm or a powerful hurricane, it blew up suddenly and threatened to rip with destructive force through the heart of my life.

For many months, everything I held to be dear was under threat: my home, my work, my relationships, my sense of place in the world, my future. And while coping with the inevitable practical changes that the circumstances of grief brought, I also had to deal with its intense emotional fall-out and the deep cuts to my own heart.

Of course, grief comes to us in different ways, whether it be through bereavement, loss of a friendship, or emotional or physical pain. Grief may have crept up on you slowly or it may have come as a sudden shock. Yet however grief visited you and in whatever guise, I am convinced that the effect it has on the human spirit is the same. Whatever its outer covering, you are not alone in your experience of pain, for grief visits the life of every person.

Despite this, our culture ill-prepares us for the inner journey of grief, which is always, at first, an experience of loss. In a world dominated by celebrity smiles and quick-fix solutions, we are left alone to chart the choppy and apparently dangerous seas of grief. We may feel powerless, uncertain and alone.

But the truth is, we are not alone and we are not without power. Grief need not be a fearful enemy; instead it can be a benevolent, if strange, visitor. In the vulnerability that grief brought, I came to know the true character of friends and family and the generosity of heart and spirit that real friends unthinkingly offer. I learned who I could trust with my life (and who I could not). I discovered the value of tears and the power of redemption. I saw that it was often more strong to be weak and dependent than vainly to try to prove one's independence. I realized that sometimes silence speaks as eloquently as words, and that the kingdom of joy, peace and love is gained not by force, as some say, but by gentleness. I learned that forgiveness truly frees us and that mercy pursues each one of us, desiring with passion to lavish its generous gifts in our humble and hurting hearts.

As I walked the paths of grief, I discovered for myself what every good and wise person has always suggested: that grief can be a gift which, if used well, will lead us towards greater wholeness and more meaningful beauty. It is not a way we willingly choose, but if forced onto it, we could find that grief is a dark path we may find strewn with surprising and bright treasures. For me, grief hollowed and hallowed a more profound space for life within me. Suffering is an elegant tool in the hand of the divine and we can surrender to the work it wants to do in our souls without undue fear.

I read this the other day. Let it encourage you.

So in the hardships we underwent... we want you to be quite certain... that we were under extraordinary pressure, beyond our powers of endurance, so that we gave up all hope even of surviving. In fact, we were carrying the sentence of death within our own selves, so that we should be forced to trust not in ourselves but in God, who raises the dead. He did save us...

2 Corinthians 1:8–10

I have been to this place; and perhaps it is a place you, or others you love, are entering. My message to you is this: I entered the furnace of grief unwilling and afraid, yet I emerged with my soul singing. And so, I hope, may you.

Suggested ways to use this book

The book is divided into nine paths. Each path has an introductory comment, a Bible passage with questions, an imaginative meditation, a prayer, a poem and a range of quotes about the subject of grief from, mostly, well-known authors. The aim of the book is that you feel you are sitting with a trusted, loving and very non-judgmental friend. You should feel free to explore and express whatever emotions and thoughts are arising in you. Some of these feelings and thoughts will inspire you. Some of them will come to the surface as pain and part of your process of healing. And some of them may challenge you gently to grow in new and, perhaps, unforeseen ways.

Introduction

This is a short section designed to help you begin to think about each particular path. It offers an introduction to the path with key features you may like to consider, and is drawn from personal experience.

Meditation

Each Bible passage has been chosen for its relevance to the path in question. I suggest you read the passage slowly, allowing any words or thoughts from it to hold your attention. You may like to repeat words or phrases to yourself, letting them sink fully into your mind and heart. Do not rush this. Allow the passage to speak to you and your situation.

When you feel you have gleaned all possible nourishment from the Bible passage, you may like to move on to the questions attached to it. Use them as a way of turning the Bible passage over in your mind and entering into its truths more fully. If the questions don't appeal to you, skip them. But if there are particular questions which arrest your attention, make a response to them in whatever way is most suitable for you; for example, in a journal or through prayer.

Imagine

I suggest you read through the imaginative meditation before you do it, so you have a good idea of what you are going to contemplate. When you are ready, close your eyes and use the meditation as a basis for exploring each path more imaginatively and creatively.

Each meditation also has a few questions attached to it. Again, these are designed to help, not hinder you. You don't have to have an immediate answer to the question, but it may be something you want to return to in subsequent days, allowing answers and wisdom to come from the deep places within you.

Prayer

Each path has its own short prayer. Speaking others' prayers is effective and may be a means of articulating your own grief in a helpful way. Grief and the circumstances surrounding it are often tiring, so you should feel free to take the restful path. If a prayer particularly speaks to you, you may like to copy it out and place it somewhere prominent, where you can read it easily and spontaneously over a period of time. If you wish to pray your own prayers, remember that you can express yourself however you wish. And remember, too, that if you speak slowly, gently, even hesitantly, you will still be heard.

Poem

Each path has its own short poem written from personal experience. You may like to use the poem as the basis for contemplation.

Inspirations

The quotes in each path have not been randomly selected. Some quotes grab us and sum up what we are thinking and feeling at any one time. This is the power of words. Allow others' words to inspire and strengthen you, even as you walk the paths in this book. The people behind these words know the reality of the path you are on and are included in this book deliberately to encourage you. You may like to stick relevant quotes around your home and workspace.

Finally

Do not judge yourself as you travel these paths. Treat yourself with reverence and love, as one who passes through a dark valley.

You are on a demanding journey, but you are on the way to a summit you might not otherwise experience. May you be richly blessed and profoundly healed as you travel. My hope is that you will be able to reframe your experience of grief as one that, although painful, ultimately brought you to the thresholds of new life.

Vulnerability

Opening our hearts

Vulnerability does not get a good press in our culture. On the contrary, it is seen as a virtue to be constantly strong, in control and independent. There is nothing wrong with strength and independence, but if we lose sight of our own vulnerability, we have lost the very thing that can enable us to enter into the deep, fruitful and satisfying relationships that our hearts and minds dream are possible and for which we secretly long.

Grief does not allow us the luxury of pretending that we are strong. It strips away the illusion that we are in control. For a while, it may also take away our independence. For a terrifying moment, this may be all we see. Such emptiness and such powerlessness, as we experience them, may not feel pleasant at all.

We may also feel deeply cut by our grief. Here, again, we face a choice. Do we cover up our feelings of loss and pain, pretending that all is well when we are far from well, or do we bring our heart out into the open, among those we trust and who really love us?

If we choose to express our heart to others, we may be surprised. We may find that instead of rejection, we experience profound acceptance. We may discover that instead of criticism, we receive honour. We may feel that what we bring – hurt, pain, anger – is ugly, but to our amazement, we find that others name it as beautiful.

To experience such acceptance as this is profoundly healing in its own right, and we should not underestimate the gifts of grace that our friends and family can give us in a period of grief. Yes, we may need times of solitude. We

may strongly desire moments of aloneness with our grief, and this is perfectly acceptable, even necessary.

But our friends and families may also be aching to share with us the burden of grief that they see us carrying. We cannot close the door to them. We should not close the door to them. Our hearts are beautiful, rich and profound places. They are places from which not only we ourselves but also countless others can experience true blessing – even in a time of grief.

Yet truthful vulnerability requires great courage. It is not easy to trust when we have experienced loss. It is not always easy to allow ourselves to be held – physically or

emotionally. It is not always easy, even, to express what is going on in our hearts. But we must try. We may be surprised by the insights and gifts that arise from our openness.

Old friendships may deepen. New friendships may form. We will become even more connected to those around us and experience a depth of friendship that bears the blessing and mark of longevity. I have such friends and I am such a friend. All of us take a risk when we are vulnerable. But our risk is rewarded and our hearts are forever accepted.

Moreover, we open ourselves in new ways to the divine. We lie in our divine lover's arms and experience tenderness, peace and gentleness. We are allowed to cry and grieve, and we find that our desolation is replaced by hope and courage. Our gentle hearts are allowed to come home to themselves. We are invited to give up all posturing, all bluster, all pretence. Seen in this light, vulnerability becomes a thread of grace running through our lives, which knits us together with others and with the divine.

In this way, vulnerability becomes a great strength in our lives. We do not flit from relationship to relationship, job to job, house to house. Our lives regain balance, focus, solidity and rest. Our true selves are known and, likely, we are loved.

Meditation

Read

But a Samaritan traveller who came on him was moved with compassion when he saw him. He went up to him and bandaged his wounds, pouring oil and wine on them. He then lifted him onto his own mount and took him to an inn and looked after him.

Luke 10:33–34

Near the cross of Jesus stood his mother, his mother's sister, Mary the wife of Clopas, and Mary Magdalene. When Jesus saw his mother there, and the disciple whom he loved standing near by, he said to his mother, 'Dear woman, here is your son,' and to the disciple, 'Here is your mother.' From that time on, this disciple took her into his home.

John 19:25–27

He was despised and rejected by men,
a man of sorrows, and familiar with suffering.
Like one from whom men hide their faces
he was despised, and we esteemed him not.
Surely he took up our infirmities and carried our sorrows.

Isaiah 53:3–4a

By his wounds you have been healed.

1 Peter 2:24

Consider

Can you believe that people you don't know will have compassion on you? Can you choose to accept their help, as the injured traveller accepted the help of the Samaritan?

Can you believe that circumstances and

relationships will come your way unbidden, which will bring comfort and hope to you?

Jesus is particularly close to us when we suffer. He is familiar with suffering and understands the emotional pain we experience. Can you let him come close to you with the consolation you need? Maybe he is even carrying some of your suffering for you.

Imagine

Imagine that you have sustained a physical injury – for example, a broken leg. You must lie in bed while your leg heals. Imagine that friends and family, even kind strangers, come to the place where you lie. They bring you gifts – maybe material things you need, or presents that cheer you, or simply gifts of their time, presence and love.

As you imagined this scene, how did you feel? What gifts did people bring? Did you feel grateful or did you experience feelings of resistance? How can you cultivate an open attitude to acts of kindness and love which may come your way?

Your grief is a form of injury, which will heal. Perhaps you are at the start of the journey of grief. Be deeply reassured that those who love you will come to you and care for you. If you are nearing the end of your journey of grief, you may like to reflect on how vulnerability could enrich your life when your time of grief is over.

Consider how you can apply the path of vulnerability to your life right now.

Prayer

O God, I feel my brokenness keenly. Help me not to hide this brokenness or to be ashamed of it. Help me to accept your loving care and the kindness of others. You long to hold, heal and cherish me. You come in great gentleness and great love, directly and through others. Do not let me refuse your care or the kindness of others. May the gift of vulnerability enrich my life now and in the future. Amen.

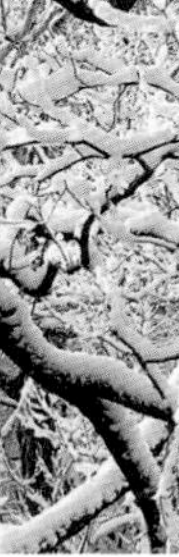

Poem

Death comes, but life comes stronger

A man died
In this bed
I sleep in, and

Today I found
A seagull
Washed up
In the grit.

Death surrounds me
And winter advances.

Yet when we met last year,
And he shook my hand,
Mortality whispered,

'There is only life,

There is only life.'

Inspirations

Friendship is a sheltering tree.

Samuel Taylor Coleridge

God, why do I storm heaven for answers that are already in my heart? Every grace I need has already been given me. Oh, lead me to the Beyond within.

Macrina Wieherkehr

There is a love no words of love can reach;
Heavy the waves that superincumbent press,
But as we labour here with constant stress,
Hand doth hold out to hand not help alone,
But the deep bliss of being fully known.

Sarah Williams

It takes heroic charity and humility to let others sustain us when we are absolutely incapable of sustaining ourselves. We cannot suffer well unless we see Christ everywhere, both in suffering and in the charity of those who come to the aid of our affliction.

Thomas Merton

Never apologize for showing feeling. When you do so, you apologize for the truth.

Benjamin Disraeli

Let's not forget that the little emotions are the great captains of our lives and we obey them without realizing it.

Vincent Van Gogh

Any emotion, if it is sincere, is involuntary.

Mark Twain

I long for household voices gone,
For vanished smiles I long,
But God hath led my dear ones on,
And He can do no wrong.

I know not what the future hath
Of marvel or surprise,
Assured alone that life and death
His mercy underlies.

And if my heart and flesh are weak
To bear an untried pain,
The bruisèd reed He will not break,
But strengthen and sustain.

No offering of my own I have,
Nor works my faith to prove;
I can but give the gifts He gave,
And plead His love for love.

And so beside the Silent Sea
I wait the muffled oar;
No harm from Him can come to me
On ocean or on shore.

I know not where His islands lift
Their fronded palms in air;
I only know I cannot drift
Beyond His love and care.

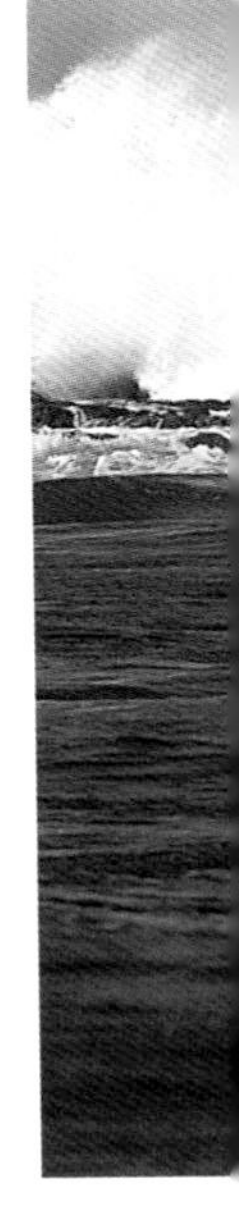

O brothers! if my faith is vain,
If hopes like these betray,
Pray for me that my feet may gain
The sure and safer way.

And Thou, O Lord! by whom are
seen
Thy creatures as they be,
Forgive me if too close I lean
My human heart on Thee!

John Greenleaf Whittier

We turn to God for help when our foundations are shaking, only to learn that it is God who is shaking them.

Charles C. West

Kindness is the language which the deaf can hear and the blind can see.

Mark Twain

God is closest to those with broken hearts.

Jewish saying

Though we travel the world over to find the beautiful, we must carry it with us or we find it not.

Ralph Waldo Emerson

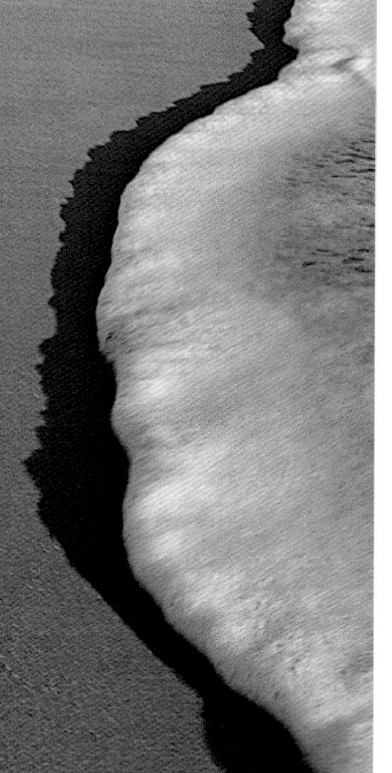

When we were children, we used to think that when we were grown-up we would no longer be vulnerable. But to grow up is to accept vulnerability. To be alive is to be vulnerable.

Madeleine L'Engle

The greatest good you can do for another is not just to share your riches but to reveal to him his own.

Benjamin Disraeli

Man is fond of counting his troubles, but he does not count his joys. If he counted them up as he ought to, he would see that every lot has enough happiness provided for it.

Fyodor Dostoyevsky

We tend to forget that happiness doesn't come as a result of getting something we don't have, but rather of recognizing and appreciating what we do have.

Frederick Keonig

Open your mind to God's wisdom, open your soul to God's peace, open your heart to God's love and all three will stay with you forever.

Mary Stavros

Then come the wild weather, come sleet or come snow,
We will stand by each other, however it blow.

Simon Dach

For friendship, of itself a holy tie,
Is made more sacred by adversity.

John Dryden

Silence

The healing of no words

Silence is often something we associate with punishment and not with blessing. We remember being told to be quiet, be silent, stop talking. Often these memories are ones in which we are being brought into line or disciplined. Silence does not always evoke images of nurturing care, or of being accepted and held.

Yet it is just such nurturing silence that is on offer to us when we grieve. We discover, in our pain, our need for a lack of words. We discover, even if belatedly, our need for quiet, for contemplation, for reflection. Our torn hearts and minds cry out, not for the healing of words, but for the healing of no words.

It is out of this quiet, wordless place that new insights begin to arise. As we make space for reflection we find that it is not a fearful, empty space that we are entering. Rather, we feel as if we have come into the warm embrace of someone who loves us and understands us deeply. We find that there is no need for expression, for we are already understood. We find that there is no need for words, for we are already heard.

We find ourselves held for as long as we need to be held. Our hearts quieten, as the psalmist says, like a child at its mother's breast. The heat, passions and rush of our daily lives disappear and are replaced instead by a gentle creativity and appreciation for life.

It is as if we enter a quiet, still and shaded forest, after days in the glare of a hot sun. We may experience again the sweetness of sleep.

We discover, too, our need for mystery. Words do not always carry with them the possibility of mystery, particularly when they are rushed and unconsidered. Words of this kind may not be paths for us, but simply dead ends. Yet silence is pregnant with mystery and therefore with possibility. We are not made to understand all, to know all, to remember all. We are made for silence and forgetting and uncertainty.

The poetry of our hearts longs to see our lives not in the bright and certain glare of neon, which is so often harsh and unforgiving, but in dappled light, whose patterned and gentle shapes secretly delight us. This is the truth of our hearts. This is the creativity of our lives.

We enter silence with courage, and as we do so, we find that our grief and anxieties begin to lose their grip on us. We let them go and do not need to name or analyze them. As we enter silence, we find that what we no longer need falls out of our open hands. We choose not to possess our grief – and find we are not possessed by it. In choosing silence, we choose freedom.

And yet there is more, for silence is a lavish giver. We start to experience a new, supple, deeper trust and the stirrings of a fresh optimism. We taste new joy, new contentment, new peace, new energy. We may not have asked for these things, but in our simple act of openness, we receive them. All these gifts have come wordlessly and mysteriously to us. These great gifts come to us from silence, which has been to us not a reprimand, but a blessing, as we discover that grief secretly leads us on a wordless path to peace.

Meditation

Read

Thus, before they call I shall answer,
before they stop speaking I shall have heard.

Isaiah 65:24

Your Father knows what you need before you ask him.

Matthew 6:8

When Job's three friends... heard about all the troubles that had come upon him, they set out from their homes and met together by agreement to go and sympathize with him and comfort him. When they saw him from a distance, they could hardly recognize him; they began to weep aloud, and they tore their robes and sprinkled dust on their heads. Then they sat on the ground with him for seven days and seven nights. No one said a word to him, because they saw how great his suffering was.

Job 2:11–13

I have stilled my soul, like a child at its mother's breast.

Psalm 131:2

Be still, and know that I am God.

Psalm 46:10

Consider

How can you cultivate silence in your life right now? Could you give yourself to, say, twenty minutes of silence a day? Shut your door, unplug your phone, take off your shoes. Do whatever you need to do to enter the embrace of silence.

If you could believe that God knew what you needed before you asked, how would this change the way you prayed? Can you recall times when God answered your prayers and your needs even before you had expressed them?

Can you re-envision silence as a place of love, care and deep understanding?

Are there people in your life who can appreciate your need for silence, even when you are with them? Can you seek them out or allow yourself to be sought by them? Can you allow them to sit with you and to grieve with you?

Imagine

Imagine lying on your back in a warm, sunny field. The sky is summer blue and scattered with beautiful white clouds, which drift by gently. Idly, you watch the clouds pass over you. You experience deep peace and

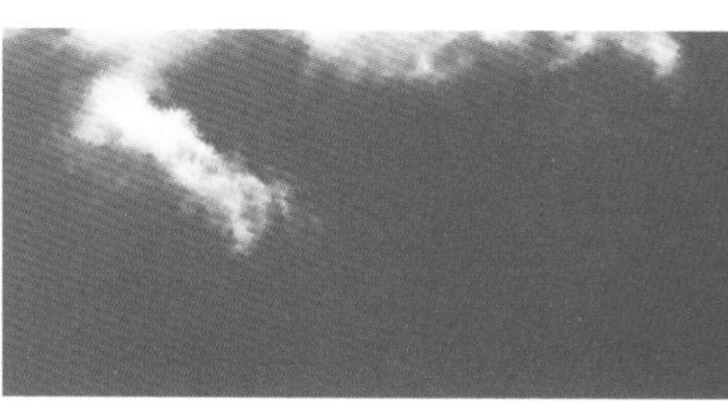

happiness. Insights and ideas may emerge unforced as you mentally freewheel, but you do not have to hold on to these.

Now think of silence as staring at the sky. Your thoughts and emotions are the clouds that pass over you. You do not need to hold on to them, but can simply watch them pass you by. As you watch in this detached way, your mind and body rest and you begin to feel a profound sense of calm. If insights and ideas surface, trust that what you need to remember will return to you at the end of your period of rest and silence.

Consider how you can apply the path of silence to your life right now.

Prayer

O God. Here I am. I rest in you. Amen.

Poem

The contemplative

Do not ask for understanding.
(It will come.)
Do not ask for insight.
(You will see.)
But –

Lie on your bed.
Darkly whisper
A word of holy love.

All things are given.

Inspirations

I grew up among wise men and found that there is nothing better for man than silence.

Proverb

Silence is also speech.

Yiddish proverb

The fruit of silence is tranquillity.

Arabic proverb

Silence is the element in which great things fashion themselves together; that at length they may emerge, full-formed and majestic, into the daylight of Life, which they are thenceforth to rule.

Thomas Carlyle

The holiest of all holidays are those
Kept by ourselves in silence and apart;
The secret anniversaries of the heart,
When the full river of feeling overflows;–
The happy days unclouded to their close;
The sudden joys that out of darkness start
As flames from ashes; swift desires that dart
Like swallows singing down each wind that blows!

Henry Wadsworth Longfellow

It is the silence between the notes that makes the music; it is the space between the bars that holds the tiger.

Traditional

With silence only as their benediction,
God's angels come
Where in the shadow of a great affliction,
The soul sits dumb!

John Greenleaf Whittier

We need to find God, and he cannot be found in noise and restlessness. God is the friend of silence. See how nature – trees, flowers, grass – grows in silence; see the stars, the moon and the sun, how they move in silence... We need silence to be able to touch souls.

Mother Teresa

In silence man can most readily preserve his integrity.

Meister Eckhart

In the school of the Spirit man learns wisdom through humility, knowledge by forgetting, how to speak by silence, how to live by dying.

Johannes Tauler

I swear to you there are divine things more beautiful than words can tell.

Walt Whitman

He that would live in peace and at ease, must not speak all he knows, nor judge all he sees.

Benjamin Franklin

Strength is born in the deep silence of long-suffering hearts; not amid joy.

Felicia D. Hemans

Prayer is not a way of making use of God; prayer is a way of offering ourselves to God in order that He should be able to make use of us. It may be that one of our great faults in prayer is that we talk too much and listen too little. When prayer is at its highest we wait in silence for God's voice to us; we linger in His presence for His peace and His power to flow over us and around us; we lean back in His everlasting arms and feel the serenity of perfect security in Him.

William Barclay

Learn to get in touch with silence within yourself, and know that everything in this life has purpose. There are no mistakes, no coincidences, all events are blessings given to us to learn from.

Elizabeth Kubler-Ross

Much silence makes a powerful noise.

African proverb

Great souls endure in silence.

Friedrich Schiller

And if tonight my soul may find her peace
in sleep, and sink in good oblivion,
and in the morning wake like a new-opened flower
then I have been dipped again in God, and new-created.

D. H. Lawrence

Let me rest in your will and be silent. Then the light of your joy will warm life. Its fire will burn in my heart and shine for your glory. This is what I live for.

Thomas Merton

Have courage for the great sorrows of life and patience for the small ones; and when you have laboriously accomplished your daily task, go to sleep in peace.

Victor Hugo

Only in quiet waters do things mirror themselves undistorted. Only in a quiet mind is adequate perception of the world.

Hans Margolius

It is only when we silent the blaring sounds of our daily existence that we can finally hear the whispers of truth that life reveals to us, as it stands knocking on the doorsteps of our hearts.

K. T. Jong

True silence is the rest of the mind; it is to the spirit what sleep is to the body, nourishment and refreshment.

William Penn

We visit others as a matter of social obligation. How long has it been since we have visited with ourselves?

Morris Adler

Nowhere can man find a quieter or more untroubled retreat than in his own soul.

Marcus Aurelius

When you pray, rather let your heart be without words than your words without heart.

John Bunyan

Mercy

We dream again

Grief lays bare our lives, not with the harsh light of exposure but with the benign intention of healing. We may see parts of our own lives that are cracked, dry or neglected. But just when we are tempted to grieve even more deeply, mercy arrives. Mercy, in supreme kindness, shows us the treasures we have lost, unduly forfeited or had stolen from us – and it offers these inner treasures back to us.

In our humility we discover a new way of being. We open empty hands and return with a fullness of spirit we had not envisioned. We are taken in unfamiliar directions. Our suppleness to the divine Spirit in this newly broken, newly mended state, makes fresh shapes and patterns in our lives. It is the finger of mercy which traces this new beauty, where there had not been beauty in us before.

Through the experience of grief, we are broken and remade. The remaking may resemble old, old ways of being and it may initiate us into something new. We experience a taste of wholeness and an unexpected sense of homecoming – coming home, literally, to ourselves.

We are not simply put back together the way we were. In particular, where our grief has been the result of sudden or violent pain, the broken parts of our lives are not merely glued back together. We do not become once again the sum of our parts. Somehow, by some mysterious grace or quiet miracle, we are remade more whole. We lose something – yes, of course, this is the reason for our grief – but mercy wants to press something greater on us.

And in this way we experience the divine generosity. Tentatively, we open ourselves up to new experiences, new pathways.

We hear words like 'lavish' and 'cherish' and begin to wonder if our understanding of the divine is too limited. We begin quietly to reframe our grief as an experience of goodness. To our great surprise, we hear a whisper in the depths of our hearts that our own welfare is truly important. The day comes when we dream again.

For me, mercy has always been important. I do not believe in returning hate for hate, violence for violence, death for death. I strongly believe in the power of redemption and that good overcomes every grief and every evil. But this became even more clear for me

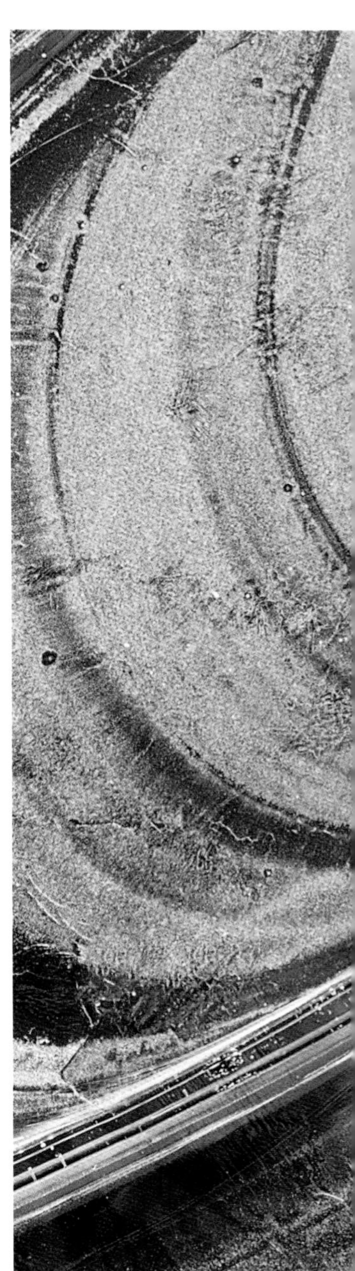

when I passed through my own valley of grief.

Here, I found that mercy offered me a personal invitation to joy and to wholeness in the midst of an experience that, by all reckoning, should simply have been one of great sorrow and brokenness. In truth, sometimes instead of mourning I found that I was being invited to dance and to sing. I discovered that instead of unrelenting grief, I was touched with happiness and thanksgiving. I began to realize that the loss I was experiencing, although profound and heart-breaking, could work in some mysterious way for my own benefit and for the benefit of others. Friends commented on how much freer and more joyful I was becoming. This was mercy at work. Where I had expected only death, I now saw glimpses on the horizon of life and hope and possibility, too.

Thus mercy comes to mend all our griefs, and our lives. We do not live forever with wounds that are unhealable or cracks that cannot be fixed. Instead we find life coming to us in the most unexpected of ways, at the most unexpected of times and in the most unexpected of circumstances. And so, in this way I discovered for myself that those who give mercy are the ones who become the glad and grateful recipients of it themselves.

Meditation

Read

Blessed are the merciful, for they will be shown mercy.
Matthew 5:7

One of the criminals who hung there hurled insults at him: 'Aren't you the Christ? Save yourself and us!' But the other criminal rebuked him. 'Don't you fear God,' he said, 'since you are under the same sentence? We are punished justly, for we are getting what our deeds deserve. But this man has done nothing wrong.'

Then he said, 'Jesus, remember me when you come into your kingdom.'

Jesus answered him, 'I tell you the truth, today you will be with me in paradise.'
Luke 23:39–43

And he said, 'I will make all my goodness pass before you, and will proclaim before you the name, "The Lord"; and I will be gracious to whom I will be gracious, and will show mercy on whom I will show mercy.'
Exodus 33:19

Surely goodness and mercy shall follow me all the days of my life, and I shall dwell in the house of the Lord forever.

Psalm 23:6

Consider

Can you be open to new invitations? For the second criminal, to be invited into paradise must have seemed beyond imagining for one who had simply asked to be remembered. If you have experienced mercy already, how has it surpassed your expectations?

In your suffering, can you still show an attitude of mercy, as Jesus did?

Can you believe that mercy is following you? How could you let God show his mercy to you right now?

Imagine

Imagine that you love to go to art galleries. On a particular day you hope to see your favourite artwork, but it is missing. No matter, because you have enough money to buy a small print of it. You go to the gallery shop and pick up the print, then head towards the counter to make your purchase. The shop assistant looks at you strangely and then whispers something to a security attendant nearby. You are asked politely to accompany the security attendant, leaving your print behind. Bewildered and perhaps a little anxious, you are led into a secret part of the gallery and brought face to face with the gallery's owner. The owner explains with a smile that you are to be given your favourite artwork! He shows you the artwork which you love and asks you to accept it as a completely free gift.

How did you feel when you realized that you were being given such an extravagant gift? Can you believe that mercy will be this wide and generous to you?

Consider how you can apply the path of mercy to your life right now.

Prayer

O God of mercy, you know what it is to experience grief. You do not come to my emotions as a stranger or an observer. You come as a friend and a healer. Help me to see that grief need not be an enemy, but an emissary of your mercy. Your every thought towards me is for my welfare. I choose mercy and wait for your wide blessing. I trust you. Amen.

Poem

Beneath the hard earth
The seeds are dreaming

And their skins are creaking
With the songs of life.

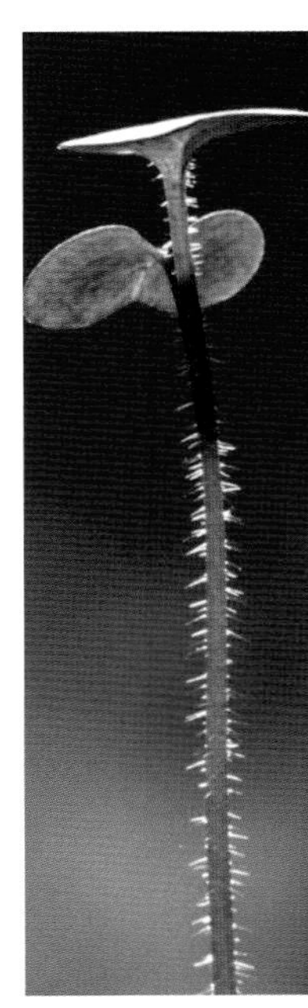

Inspirations

The quality of mercy is not strain'd,
It droppeth as the gentle rain from heaven
Upon the place beneath.
It is twice blest: it blesseth him that gives and him
that takes.
'Tis mightiest in the mightiest: it becomes

The throned monarch better than his crown;
His sceptre shows the force of temporal power,
The attribute to awe and majesty,
Wherein doth sit the dread and fear of kings;
But mercy is above this sceptred sway,
It is enthroned in the hearts of kings,
It is an attribute to God himself;
And earthly power doth then show likest God's,
When mercy seasons justice.
Therefore, Jew, though justice be thy plea, consider this,
That in the course of justice none of us
Should see salvation: we do pray for mercy;
And that same prayer doth teach us all to render
The deeds of mercy.

William Shakespeare

God gives his wrath by weight, and without weight his mercy.

George Herbert

In case of doubt it is best to lean to the side of mercy.

Proverb

Yet then from all my grief, O Lord,
Thy mercy set me free,
Whilst in the confidence of pray'r
My soul took hold on thee.

Joseph Addison

The brave love mercy and delight to save.

John Gay

The things which must be, must be for the best,
God helps us do our duty and not shrink,
And trust His mercy humbly for the rest.

Lord Lytton

Being all fashioned of the self-same dust, let us be merciful as well as just.

Henry Wadsworth Longfellow

Open thy gate of mercy, gracious God,
My soul flies through these wounds to seek out thee.

William Shakespeare

I have always found that mercy bears richer fruits than strict justice.

Abraham Lincoln

Today we are afraid of simple words like goodness and mercy and kindness. We don't believe in the good old words because we don't believe in good old values anymore. And that's why the world is sick.

Lin Yutang

Where Mercy, Love, and Pity dwell
There God is dwelling too.
For Mercy has a human heart,
Pity a human face,
And Love, the human form divine,
And Peace, the human dress.

William Blake

The most valuable things in life are not measured in monetary terms. The really important things are not houses and lands, stocks and bonds, automobiles and real estate, but friendships, trust, confidence, empathy, mercy, love and faith.

Bertrand Russell

The reason is that we do not know truly that our Lord is the ground from which our prayer springeth; nor do we know that it is given us by his grace and his love. If we knew this, it would make us trust to have of our Lord's gifts all that we desire. For I am sure that no man asketh mercy and grace with sincerity, without mercy and grace being given to him first.

Julian of Norwich

Hate shuts her soul when dove-eyed mercy pleads.

Charles Sprague

How shall I praise th' eternal God,
That Infinite Unknown?
Who can ascend his high abode,
Or venture near his throne?
The great invisible!
He dwells conceal'd in dazzling light:
But his all-searching eye reveals
The secrets of the night.
Those watchful eyes that never sleep,
Survey the world around;
His wisdom is the boundless deep,
Where all our thoughts are drown'd.

He knows no shadow of a change,
Nor alters his decrees;
Firm as a rock his truth remains,
To guard his promises.
Justice, upon a dreadful throne,
Maintains the rights of God;
While mercy sends her pardons down,
Bought with a Saviour's blood.
Now to my soul immortal King,
Speak some forgiving word;
Then 'twill be double joy to sing
The glories of my Lord.

Isaac Watts

No one is safe by his own strength, but he is safe by the grace and mercy of God.

St Cyprian

So long as we judge ourselves by human comparisons, there is plenty of room for self-satisfaction, and self-satisfaction kills faith, for faith is born of the sense of need. But when we compare ourselves with Jesus Christ, and through Him, with God, we are humbled to the dust, and then faith is born, for there is nothing left to do but to trust to the mercy of God.

William Barclay

Turn thine eyes to Christ, and see there the exceeding mercy of thy most kind and loving Father.

William Tyndale

The man whose prayer is so pure that he never asks God for anything does not know who God is, and does not know who he is himself: for he does not know his own need of God. All true prayer somehow confesses our absolute dependence on the Lord of life and death.

Thomas Merton

Jesus, as a mother you gather your people to you: you are gentle with us as a mother with her children. Often you weep over our sins and our pride: tenderly you draw us from hatred and judgement. You comfort us in sorrow and bind up our wounds: in sickness you nurse us, and with pure milk you feed us. Jesus, by your dying we are born to new life: by your anguish and labour we come forth in joy. Despair turns to hope through your sweet goodness: through your gentleness we find comfort in fear. Your warmth gives life to the dead: your touch makes sinners righteous. Lord Jesus, in your mercy heal us: in your love and tenderness remake us. In your compassion bring grace and forgiveness: for the beauty of heaven may your love prepare us.

St Anselm of Canterbury

Let us not be discouraged when the hand of God layeth heavy ones upon us. We ought to judge of the violence of our disease by the violence of the remedies which our spiritual physician prescribes for us. It is a great argument of our wretchedness and of God's mercy, that, notwithstanding the difficulty of our recovery, He vouchsafes to undertake our cure.

François Fénélon

With thee, 'tis one to behold and to pity. Accordingly, thy mercy followeth every man so long as he liveth, whithersoever he goeth, even as thy glance never quitteth any.

Nicolas of Cusa

We may suffer the sins of our brother; we do not need to judge. This is a mercy for the Christian.

Dietrich Bonhoeffer

Anger

Of wolves and lambs

Every experience of grief carries with it the natural potential for anger. We feel angry at circumstance: why did these circumstances contribute to this loss I am experiencing? How could it have been different if circumstances had been different? We feel angry with other people: what if that person had done less or more, or been involved or not been involved? And perhaps, too, we feel an element of anger with ourselves: what if I had been able to avoid this situation? Why did I not see this coming and prepare myself better?

Such speculation, however, is rarely fruitful and may instead lead us into an ever-narrowing mental maze. We do not live in a 'what if' universe, as good as the gift of imagination may be. We do not live in alternative worlds, where other outcomes are possible. We live here, we live now, and when we are grieving, we live in pain.

Yet anger, managed properly, does have its legitimate place in our grieving, because it takes us to a place of honesty. Honesty, we then find, is the surprising springboard to acceptance. So we need to face clearly the experiences that bring with them anger and pain. If we bury them, all we do is poison our own lives and our future happiness.

Thus we need to (and can) sit with our anger. We do not suppress it and we do not express it in harmful ways. We can accept that we feel angry, that we feel bitter, that we feel resentment at the way life has treated us. To do so shows that we bear in our souls the divine mark which ultimately longs for blessing and delight – that same divine mark which, although it understands our grief in a profound and compassionate way, silently declares that loss and grief are not the way life was intended to be. Our cry against grief is a cry for well-being. It is the cry of a healthy heart.

The order of this world, the order of grief and anger, will pass away. As we allow our anger to surface, we can begin to experience some of that ultimate healing and release. We discover both that the gift of forgiveness is powerful and that forgiveness is a powerful act. Forgiveness is nothing more than letting go. We name the sources and objects of our anger – people, places, events – and we choose to let them go. We open our hands,

emotionally and, if necessary, in a physical act of surrender, and allow what has hurt us to pass out of our possession. We give up the fleeting sense of strength we experience as anger floods our bodies. Instead we choose the abiding strength of a gentle heart.

As we do so, the weight falls from our shoulders and the scales fall from our eyes. Our burden of anger has been acknowledged and it has been laid down. Only we can make this act of surrender. No one else can do it for us.

So then we rise, invigorated by a new sense of freedom, a new sense of potential, a fresh vision. We do not revisit the past any more – our eyes are no longer fixed on horizons that have already gone by. Vengeance does not occupy our thoughts and we do not seek actions in the present that are tied to events of the past. We are free.

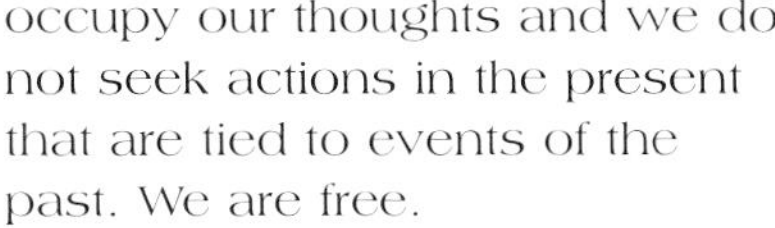

Now we look to new horizons and new possibilities. Our bodies and hearts find strength as we begin to walk and run in uncharted paths. Anger is replaced by adventure.

Our lives always have the potential for grief and they have the potential for anger. But we are not drawn to violence. On the contrary, we long for peace-filled landscapes.

Acknowledging, experiencing, accepting and letting go of our anger is the path that leads to such new and sun-lit pastures. It is a gentle but demanding pathway, yet well worth the effort, for ultimately it leads to our souls' freedom.

Meditation

Read

The wolf and the young lamb will feed together,
the lion will eat hay like the ox,
and dust be the serpent's food.
No hurt, no harm will be done
on all my holy mountain,
Yahweh says.

Isaiah 65:25–26

A fool gives full vent to his anger,
but a wise man keeps himself under control.

Proverbs 29:11

My dear brothers, take note of this: Everyone should be quick to listen, slow to speak and slow to become angry, for man's anger does not bring about the righteous life that God desires.

James 1:19–20

Consider

Can you envision your anger and your bitterness as a fierce wolf and your gentleness and your desire for peace as a small lamb? Can you let them lie down together – allow them both to be in your heart? As you let the wolf lie down with the lamb, what feelings do you experience (for example, relief, acceptance, a release of tension)?

The next time conflicting feelings arise in you, can you allow them both to exist side by side?

Do you believe that it is better to express every angry feeling? Psychology experts agree with ancient wisdom: it is not best to express all of your anger all of the time.

Can you re-envision anger, not as something powerful but as something weak? Anger may not achieve what you want it to achieve – yet forgiveness might.

Imagine

Imagine you are bound by strong, leather straps. Each strap can be traced to a person or event (or even to God). In your mind, deliberately trace each strap to its source. As you face each source, speak out the words: 'I forgive you. I give up all thoughts of my own vengeance against you. I let you go.' Imagine the straps that have been holding you unwinding from your body. Do this until every strap that has bound you is gone. Then rest.

How did you feel as you imagined yourself tightly bound in your anger? Was it easy or difficult to trace your anger to its source? If you were able to forgive, what sensations did you feel as you did so?

You may like to repeat this meditation every time a situation or person angers you, until you are completely free.

Consider how you can apply the path of anger and forgiveness to your life right now.

Prayer

O God of justice, I long for wholeness, but I know this won't come unless I am honest with you. I feel angry. It is a relief to admit this to you. Help me to know what to do with this anger. Where I have been hurt, help me to let anger and pride fall out of my hands. I want to let slip the weapons of war. I trust that by emptying my hands of vengeance, I open my hands to your rich blessing. Even though I am angry, I will not refuse you. Free me. Amen.

Poem

Beauty without cruelty

Throwing off the dark shroud
Of my own quite
Righteous indignation,

One night
I heard stars singing
And blossom growing
From dead branches.

Inspirations

The difficulties of life are intended to make us better, not bitter.

Anonymous

Honesty is the first chapter of the book of wisdom.

Thomas Jefferson

If you kick a stone in anger, you'll hurt your own foot.

Korean proverb

I have found the paradox that if I love until it hurts, then there is no hurt, but only more love.

Mother Teresa

When there is no enemy within, the enemies outside cannot hurt you.

African proverb

No one can get inner peace by pouncing on it.

Harry Emerson Fosdick

Resentment is like taking poison and waiting for the other person to die.

Malachy McCourt

A rattlesnake, if cornered, will become so angry it will bite itself. That is exactly what the harboring of hate and resentment against others is – a biting of oneself. We think we are harming others in holding these spites and hates, but the deeper harm is to ourselves.

E. Stanley Jones

Without forgiveness life is governed by an endless cycle of resentment and retaliation.

Roberto Assagioli

Peace cannot be achieved through violence. It can only be attained through understanding.

Ralph Waldo Emerson

Anger ventilated often hurries toward forgiveness; and concealed often hardens into revenge.

Edward G. Bulwer-Lytton

He who cannot forgive breaks the bridge over which he himself must pass.

George Herbert

While grief is fresh, every attempt to divert only irritates. You must wait till it be digested, and then amusement will dissipate the remains of it.

Samuel Johnson

Anger is the most impotent of passions. It effects nothing it goes about, and hurts the one who is possessed by it more than the one against whom it is directed.

Edward Hyde Clarendon

Anger, even when it punishes the faults of delinquents, ought not to precede reason as its mistress, but attend as a handmaid at the back of reason, to come to the front when bidden. For once it begins to take control of the mind, it calls just, what it does cruelly.

St Gregory

Holding on to anger, resentment and hurt only gives you tense muscles, a headache and a sore jaw from clenching your teeth. Forgiveness gives you back the laughter and the lightness in your life.

Joan Lunden

Anybody can become angry – that is easy; but to be angry with the right person, and to the right degree, and at the right time, and for the right purpose, and in the right way – that is not within everybody's power and is not easy.

Aristotle

He who angers you conquers you.

Elizabeth Kenny

How much more grievous are the consequences of anger than the causes of it.

Marcus Aurelius

His heart was as great as the world, but there was no room in it to hold the memory of a wrong.

Ralph Waldo Emerson

Bear and forbear.

Ovid

Forgiveness is better than revenge.

Pittacus of Mitylene

Forgiveness is the fragrance of the violet which still clings fast to the heel that crushed it.

Proverb

I pardon him as God shall pardon me.

William Shakespeare

The weak can never forgive. Forgiveness is the attribute of the strong.

Gandhi

Forgiveness is a game only saints play.

Kabir

Anger is momentary madness, so control your anger or it will control you.

Horace

Just for today, I will let go of anger. Just for today, I will let go of worry. Today, I will count my many blessings. Today, I will do my work honestly. Today, I will be kind to every living creature.

Mikao Usui

Let your love be stronger than your hate or anger. Learn the wisdom of compromise, for it is better to bend a little than to break.

H. G. Wells

Consider how much more you often suffer from your anger and grief, than from those very things for which you are angry and grieved.

Marcus Antonius

Weakness

When birds sing at night

Grief is always a blow of some kind to our hearts and lives, however well anticipated it may have been or however slow and languid in coming. We do not experience grief as a source of strength, at least initially. More likely, we experience our pain as something that weakens us and drains strength and emotion out of us.

At this point, we face a choice. We can choose to ignore our feelings of weakness. We can look for substitute props – relationships, activities, more work. We can choose to find distractions – more television, more busyness, more interests. We can choose to gain our strength illegitimately – from anger, from violence, from drugs, from using others. But if we do so, we avoid the real issue, which is to admit that we are weak.

To admit that we are weak is not a fashionable idea. We live in a culture that tells us that only the strong succeed. Suffering is not part of the strength equation. So we push away our weakness, or we deny it or stifle it. Yet by doing this, we only succeed in pushing away, denying or stifling our very selves. There is only one solution to weakness – and that is to embrace it.

Embracing our grief-induced weakness is the path of sanity itself. If the trauma we had gone through were physical, we would quickly acknowledge ourselves to be weak. So it is with our emotional selves. Grief has come as a trauma to our hearts. We are weakened and need tender loving care. We need to learn to be gentle with our hearts, so that we can heal and grow strong again.

Being gentle includes learning to listen to our hearts. Our minds are so used to being in control that the whispers of our hearts are rarely heard. We need to take time to ask: how do I *really* feel right now?

The answers may surprise us. As we give ourselves the gift of listening and acceptance, not judging our hearts, we may hear the first stirrings of joy or laughter. Have you heard a bird sing at night? I have. Just so, our grief-stricken hearts may surprise us with a brief song of joy or a shout of delight, even in the most heart-wrenching pain of grief.

We come to realize that even in dark times, we can be overwhelmed by the goodness of life. Fields still glisten with frost, friends still send messages of encouragement, the moon still rises in a day-blue sky. Our pleasures may not be large by the world's standards, but they are deep and true and, if we had not embraced our weakness, we may simply have missed them.

It is only when we accept our weakness that such whispers of joy and beauty can be heard. And as our hearts grow stronger and our desire to embrace our hearts grows more committed, these shouts and whispers become louder and more robust. In time, our sad songs become whole symphonies of hope, victory and joy.

But we cannot leap-frog over our weakness to get to these places – nor would we want to. Weakness takes us by the hand and leads us to our hearts, where refreshment and healing and new gifts await us. Who would want to miss such a journey? When the scaffolding of grief is gone from our lives, new beauty remains. Weakness is the friend who has introduced us to this enduring beauty.

Meditation

Read

In the same way, the Spirit helps us in our weakness. We do not know what we ought to pray for, but the Spirit himself intercedes for us with groans that words cannot express.

Romans 8:26

But he said to me, 'My grace is sufficient for you, for my power is made perfect in weakness.' Therefore I will boast all the more gladly about my weaknesses, so that Christ's power may rest on me. That is why, for Christ's sake, I delight in weaknesses, in insults, in hardships, in persecutions, in difficulties. For when I am weak, then I am strong.

2 Corinthians 12:9–10

Blessed is he who has regard for the weak; the Lord delivers him in times of trouble.

Psalm 41:1

Consider

Can you believe that God wants to help you in your very weakness? Can you allow God to come close to you and to support you in whatever way you need? Let yourself be honest both about your weaknesses and about your needs.

Can you see your position of weakness as one of great strength and as a gift, because you are being invited not to rely on yourself but on God? How could you re-envision your weakness as a place of power?

Can you believe that God honours those who have regard for you when you are weak? Would you like to be the kind of person who is blessed because they do not despise or dismiss the weak? Or perhaps weakness will continue to be a feature of your life which draws others to you and therefore to God?

Every time you feel stressed, powerless or weak, try repeating this to yourself: Jesus, I trust in you.

Imagine

Imagine that you see a tiny and fragile animal – perhaps a mouse. Imagine that it is being held in tender, warm, encompassing hands. The mouse allows itself to be still, small and protected.

How did you feel as you imagined this? Did you relate more to the mouse or the hands? If you related to the mouse, can you accept that there are small and weak parts of you which can be held and cherished? If you

related more to the hands, what is it that you want to hold with tender care (for example, parts of yourself, vulnerability in others)? How can you honour the small and humble in yourself and others?

Consider how you can apply the path of weakness to your life right now.

Prayer

O God of great strength and great weakness, I am weak, weak, weak. Yet you do not despise my weakness. You love small and gentle. Just so you love my heart. Hold me, strong God. Let me lean on you and into you. Embrace my weakness, not to transform it, but to love it. Amen.

Poem

Grief

He is trying
To fill
The big loss
With the big things.

But only
The small –

A child's laugh,
His dog's eyes shining –

Will do it.

Inspirations

Man's greatest achievement is in allowing God to help him.

Søren Kierkegaard

In a gentle and unvexed spirit, be lost in your own weakness.

Jean-Pierre de Cassaude

Let's not forget that the little emotions are the great captains of our lives and we obey them without realizing it.

Vincent Van Gogh

Every day we slaughter our finest impulses. That is why we get a heart-ache when we read those lines written by the hand of a master and recognize them as our own, as the tender shoots which we stifled because we lacked the faith to believe in our own powers, our own criterion of truth and beauty. Every man, when he gets quiet, when he becomes desperately honest with himself, is capable of uttering profound truths. We all derive from the same source. There is no mystery about the origin of things. We are all part of creation, all kings, all poets, all musicians; we have only to open up, to discover what is already there.

Henry Miller

O Lord, help me to believe the truth about myself, no matter how beautiful it is.

Macrina Wieherkehr

God can heal a broken heart, but He has to have all the pieces.

Anonymous

I have been driven many times to my knees by the overwhelming conviction that I had nowhere else to go.

Abraham Lincoln

Too many people overvalue what they are not and undervalue what they are.

Malcolm S. Forbes

How far you go in life depends on your being tender with the young, compassionate with the aged, sympathetic with the striving and tolerant of the weak and the strong. Because someday in your life you will have been all of these.

George Washington Carver

Make it a practice to judge persons and things in the most favourable light at all times and under all circumstances.

St Vincent de Paul

God is our true Friend, who always gives us the counsel and comfort we need. Our danger lies in resisting Him; so it is essential that we acquire the habit of hearkening to His voice, or keeping silence within, and listening so as to lose nothing of what He says to us. We know well enough how to keep outward silence, and to hush our spoken words, but we know little of interior silence. It consists in hushing our idle, restless, wandering imagination, in quieting the promptings of our worldly minds, and in suppressing the crowd of unprofitable thoughts which excite and disturb the soul.

François Fénélon

We must embrace pain and burn it as fuel for our journey.

Kenji Miyazawa

Some of us think holding on makes us strong; but sometimes it is letting go.

Anonymous

God is whispering to us well-nigh incessantly. Whenever the sounds of the world die out in the soul, or sink low, then we hear these whisperings of God. He is always whispering to us, only we do not always hear, because of the noise, hurry, and distraction which life causes as it rushes on.

Frederick W. Faber

Tears

Cry me a river

Our culture applauds perma-white smiles in happy-ever-always lifestyles. Tears are for the weak, the wimps and the ugly – or so the message goes. We may be told that real men don't cry and only manipulative women do. And so, our griefs are buried. Yet our unshed tears continue to burden our hearts, even if we can't name our burdens accurately (as we often can't).

At best, such undealt with pain surfaces as mild anxiety, a feeling of discontent or a nagging dissatisfaction with the world. At worst, we walk the earth with unnamed pain in our hearts, closing our eyes to beauty and our hearts to love, and depriving the world of the gifts we could offer.

We may fear facing such emotion. What if we can't stop crying once we start? We ask: would we find our way back, were we to set sail on the salty sea of our tears? The truth is more beautiful. Setting sail in this way may be the very thing that leads to the safe and gentle harbours that our storm-tossed hearts secretly desire.

And often, to our amazement, we find that when we cry, we weep not into a void or an abyss but into the soft embrace of the divine comforter, who catches, keeps and values our tears, and whose compassion then heals us and redeems us. That same compassion also substitutes new treasures for our pain, or reminds us of old treasures we had forgotten are ours.

Yes, to cry is frequently painful, but contrary to the values of our culture we find that, rather than weakening us, our tears strengthen us. They wash our hearts clean and clear. Any grit of bitterness disappears. To put it

another way, when we cry, we emerge as from a refreshing dip in a clear river – fresh, shining, more bright.

Tears cannot destroy – that is their beauty. When they come from a heart that is honest and true, they can only heal us and our world. It takes courage to cry. If your heart wants to weep, let the tears flow.

I have cried in solitude and with friends. I have cried in front of one who wished to be my worst enemy. I have cried with my face to the ground and with my head held high. Crying can be as much a prayer as are words or a song, and I have come to know that my tears are received with compassion and care by the divine lover of my soul.

Tears also take us on a journey. Only a heart that is free rushes like water. A heart of stone must stay where it is. Our suffering tears never take us back simply to where we were, but move us to new places, more beautiful than we have known before. This is the way of redemptive suffering, and tears are the gentle current that carries us home – closer to our freedom and to our wholeness.

In reality, we who have cried our griefs can say: tears are a gift to be received with gratitude and fortunate is the one who receives such a gift.

Meditation

Read

Jesus wept.

John 11:35

Blessed are those who mourn,
for they will be comforted.

Matthew 5:5

I will turn their mourning into gladness; I will give them comfort and joy instead of sorrow.

Jeremiah 31:13b

Consider

Use one of these short thoughts or affirmations throughout the day. You could choose one to repeat to yourself. You may find this is a source of encouragement, hope and comfort. Or they may help you to access the emotion in your heart which you want to express through tears.

If you know that you have unexpressed tears in your heart, think about a safe place where you could let them go. You may like to cry alone, before the God who loves you, or with a trusted friend. Value yourself enough to give yourself this space as many times as you need it.

Can you believe that your emotions can be sacred? Jesus was not afraid to cry.

Tears are a natural part of our lives. Scientists have proven that they are stress-busters which take harmful chemicals out of our bodies. Can you give thanks for the gift of tears?

Where would you like your tears to take you – into greater joy, greater wholeness, greater peace? Can you believe that your tears are a river which will carry you to these places?

Imagine

Imagine you are a pressure cooker. The heat is all around you and you feel steam and stress building up inside you. Now imagine someone comes to release that stress through your safety valve. You let the steam – the stress, strain and pain of your life – escape. How does it feel?

This is what it is like to cry well. Tears are our natural safety valve. Rather than throwing us into a wailing madness (as our minds may try to warn us), tears are the very path of sanity itself. Anytime you feel like burying your tears, remember that they keep you sane, healthy, alive and well.

Consider how you can apply the path of tears to your life right now.

Prayer

Divine comforter, I bring my heart's anguish and my mind's anxiety to you. My only prayer is my tears. I know you accept such a humble offering. Enfold me in your comfort, you who are the best listener, the most faithful friend and the greatest healer. I abandon myself to your embrace. God of my entire being, here I am, just as I am. Amen.

Poem

This suffering Summer

The deep dusk
Climbs down an old, worn cliff path.

Swallows are calling.

I stand in the shallows
Of the cool North Sea,
A yellow kite, furled, in my belt.

And all the while,

My heart so slowly
healing,
healing,
healing.

Inspirations

Whenever you find tears in your eyes, especially unexpected tears, it is well to pay the closest attention. They are not only telling you something about the secret of who you are, more often than not, God is speaking to you through them of the mystery of where you have come from and summoning you to where, if your soul is to be saved, you should go to next.

Frederick Buechener

When tears come, I breathe deeply and rest. I know I am swimming in a hallowed stream, where many have gone before. I am not alone, crazy or having a nervous breakdown. My heart is at work. My soul is awake.

Mary Margaret Frik

Grief brims itself and flows away in tears.
Traditional

Let tears flow of their own accord: their flowing is not inconsistent with inward peace and harmony.
Seneca

Our eyes are here for seeing
But our hearts are here for joy.
Rumi

Think not, thou canst sigh a sigh,
And thy maker is not by.
Think not, thou canst weep a tear,
And thy maker is not near.

O! he gives to us his joy.
That our grief he may destroy
Till our grief is fled and gone
He doth sit by us and moan.
William Blake

Their eyes, having grieved all grief, were clear.
Wendell Berry

Our very weakness itself may be a privileged occasion for us to experience the power of the Spirit.
Raniero Cantelamessa

The Spirit brings consolation that is true, perfect and in proportion. It is true, because he brings consolation where it is more in place, that is, in the soul and not to the flesh as the world does. The word, in consoling the flesh, actually afflicts the soul, like an incompetent inn-keeper who stables the horse well, but neglects the rider. It is perfect, because, whatever the tribulation, it is effective, unlike the consolation of the world that for every way it soothes brings two new sorts of trouble, like someone who sews up a rent in an old cloak and causes two new tears on either side of it. And it is in proportion, because the greater the tribulation, the greater the consolation, unlike the world that consoles and flatters when one is prosperous, but ridicules and condemns when one falls on hard times.

St Bonadventure

There are times when God asks nothing of his children except silence, patience and tears.

C. S. Robinson

Let your tears come. Let them water your soul.

Eileen Mayhew

Heaven knows we need never be ashamed of our tears, for they are rain upon the blinding dust of earth, overlying our hard hearts.

Charles Dickens

Tearless grief bleeds inwardly.

Christian Nevell Bovee

Time engraves our faces with all the tears we have not shed.

Natalie Clifford Barney

Heavy hearts, like heavy clouds in the sky, are best relieved by the letting of a little water.

Antoine Rivarol

To weep is to make less the depth of grief.

William Shakespeare

Tears are the silent language of grief.

Voltaire

Dear Lord, though I be changed to senseless clay,
And serve the Potter as he turn his wheel,
I thank Thee for the gracious gift of tears!

Thomas Bailey Aldrich

Thank God for grace,
Ye who weep only!
If, as some have done,
Ye grope tear-blinded in a desert place
And touch but tombs – look up!
Those tears will run
Soon in long rivers down the lifted face,
And leave the vision clear for stars and sun.

Elizabeth Barrett Browning

We look through gloom and storm-drift
Beyond the years:
The soul would have no rainbow
Had the eyes no tears.

John Vance Cheney

No radiant pearl, which crested Fortune wears,
No gem that twinkling hangs from Beauty's wars.
Not the bright stars which Night's blue arch adorn,
Nor rising suns that gild the vernal morn,
Shine with such lustre as the tear that flows
Down Virtue's manly cheek for others' woes.

Erasmus Darwin

There is nothing I can give you, which you have not;
But there is much, very much, that
while I cannot give it, you can take.
No heaven can come to us unless our hearts find rest
in today.
Take heaven!
No peace lies in the future which is not hidden in this
present instant.
Take peace!

The gloom of the world is but a shadow.
Behind it, yet within reach, is joy.
There is a radiance and glory in the darkness, could we
but see,
and to see we have only to look.
I beseech you to look.

Life is so generous a giver, but we,
judging its gifts by their covering,
cast them away as ugly, or heavy or hard.
Remove the covering, and you will find beneath it
a living splendor, woven of love, by wisdom, with power.

Welcome it, grasp it,
and you touch the angel's hand that brings it to you.
Everything we call a trial, a sorrow, or a duty,
believe me that angel's hand is there; the gift is there,
and the wonder of an overshadowing presence.
Our joys too: be not content with them as joys.
They, too, conceal diviner gifts.

And so, at this time, I greet you.
Not quite as the world sends greetings,
but with profound esteem and with the prayer that for you
now and forever,
the day breaks, and the shadows flee away.

Fra Giovanni

Surrender

Faith in a storm

At first, we do not know grief as a benign friend or as a gentle emissary. Instead, we experience grief darkly. We stand as if in a storm and feel our lives, even the very core of them, shaken. It is as if we see trees bending, about to break, and we deeply fear that this bending and breaking will happen to us. If we are honest, we experience stormy and turbulent sensations in our hearts. Fear holds us in its cold grip. Our cries may be

simple: 'Help me, protect me, stop this storm.'

My own sorrow and grief was like just such a storm, yet in the midst of it I had a strange experience. I went on holiday. And going on holiday for me was like entering the eye of a storm. Everything quietened down. All noise subsided. All threat departed. My whole body, held so tensely for so long, began to relax. I experienced calm, peace and lightness of heart. I slept well, ate well and smiled again.

And truthfully, I thought, 'Is that it?' I realized the profound truth that my sufferings were indeed to be light and transitory. I looked at myself and found, to my amazement, that I was essentially unscathed. Later, when I returned from holiday, the eye of the storm had passed over me and I had at least another six months of challenge and suffering ahead of me. But this time, my heart was more calm. I was able to observe the storm from a more safe, sheltered and peaceful place. The power of the storm did not depart but my great fear of it had lessened. Calmness brought with it the beginnings of a slow courage.

Such experiences are vital. Grief is demanding, draining and exhausting. We must take care of ourselves. We cannot always stand in the storm. We must honour our bodies and their needs. As we do so, we realize that courage comes to us in unexpected ways. It may come as we nurture and care for ourselves. It may come as we take time out. Courage may not come as we prepare for battle and it probably won't come with sleepless nights of worry.

We tend to imagine courage as a brave lion, but I have discovered that it is more like a sheltering bird. Great cowardice can motivate seemingly daring deeds, yet it takes courage to rest, to relax, to pass time peacefully, especially when there is a storm raging about us. It takes courage quietly to place ourselves in the hands of the divine and to stay there.

Yet this courageous resting and self-caring is what we are called to. We are called, essentially, to a kind of trustful surrender. We leave some of it up to the divine.

No longer must we always fight and complain. Our lamentation is replaced by trust, deep inside us. The circumstances of our lives may not change, but our attitude to them does. We cease struggling and instead allow the divine physician to work healing in us in whatever way and through whatever means he chooses – even if those means should include hardship and grief.

We begin to realize that everything – every good and every evil – can work to our benefit. Sometimes darkness comes so that we can rest or so that we can see stars we would miss were the light in our lives more bright. We find that grief, properly yielded to, can heal us, teach us, renew us, soften us, free us, mature us. We do not run away, however great the desire to do so. Instead we lie down where we are. And we wait for the storm to blow itself out, as all storms do and as my storm eventually did.

And so, sometimes, we must close our eyes both literally and metaphorically. We surrender to the circumstances of our lives, here, in this place. Slowly, we begin to understand the great why of what is happening to us. No longer do we wrestle with fate. Instead, we ask it to bless us. It does. In time, we may find our first cries of fear have been transformed into gentle and heartfelt whispers of thanks.

Meditation

Read

One day Jesus said to his disciples, 'Let's go over to the other side of the lake.' So they got into a boat and set out. As they sailed, he fell asleep. A squall came down on the lake, so that the boat was being swamped, and they were in great danger.

The disciples went and woke him, saying, 'Master, Master, we're going to drown!'

He got up and rebuked the wind and the raging waters; the storm subsided, and all was calm. 'Where is your faith?' he asked his disciples.

Luke 8:22–25

Even when you are chased by those who seek your life, you are safe in the care of the Lord your God, secure in his treasure pouch!

1 Samuel 25:29

As far as I am concerned, God turned into good what you meant for evil.

Genesis 50:20

Who among you fears the Lord
and obeys the word of his servant?
Let him who walks in the dark,
who has no light,
trust in the name of the Lord
and rely on his God.

Isaiah 50:10

Consider it pure joy, my brothers, whenever you face trials of many kinds, because you know that the testing of your faith develops perseverance. Perseverance must finish its work so that you may be mature and complete, not lacking anything.

James 1:2–4

Consider

If a storm is raging about you, can you choose to rest and to nap? Jesus was not afraid to do so. There may be a mystery to your grief and you may not yet understand why it is happening to you, but could you choose the path of faith?

The circumstances of grief may feel threatening to you. How could it reassure you to know that God keeps you safe, hidden inside his treasure pouch? If you feel in the dark, can you imagine the darkness as a place of safety, rather than a fearful place?

Sometimes we cannot name what has happened to us as good. It may indeed have been evil. Yet can you see any ways in which grief has begun to work for good in your own life – perhaps you have already grown (for example, in compassion, strength, courage, care for yourself)? Name specifically how you have grown.

If you experience grief darkly, how is it helping you to trust in God? As you trust God more deeply, what kind of effect does this have on you (for example, are you able to relax more fully, be less anxious, more insightful)? How might this deepened trust help you when your period of grief is over?

Can you continue, despite your grief, to express joy? How might this be a profound invitation, not to be defined by the circumstances of your life, but rather to become deeply free?

Imagine

Imagine you are on an epic mountaineering expedition. What started with such great hopes now appears to be ending in tragedy. You are descending a dangerous mountain alone and through a snowstorm.

You have had to leave your climbing companion on the mountain, assumed dead. You cannot see more than one or two feet in front of you. The ground could give way at any moment to a deep and fatal crevasse. Your feet slip and slide on the treacherous snow and ice. Snow flies in your face. Your body is exhausted, your mind is reeling, your emotions are in turmoil. Finally, after what seems to be an endless night, dawn begins to appear over the horizon. You stagger the final steps to the base camp you made a few days earlier. You strip yourself of your mountain gear and wade into the nearest river. Despite your extreme exhaustion, you want to wash all memories of the mountain from your body. Finally, clean, you dress and fall into a deep sleep.

As you imagine yourself in this scene, what feelings does each stage evoke? Do you feel alone and in the dark, perhaps under grave threat? Can you see that the very act of walking through your grief is an act of courage?

If you are nearing the end of your period of grief, do you feel the need to wash away the memories of the circumstances of your grief? How might you do this? Can you accept your need for rest and sleep?

Consider how you can apply the path of surrender to your life right now.

Prayer

O God, I have known what it is to be afraid. I have known what it is to feel under threat. I have known what it is to walk in darkness. And so have you. There is no dark or dangerous place where you cannot go, for you hold the keys to the whole cosmos. Whether I see you or not, you walk with me. You guide me and you protect me. Cleanse me of the negative aspects of what I have experienced. Show me the good in what has happened. Help me truly and deeply to rest and to be renewed. You honour my courage. Thank you. Amen.

Poem

Night vision

Wise people
Follow stars.
It has always been so.

Life becomes
The awesome adventure
Predestined.

Do not be too hasty
For the neon
Of certainty.

Inspirations

To go in the dark with a light is to know the light.
To know the dark, go dark. Go without sight,
and find that the dark, too, blooms and sings,
and is travelled by dark feet and dark wings.
Wendell Berry

Let us imagine our confusion when we appear before God and understand the reasons why he sent us the crosses we accept so unwillingly. The death of a child will then be seen as its rescue from some great evil had it lived, separation from the woman you love the means of saving you from an unhappy marriage, a severe illness the reason for many years of life afterwards, loss of money the means of saving your soul from eternal loss. So what are we worried about? God is looking after us and we are full of anxiety! We trust ourselves to a doctor because we suppose he knows his business. He orders an operation which involves cutting away part of our body and we accept it. We are grateful to him and pay him a large fee, because we judge he would not act as he does unless the remedy were necessary and we must rely on his skill. Yet we are unwilling to treat God in the same way! It looks as if we do not trust his wisdom and are afraid he cannot do his job properly. We allow ourselves to be operated on by a man who may easily make a mistake – a mistake which may cost us our life – and we protest when God sets to work on us. If we could see all he sees we would unhesitatingly wish all he wishes. We would beg him on bended knee for those afflictions we now ask him to spare us.

St Claude de la Columbiere

Sleep that knits up the ravelled sleave of care
The death of each day's life, sore labour's bath
Balm of hurt minds, great nature's second course,
Chief nourisher in life's feast.

William Shakespeare

At length Gandalf rose. 'The hands of the King are hands of healing, dear friends,' he said. 'But you went to the very brink of death ere he recalled you, putting forth all his power, and sent you into the sweet forgetfulness of sleep. And though you have slept long and blessedly, still it is now time to sleep again.'

J. R. R. Tolkein

There is more refreshment and stimulation in a nap, even of the briefest, than in all the alcohol ever distilled.

Edward Lucas

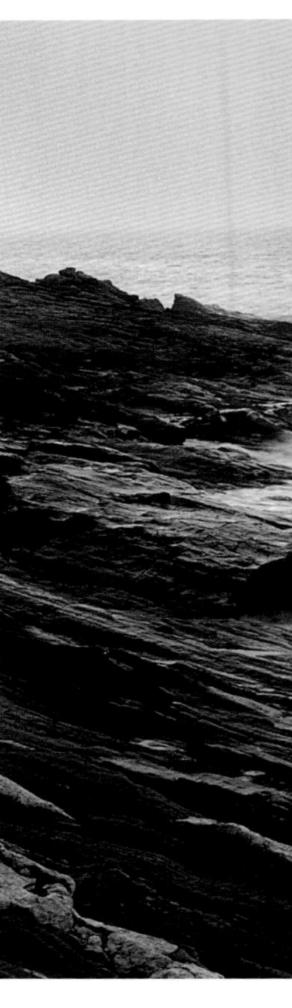

The best bridge between despair and hope is a good night's sleep.

E. Joseph Cossman

Do not let ourselves be troubled when we are sometimes beset by adversity, for we know it is meant for our spiritual welfare and carefully proportioned to our needs, and that a limit has been set to it by the wisdom of the same God who has set a bound to the ocean. Sometimes it might seem as if the sea in its fury would overflow and flood the land, but it respects the limits of its shore and its waves break upon the yielding sand. There is no tribulation or temptation whose limits God has not appointed so as to serve not for our destruction but for our salvation.

Jean Baptiste Saint-Jure

The truth is the only thing worth having, and, in a civilized life like ours, where so many risks are removed, facing it is almost the only courageous thing left to do.

E.V. Lucas

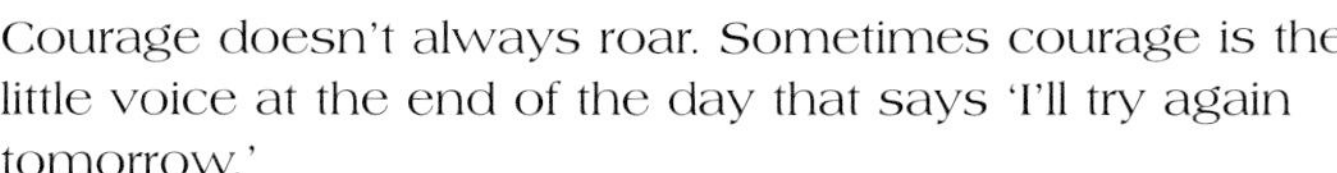

Courage doesn't always roar. Sometimes courage is the little voice at the end of the day that says 'I'll try again tomorrow.'

Mary Anne Radmacher

It is curious that physical courage should be so common in the world and moral courage so rare.

Mark Twain

To live with fear and not to be afraid is the final test of maturity.

Edward Weeks

Smooth seas do not make skilful sailors.

African proverb

I have call'd thee Abba, Father;
I have stay'd my heart on thee:
Storms may howl, and clouds may gather,
All must work for good to me.

Henry Francis Lyte

We run away all the time, to avoid coming face to face with ourselves.

Anonymous

To sit with a dog on a hillside on a glorious afternoon is to be back in Eden, where doing nothing was not boring – it was peace.

Milan Kundera

A person often meets his destiny on the road he took to avoid it.

Jean de la Fontaine

We can easily manage if we will only take, each day, the burden appointed to it. But the load will be too heavy for us if we carry yesterday's burden over again today, and then add the burden of the morrow before we are required to bear it.

John Newton

I know God will not give me anything I can't handle. I just wish that He didn't trust me so much.

Mother Teresa

When it is dark enough, you can see the stars.

Ralph Waldo Emerson

There is no education like adversity.

Benjamin Disraeli

There is in every true woman's heart a spark of heavenly fire, which lies dormant in the broad daylight of prosperity; but which kindles up, and beams and blazes in the dark hour of adversity.

Washington Irving

There are times in everyone's life when something constructive is born out of adversity, when things seem so bad that you've got to grab your fate by the shoulders and shake it.

Anonymous

Prosperity is not without many fears and distastes, and adversity is not without comforts and hopes.

Francis Bacon

It is better to drink of deep griefs than to taste shallow pleasures.

William Hazlitt

Happiness is beneficial for the body, but it is grief that develops the powers of the mind.

Marcel Proust

There are two things that one must get used to or one will find life unendurable: the damages of time and injustices of men.

Nicolas Chamfort

One's suffering disappears when one lets oneself go, when one yields – even to sadness.

Antoine de Saint-Exupéry

We have no right to ask when sorrow comes, 'Why did this happen to me?' unless we ask the same question for every moment of happiness that comes our way.

Anonymous

Time

Past, present, future

When grief enters our lives, our first thoughts may be for immediate survival or relief. We do not have the luxury of time to look to the past and our fearful hearts may not have the strength to envision a new future. So we cope. We deal with our day-to-day demands and fall exhausted, at the end of the day, into an uneasy sleep.

But the time comes when our immediate needs are met. We have carved out some kind of day-to-day existence. We do survive and we continue to live, even if we live with unresolved heartache or difficulty. Now we are tempted to re-enter the past. We ask speculative questions, to which there are often no answers. We wonder if our path could have been different. In time, we may receive unexpected answers to our questions. In time, we may see that what has happened to us has come from the hands of One who loves us. But for a while, we walk alone the paths of mystery and darkness.

This is a natural part of grief and, although there are no easy answers, it is a way for our hearts and minds to come to terms with what has happened. To put it another way: mulling over the past is a way of sorting through our experience. As long as we don't become stuck there, it can be healthy.

Eventually, our thoughts do not seek out old pains to form new regrets. We smile again, as we begin to recall the good we have already received. The past is no longer a place for recrimination or bitterness, even if our memories have a bitter-sweet quality to them. But equally we must remember that the past is a country we cannot re-enter, either to change it or to live in it. We cannot dwell with ghosts.

Our hearts' wisdom knows this. And so, as time goes on, we begin to stir and to look, even if tentatively, towards the future. We hear a call to the optimist in us to live again, although the call may initially touch pain in us where we have been cut with challenge and suffering. Yet still the divine invites us to dream and to daydream.

At first, we may be resistant. We want to refuse because we want to protect ourselves. Grief may have taken from us cherished dreams. We may not, at first, be willing to risk ourselves again in this way. Also, our healing may come slowly, particularly if our pain has been deep. Yet there is nothing wrong with this caution. We should not feel forced to hurry along this path. Instead we are invited to travel slowly, tentatively, gently. The divine does not rush us, even if it insists that we have life.

Yet as we travel, we find the courage to let go of our old pain. We gather into our hands good things now – from the past, the present and the future. Our despair is left at the roadside. We learn to wait in joyful hope. We embrace all that is and all that is becoming. We begin to rest and to sleep well. Our weariness softly departs.

So, as our hearts grow stronger, our desire to live now and in the future grows. There comes a time when peace blossoms in the soul. We begin to want to forget the past – which is, of course, an invitation to liberation. Now we are no longer carried. To our delight, we may hear the call to rise and to run. We step out of a small, sheltered, blessed place. We open ourselves to life in all its fullness and all its glory and all its tragedy once again.

We are healed.

Meditation

Read

So he called one of the servants and asked him what was going on. 'Your brother has come,' he replied, 'and your father has killed the fattened calf because he has him back safe and sound.' The older brother became angry and refused to go in. So his father went out and pleaded with him.

Luke 15:26–28

So Jacob was left alone, and a man wrestled with him till daybreak. When the man saw that he could not overpower him, he touched the socket of Jacob's hip so that his hip was wrenched as he wrestled with the man. Then the man said, 'Let me go, for it is daybreak.' But Jacob replied, 'I will not let you go unless you bless me.'

Genesis 32:24–26

When he had said this, Jesus called in a loud voice, 'Lazarus, come out!' The dead man came out, his hands and feet wrapped with strips of linen, and a cloth around his face. Jesus said to them, 'Take off the grave clothes and let him go.'

John 11:43–44

But one thing I do: forgetting what is behind and reaching forward to what is ahead, I pursue as my goal the prize promised by God's heavenly call in Christ Jesus.

Philippians 3:13–14

Consider

When the prodigal son returned, in Luke's account of Jesus' story, the elder son was resistant. His refusal was strong. Do you hold a sense of refusal in your heart, perhaps where you have been wounded or disappointed? Can you bring that refusal honestly to God? Would it surprise you to learn that God wants to speak and even to plead with you?

Jesus cried to Lazarus to 'come out' of his tomb. The time comes in every experience of grief when God calls us out of a small, dark place – the safe place of our healing. This is the call to resurrected life. Perhaps this call is coming or is now here for you?

Paul in his letter to the Philippians declares that it is good to forget the past. Do you agree? Do you feel the desire to reach forward for what is ahead? If so, can you do so with joy and confidence?

Imagine

Imagine that you hold in both your hands full carrier bags. Where they are heavy, they cut into your fingers. Your whole body is weary with the weight of carrying them.

Suddenly you find yourself standing before a man. He stands in the pose of a cross: arms outstretched, hands open. Silently he invites you to place your hands directly onto his hands. You know that as you do this your mind, body and heart will experience freedom.

But you cannot do it while you are holding onto your full and heavy bags. You face a choice. What will you do?

What feelings arose in you as you contemplated this scene? Did you imagine letting go of your baggage with relief or with fear? What would it mean for you to place your hands in the healing hands of freedom right now? (Remember, you can admit your fears to the One who loves you.)

Consider how you can apply the path of time to your life right now.

Prayer

O God of freedom, I come to you weary with all I have experienced. I cannot resolve the past, only accept it. Give me insight to see the good in the grief I go through. Give me courage to dare to dream again and be with me in my dreaming. I place my whole life in your hands. Guide me. Create me. Shape me. Call me to life and I will live again. Amen.

Poem

Now

Where the mind stops,
The heart goes on,
Enters the wild country.

Awake!
Morning is here and
The wood pigeon is calling our names:

Be-love-d,
Be loved,
Beloved.

Inspirations

There is no despair so absolute as that which comes with the first moments of our first great sorrow, when we have not yet known what it is to have suffered and be healed, to have despaired and have recovered hope.

George Eliot

Do not weep. Instead let us pray together with joy.

Pope John Paul II

The longest night is past.

Wendell Berry

The imperfect is gone and the perfect is struggling forth.

W. B. Yeats

Life is divided into three terms – that which was, which is, and which will be. Let us learn from the past to profit by the present, and from the present to live better in the future.

William Wordsworth

Again the blackbird sings; the streams
Wake, laughing, from their winter dreams,
And tremble in the April showers
The tassels of the maple flowers.

John Greenleaf Whittier

Nor deem the irrevocable Past,
As wholly wasted, wholly vain,
If, rising on its wrecks, at last
To something nobler we attain.

Henry Wadsworth Longfellow

But how carve way i' the life that lies before,
If bent on groaning ever for the past?

Robert Browning

Things which seem evils, hardship, toil, discipline, unpopularity, even persecution, are seen in their glory when they are seen in the light of God.

William Barclay

For the hopes of men have been justly called waking dreams.

St Basil

The past should be a springboard, not a hammock.

Irving Ball

The world is charged with the grandeur of God.
It will flame out, like shining from shook foil;
It gathers to a greatness, like the ooze of oil
Crushed. Why do men then now not reck his rod?
Generations have trod, have trod, have trod;
And all is seared with trade; bleared, smeared with toil;
And wears man's smudge and shares man's smell: the soil
Is bare now, nor can foot feel, being shod.
And for all this, nature is never spent;
There lives the dearest freshness deep down things;
And though the last lights off the black West went
Oh, morning, at the brown brink eastward, springs –
Because the Holy Ghost over the bent
World broods with warm breast and with ah! bright wings.

Gerard Manley Hopkins

The future belongs to those who believe in the beauty of their dreams.

Eleanor Roosevelt

I thank you God for this most amazing day, for the leaping greenly spirits of trees, and for the blue dream of sky and for everything which is natural, which is infinite, which is yes.

E. E. Cummings

And this, our life, exempt from public haunt, finds tongues in trees, books in the running brooks, sermons in stones, and good in everything.

William Shakespeare

The whole world is charged with the glory of God and I feel fire and music under my feet.

Thomas Merton

In dreams and in love there are no impossibilities.

Janos Arany

I believe that imagination is stronger than knowledge – that myth is more potent than history. I believe that dreams are more powerful than facts, that hope always triumphs over experience, that laughter is the only cure for grief. And I believe that love is stronger than death.

Robert Fulghum

It is not God's way that great blessings should descend without the sacrifice first of great sufferings. If the truth is to be spread to any wide extent among the people, how can we dream, how can we hope, that trial and trouble shall not accompany its going forth?

John Henry Newman

O Lord our God,
Who has called us to serve You,
In the midst of the world's affairs,
When we stumble, hold us;
When we fall, lift us up;
When we are hard pressed with evil, deliver us;
When we turn from what is good, turn us back;
And bring us at last to Your glory.

St Alcuin

Honour and glory are indeed due to God and to Him alone, but He will accept neither of them if they be not preserved in the honey of love. Love is sufficient of itself; it pleases by itself and on its own account. Love seeks no cause beyond itself and no fruit. It is its own fruit, its own enjoyment. For when God loves us He desires nothing but to be loved. He loves for no other reason, indeed, than that He may be loved, knowing that by their love itself those who love Him are blessed.

Bernard of Clairvaux

We are healed of a suffering only by experiencing it in full.

Marcel Proust

Letting go

The invitation

At some point, we have to let go. We travel as though through a foreign country, and one day we reach the borderlands of this country called grief. Our journey has been heroic and has called on every reserve of courage and conviction we have. But we must not hold on to our grief as a way of holding on to these riches.

We reach the frontier land because the divine One who loves us and delights in our enjoyment has drawn a line. That line is this border. And now? We are invited to travel on.

But we do not let go of the riches we have attained. We remember our new and deeper connections to those around us and we celebrate them. We value silence and we seek it out for the insights it can give us. We choose attitudes of mercy in every situation. We accept that we may feel angry, but know that we are not bound by anger. Instead we embrace the freedom to which frequent forgiveness invites us. We cry when we need to and our hearts are always refreshed by our tears. We know how to wait and that patience often achieves what power cannot. We know with conviction that all our tears and all our pain will one day be wiped away forever. We experience some of this tender healing now. We choose to love, knowing that we may yet suffer again, but we do not close our hearts to life and to beauty. We fear suffering no longer.

Yet we do move on. For me, that invitation to let go of my grief meant stepping into a land called laughter. The next few months, after the most grievously painful period of my life, were filled with laughter and with joy. I entered a country of light, after months in a dark and dangerously lawless place. In my grief I could not have imagined, or believed, that such a place existed, let alone that it would welcome me in and accept me as one of its own. But this is exactly what happened.

I suppose I entered a kind of heaven after a kind of hell. This time my courageous and mended heart was called not to mourn and to weep, but to rejoice. I passed from death to life. In a way, maybe, I was practising resurrection.

And so I grasped once again the hand of wisdom, who had become my precious travelling companion, and I set forward resolutely. But there was a newness in me, too. I didn't want a small, self-centred life. I looked to the heavens and said: If the choice is between love with grief or no love and no grief, I choose love.

And so, on a certain day, I stood with my hands open, crying my last grief on that borderland of suffering, giving thanks for everything providence had given me, acknowledging my own absolute weakness and dependence on the divine, offering myself with tears and urgency.

I offered myself in this way because I had come to love deeply the One who loved me with an everlasting love and who, I willingly acknowledged, had carried and guided me throughout my journey of grief.

I offered myself and the divine One simply said one word: laugh.

Meditation

Read

Listen, I tell you a mystery: We will not all sleep, but we will all be changed – in a flash, in the twinkling of an eye, at the last trumpet. For the trumpet will sound, the dead will be raised imperishable, and we will be changed. For the perishable must clothe itself with the imperishable, and the mortal with immortality.

1 Corinthians 15:51–53

Our mouths were filled with laughter,
our tongues with songs of joy.
Then it was said among the nations,
'The Lord has done great things for them.'

Psalm 126:2

The Lord will march out like a mighty man,
like a warrior he will stir up his zeal;
with a shout he will raise the battle cry
and will triumph over his enemies.

Isaiah 42:13

Let us fix our eyes on Jesus, the author and perfecter of our faith, who for the joy set before him endured the cross, scorning its shame, and sat down at the right hand of the throne of God.

Hebrews 12:2

She is clothed with strength and dignity;
she can laugh at the days to come.

Proverbs 31:25

Consider

Can you see the culture of death – loss, betrayal, bereavement, suffering, breakdown, death itself – as the enemy at which God laughs? And which God overcomes?

Can you give thanks for all that you have learnt and been given in your own time of suffering? Can you name some of your new gifts – perhaps hope or strength, gentleness or joy?

When the worst you can imagine happening happens to you, what then? How are you being invited to live now – more boldly, more freely, more hopefully? Name your invitation.

Can you believe that grief is not the last word of your life?

Imagine

Imagine that you are escaping from a dangerous country, where your life is in danger. You are being led silently and quietly by a member of the Resistance towards the docks, where a ship bound for a free country is waiting. Quickly you board the ship. It is night. All is dark. You hide under some old sacking on the ship's deck. You do not sleep during the night, for until you reach your destination you are still in danger.

Finally, as the first rays of the dawn appear, you catch a glimpse of the cliffs of your home country. The ship docks. Night-time is past. You disembark from the ship in the busy light of day. Already the dockside is full of hustle and bustle. What do you do now?

How did you feel as you went on this imaginative journey? Can you see any parallels between your experience of grief and your meditation on escaping from a dangerous country (for example, darkness, uncertainty, a sense of foreboding, sleeplessness)? What feelings arose in you as you contemplated arriving home? What did you want to do when you had disembarked from the ship (for example, cry, find old friends, laugh, sleep) and what could this tell you about where you are to go next?

Consider how you can apply the path of letting go to your life right now.

Prayer

O God of adventure, you have blessed me even in times of great pain. Help me, though, not to settle here. You invite me to travel on. I hear your call to new horizons. Give me courage for new journeys. I travel with you. Thank you for your help, your love and your constant presence. Amen.

Poem

Firefly

One day I'll leap
Like a spark,
From this lump of peat,
The earth,

Like a spark,
Lit from within
By divine light.

The divine kiss
Of life
Will bring me to life
From death.

I shall not die
But leap
From life to Life.

Inspirations

The robbed that smiles, steals something from the thief.
William Shakespeare

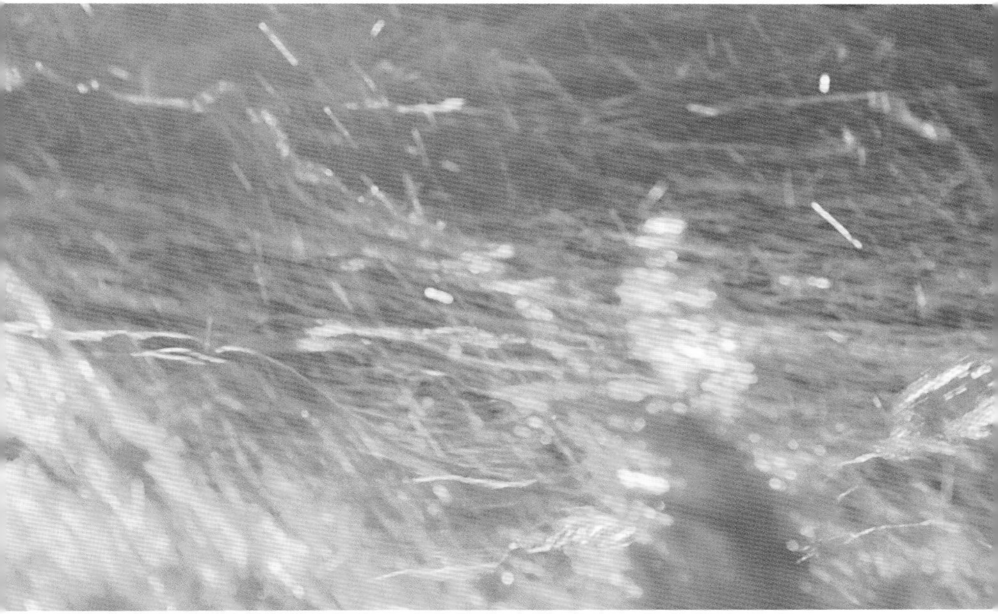

The most completely lost of all days is that on which one has not laughed.

Catullus

A good laugh and a long sleep are the best cures in the doctor's book.

Irish proverb

If I had a formula for bypassing trouble, I would not pass it round. Trouble creates a capacity to handle it. I don't embrace trouble; that's as bad as treating it as an enemy. But I do say meet it as a friend, for you'll see a lot of it and had better be on speaking terms with it.

Oliver Wendell Holmes

The problem is not that there are problems. The problem is expecting otherwise and thinking that having problems is a problem.

Theodore Rubin

Every path has its puddle.

English proverb

A good laugh is sunshine in a house.

Anonymous

If you're in a bad situation, don't worry it'll change. If you're in a good situation, don't worry it'll change.

John Simone, Sr

Everybody needs beauty as well as bread, places to play in and pray in, where nature may heal and give strength to body and soul.

John Muir

We acquire the strength we have overcome.

Ralph Waldo Emerson

I count life just a stuff to try the soul's strength on.

Robert Browning

Better keep yourself clean and bright; you are the window through which you must see the world.

George Bernard Shaw

What do I need today? Strength? Peace? Patience? Heavenly joy? Industry? Good temper? Power to help others? Inward contentment? Courage? Whatever it be, my God will lavish it upon me.

Amy Carmichael

We have to laugh. Because laughter, we already know, is the first evidence of freedom.

Rosario Castellanos

If you don't learn to laugh at trouble, you won't have anything to laugh at when you're old.

Ed Howe

Like a plant that starts up in showers and sunshine and does not know which has best helped it to grow, it is difficult to say whether the hard things or the pleasant things did me the most good.

Lucy Larcom

Laughter is the sun that drives winter from the human face.

Victor Hugo

Laughter is the closest thing to the grace of God.

Karl Barth

The soul of one who serves God always swims in joy, always keeps holiday, is always in the mind for singing.

St John of the Cross

Enjoy thankfully any happy hour heaven may send you, nor think that your delights will keep till another year.

Proverb

Not everything that is more difficult is more meritorious.

St Thomas Aquinas

Crosses are ladders that lead to heaven.

Proverb

Vexations, duly borne,
Are but as trials, which heaven's love to man
Sends for his good.

Italian proverb

The feeling remains that God is on the journey, too.

Teresa of Avila

And lo! Even as he laughed at despair he looked out again on the black ships, and he lifted up his sword to defy them. And then wonder took him-and a great joy; and he cast his sword up in the sunlight and sang as he caught it.

J. R. R. Tolkein

Text acknowledgments

pp. 5, 18, 29, 39, 50, 60, 68, 80, 81, 92, 93, 103–104 Scripture quotations taken from the *Holy Bible, New International Version*, copyright © 1973, 1978, 1984 International Bible Society. Used by permission of Zondervan and Hodder & Stoughton Limited. All rights reserved. The 'NIV' and 'New International Version' trademarks are registered in the United States Patent and Trademark Office by International Bible Society. Use of either trademark requires the permission of International Bible Society. UK trademark number 1448790.

pp. 10, 18, 29, 50 Scripture quotations taken from the *New Jerusalem Bible*, published and copyright © 1985 by Darton, Longman and Todd Ltd and les Editions du Cerf, and by Doubleday, a division of Bantam Doubleday Dell Publishing Group, Inc. Used by permission of Darton, Longman and Todd Ltd, and Doubleday, a division of Random House, Inc.

pp. 39, 40 Scripture quotations are from The Holy Bible, English Standard Version, published by HarperCollins Publishers, copyright © 2001 Crossway Bibles, a division of Good News Publishers. Used by permission. All rights reserved.

pp. 80, 81, 93 Scripture quotations are taken from the *Holy Bible, New Living Translation*, copyright © 1996. Used by permission of Tyndale House Publishers, Inc., Wheaton, Illinois 60189. All rights reserved.

p. 84 Extract taken from 'To Know the Dark' from *The Selected Poems of Wendell Berry*. Copyright © 1998 Wendell Berry. Reprinted by permission of Counterpoint Press, a division of Perseus Books Group.